PR… ROME

‘A n… perceptive book that interrogates “the stories that we tell ourselves about who we are”’
Tobias Jones, *Observer*

‘Roman roads run everywhere, and Fletcher has been on most of them . . . It has been her labour of love to crisscross an entire continent . . . Fletcher’s book . . . presents a familiar panorama – of Europe since antiquity – but from an unfamiliar, even original perspective . . . The roads themselves are Fletcher’s stars: sources of prosperity but also danger, stages on which to compete for and assert status, vectors of destiny that take men from where they cannot stay to where they must go . . . The camaraderie she generates with fellow travellers, dead as well as living, engages and inspires’
Miles Pattenden, *Literary Review*

‘Elegantly plotted . . . It is no easy task to condense twenty-five centuries of history into 300 pages and Fletcher, whose area of expertise is Renaissance Europe, rises to the challenge . . . For modern Grand Tourists, Fletcher’s book will provide an enjoyable distraction when the journey to Rome gets dull’
Patrick Kidd, *The Times*

'Very readable . . . these routes are almost a natural part of the landscape. The reader departs the book with a feeling that they have been there for an unimaginable time, travelled on by a cast of vivid characters. It is a compelling image, in an enjoyable book'
Robert Wright, *Financial Times*

'Catherine Fletcher's mastery of history and storytelling converge beautifully in this captivating exploration of the Roman roads. She expertly leads us on a journey that reaches from Rome to Spain to Constantinople, and from the remote past into the present. A must read for tourists and armchair travellers alike'
Ross King

'[A] rich narrative of the long afterlife of Rome's roads'
Michael Prodger, *New Statesman*

'In her magnificently imagined and vividly composed book . . . we journey the thousands of miles of Roman roads from 500 BCE to the present and are never made timeless or homeless'
Richard Bosworth

'Fletcher has a knack for identifying the poignant and the picaresque, which keeps the book unpredictable and entertaining. Fletcher is a charming writer'
Kyle Harper, *Wall Street Journal*

CATHERINE FLETCHER

Catherine Fletcher is a historian of Renaissance and early modern Europe and the author of several previous books, including *The Beauty and the Terror: An Alternative History of the Italian Renaissance*, which was a book of the year (2020) in *The Times*. Catherine is Professor of History at Manchester Metropolitan University and broadcasts regularly for the BBC.

ALSO BY CATHERINE FLETCHER

Our Man in Rome: Henry VIII and his Italian Ambassador
(also published as *The Divorce of Henry VIII: The Untold Story*)

Diplomacy in Renaissance Rome: The Rise of the Resident Ambassador

The Black Prince of Florence: The Spectacular Life and Treacherous World of Alessandro de' Medici

The Beauty and the Terror: An Alternative History of the Italian Renaissance

CATHERINE FLETCHER

The Roads to Rome

A Journey Into Europe's Past

VINTAGE

1 3 5 7 9 10 8 6 4 2

Vintage is part of the Penguin Random House group of companies

Vintage, Penguin Random House UK, One Embassy Gardens,
8 Viaduct Gardens, London SW11 7BW

penguin.co.uk/vintage
global.penguinrandomhouse.com

Penguin Random House UK

First published in Vintage in 2025
First published in hardback by The Bodley Head in 2024

Map by Bill Donohoe

Printed and bound in Great Britain by Clays Ltd, Elcograf S.p.A.

The authorised representative in the EEA is Penguin Random House Ireland, Morrison Chambers, 32 Nassau Street, Dublin D02 YH68

A CIP catalogue record for this book is available from the British Library

ISBN 9781529932690

Penguin Random House is committed to a sustainable future for our business, our readers and our planet. This book is made from Forest Stewardship Council® certified paper.

MIX
Paper | Supporting responsible forestry
FSC® C018179

To those who wore out life and limb to
cut through marsh and forest.

Contents

NORTH SEA
The Antonine Wall
St. Mary, Whitekirk
Corbridge
York
Manchester
UNITED KINGDOM
Wroxeter
Wall
Cirencester
London
Bath
ATLANTIC OCEAN
BELGIUM
GERMANY
Paris
Vienna / Carnuntum
FRANCE
Bern
AUSTRIA
SWITZERLAND
THE ALPS
HU
Valence
Milan
Pavia
Avignon
Orange
Turin
Nîmes
Nice
Genoa
Ravenna
Arles
Monaco
Rimini
ITALY
Furlo
R. Douro
Viterbo
Monte Sant'Angelo
SPAIN
ROME
Anzio
Bar
Terracina
Barcelona
Montecassino
Tarragona
Pozzuoli
Valencia
Benevento
Seville / Italica
Córdoba
MEDITERRAN
Cádiz
Tangier
Timgad
1 Via Augusta
2 Via Flaminia
3 Via Appia (Appian Way)
4 Via Egnatia
5 Via Militaris/Via Diagonalis
0 400 km
0 400 miles

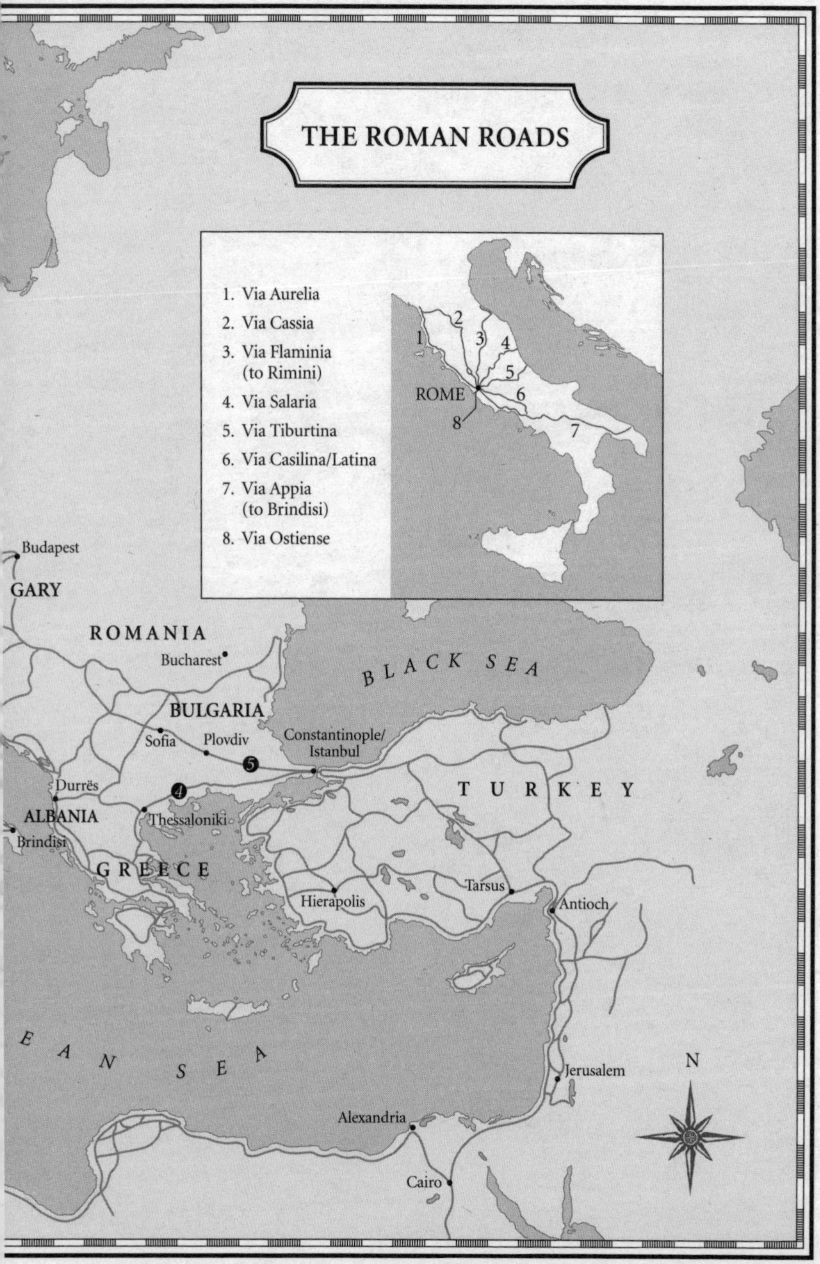
THE ROMAN ROADS
1. Via Aurelia
2. Via Cassia
3. Via Flaminia (to Rimini)
4. Via Salaria
5. Via Tiburtina
6. Via Casilina/Latina
7. Via Appia (to Brindisi)
8. Via Ostiense
ROME
Budapest
GARY
ROMANIA
Bucharest
BLACK SEA
BULGARIA
Sofia
Plovdiv
Constantinople/ Istanbul
Durrës
ALBANIA
Thessaloniki
Brindisi
TURKEY
GREECE
Tarsus
Hierapolis
Antioch
EAN SEA
Jerusalem
N
Alexandria
Cairo

Introduction

'All roads lead to Rome.' It's a medieval proverb: its first recorded expression is found in the works of a French poet, Alain de Lille. 'A thousand roads lead men forever to Rome,' he wrote, almost a millennium ago. *Mille vie ducunt homines per secula Romam.* An English version came two centuries later, in Chaucer: 'right as dyvers pathes leden dyvers folk the right weye to Rome'.[1] The proverb has a broader meaning, of course, but for the ancient Romans it had a rather literal truth. Sometime after 20 BCE, the Emperor Augustus inaugurated a monument known as the Golden Milestone in the Forum. This was, wrote Plutarch, 'the point at which all roads ended'.[2] One way or another, those roads led to Rome.

The queen of the roads – to quote another ancient writer, Statius – was the Appian Way, leading south and east from Rome to the Adriatic port of Brindisi on Italy's heel.[3] It runs now between glorious ruins and famous pines, amid the remnants of suburban villas and aqueducts, its picturesque pavements above the corridors of catacombs, their niches of memory filled with the bones of the dead. There's a backdrop of mountains, a view towards the city; its palette shifts with the weather from soft mist to stark sun. It has the sort of calm beauty a Grand Tourist might have drawn or painted. There's a special light here, a pink haze that clears to reveal ruins in red brick, their lines interrupted by intricate patterns, the secrets of their engineering. Sometimes the trees sway in a breeze: sometimes the prevailing winds impart to them a permanent direction. There are never many people in the pictures of this quintessential landscape, just a traveller or two, or a peasant in his vineyard. This is a world of layers, a palimpsest of history. Travellers have come here, walked or ridden or driven, for over two millennia. Here I am, you may think, with everyone who walked this path before me, their footsteps imagined over flagstones. There are ghosts along these roadsides, in the memorials and tombs. Here are the lost, the missing, the crossroad haunts. Along the way were shrines to those who watched over the travellers: the goddess Hekate first, St Christopher later. For all the beauty of the Roman campagna, the roads were dangerous places.

The Appian Way has a soundtrack, too. Ottorino Respighi's tone poem *Pines of Rome*, written a century ago, recalls the trees of Rome's romantic settings, from the Borghese Gardens to the catacombs and Gianicolo hill. In its final movement a legion marches in triumph towards the city, down the Via Appia. Robert Graves' 1934 novel *Claudius the God* describes the eponymous emperor standing outside the Temple of Capitoline Jove, pointing towards the Appian Way. 'Do you see that?' he asks. 'That's part of the greatest monument ever built, and though monarchs like Augustus and Tiberius have added to it and kept it in repair, it was first built by a free people. And I have no doubt that it will last as long as the Pyramids, besides having proved of infinitely more service to mankind.' He goes on:

> The Roman Road is the greatest monument ever raised to human liberty by a noble and generous people. It runs across mountain, marsh and river. It is built broad, straight and firm. It joins city with city and nation with nation. It is tens of thousands of miles long, and always thronged with grateful travellers.[4]

Some decades later, when the characters of Monty Python's *Life of Brian* discussed what on earth the Romans had ever done for us, the roads came high up the list: 'Well, yes, *obviously* the roads . . . the roads go without saying.' Many roads do go without saying. They're not aesthetically exciting. They're functional and mundane. We notice roads when they have problems – a traffic jam or accident. When the journey is smooth they're not worthy of comment. (I noted, while researching, how rarely the word 'road' is indexed.) And yet for centuries the Roman roads have been a source of fascination.

This book is about how that fascination came to exist, and about its implications in both past and present. Besides the obvious practical uses, why have Roman roads been such a persistent cultural presence across so much of Europe? In part, it's because the Romans themselves decided that they should be. Graves' Claudius had a point when he called the roads monuments: the milestones beside them kept the names of patrons and emperors alive long after the Romans were gone. The longevity of the road network is remarkable, and its staggering scale conveys Roman power on a level no individual building, however grand, can match. I recall, as a child, in between games of I-Spy noting these roads from the sticky back seats of my parents' old Renault 12. As we drove through England, every time we reached a straight stretch my father would announce it as a Roman road. He had read Classics at Oxford and I suppose at the very least that should equip you to know a *via romana* when you're driving down one. One such road was called Watling Street, though I later learnt that it predated the Romans and they'd remodelled an older, British route. The name 'Watling' didn't sound very Roman to me, but its status could be verified by unfolding the map, memorising the order of the folds so as to close it properly later, and checking for the sans serif capitals that in the Ordnance Survey marked each ROMAN ROAD, sometimes beside its proper name. It mattered, this history, to the mapmakers of the British state. As Britain conquered its own empire, its rulers sought to cultivate a link to ancient Rome and the roads provided physical proof of that connection.

Over the centuries, the roads have been a model for more than one aspiring great power. Together with river and sea routes, the original network enabled the very existence of a Roman Empire, and became essential to its management. Effective government depends on communication. Replacing old packed-earth tracks, roads topped with compressed gravel (or 'metalled') made travel for Rome's governors and officials newly efficient and feasible. By switching horses at each posthouse, couriers could travel fifty to sixty miles a day. An army marching on a metalled road, even in poor weather, could manage twenty-five. Distance is a problem for an imperial order if troops can't get there for a month, so for potential rebels, the knowledge that an imperial force is only twenty-four hours away is a sobering deterrent. Claudius' 'greatest monument to human liberty' clearly needs some qualification.

Precise figures for the extent of the Roman road network are hard to come by, and depend on which roads are counted. Around 100,000 kilometres seems a fair estimate. Certainly the network extended across Europe, through the Near East and all around the Mediterranean, and perhaps as important as its exact size was the impression it made on contemporaries.[5] Along with aqueducts and drains, roads were one of the three features of the Roman Empire that according to Dionysius of Halicarnassus, a Greek historian and contemporary of Augustus, marked its 'extraordinary greatness'.[6] In the eighth and seventh centuries BCE the Assyrians had a substantial road network, but the precedent most familiar to the Romans was in Persia, the Royal Road constructed in the fifth century BCE under King Darius the Great. It ran between Susa and Sardis, crossing the area now covered by Turkey, Iraq and Iran.[7] There were major road projects in China, too, under the Han Dynasty (*c.*200 BCE to 200 CE), which likewise had long, straight roads built. They were not paved, however, so there is less archaeological evidence to complement the surviving descriptions, which place them at perhaps fifty feet (15.2 m) wide, far more substantial than the Roman standard of eight to sixteen feet (2.4–4.8 m).[8]

The Roman project, however, would outlast that of the Han. Begun in 312 BCE, the Via Appia initially ran the 132 Roman miles to Capua, a pre-Roman settlement a little way north of Naples. This was a distance of 196 km: the Roman mile, at 1,478 metres, is a little shorter than the modern mile, at 1,609. The first 90 km stretch of the Appia, to Terracina, completed in five or six years,[9] was almost exactly straight. (Today's equivalent, the Strada Statale or state road 7, still is.) Following further conquests in southern Italy, around a half-century later the Appia was extended to cross the peninsula from Capua to Barletta on the Adriatic coast, then running south along that coast to Brindisi, which made its full length 385 Roman miles (569 km).[10] The Via Appia is the first of the Roman roads to bear the name of its creator: earlier highways had been named for their destination or purpose. Appius Claudius, censor of Rome, is memorialised in the manner of a Macedonian king.[11] His nickname Caecus indicates he became blind in later life, and there's a story – though it's not confirmed in the ancient sources – that he tested his new pavements by walking along them in bare feet.[12] Whether or not that's true, this was not his only infrastructure project: he was also responsible for an aqueduct, the Aqua Appia. So significant was the road initiative, however, that it prompted one of the earliest issues of currency in the name of the Roman state – in order to pay for it – while Appius was rewarded with a statue in the Forum. The development of roads created a shift in the mental world of Romans: it became possible to move both people and things at greater speeds and in new ways. Roads changed understandings of space and expanded the horizons of empire. Settlements that had once been divided were now connected. Once complete, the Appia ensured that anyone travelling from southern Italy to Rome would, even prior to arrival, gain a sense of Roman power.[13]

Even in these early years, the roads' symbolism mattered in making newly conquered territories Roman,[14] and long after the empire had gone they remained written into its landscapes. For thousands of miles across Europe and around the Mediterranean, modern motorways shadow their routes. On a cultural level, too, this heritage has been important over centuries. In much of Europe, the eastern Mediterranean and North Africa, there's no need to travel abroad to find a physical connection with this deep past: its stones are buried in a local field or nearby town. Time after time, writers have used the Roman roads as a metaphor to inform tales of imperial might and European identity, have had fictional characters stride and stroll their pavements. Artists have painted them. Archaeologists have dug them up, measured them, recorded their inscriptions. Rulers have planned their own new roads to stand in the great Roman tradition. Though the roads' symbolism fades from the medieval records, travellers were evidently still making use of them in the millennium between the Gothic Wars and the Renaissance, and since at least the fifteenth century the Via Appia has found a place on tour itineraries. Leading as they do to the empire's surviving monuments and the ruins of its towns, the roads transport us to the past, into the history and geography of Rome.

Some twenty-odd years after those journeys with my family, I had the dubious privilege of driving the rather battered minibus belonging to the British School at Rome. We'd make the circuit of the GRA, the

Grande Raccordo Anulare that rings the city, counting off the ancient street names as we went. Via Cassia, Via Salaria, Via Nomentana, Via Flaminia, Via Tiburtina. It's a strange experience to be so sharply conscious of the history of the routes you take, even if you're taking them at a speed inconceivable to their builders. (Or a perfectly recognisable speed, should it happen to be rush hour.) On the other hand, sometimes the old roads are reconfigured into a space for stressed-out modern lives to slow down, for weekend walks along Sunday's pedestrianised Via Appia towards the cycle routes of its country park, a space to recapture leisure and pleasure, or to experience the spine-tingling catacombs, as tempting as any white-knuckle theme-park ride. Even before I came to the Via Appia I had heard of its most famous monument, the tomb of Caecilia Metella. I don't recall whether this daughter of a consul existed in a textbook or in the stories of my Latin teacher, but I can visualise her tomb now, a circular mausoleum clad in marble. More than a millennium after its erection, the Caetani barons of Rome built a castle to adjoin it, the better to control who passed along the road. It was threatened with demolition in the later sixteenth century, but city officials intervened to save it and in 1808 the sculptor Antonio Canova built his own monument to preserve remains discovered nearby.[15] The roads may be ancient, but they're not unchanged.

Yet even as the stone erodes, new travellers make new memories as they come to see the sights, to trade, to migrate and move, to enjoy escape and enlightenment, to resist, to conquer. With roads come all manner of people. They bring tourists and traders and government officials; walking itself becomes an act of piety for pilgrims. Some people do not travel but rather work the roadsides: innkeepers and chambermaids, ostlers, toll-men, the labourers who mend the metalling, the highway robbers, highway police, guides and spies. And they've done so over centuries. Flights and motorways have been with us less than a hundred years; railways only 200. For much of Europe's history this road network has been the means of national and international travel.

I travelled the roads too, looking at the way their remains are presented today. The Via Augusta, the Via Militaris or Diagonalis, the Via Egnatia, the Via Appia, the Via Flaminia, and more, from Manchester to Cádiz, to Istanbul, and back to Rome. The Roman road network stretched further, of course, but modern public transport – at least on the ground – doesn't match it, and then there's present-day politics. For the Romans it was twenty-seven miles down the coast from Tyre to Acre, but today the crossing between Lebanon and Israel is closed, and travellers are obliged to drive via Syria and Jordan, more than ten times the distance. Nor did any tour operator offer a trip along the North African highway within my research schedule, which ruled out one chapter I had hoped to write. This journey has been my way of exploring the physical links between past and present, of seeing for myself the continuing cultural presence of the ancient routes.

Across Europe there have been lively public debates about how to deal with the legacies of modern empires, from the Sarr-Savoy report in France on the restitution of African cultural heritage, to research in Britain on the colonial connections of National Trust properties, to a project in Italy that maps public monuments with links to empire. Yet Roman roads were the work of an empire too, and by looking at how travellers related to that empire, we can better understand how they related to others, whether Holy Roman, French, British or Italian. Perhaps by standing back and taking a long view of the foundational European empire, we might find new perspectives.

Despite the scale and longevity of the road network, when I began writing this book, I found less existing research than I'd expected. There is a good deal of scholarship on the Roman roads in the ancient period itself and some outstanding work on Fascist-era road projects. For the centuries in between, however, the references tend to be tangential. I found my mentions of roads in passing, in books about the Renaissance or Grand Tour, in biographies of Napoleon and Garibaldi, and went back to the sources for myself to understand the detail. I look at what these travellers say about roads, and also feature some whose interest lies elsewhere. Absences can be as significant as presences. Because the roads go without saying, ideas about them are often found in the margins of a broader cultural phenomenon, the journey to Rome. The two are so far intertwined that I have found it impossible to tell the story of the roads without also considering how that story fits into the wider experience of travel.

Given that all sorts of histories attract researchers, it's worth asking why so much of the roads' history has gone without studying. My suspicion is that it is lost in a gap between the many archaeological studies of their routes and construction on the one hand, and an emphasis in works of later centuries on the impact of high classical culture – art, literature and philosophy – on the other.[16] Nor do roads sit comfortably in the realm of 'memory studies', which has tended to focus on those memories with a recent or continuous genealogy. There are collective memories attached to certain sites on the Roman roads, often for their twentieth-century importance, but the cultural significance of the road network also operates at a deeper level, more mythologised and more visceral.

To understand the roads, I turned to an idea expressed by two authors in the early nineteenth century. One is Germaine de Staël, whose 1807 novel *Corinne, or Italy*, inspired by her own travels, tells the story of a love affair between the half-Italian Corinne, a poet, and Oswald, Lord Nelvil. Corinne is a personification of Italy and the work is centrally concerned with recent politics and the European past.[17] Visiting the Forum, Corinne declares:

> The eyes are all powerful over the soul; after seeing the Roman ruins, we believe in the ancient Romans as if we had lived in their day. Intellectual memories are acquired by study. Memories of the imagination stem from a more immediate, more profound impression, which gives life to our thoughts and makes us, as it were, witnesses of what we have learned.[18]

Samuel Rogers, writing a journal of his travels to Italy in 1814, likewise wrote of imagination:

> Of Antient Rome its roads, & aqueducts its walls & watchtowers, its seven hills its campagna, & the mountains that skirt it, the river that crosses it & the sea that opens beyond it, still remain to us. Many of these things are not only unchanged but unchangeable. The snow at this moment shines on Soracte, the Tiber winds along from the Apennines to the Tyrrhene sea, & the sun still continues to rise & set in the same places. What materials then are left for the Imagination to work with![19]

The journey to Rome can be about historical study, but the roads are also a place to imagine, perhaps to dream. Some writers will cite their ancient sources but many more summon up hazier ghosts of the past. They do so, however, with a shared repertoire of visual references. (Rogers' snowy Mount Soracte is an allusion to the Roman poet Horace.) The journey to Rome is a performance: it has a script. Or rather, it has two: one is focused on the ancient pagan sites, and one is a Christian pilgrimage. Many travellers incorporate both, the emphasis changing with politico-religious circumstance as well as personal preference. In the more modern period these scripts are adapted. Every generation gives the journey a new twist. As the world became modern, the presence of roads became a marker of civilisation and progress. Yet while some stories of the roads endorsed imperial projects, others resisted them. If the stones themselves are unchanged (beyond their slow erosion) the tales of them are not. This is not quite history, and not quite memory. We might call it collective historical imagination.[20]

A millennium and a half after the last Roman emperor was deposed, the roads continue to matter. Barely a week goes by without a report on a newly discovered Roman road. It's perhaps because the roads are so omnipresent in our culture that we rarely ask why they have this grip on our imagination. Many travellers simply look ahead to their destination. Beyond those roads that have been picked out for preservation (like the section of the Via Appia immediately south of Rome) or formalised as cultural routes (the Via Francigena), they don't offer tourists a spectacle like the Colosseum or Hadrian's Wall, the Arena at Nîmes or the theatre in Cádiz. Still, we're intrigued. As I follow the roads from north to south and east to west, and through more than two millennia of history, I'm going to look down and ask how and why – across the centuries – these simple slabs of stone have retained such power. Reflecting on his own walk on the Appian Way, Charles Dickens observed that here is 'a history in every stone that strews the ground'.[21] He was right. The story of the Roman roads is the story of Europe and its neighbours, told from beneath our feet.

PART I

An Imperishable Monument, 350 BCE–500 CE

I

Romans on the roads

To understand why the Roman roads came to carry such significance, we need to start with the basics: the practicalities of their construction and their imprint on the natural and cultural landscape. The first Roman road known to have been paved was not a long-distance route, but a shorter stretch in town, the Clivo dei Publicii, which can still be walked today. Named for Lucius and Marcus Publicius, the public officials who established it in 238 BCE (during the Republican period, nearly two centuries before Julius Caesar came to power), it leads up onto the Aventine hill from the Circus Maximus, though the original Clivus Publicius continued further down to the Forum Boarium, Rome's cattle market.[1] The commission of a road put the name of these men quite literally on the map. The modern road is not inspiring: the flagstones are gone, or buried, and busy traffic at a nearby intersection clogs the air with exhaust fumes. This is one of the cheaper central places to park and cars are lined up on both sides of the street, miniature Smart two-seaters turned nose-in, against what might be ancient walls. There a line of people has formed waiting to peer through the famous keyhole that frames a view of St Peter's Basilica. The view, not the street, is the highlight of this part of town. There's nothing to mark the road's interest.

The Circus Maximus is ready with staging for an upcoming rock concert. I cut down around the Palatine hill to the Forum, where all that remains of the Golden Milestone is a plinth marked with a plaque. Archaeologists aren't convinced that these unassuming chunks of stone are even related to the monument: they seem too large for something in the shape of a milestone, unless it was absolutely giant. Nor are they sure what exactly was inscribed on it. The theory that it gave roads and distances is a modern one. One possibility is that it listed those roads leading from Rome and the *curatores viarum* responsible for their upkeep.[2]

Whatever the Milestone looked like, ancient Rome depended on an effective transport network to bring in supplies from the surrounding area, from food to building materials. The Via Salaria provided a route in one direction to the coastal salt marshes of Ostia (in Latin *sal* means salt), and in the other led up into the Apennines, the mountainous spine of Italy.[3] Some essential goods could be transported by river, for example, along the Anio (now Aniene) from the hilltop town of Tivoli that lay to Rome's east. But in 30 BCE the road to Tivoli, the Via Tiburtina, was widened, suggesting that the river was no longer an adequate means of transport for the travertine produced by its quarries for projects like the Colosseum.[4]

In building the roads, the Romans did not start from nowhere. There were significant networks already on the Italian peninsula, and in some places, such as southern Etruria, road engineers had a level of skill to match the early Romans. The Etruscan town of Marzabotto, for example, near Bologna, has a street design on a grid with drains to either side of its roads. Where the Romans departed from these predecessors was in the development of longer-distance routes linking Rome to its newly conquered territories.[5] The Via Latina, which led south to Benevento, connected the city with Latium (now Lazio). While the Via Appia is better known, the Via Latina – established a few years earlier – was the first 'planned' Roman road.[6] (It formed part of what is now the Via Casilina.) Those who benefited most from the road network in its earliest stages, the sixth to fourth centuries BCE, were the people who travelled to Rome for political reasons. Road building also redistributed resources back to the regions, but the main early links were between the centres of western and central Italy, particularly the wealthy coastal cities. Metalled roads made the largest difference to those who used wheeled transport, that is, the better-off, and moreover guaranteed their safety thanks to the administrative role of the army in road management. Roads helped, in short, to unify the Italian elites.[7]

Roads were also vital in the conduct of war, which saw many less wealthy people travel extended distances. As the Greek historian

Polybius' account of the Punic Wars between Rome and Carthage makes clear, they were the means of moving masses of soldiers across the lands of the growing empire (numbers during the Second Punic War of 218–201 BCE are estimated at 700,000). During the siege of Eryx in western Sicily (244 BCE), the Carthaginians found themselves 'between two hostile armies, and their supplies brought to them with difficulty, because they were in communication with the sea at only one point and by one road, yet held out with a determination that passes belief'.[8] Leading his troops through Gaul and into northern Italy, the Carthaginian commander Hannibal thwarted the locals' attempts to block the Alpine passes thanks to intelligence that at night the Gauls left their posts and retreated to the nearest town, allowing him to sneak men through. At one point the Carthaginian army built a new road to help in their descent of the Alps. It took a single day to make a path for horses, but three days' 'difficult and painful labour' to get it fit for Hannibal's famous elephants.[9]

During peacetime, soldiers worked on road construction and in fact road-building was largely the responsibility of armies, although enslaved labourers were also sometimes employed, especially in the aftermath of conquest. The Via Appia, built primarily by Roman citizens and freedmen, was in this regard unusual, yet even it has military connections: its route followed that of soldiers returning from the first Samnite War (343–340 BCE) and took in the town of Terracina, originally a Roman army colony, located on a vital pass.[10] Moreover, while the Appia linked Rome with its allies, it avoided potentially hostile cities in Lazio.[11]

I take a walk out from Rome towards the Appia over worn *sampietrini* – the flat, square cobbles that cover Rome's roads. A double archway bids me farewell at the city walls; I cross beneath imposing red brick towers, on to what's now called the Via Appia Antica: the Ancient Appian Way. (The New Appian Way is a dual carriageway.) To my right, a column presses into the wall. This is the first milestone, in fact a replica, marking the distance of one mile from the Golden Milestone in the Forum and the road's restoration in the late first century CE. It's a fair walk to find the picturesque section that begins at the church of Santa Maria in Palmis, located at the junction of the Via Appia and Via

Ardeatina. This is where you'd turn off to visit the memorial to the victims of the Nazi reprisals at Fosse Ardeatine. Santa Maria is better known by its nickname 'Domine Quo Vadis?' – acquired from an apocryphal legend of St Peter that echoes Peter's denial of Christ in the Crucifixion story. The saint, fleeing persecution in Rome, encounters Christ on the road. He asks the question that gives the church its name, 'Lord, where are you going?' Christ replies that he is going to Rome to be crucified again, prompting Peter to turn round and face his own fate. A paving stone said to bear the imprint of Christ's foot is now in the nearby Basilica of St Sebastian; most likely it's an earlier votive offering, and not a Christian relic at all.

A little further down a dangerous stretch of road (there's no pavement and high walls on either side) this intermingling of pagan and Christian is to be found in the catacombs. Long associated with persecution of Christians, they're now understood quite differently, as burial places for Romans of all religions: pagans, Christians and Jews. They're an important site of pilgrimage nonetheless: at least fourteen popes are buried at the catacombs of St Callistus and tour buses bring parties to pay homage. That is not to say, however, that the Via Appia lacks a bloody history. In 73 BCE, following the defeat of Spartacus' army, the remaining 6,000 men were 'captured and crucified along the whole road from Capua to Rome'.[12]

Yet the Via Appia was by no means only a site of death and memory. It was a place of pleasure too. Not far from the catacombs are the remnants of the Villa of Maxentius, the pagan emperor defeated by the Christian Constantine at the Battle of Milvian Bridge. Alongside them lies a stadium that accommodated about 10,000 visitors to the chariot races. (Its obelisk is now in Rome's Piazza Navona.) It's 310 Roman feet (92 m) wide and more than three times as long, covered in grass, clover, fungi, and twigs that crunch underfoot. A carpet of pink-tinged daisies covers one part of the old track, big ones, flowers an inch across, interrupted by the occasional molehill. A clattering of jackdaws, grey and black, shifts as I make the circuit. Eventually they take off for the trees, where they perch cawing as a thread of aeroplanes descends overhead to Ciampino.

Back on the road, the tomb of Caecilia Metella lies soon beyond, and now the *sampietrini* give way briefly to old flagstones as I step into the iconic landscape: an old stone road between Roman pines and cypress trees. I take it down to the Parco Appia Antica, a big country park that sprawls beside it. Green parakeets fly out screeching from a tree. This land was taken over in the sixteenth century by the Caffarelli family of Rome, who built themselves an ample farmhouse. I'm not here for the Caffarelli, though, but to find the nymphaeum of Egeria: a ruin that attracted travellers including Goethe and Byron. The latter wrote in *Childe Harold's Pilgrimage* of the spring and its nymph:

> The mosses of thy fountain still are sprinkled
> With thine Elysian water-drops; the face
> Of thy cave-guarded spring, with years unwrinkled,
> Reflects the meek-eyed genius of the place,
> Whose green, wild margin now no more erase
> Art's works, nor must the delicate waters sleep,
> Prison'd in marble; bubbling from the base
> Of the cleft statue, with a gentle leap
> The rill runs o'er, and round, fern, flowers, and ivy, creep.[13]

The ivy still creeps up the ruins today, and the nymphaeum remains glorious with the sound of running water from its spring and the slight breeze in the canopy of trees that hangs above its diagonal patterns of brick, though its delicate waters may be struggling to sleep under the Ciampino flight path. Past another milestone and I arrive at the Villa of the Quintilii. Once the luxurious home to a senatorial family – two of whom were killed for allegedly conspiring against the Emperor Commodus – it now has only a handful of fully standing walls.

With an area's incorporation into the Roman Empire, roads attracted broader use,[14] serving for governance, facilitating trade and economic development. As public works projects they provided employment. These later roads connecting recently subdued areas with the imperial centre are often referred to as the 'consular' roads after the officials responsible. By the first century CE, according to Siculus Flaccus, a surveyor, they were 'under the charge of administrators [*curatores viarum*]', who would commission repairs, and local landowners were required to contribute to the cost of maintenance. These major roads existed alongside minor ones, built for access to villages and likewise maintained by local landowners, and private roads, used to reach private estates and not for public use.[15] A milestone now in the Capitoline Museums, from the first century BCE, marks a private road owned by the Camilla tribe.[16] Other routes known as the *calles publicae* were used primarily for the movement of flocks of sheep.[17] (*Calle* remains the name for streets in the city of Venice.) Indeed, even some major roads were associated with the movement of sheep flocks. The Via Tiburtina, which connected Tivoli and Rome, incorporated a tunnel underneath the sanctuary of Hercules outside Tivoli in which sheep would be counted for tax purposes.[18]

A poem by Statius, also from the first century CE, describes (if perhaps with some artistic licence) the labour needed for roadbuilding:

> How numerous the squads working together! Some are cutting down woodland and clearing the higher ground, others are using tools to smooth outcrops of rock and plane great beams. There are those binding stones and consolidating the material with burnt lime and volcanic *tufa*. Others again are working hard to dry up hollows that keep filling with water or are diverting the smaller streams.[19]

There are no accurate figures for the number of workers involved in the construction of the road network: one transportation specialist has estimated that a workforce of 25,000 to 36,000 would have been needed to complete the initial 185 km of the Via Appia to the recorded five-year schedule.[20] In the absence of mechanised equipment, it was an astonishing achievement, requiring sophisticated skills from surveyors and masons as well as plain heavy labour. Road materials were adapted to local conditions: volcanic tufa on the Via Appia, but elsewhere whatever came to hand. Straight, level roads were famously preferred, as in that stretch of the Via Appia south of Rome, which traversed the steep Alban Hills as well as the Pontine Marshes. For military purposes straight roads made sense: they meant shorter marches. They saved on the cost of materials and were simpler to survey, but also created technical challenges. Natural rock strata sometimes provided a solid foundation but in other cases one had to be artificially constructed. On marshy ground causeways were built with timber; elsewhere, such as on the Via Appia near Terracina, cuttings were required to ease the route; hills were flattened and valleys filled. Even the more routine elements of roadbuilding were taxing. Sometimes gravel could be obtained from the drainage ditches that were dug on either side of the road; sometimes stone had to be transported from some miles away.

The documentation for the early stages of road-building is limited. No one left behind a 'how-to' guide for Roman engineers, and the constant rebuilding and maintenance of the roads has complicated their archaeology. In their simplest form, the roads were not paved but consisted simply of a raised section (the agger) with ditches to either side and two layers of metalling on top. The first of these consisted of larger stones, then came the *glarea* – gravel that traffic would compress to a smooth surface. Culverts under roads were used to avoid fords.[21] Exactly how the Roman surveyors planned their roads is a matter of debate. There are numerous theories, involving a range of surveying instruments including one called a *dioptra*, similar to a modern theodolite, as well as a *groma*, a simple instrument consisting of a right-angled cross on top of a stake from which plumb-lines were hung, enabling straight lines to be accurately laid. Geometrical skills were reasonably widespread thanks to the tax system that required precise measuring of land parcels. These survey methods may have led to the preference for straight roads, simply because (to quote Hugh Davies, a highway engineer and historian of the roads) it was more 'mathematically convenient'.[22]

Subsequent ancient writers often attributed to Appius Claudius the project of paving the Via Appia. A Greek historian, Diodorus Siculus, credited him with having 'paved with brilliant stone the greater part of the road that from him bears its name of Appia, from Rome to Capua, for a distance of one thousand stadia, levelling heights and filling holes and depressions in the land with appropriate works; and although he exhausted the public purse, he left behind an imperishable monument in memory of himself, having aspired to the common good'.[23] In fact, however, the archaeological evidence suggests that there was little paving prior to the first century CE.[24] Early on (even up to the reign of Trajan, 98–117 CE) the southern sections were paved with *glarea*.[25] The description by another Greek writer,

Plutarch, of the works of Gaius Gracchus in 123–121 BCE is in fact very close to what Diodorus thought Appius had done:

> The roads were carried straight across the countryside without deviation, were paved with hewn stones and bolstered underneath with masses of tight-packed sand; hollows were filled in, torrents or ravines that cut across the route were bridged; the sides were kept parallel and on the same level – all in all, the work presented a vision of smoothness and beauty.[26]

These images of the roads as an 'imperishable monument' to the 'common good', even 'beautiful', were thus already present, at least to outside observers, in Roman times. From the start, roads made both connections and reputations. Far in the future, they would become material for modern imaginations, as writers penned their reflections on both the Roman Empire and their own contemporary worlds.

Following the construction of the Via Appia, there was a hiatus of more than half a century in long-distance road-building before work on the Via Aurelia, leading north along the coast from Rome, commenced around 241 BCE. It was followed about two decades later by development of the Via Flaminia, which crossed the peninsula from Rome to Ariminum (Rimini), a colony on the Adriatic coast.[27] Like the Via Appia, the Via Flaminia linked Rome with existing colonies: not only Rimini, but also the earlier and closer colony of Narnia (Narni). (C. S. Lewis, author of children's books about the mythical land of Narnia, is supposed to have picked the name from a classical atlas.)[28] Some of the milestones that later stood on or near the Via Flaminia can be seen in the museum at Fano today. Formerly Fanum Fortunae, a colony so named for its temple to the goddess Fortuna, Fano lies south-east of Rimini on the Adriatic coast. These unassuming but distinctive stone columns vary from waist- to shoulder-height and date from the fourth century CE. They include in one case the distance – 179 miles – to Rome, and in all cases the name of the ruling emperor.[29] It was as important – if not more so – for travellers to know who was in charge as how far they had to go.

Over the centuries, as the network was extended across the growing empire, there were some remarkable feats of engineering. Over the

Carapelle river, near Foggia in Puglia, a 700-metre-long viaduct was built with ten arches to allow the road to pass through. At Cumae, near Naples, a 1,000-metre tunnel known as the Grotta di Cocceio connected the town to the Roman naval base at nearby Lake Averna. Surveying techniques, involving theodolites and sundials, were sufficiently advanced to allow tunnels to be dug from both ends, although a water tunnel in Saldae (Béjaïa in modern Algeria) had to be rebuilt because the ends didn't meet at the first attempt.[30] Such spectacular projects, however, were not ubiquitous. Elsewhere, and especially outside Italy, terracing allowed roads to curve around hillsides, avoiding river valleys with their risk of flooding, and cuttings were used sparingly.[31] In the centuries to come, tourist after tourist would gaze in fascination at the bridge over the Nera river in Narni, built under Augustus to carry the Via Flaminia across its deep valley. Elsewhere, ancient engineering remained in use for millennia. A forty-metre tunnel at Furlo in the Apennines, built under Vespasian to accommodate the Via Flaminia, was still in routine use until the 1980s when a modern bypass was built.[32]

I'm far from the first tourist to make the Furlo trip. In the sixteenth century, French essayist Michel de Montaigne visited on his travels through Italy, noting an inscription in honour of Vespasian (hidden by later construction). 'All along this road, the Via Flaminia, which leads to Rome,' Montaigne wrote, 'are traces of the great stones used for paving, but most of these are buried; and the road, which was originally forty feet wide, is now not more than four.'[33] Occupying the narrow gorge between the Pietralata and Paganuccio mountains, beside the Candigliano river, the Furlo Pass is a spectacular drive, if not always an easy one, especially with a poorly-programmed GPS. Nets and fencing have been put up to catch rocks falling from the cliffs that soar above the narrow road; signs require drivers to carry snow tyres between November and April. In September, though, the mountains are green and lush, and the water below a clear aquamarine, although its level is now much higher than it would have been when the tunnel was originally constructed. The river was dammed between 1919 and 1922 when a hydroelectric power plant was built, its concrete wall curving round across the valley. Notices remind visitors: no boating, no bathing, no fishing, no drones. We park the car and walk the tunnel. There are two, in fact, the larger and still passable one commissioned by Vespasian, and the smaller probably built under Augustus but currently closed to pedestrians. The first might just have accommodated two carts side by side, but now it's controlled by traffic lights, with cars taking their turn in each direction beside the sightseers. It's remarkable to think that our modern vehicles, steel and aluminium and plastic, are speeding through the same tunnel that the Romans once cut.

Further along, minus the unhelpful GPS, we're heading back to Rimini on the SS16, the present-day Via Flaminia. The dissonance between past and present sharpens. There are signs to Lidl at no. 387. For a little while we follow an advertising van, its billboards promising that Giorgia Meloni, leader of the Brothers of Italy party, variously labelled post- or neofascist, certainly on the populist right, is 'Ready to Reawaken Italy'.[34] Elections are less than a fortnight away and Meloni is front-runner in the polls. Back in Rimini itself, an arch (properly, a gate in the city walls) pays tribute to Augustus, 'son of the divine Julius, acclaimed victorious commander seven times, consul seven times, and consul-elect for an eighth time, for having restored, on his own decision and authority, the Via Flaminia as well as the other most splendid roads of Italy'.[35] The remains of the inscription can be seen above the pediment, while below it are four sculpted heads representing Jupiter, Apollo, Neptune and the personification of Rome. Fluted pilasters with leafy Corinthian capitals complete the grand entrance. The inscription's authenticity is confirmed by coins dating between 18 and 16 BCE which refer to the road-building project.[36] Today, the arch stands grand and isolated. Only a remnant of the old city walls remains to either side, and a line of battlements above, their red brick a contrast with the marble of the gate. A nearby panel explains that this is thanks to clearance works in the 1930s. Now, the arch is a perfect spot for selfies as tourists enter the old town. Not far away, a little rectangular pillar, its origins uncertain though it was known by 1555, purports to mark the spot where Julius Caesar addressed his troops after they had crossed the Rubicon (the river lies just north of the city), a reminder of the road's military significance.

By that time, however, the Via Appia was almost 300 years old, and even the queen of the roads was not immortal. Shortly after the turn of the first to second century CE, the Emperor Trajan initiated a programme of major improvements to the roads between Rome and the south. His new route, known as the Via Appia Traiana or simply the Via Traiana in the emperor's honour but largely following the route of the then 300-year-old Via Minucia, departed from the old Via Appia at Benevento. There a triumphal arch, marking Trajan's victories in Dacia (now primarily Romanian territory), and incorporating a relief of the sacrifice made for the new road, still stands. Rather than the old southerly approach to Brindisi via Taranto, the Traiana took a more northerly and more direct route, crossing to Bari via Canosa before continuing down the coast.[37]

Writing in the second century CE, the Greek physician and philosopher Galen described the improvements:

> [Trajan renovated the] muddy roads covered with stones and brambles, overgrown, steep, marshy, dangerous to ford, overly long and difficult . . . by raising them up with viaducts and paving them, removing all encumbrances and endowing them with bridges, shortening the route where it had been excessively long, cutting into the land to lower the road where it had been too sharply inclined, avoiding mountainous, wooded, or desert areas, and favouring inhabited sites.[38]

Further to the north, where the empire was expanding, a milestone erected in the Danube region during the reign of Trajan celebrated not only the emperor but also the engineering:

> Emperor Caesar Nerva Trajan Augustus Germanicus, son of the deified Nerva, pontifex maximus, in his fourth year of tribunician power, father of his country, consul for the third time, mountains having been cut through and the bends removed, constructed this road.[39]

How, then, did a Roman traveller experience the roads? For a start, with offerings to the gods in the hope of safe passage. In the Capitoline Museums, I find a votive tablet engraved with pairs of feet pointing in both directions to represent outward and return journeys, along with an inscription to the goddess Caelestis in fulfilment of the vow from the man who made it, Jovinus.[40] It's a simple object, but an evocative one. I wonder whether the maker drew around Jovinus' own feet, whether his journey left him with blisters, if he made it in a blaze of sun or a cooling breeze or had to plough on through heavy showers as dusty gravel turned to mud or water planed on rutted stone, counting off the milestones as he passed. At one roadside shrine at Ponte di Nona, a small crossing point on the Aniene river on the road from the hill town of Tivoli to Rome, numerous votive offerings of clay feet have been found, left perhaps in the hope that no accident would befall the traveller's lower limbs.[41] Speeds of travel varied considerably. Walkers might manage twenty Roman miles a day (29.6 km). When litigants were summoned to appear in court, the dates of hearings were set on the basis that they could travel at that speed.[42] It was physically hard work, however, especially over long distances. My longest single day walking on my travels is a twenty-four-kilometre stretch, taking in part of the old Via Cassia, and after that I definitely need a day off. Probably would have lost my court case.

It was easier and faster to ride, if one could: messengers probably managed between fifty and eighty miles a day, which meant most Italian towns would receive letters from Rome within five days. These were the equivalent of today's public postal workers or private courier services. Train and coach drivers, and chauffeurs, all have ancestors on these roads, though their stories are rarely reported in the ancient sources. The biographies of emperors, in contrast, offer records: Julius Caesar apparently managed a hundred miles a day over eight days, and Tiberius Nero an astonishing 182 miles in a day in an urgent case of family illness.[43] More realistically, non-professional travellers with the luxury of a horse or wheeled transport might do thirty-five to forty miles a day on the fast roads.[44] Those who could afford it had litter-bearers, or drivers on their staff.[45] The *raeda* (an open carriage that could also transport goods) was a popular option with elite men; women typically travelled more slowly in the closed carriage known as a *carpentum*. Indeed, women faced punitive taxes for using expensive vehicles: more than ten times the usual rate.[46] Another option, slower again, was the litter, where the number of bearers showed off the occupant's status: eight was definitely a mark of prestige. Retinues were essential to the identity of the elite. An entourage of thirty enslaved attendants, working to clear the road ahead of a wealthy traveller, was about normal in the late first century BCE.[47] The staffing of Rome's road network reflected the fact that this was a slave society.

There were all sorts of reasons to travel to ancient Rome. During the Republic travel was necessary in order to vote, and that's still true in Italy today. Postal voting is limited to those living abroad. Taking trains ahead of the election I hear advertisements for discount tickets for students, or people in temporary jobs, returning to their official home address for polling day. One had to judge the issue worthwhile in order to bother setting out, but plenty of people do and did.[48] The journey of Mary and Joseph to participate in a Roman census is at the heart of the Christmas story. Others travelled for private business reasons: to take goods to market, for example. (Though it was generally much cheaper to send merchandise by river or sea, and of course the Roman Empire was centred on the Mediterranean, sellers still had to get it to a port.)[49] People went to visit religious sites, where they might consult an oracle; they attended festivals. Some journeyed further afield, to Greece, for example, and its shrines and schools. Travel was an onerous business, so if it became necessary for work, or political participation, travellers might choose to mix in other activities en route.[50]

It was, however, elites who had the time and luxury to best enjoy a new form of travel pioneered by the Romans: the annual holiday. This was generally a trip to the seaside or the mountains, though a handful of adventurous souls went off to explore.[51] Inevitably, there were debates about the merits of travel. Seneca in particular thought that it was not a good thing to be restless and unsettled.[52] More happily, good transport routes helped villa life become integral to Roman high society. Ideally, one needed two villas: a place on the coast and another in the mountains for those days when even the seaside got too hot.[53] Pliny the Younger had a seafront villa, which he described to a friend:

> It is seventeen miles from Rome, so that it is possible to spend the night there after necessary business is done, without having cut short or hurried the day's work, and it can be approached by more than one route; the roads to Laurentum and Ostia both lead in that direction, but you must leave the first at the fourteenth milestone and the other at the eleventh. Whichever way you go, the side road you take is sandy for

> some distance and rather heavy and slow-going if you drive, but soft and easily covered on horseback. The view on either side is full of variety, for sometimes the road narrows as it passes through the woods, and then it broadens and opens out through wide meadows where there are many flocks of sheep and herds of horses and cattle driven down from the mountains in winter to grow sleek on the pastures in the springlike climate.[54]

It was not only the destination that mattered, then, but the journey itself with its pleasant views, while the existence of milestones allowed Pliny to issue precise directions.[55] Ideally a villa should be close not only to a road but also to a town (for markets and labour) and a port or river (for export). Those along the busy coastal strip south of Rome were well placed for all three.[56] Such was the fashion for villa life that late in the first century CE, Martial joked about farm owners who kept country estates merely for the look of things and had to bring food with them when they visited. The target of his epigram, Bassus, was 'carrying with him all the riches of a favoured country spot': cabbages, leeks, lettuces and beetroots, thrushes, a hare and a suckling pig. He even had his footman bring a supply of eggs.[57]

Not far from Pliny's villa, another Roman site gives an even better impression of the kind of facilities travellers might have enjoyed in a larger town. Ostia Antica is located on the Tiber at the intersection of the Via Ostiense and Via Laurentina. It connected not only roads but also sea routes, and at its peak was home to 50,000 residents and hosted offices of multiple trading firms. So big is the archaeological site today that even in high season it can still feel quiet as the sea breeze kicks up needles dropping from the Roman pines. In the 'Square of the Corporations' one floor mosaic with a picture of a ship advertises 'Navi Narbonenses', with leaves to either side indicating wishes for a safe journey. That should mean something like Narbonne ships, though the Latin isn't quite right and it turns out the 'Navi' was inserted by a restorer who'd clearly skipped a lesson on the rules for abbreviations.[58] Those arriving at the sea port could pick up the Roman equivalent of a taxi: a two-wheeled gig drawn by a pair of mules. These are illustrated on a mosaic in the 'bathhouse of the coachmen', where the mules are given names including Pude[n]s

('Modest'), Podagrosus ('Arthritic'), Potiscus (perhaps 'Thirsty'), and Barosus ('Silly').[59] While waiting for a carriage, travellers might have enjoyed Ostia's well-preserved wine bar, the Thermopolium (literally, hot food spot) di Via di Diana. Behind its three arches are a dining room with a black and white geometric mosaic floor, a bar area, kitchen space and courtyard for outdoor food, all easily imagined filled with chattering diners and the chime of drinking cups. Set into the floor is a round stone compartment for keeping items cool, while above a set of shelves perhaps meant for storage are images of a drinking cup and food, including what looks like a carrot. I'm wondering if this refers to crudités with the drinks, but one ancient recipe suggests cooking carrots with cumin, so it could also have been a hot and spicy veggie snack.

Slumming it in bars could be avoided if, like Cicero, you owned at least six out-of-town properties. I head south from Rome via one place associated with him, Bovillae. About eleven miles south-east of the city and now known as Frattochie, it was the site of the clash between Cicero's client Milo and Milo's political rival Clodius in which the latter was killed.[60] Conventions of travel were a point of contention in the subsequent trial. In Milo's defence, Cicero argued that because Clodius was travelling without an entourage, he must have been up to no good. Others, however, pointed out that in fact Clodius and his three companions had a retinue of thirty slaves armed with swords, typical for a traveller of his rank.[61] Cicero's defence proved unsuccessful and Milo was exiled.

Today, Frattochie is at the far end of the walkable/cyclable section of the Via Appia Antica. The track – only a small section of it paved at this stage – leads down a hill, straight as ever, the busy main road screened off by pines and poplars. To one side stands a stone mausoleum, marble cladding long lost, topped by a nineteenth-century brick tower that served as a trig point. (The tomb of Caecilia Metella was similarly used by surveyors.) A better illustration of a Roman road, however, is to be found beneath ground level. Across the current Strada Statale or SS7, it lies beneath a branch of McDonald's, visible through the restaurant's specially constructed glass floor. A side street that fell out of use and was buried early in the Appia's life, it's remarkably well preserved, showing the distinct camber and drainage channel to either side of the paving, as well as three roadside burials. No grand tombs for these people, only plain graves.

A little further south-east lies a key site on one of the most famous literary journeys on a Roman road, that of Horace, who in his *Satires* (published in the 30s BCE) described a stop at a 'modest inn' at Ariccia (Lat: Aricia) in the Alban Hills. Nearby was a sanctuary of Diana, a popular destination for visitors.[62] Further south, Horace and his companion reached the start of the canal that ran parallel to the Appia through the Pontine Marshes, where his description evokes more a raucous service station than the peaceful romance of modern ruins:

> Next came Appii Forum, crammed with boatmen and stingy tavern-keepers. This stretch we lazily cut in two, though smarter travellers make it in a single day: the Appian Way is less tiring, if taken slowly . . . Then slaves loudly rail at boatmen, boatmen at slaves: 'Bring to here!' 'You're packing in hundreds!' 'Stay, that's enough!' What with collecting fares and harnessing the mule a whole hour slips away.[63]

The Via Appia is as straight here as you imagine, the dullest drive, but with a speed limit of 60 km per hour (if, unlike most, you choose to respect it) you do get a view of the landscape. Side roads are labelled by the mile: *migliara*, with a number. They criss-cross the marshes in a grid, like the squares of a maths exercise book, drainage ditches to either side, all too easily flooded. East from Terracina towards Itri, however, this is no longer a dead straight road. It curves up through the mountains to make the crossing. As I reach the summit the heavens open and water streams across the road as it snakes up and then downhill. My reward, though, is a stunning view of Itri's medieval castle as I approach the town. The rain has eased and it stands fairy-tale golden before a mountain shrouded in mist. Over Formia there's a rainbow.

Tradition has it that a tomb at mile 85 of the Appian Way is that of Cicero, though scholars are sceptical. The story goes, however, that he was murdered on the road. According to Seneca's summary of Livy, 'as he leaned out of the litter and craned his neck without a shudder, his head was severed'.[64] The mausoleum named for Cicero today is a round stone construction but there's nowhere to park and so I don't get more than a glimpse before I turn back west along the Via Flacca.

That leads me past the splendid fortress on the coast at Gaeta, a formidable landmark jutting out on its peninsula, its forbidding bastions atop steep cliffs, and through the tunnels that now take the road through the mountains.

By the end of the third century BCE, the major radial routes out of Rome were in place. The Via Ostiense, leading to the port of Ostia. The Via Aurelia, north up the coast towards Genoa. The Salaria, Flaminia, Tiburtina. The Via Latina and the Via Appia. They still exist today, marked on street signs, sometimes close to their old locations, sometimes thoroughly updated. While some philosophers sounded notes of caution, the control of nature that such engineering represented was perceived, at least in literature, as a human triumph.[65] As the geographer Strabo (another Greek) observed: 'The Romans have provided for three things that the Greeks, on the other hand, neglected: roads, aqueducts, and sewers.'[66] Hardly a trio to evoke romantic sentiment, but one that fitted very well with Diodorus Siculus' assessment that the Appia served the 'common good'. As gravel and stone flags criss-crossed Italy they secured the Romans' connections, but more than that, milestones marked the growing empire's presence. Mountains, marshes and rivers were still challenges to the traveller, but through their grip on the landscape the road builders were showing how nature might be conquered.

2

Journeys through the empire

In 1852, builders in the Tuscan town of Vicarello were working on a redevelopment of its thermal baths. The project threw up a spectacular archaeological find: about 5,000 bronze coins and proto-coins (Etruscan, Greek and Roman) and a range of other metal objects, including artefacts in gold, silver and bronze.[1] Among them were four silver cups, now in the Museo Nazionale Romano at Palazzo Massimo in Rome. Made to the shape of milestones, these 'Vicarello cups' or 'Itinerary cups' are between 9.5 and 11.5 cm tall. Each is engraved with a travel itinerary listing stops between Cádiz and Rome, a journey of 1,840 Roman miles (2,723 km). The four itineraries differ in some details, perhaps reflecting the construction or repair of alternative roads,[2] but all present broadly the same route from Cádiz to Córdoba, Valencia, Tarragona, then picking up the Via Domitia through southern Gaul – Narbonne, Nîmes, Turin – crossing the Italian peninsula on the Via Aemilia from Piacenza and Bologna to Rimini, and following the Via Flaminia south past Narni for the final stretch to Rome.[3] By connecting up a series of existing routes in Hispania (some of them used by Hannibal two centuries earlier during the Second Punic War), the Emperor Augustus (63 BCE–14 CE) and his officials had created a major thoroughfare.[4] This new Via Augusta linked the Iberian provinces into the Roman road network.

The cups had been presented as a votive offering at the sacred spring of Aquae Apollinares, dedicated to Apollo and the Nymphs, to Aesculapius, god of medicine and Silvanus, god of the countryside. Aquae Apollinares was a longstanding site with a bath complex and gymnasium, but who made the offering we can only speculate. Recent scholarship has suggested that perhaps the owner was connected to the silver mines of Hispania, possibly someone who benefited from the improvement of the Via Augusta in the first half of the first century CE (though some experts date the cups earlier); even if there was no direct link, the silver of the cups might have evoked Hispanic origins.[5] Their milestone shape is notable, too, because milestones – along with arches and bridges – distinguished Roman roads from others. Even where the empire had taken over an old route, these markers were an unavoidable visual expression of the new power. As one emperor succeeded another, clusters of milestones recorded their rule. And, importantly, no other empire had them.[6]

Following the Vicarello itineraries, we get a sense of the roads' importance for the practical functioning of the Roman Empire, but also of their modern cultural significance. I start at the southern Spanish port of Cádiz, west of the Strait of Gibraltar, for the Romans the end of the earth.[7] Before it became the Roman Gades, Cádiz had been a Phoenician colony, Gadir; alongside Tyre and Carthage it was one of the three major ports of the Phoenician Empire. The Romans had begun their conquest of Iberia in the third century BCE, expanding south from a bridgehead at Tarragona. The colonists were attracted by access to silver, lead and tin mines. They also developed a fishing industry, particularly for tuna, producing salt fish and garum. The merchants of Cádiz became important enough that seats were reserved for the Gaditani in the Colosseum.[8]

Among the wealthy of Cádiz were the Balbi family, known for their patronage of theatres in both their home city and Rome. Their Roman theatre was buried beneath later construction but came to light in the late 1930s, during the extensive remodelling of Rome sponsored by the Fascist regime.[9] The Balbi had successfully navigated the politics of the later Roman Republic, though not without allegations of corruption.[10] Their Cádiz theatre once seated 10,000 spectators. Beneath its worn stone tiers, a curving corridor shades me from the sun. In the visitor centre a surviving piece of ancient graffiti labels Lucius Cornelius Balbus a thief. His uncle, also named Lucius Cornelius, had been the subject of a court case challenging his citizenship, in which Cicero successfully defended him. In the course of doing so, in fact, Cicero used a metaphor of the roads:

> What reason is there why a citizen of Gades should not be allowed to become a citizen of Rome? For my part, I think none at all. For since from every state there is a road open to ours, and since a way is open for our citizens to other states, then indeed the more closely each state is bound to us by alliance, friendship, contract, agreement, treaty, the more closely I think it is associated with us by sharing our privileges, rewards, and citizenship.[11]

Here is evidence for one elite perception of the road network: as drawing together the city states of empire.

I follow the itinerary of the cups north from Cádiz to Seville, by train. There's an unhappy dog across the aisle, in a Covid mask, over his face, around his ears. Masks are still mandatory on trains here. We're travelling faster than the Romans, but troubles of disease and the need to transport animals would hardly have been unfamiliar problems.

The train dips underground between Cádiz and Estadio and wheels around the lagoon, past Puerto de Santa María. I wonder how the Vicarello travellers crossed these rivers: were there bridges, or did this, like the Appia canal, require a boat? We pass salt pans, another industry with ancient roots, vital for preserving fish and meat before refrigeration. The natural salt lagoons in this area were in use well before the Romans got here.[12] At El Puerto there's a vinegar factory: salt and vinegar, makes sense. We pass a wind farm, with modern, sleek white windmill blades, and a field of solar panels, silvery black. The Romans might theoretically have had windmills, but there's little evidence they did, favouring watermills instead.

The station at Jerez de la Frontera is stunning, decorated with polychrome tiles, blue and white with images of Athena and Scipio Africanus. A woman in the seat in front is snapping pictures of the tiles. 'That's the Roman emperor who was born in Africa,' says the man beside her, who I suspect has confused Scipio with Septimius Severus. Scipio was a general, not an emperor, and was born in Rome. He's commemorated here (I'm guessing) for his role in the Roman conquest of Iberia in the Second Punic War, a little before 200 BCE. He got the name 'Africanus' after his most famous victory: against Hannibal's troops at the Battle of Zama in what's now Tunisia. I resist the temptation to interfere. The train speeds through gentle hills, punctuated by tall concrete grain stores, through fields spanned by spidery metal irrigators. Houses come in white and pale earth colours, reflective of the sun. Plane trails cross blue sky. We pass olive groves and what look like commuter towns. There's a stop called Dos Hermanas. I wonder who the two sisters were.

Like Cádiz, Seville (to the Romans Hispalis) was a Phoenician port before the Romans got here. It lies inland from the coast on the Guadalquivir river, which was navigable by boat. The city centre has a small Roman site, featuring amphorae for transporting salt fish, discarded oil lamps, and earthenware water jugs. Around the displays are in-situ mosaic floors with imagery that gives the houses here their names: the House of the Nymph, of Bacchus, of the Columns, of Oceanus, the Ivy House. The more important Roman settlement locally, however, was Itálica, a few kilometres north, founded in 206 BCE, birthplace of the Emperor Trajan, and perhaps of Hadrian too.[13] The ruined amphitheatre is well kept, as are the mosaics of its lost houses. Itálica is close by the Sierra Norte mining area, with its link to the Vicarello cups. There must have been carts of silver ore somewhere on these roads, even long before the traveller had those cups made up, but now Itálica is quiet enough to hear the birdsong above a distant motorway, and calm enough to attract butterflies. Its geese are lazing in the shade. A splendid road runs through the ancient city, and even where the paving slabs are gone, its line is visible in the stretch of field leading to the newer town of Santiponce, where it disappears with its ghosts beneath the buildings.

From Seville both road and river lead to Córdoba. I go for the train, but almost miss it as I linger over coffee in the station. The experience of the medium-distance train from Cádiz has misled me. This one, in contrast, is high-speed, and that means there's security. Bags through an X-ray machine. I spot a couple jumping the queue, follow suit, and make the train with a minute to spare. It's less than twenty years since the 11 May bombings of trains into Madrid, and the threat of terrorism hasn't disappeared.

Ancient history and literature has numerous accounts of peril on the roads. Livy described a 'conspiracy of shepherds' in Puglia, 'whose banditry had made roads and public pasture lands unsafe'. The governor 'convicted some seven thousand men; and many of them fled from there and many were put to death'.[14] Corrupt guards in league with bandits, nuisance drunks and donkey thieves were all reported on the roads.[15] Apuleius, a writer of the later second century CE, included in his *Metamorphoses* the story of a traveller who hoped to leave his inn before daybreak. The porter advised against it. Not in the hours of darkness: 'Don't you know that the roads are infested with robbers?'[16] While human assailants were one risk, wild animals were another, at least in the literary imagination. Apuleius' characters were warned of 'bands of large wolves with heavy-laden, enormous bodies, accustomed to plunder at will with extremely fierce savagery'. Such was their 'insane hunger' that 'along the route that we had to follow lay half-eaten human bodies, and the whole area glistened with white bones stripped of their flesh'. The wolves disliked sunshine, however, and by travelling in the daylight, 'not strung out like a ribbon, but in a tight wedge-shaped convoy', those on a journey might protect themselves.[17]

The Emperor Tiberius probably could not do a great deal about flesh-eating wolves, but he could tackle the human problem. According to Suetonius: 'He gave special attention to securing safety from highway banditry and lawless outbreaks. He stationed garrisons of soldiers nearer together than before throughout Italy.'[18] During wartime and other crises, travellers might avoid major roads altogether, resorting instead to the *calles publicae* more usually used for moving flocks of sheep.[19] A less scrupulous person determined to prevent pursuit might even sabotage the post service by killing or laming the horses: the future Emperor Constantine is said to have deployed this tactic on hearing that his father was close to death.[20] Travellers could take precautions, for example by dressing down and keeping expensive jewellery out of sight, as well as ensuring they had an adequate entourage. In 296 CE, Ploutegenia was due to visit her husband Paniskos in Koptos (Qift, about 43 km north of Luxor on the east bank of the Nile). 'If you find an opportunity,' he told her, 'come here with good men . . . Bring your gold ornaments with you on the trip, but do not wear them on the boat.'[21] I do much the same, leaving my diamond ring at home. My entourage is virtual, but the threat of bad reviews on social media is a handy weapon for the modern traveller, as are the posts from the night bus to ensure the world knows my whereabouts.

No quantity of protection, however, could safeguard the careless traveller who failed to prepare for a voyage. Seneca the Younger described how the army of Cambyses, king of kings of the Achaemenid (Persian) Empire, faced disastrous consequences when he failed to check the geography of enemy territory:

> Without providing supplies, without investigating the roads, through a trackless and desert region he hurried against [the enemy] his whole host of fighting men. During the first day's march his food supplies began to fail, and the country itself, barren and uncultivated and untrodden by the foot of man, furnished them nothing.[22]

In desperation, the troops turned to cannibalism. Cambyses would have done better to consult an itinerary: these are known to have been used in wartime.[23] Indeed, in a treatise on military matters written probably in the first half of the fifth century CE, Vegetius specifically recommended that commanders do so, in order to learn about distances and road conditions, and so that they:

> Might take into account shortcuts, branch-roads, hills, and rivers. So much so, that more ingenious commanders are claimed to have had itineraries of the areas in which their attention was required not so much annotated but even illustrated, so that the road for setting out might be chosen not only by a mental consideration but truly at a glance of the eyes.[24]

Several itineraries survive, including the Antonine Itinerary, which describes routes across the Roman Empire. Though sometimes associated with the Emperor Antoninus Pius (r. 138–161 CE), its name more likely refers to Marcus Aurelius Antoninus (r. 198–217 CE), better known as Caracalla. The surviving version must, in any case, have been completed later in the third century.[25] These lists of stops were not only handy for military planning but also for more general travellers, who could consult them to confirm distances between stopping points, whether waystations or towns, and to estimate the likely duration of a journey.[26] For the duration of my journeys I rely on railway timetables, which bar the odd delay are fairly safe. My train north from Seville speeds through morning mist, scenic for me, though poor visibility was less than ideal for someone riding post. It's spring, and thin threads of green rise from seedlings in ploughed fields. A short walk from the station in Córdoba I get a glimpse of Roman road with its familiar stone paving. It lies beneath ground level in a little set of gardens, outside the old line of the city walls, between two cylindrical brick mausoleums from the first century CE.

Córdoba is part of the same Sierra Morena mining area that was so attractive to the Phoenicians, Greeks and Carthaginians before the Romans, but as the Roman city of Baetica it also exported other goods. Most of the Roman layer is now beneath ground: the remnants of the theatre beneath the museum; the amphitheatre beneath the Faculty of Veterinary Sciences; an early Christian basilica beneath the Mosque-Cathedral. (Now officially the latter, this is one of the most chaotic religious buildings I've experienced: a full-on baroque church plopped in the middle of a giant mosque.) An exception to the below-ground rule is a Roman temple, three sides of a rectangle marked out by fluted columns, their Corinthian capitals rising against blue sky amid the modern buildings. To the south, the restored stone arches of a long, low Roman bridge stretch across the Guadalquivir river.

Past Valencia, and the Euromed train streaks up the coast to Barcelona Sants. Two hours and forty minutes, glancing out to my right for glimpses of the sea. The railway stays firmly inland, at least at first, and the sights lean industrial: a ceramics factory, distant blocks of flats. In the west, hills rise steep from a plain. I spot cranes at a port and a ship out beyond. The orange trees are blooming, but sealed into an air-conditioned train I can't smell the blossom as an outdoor traveller might. The gardens of the Alcázar in Córdoba had the scent of citrus trees and lilies. That's one way travel's changed. An hour out of Valencia and the sun is gone. All I can see are car headlights on the road to our right, and my reflection back from the window. For most of history travel by night was a risky option: an option nonetheless, especially with clear skies and moonlight, and if a traveller was familiar with the roads, but as Apuleius' porter knew, not one to take lightly.

Barcelona, or Barcino, is in fact off the main Via Augusta, which skirts it a little way inland. Most of Barcelona's Roman road is lost, but its visitor centre has an interactive display showing the roads that linked the city with Rome: the Augusta, Domitia, Aemilia and Flaminia. On the wall is a copy of the Peutinger Map, all seven metres of it. This map, which survives in a thirteenth-century copy measuring 672 by 33 cm, most likely dates from the fourth century CE, sometime after the Antonine Itinerary. It draws together information from itineraries into a visual representation covering an area from Britain to India.[27] At its centre is Rome. The map has sometimes been taken to be a military itinerary, but the most recent scholarship suggests that it probably had a decorative function, perhaps for an imperial palace around 300 CE, and that it was commissioned to celebrate the reach of Roman power.[28] The absence of reference to Christian sites makes a later date less plausible.[29] (This was far from the only known map of the empire: Augustus had apparently had one in Rome, which later inspired Theodosius II to commission a similar one.)[30] Whoever made the map must also have had good access to information about the routes, and perhaps had to compile it himself, undertaking additional research on the areas not covered by the Antonine Itinerary.[31] Whatever the precise process, the map's design served to highlight the importance of the roads to Rome.[32]

Outside the Barcelona visitor centre is the Sepulchral Way, a little strip of what would have been a Roman road just outside the city walls, though no pavement survives. Its line is marked outdoors by red brick and in the visitor centre by red tile. As in Córdoba, the line is made visible by tombs: smaller, these, than the cylindrical mausoleums there. The guide tells me that often inscriptions would be addressed to travellers, asking them to stand and reflect. One, cited in the visitor centre, reads: 'Fare thee well, traveller who has not ignored me, read this carefully, here I lie.' The memory of the deceased would live on in the memory of the passer-by.

Not far from Barcelona is a much more important Roman city. A World Heritage Site since 2000, Tarragona, once a Roman provincial capital, sits right on the Mediterranean coast. The Romans built a military base here at the start of the Second Punic War, 218 BCE, from which they began their campaign to conquer Iberia. This is one place where the name Via Augusta is still in use, marked by a street sign on crumbling plaster. Mopeds line the road, and cars pause at overhead traffic lights.

We're not far from the sea. The weather's warm today, but I wonder how this road did in a winter storm. The line of the Via Augusta, I learn, changed early on in its history when the town's main attraction, the amphitheatre, was carved into the rising rocks beside the water. It's Maundy Thursday, and from above the tiered seats I look down to crowds of tourists, and out to a splendid view of the Mediterranean. There's a sea breeze and succulents. The gardens above the amphitheatre are planted with Roman selections: roses, lavender, rosemary and thyme. The past has a warm scent here. Inside the amphitheatre are the layers of history so characteristic of ancient sites: a smaller Visigothic building commemorating three Christian martyrs, Bishop Fructuosus and his deacons Augurius and Eulogius, burned alive here in 259 CE; a twelfth-century church, built after Christianity was re-established here; a later monastery and finally a nineteenth-century prison.

I walk up the hill, to take the 'archaeological walk' around the walls, which have been reinforced to withstand artillery. Along the way I spot a statue of Augustus, a bronze copy of a Roman original, presented by the Italian government in 1934, removed temporarily during the Spanish Civil War, and reinstalled during a visit by the Italian foreign minister in 1939, when he toured in support of the Franco regime. It's a reminder of the ways that ancient history was deployed in the service of diplomacy; they're a little more upfront about the past here than in Rimini and the interpretation refers explicitly to fascism. At another Roman site, there's a more sinister reminder of twentieth-century history, and this one jars because I haven't been expecting it. While I can breeze through the tales of third-century martyrs, however painful their fate, modern horrors hit differently. The ancient Praetorian Tower was used under Franco as a prison. Between 1939 and 1945 650 people were taken out to be shot from the room now known as the hall of the Hippolytus Sarcophagus for the ancient sculpture that it houses. Dozens more died as a consequence of poor conditions: the building should have held only about a hundred prisoners, but more than twelve times that number were forced in.[33] The early Christians in the amphitheatre are far enough away from memory that their death seems an abstraction, but these people were the same age as my grandparents.

*

From Hispania, a traveller to Rome could follow the stops of the Via Augusta around the coast to Arles in southern France. Here, as on Barcelona's sepulchral way, there are once more tombstones, at the Alyscamps.[34] The name alludes to the Elysian Fields and the area was a Roman necropolis. It lies to either side of the Via Aurelia, which once led into Arles, heading straight for the city's spectacular amphitheatre. (This Via Aurelia ran to the south of the Via Domitia, and connected Arles with Nîmes to the west and Marseilles to the east, where travellers could then continue on the seaside route to Italy.) A milestone in the museum at Arles marks the road's renovation in the fourth century under Constantine, and the *damnatio memoriae* of Maximian, who in 310 CE tried to seize power from Constantine: his name has been erased from the stone.[35]

To reach the Alyscamps involves a walk through the shuttered town centre, quiet until the noise of markets hits, down past the modern cemetery, its wall the remains of an aqueduct, and along a dried-out canal, still thirsty despite last night's rain. The Alyscamps itself is greener, tree-lined, atmospheric in its quiet with the scent of petrichor and the sound of birdsong. An owl hoots among the chirrups. In 1888, Van Gogh and Gauguin both painted autumnal scenes here. In 2015, one of the former's Alyscamps paintings sold for $66.3 million. To either side of the lane lie sarcophagi, mossy and worn (the best inscriptions have been moved to the museum). A modern art installation of egg-shaped stones and mirrors and thread is dotted between them and continues inside the twelfth-century church of Saint-Honorat at the lane's end. The church commemorates Genese, a third-century Roman clerk said to have been martyred for refusing to sign the death sentences of persecuted Christians. This little building ends the Via Aurelia now, but it also marks the start of another, later road: the pilgrim route to Santiago de Compostela.

Twenty miles or so away, in Nîmes, is another ancient arena. I'm struck by the standardisation of these places: forum, theatre, amphitheatre, baths, walls, gates, roads. I wonder how much that struck ancient travellers, or whether the consistency made journeys simpler: inside the empire you knew what to expect, in the same way that today you can always rely on finding a McDonald's. At Nîmes the TGV arrives at Pont du Gard, named for the nearby Roman aqueduct that spans the Gardon river with its three tiers of arches, two large, one small, almost fifty metres high. A local train takes passengers to the city centre, where we're greeted at the station by a large sign showing a palm tree on top of a crocodile: the city arms, symbolising the Roman conquest of Egypt. The lettering reads COL NEM: Colonia Nemausus, the colony of Nîmes. It feels odd to me that you would keep that status as a colony on your city arms. Maybe the point is to lord it over the barbarian Gauls, the never-colonised. Nîmes sits at the junction of the Via Aurelia, leading to Arles, and the Via Domitia, the earliest paved Roman road in Gaul which connected the lowest of the Alpine passes (Col de Montgenèvre) via southern Gaul to Spain. The Domitia takes its name from Domitius Ahenobarbus, a general of the second century BCE who played a leading role in the conquest of the region: his name is known from a milestone found in Treilles.[36] Parts of the road can be seen outside the town hall in Narbonne, and in Nîmes it is marked by a plaque on rue Nationale near the Porte d'Auguste, although the most recent scholarship has questioned whether this was in fact its route.[37]

I have dinner at Le Mont Liban, a Lebanese place just around the corner where I eat falafel and drink rosé. The rosé goes well with the falafel and perfectly with the dessert, explained to me in French as a sort of crème brûlée, which turns out to be a melt-in-the-mouth milk pudding flavoured with rosewater, topped with pistachios and entirely delicious. On the walls of the restaurant are posters from the Lebanese Ministry of Tourism, one of which shows the second-century Roman temple of Bacchus at Baalbek, one of the best-preserved temples in all the empire, including Rome itself, and a reminder that crossing the Mediterranean isn't the preserve of our own age. That's a good 2,000 years during which people might have made this journey, from one end to the other of the Roman Empire.

Indeed, some did. If there's one object more than any other that illustrates the possibility of travel along the routes of the Roman Empire, it's the third-century tombstone of Regina, a British woman, now on display at the Arbeia Roman fort in the north of England, at South Shields. Erected by her husband Barates, a soldier from Palmyra, it is inscribed in Latin and Aramaic, and resembles similar tombstones from Syria.[38] The sculptor has shown Regina seated in a wicker chair, wearing a draping dress and chunky bracelets and working at her spinning (which may be a metaphor for good wifely conduct). The monument not only testifies to the reach of the Roman Empire but in documenting the marriage of this pair it reminds us that the connections made through travel were not merely abstract but involved multiple individuals, who ate, drank, complained, thieved, murdered and even fell in love along the roads. Barates' predecessors might have travelled even further north, to the line of the Antonine Wall, near Falkirk, the final frontier of the Roman Empire in Scotland. There were no paved roads there, though. A southbound traveller would pick up properly paved stone roads just north of Hadrian's Wall, with major routes running via York, Manchester or Chester then south to London and the Channel ports.

With its bilingual inscription, the tombstone also raises intriguing questions about language. While Latin certainly spread across the empire as a common language of the elite – much as business English functions today – it was by no means the daily language of the army. In the east, Latin was used in formal situations to symbolise military power but in practice the working language of the army was Greek; elsewhere, too, while officers required Latin, the rank-and-file used other vernaculars.[39] In the Danube region, near the empire's borders, several inscriptions record the work of military interpreters, responsible for communicating and perhaps also negotiating with neighbouring Dacians, Germans and Sarmatians.[40]

The travelling soldiers remind us that in the story of Rome and its roads, we are never far from war. Most of the empire's major routes can be linked in one way or another to military action, whether to facilitate conquest in the first place, or to consolidate relations afterwards. Military roads were no benign business, as Velleius Paterculus' description of Caesar's campaign in Germany makes clear.

> He . . . made aggressive war upon the enemy when his father and his country would have been content to let him hold them in check, he penetrated into the heart of the country, opened up military roads, devastated fields, burned houses, routed those who came against him, and, without loss to the troops with which he had crossed, he returned, covered with glory, to winter quarters.[41]

While not every Roman road was directly associated with a military campaign, and even those initially built for military purposes were made accessible to all, they cannot be divorced from the history of conquest and imperial expansion. The very existence of roads was essential to maintaining a military presence that required supplies and information. They also allowed Roman troops swift access to quash rebellion: no doubt that acted as a deterrent even when it never proved directly necessary.[42] Roads themselves, and the milestones along them, acted as a statement of imperial ideology, inscribing the idea of Roman rule on the landscape.[43]

The postal service, too, originated with the need for intelligence. According to Suetonius, Emperor Augustus 'at first stationed young men at short intervals along the military roads, and afterwards vehicles' so he could be speedily informed of developments in the provinces.[44] Known as the *cursus publicus*, this system facilitated state communication along the road network. In its first iteration, that involved messengers in relay, but it was later modified so that carriages were available at each station, which enabled a single individual to deliver oral messages, rather than relying on passing them from one runner to another. Messengers were generally either soldiers or imperial couriers, the latter either slaves or freedmen. By the end of Augustus' reign these *vehicula* were fully established and had space to carry passengers and a modest quantity of goods along with the couriers.[45] Official travellers were issued with paperwork to prove their right to these services, and locals were required to provide them with wagons, mules and in some cases accommodation. At the beginning of Tiberius' reign (14–37 CE), Sextus Sotidius Strabo Libuscidianus, a provincial governor, issued an edict to explain who was permitted to take advantage of this infrastructure, and who was obliged to provide it:

> Not all are entitled to use this service, but the imperial Procurator and his son. They may use up to ten wagons or three mules in place of a single wagon . . .; further, persons travelling on military service may use public transport, both those who have a diploma as well as soldiers stationed in other provinces who are passing through. A Roman

> senator may use up to ten wagons . . . A Roman knight on imperial service shall have three wagons . . . A Centurion may use one.[46]

A charming example of how this service was used, if perhaps not a typical one, was the Emperor Constantine's request to Eusebius, a church historian, to send him 'fifty copies of the sacred scriptures'. Eusebius was instructed to give Constantine's letter to his deacon, who would then be authorised to use two government wagons for transport of the books.[47] Meanwhile, in Roman Egypt, donkey drivers seem to have acted as professional couriers for private correspondence.[48]

An extensive legal framework was developed to regulate road construction and maintenance. In order to allow two carts to pass, main roads were to be eight Roman feet (2.4 m) wide where straight and sixteen (4.8 m) at a bend; later roads were often twelve feet (3.6 m) wide, which permitted two vehicles (each about four feet wide) to pass without forcing pedestrians off the paving.[49] Some major roads were, in fact, up to forty feet (12.2 m) wide. In Britain, Fosse Way was eighteen Roman feet (5.2 m) wide, while Watling Street was almost twice the size, at thirty-four Roman feet (10.1 m). Width may have reflected the likelihood of a road being needed for swift transport of troops: the larger the better, in that case.[50] Rights of way were established across private land, but even on the public roads travellers were obliged to pay tolls. Other regulations addressed issues such as water damage. While the initial cost of construction generally fell to the military, highway maintenance was the responsibility of provincial governors, who had an interest in ensuring the roads were built to need minimal repair. In the late years of the empire, the Codex Theodosianus, published in 438 CE, recorded no fewer than sixty-six laws relating to the public roads.[51]

In the early years of the *cursus publicus* system travellers were obliged to pay a set rate (rather like today's bus fares or autostrada tolls), but the practice of payment gradually dwindled. By the time the empire ended, the road infrastructure had become a burden on local inhabitants, who were still expected to provide services to travellers but could not count on any cash for their efforts.[52] On the other hand, there were economic benefits to towns that lay on major routes. Even if some services had to be provided for free, others were paid for.

Travellers might patronise local shops or pay for entertainment along the way. It is not a coincidence that the small towns of Roman Britain were concentrated along the road network.[53] Whether the benefits extended beyond the immediate environs depended very much on whether further infrastructure was developed to integrate the land around with the transport route. Towns and villages that were not linked to the modern roads faced decline.[54]

Mountains, snow, and long, long voyages: for sure, the experience of travellers in a practical sense was never universally positive. What of broader analyses? Most of those that survive are favourable. The enthusiasm comes from Greek outsiders like Dionysius of Halicarnassus and Strabo, who to the key achievements of aqueducts, roads and sewers added that the Romans 'have constructed roads through the countryside by adding both cuts through hills and embankments over valleys, so that wagons carry as much as a boat'. Roman boasts about the roads are most commonly found in inscriptions, such as that on the gate in Rimini.[55] Beyond those moments when a new route was inaugurated, the slow development of the road network over the course of centuries perhaps meant that those living nearby took it for granted, as we still do.

We rarely have access to the voices of the people who worked on construction, whether by choice, coercion or force. It does not seem to have been a desirable job. According to a story told by Plutarch, the Theban general Epaminondas was given the job of paving roads 'to insult him, that being the meanest of employments', yet he took on the task with cheer and 'made one of the most despised of charges in Thebes one to be sought after, a signal mark of distinction'.[56] It seems unlikely that this was a widespread outcome. Tacitus wrote of an incident outside Nauportus (near Ljubljana) prompted by conditions in the army, in which companies of soldiers responsible for repairing roads and bridges joined a mutiny, dragging their camp marshal from his carriage in protest at his attempt to impose 'iron discipline'.[57]

Tacitus also reports a speech by Calcagus, a Caledonian chieftain resisting Roman invasion, in which Calcagus described the Romans as the 'robbers of the world'. He went on, in an oft-quoted section:

'To plunder, butcher, steal, these things they misname empire: they make a desert and they call it peace.' This text is generally thought to represent Tacitus' own critique of the reign of Domitian, under whom Tacitus' family fell from favour. Still, while it may not be reliable as an account of any individual's words, it is notable that among Tacitus' examples of the pains of enslavement was that: 'life and limb themselves are worn out in making roads through marsh and forest to the accompaniment of gibes and blows'.[58] (The words 'in making roads' here are the translator's gloss to some condensed Latin phrasing but they represent a reasonable assumption of why captives would be made to hack through inhospitable territory.)

In the Babylonian Talmud a rabbi observes that everything the Romans had done, they had done for their own benefit: 'They established marketplaces, to place prostitutes in them; bathhouses, to pamper themselves; and bridges, to collect taxes from all who pass over them.'[59] (This is the source for the *Monty Python* scene, and by tradition it got the speaker, Rabbi Shimon ben Yoḥai, a death sentence for denouncing the government, which might explain why so few such critiques survive.) A number of petitions to emperors in the later second and third centuries CE complain about soldiers turning off the main road and harassing or extorting money from local villagers. In one incident, soldiers arrested nine peasants, put them in shackles and extracted a ransom of 'more than a thousand Attic drachmas' for one man; there is some evidence, however, that the authorities responded to petitions because in another case the governor agreed that 'if you prove that any soldier . . . has strayed off to your town, wandering about to enrich himself, he shall be punished'.[60] Perhaps we shouldn't be surprised that these incidents aren't remembered as stories of the roads are told. Many a British town has tussled over the route of a new bypass, only for objections to subside once the road's in use. Even more serious issues can slip quickly from public view. As I was writing this book I read multiple reports about the number of workers killed in the construction of facilities for the football World Cup in Qatar, but by the time the tournament came round, they'd lost their prominence. While hostility to Roman road construction, whether from labourers or locals, may have been remembered for decades, even centuries, by the time the modern histories of the roads were written, it rarely featured. Their writers aligned themselves with the Roman conquerors, and spoke of spectacle and achievement.

By the fourth century CE, when the Emperor Constantine came to power, the spokes of the Roman road network connected the capital to all parts of the empire. Setting out for Spain, or Gaul, a traveller would take the Aurelia up the coast to Genoa; for the lands around the Danube, the Flaminia through Umbria and beyond; for the south and east, the Appia, and its successor the Traiana, followed by the Via Egnatia.[61] Linked by sea to the terminus of the Via Appia at Brindisi, by around the 130s or 140s BCE the Egnatia connected Dyrrachium (Durrës, on the coast of modern-day Albania) via Thessaloniki (where travellers could pick up routes to southern Greece) to Byzantium (later Constantinople, now Istanbul).[62] These roads mapped onto older networks (which were in turn improved) so that by the first century CE Roman roads enabled travel right around the eastern Mediterranean coast to the port city of Alexandria in Egypt, and then beyond, all the way west to Tangiers.[63] The empire now circled its inland sea.

During the later Roman Empire, the pace of road construction slowed. There were a few exceptions, not least the road built under the Emperor Diocletian (r. 284–305) along the eastern frontier, from the Red Sea across what is now Saudi Arabia and into Iraq, and known as the Strata Diocletiana. Despite complaints about the state of the roads, it remained possible to travel from one to the other side of the empire. The milestones made clear whose roads you were on. Yet the meaning of the Roman roads was not static. A new experience of travel was about to open up: the Christian pilgrimage.[64]

3
Early Christian travel

The very first disciples of Jesus Christ did not practise pilgrimage, but from the fourth century onwards, as Christianity became more codified as a religion, it followed Judaism in adopting the practice of travel for religious devotion. Roman roads, in fact, have an important metaphorical weight in the Bible, where a 'highway', that is, a Roman-style raised road, was to be prepared for the return of the Messiah.[1] Christians visited the holy sites of Palestine and Egypt, but – even prior to Constantine's conversion – they also went to Rome. It was the site of the tombs of the apostles Peter and Paul, founders of the Church, and of many other martyrs' graves besides.[2] Rome was more accessible to western travellers than the Holy Land, especially after the Persian conquest of Jerusalem in 614 and the Muslim conquest in 638, and the city became known as the *altera* (other) *Jerusalem*.[3] Rome was also the centre of Church administration, and as a consequence people went there on Church business. Just as someone on a work trip today might add a day's sightseeing, so a cleric going to Rome to obtain a papal ruling might engage in the devotional activities associated with pilgrimage. As Christianity expanded across northern and western Europe, the number of such travellers increased, and while roads were not always their simplest option – maritime routes were often swifter – they certainly made use of the existing network.[4]

Following St Paul's conversion to Christianity, he had spent an extended period travelling in the Middle East:

> I went into Arabia. Later, I returned unto Damascus. Then after three years I went up to Jerusalem to see Peter, and stayed with him fifteen days ... Then I went to Syria and Cilicia ... Then after fourteen years I went up again to Jerusalem, this time with Barnabas.[5]

Various scholars have tried to reconstruct Paul's possible travel routes, which include stretches of the Via Sebaste in Anatolia.[6] His voyage to Rome, however, was the last of Paul's journeys. Late in his life, he was arrested by the Roman authorities after a dispute with Jewish leaders in Jerusalem and spent an extended period as prisoner in Caesarea on the Mediterranean coast (now in Israel). In about the year 60 Paul was sent to Rome for trial; his party landed at Pozzuoli, where they were greeted by local Christians.

At the time, Pozzuoli was a major commercial port. Located at the far northern end of the Bay of Naples, it has a Roman amphitheatre; this is the place where Caligula had a road made of barges built across the water to Baiae.[7] Now Pozzuoli has gleaming white speedboats in the harbour and ferries run to the islands of Ischia and Procida. There's a gorgeous view over lapping waves as the sun sets fiery orange behind the bay's western promontory. Paul's landing is recorded on the side of a local church beside tiles depicting the Life of Christ. The plaque, erected in 1918 by the bishop and citizens, commemorates the 'apostle of the peoples' and the seven days he spent in Pozzuoli, and wishes those who come after 'the new purest glories'. Another plaque on the church wall marks the pastoral visit of Pope John Paul II in 1990, while a further memorial, bronze on rough-hewn marble, quotes from the Acts of the Apostles to describe Paul's arrival. In a neat pun the local restaurant serves Paulaner beer with my pizza.

From Pozzuoli, Paul was sent north, most likely along the Via Domiziana, which led along the coast to connect with the Via Appia north of Mondragone. The day I drive up this road, now the SS7 *quater* ('quater' here meaning fourth variant) is Sunday 25 September. It's election day in Italy and also the day that summer ends in a downpour and all-day thunderstorms. There's a metaphor in that somewhere. Lightning cracks as I cross the Garigliano river that divides the Campania region from Lazio. There are mountains round here but it's hard to distinguish them from clouds: both are looming, and grey. I have to keep my eyes on the road, but I can see that it's marshy to either side. The road runs close up to the sea, and must have needed regular upkeep to prevent flooding. Even today it's in need of resurfacing.

There's no comment in the Acts of the Apostles on the weather Paul experienced, but we do learn that on the way to Rome:

> the brothers and sisters had heard that we were coming, and they travelled as far as the Forum of Appius and the Three Taverns to meet us. At the sight of these people Paul thanked God and was encouraged. When we got to Rome, Paul was allowed to live by himself, with a soldier to guard him.[8]

The two locations mentioned here are both on the Appian Way. Forum Appii was the Roman end of the Terracina canal, the location of Horace's complaining boatmen. The 'Three Taverns', which are featured on the Peutinger Map, are probably more accurately described as 'three shops', one perhaps a blacksmith's, one perhaps serving food, and formed the final post station on the road to Rome.

More details about travel between Anatolia and Rome are found in the life of the second-century saint Aberkios, Bishop of Hierapolis (near Pamukkale in south-western Turkey). His tombstone features one of the earliest Christian burial inscriptions, dating from the 190s and referring to him metaphorically travelling 'with Paul beside me on my wagon'.[9] A *Life of Aberkios*, written about 200 years later, fleshes out the story of his summoning to Rome in order to exorcise Lucilla, the emperor's daughter, who had been possessed by a demon. To obtain his services, the emperor had to send from Rome to Hierapolis. His messengers apparently made the journey to Brindisi in just two days, then thanks to favourable winds reached the Peloponnese within the week. 'From there,' the author writes, 'they used public horses and got to Byzantium in fifteen days in all.' Another sea voyage and further riding post (that is, hiring horses at each stop) completed their journey, in which they were assisted in the final leg by local guides and fresh horses. Aberkios agreed to make the journey, and set a date forty days ahead to meet them in Portus, very near Ostia on the coast outside Rome, which provides a useful estimate of the time travellers thought reasonable for this trip. Aberkios, who took a direct ship from Antalya to Rome, arrived in advance of the messengers, whose return was clouded by seasickness on stormy crossings.[10]

Evidence for Peter's presence in Rome is more fragmentary than that for Paul, but whatever the details, the tradition of his crucifixion there proved crucial to the city's development. The location of St Peter's Basilica is generally explained as sitting above the apostle's tomb.[11] There is certainly no doubt that it was built above a Roman necropolis. During excavations in the 1940s, remains that may have belonged to the apostle himself were identified, and in 1968 Pope Paul VI declared them authentic relics, although experts have been more sceptical.[12]

If the presence of the apostles in Rome attracted pilgrims, Roman Christians also became pilgrims themselves, using the imperial road network to travel to the Holy Land. St Helena, mother of the Emperor Constantine, is an early example, making her journey in 326.[13] The extent to which Helena influenced others to undertake pilgrimage is impossible to ascertain, but it seems very likely that she had some impact.[14] Just a few years later, a traveller we know only as the Bordeaux Pilgrim made a journey from western France to the Holy Land.[15] The surviving account is more detailed than either the Peutinger Map or Antonine Itinerary, providing information not only about overnight accommodation (*mansiones*), which offered bed, bath and board, but also the posting stages (*mutationes*) where horses could be changed and vehicles repaired, one or two between each overnight stay.[16]

The Pilgrim's itinerary lists the stops from Bordeaux via Carcassonne and Arles, then over the Cottian Alps to Turin. The Alps were integrated into the road network from about 15 BCE, with the earliest passes including the Great and Little St Bernard and Mont Cenis.[17] The journey continued via Milan, Bergamo, Brescia, Verona and Padua to reach Aquileia on the Adriatic. From there they (the Pilgrim's gender is unknown)[18] continued to Sirmium (Sremska Mitrovica in Serbia), then south-east to Sofia in Bulgaria, where I pick up the Pilgrim's route.

Sofia was known to the Romans as Serdica or Serdika. Named after a local tribe, the Serdi, it had long been settled, but was established as a Roman military camp and way station by the first century CE. Like many towns of the period, its location on the road was key to its development. Constantine was a regular visitor over several years, and even considered relocating the imperial capital to Serdica. He was reputed to have said 'Sofia is my Rome'.[19] The city lies in a valley with hills all around: walk down the central Vitosha boulevard today and the imposing mountain that gives the street its name rises dramatically behind the National Palace of Culture. Sofia's particular attraction was a hot spring, and today's regional history museum is housed in a splendid 1912 bathhouse with striped red-and-white walls and arched windows surrounded with yellow paintwork, just across the square from the remains of a Roman counterpart (which would probably have been just as colourful).

In 343, Serdica was the site of an important Church council, convened in an effort to settle the Arian Controversy, a dispute between the eastern and western branches of the Church concerning the precise relationship, in terms of time and substance, between God the Father and God the Son. This may seem an obscure theological question but it generated such heat that the eastern and western bishops refused to talk to one another and retreated to separate houses. Nonetheless, there was plenty of life in Sofia well into the sixth century. Extensive archaeological remains for this period survive, preserved after they came to light during excavations for a new metro station in 2010–12. I take the steps down to the old city level, where parts of the remains are accessible outside, while more delicate mosaics are covered over in a visitor centre and the passing metro rumbles on the far side of a wall as we circle the remains of houses. The objects found in the dig indicate the types of activity that went on at these way stations: dice and counters bring to mind the modern hotel casino, while pins and needles remind me of the traditional sewing kit. Not far away in the archaeological museum is more evidence of the Roman past: milestones, altars, funeral inscriptions, pottery and grave goods. There's an amphitheatre in Sofia too, below a hotel. Outside the metro site, visible through floor-to-ceiling windows, are the familiar slabs of flat Roman pavement, now revealed beneath Sofia's characteristic yellow brick roads. (These were installed early in the twentieth century, around the same time that they were fashionable in the USA, where they inspired L. Frank Baum's *The Wonderful Wizard of Oz*.)

The remnants of Sofia's early Christianity are most visible in the round church of St George, with its Roman temple base. I assume at first that this must be the large round building visible from outside the visitor centre, until I notice the minaret beside that. St George is in fact tucked into a rectangle of more modern buildings (I suspect nineteenth-century), and sits beside an extensive archaeological site, the predictable paved street beside foundations of multiple buildings. Inside, its dome is frescoed. The earliest images date from the ninth century, and include that of an angel, halo hovering around a heart-shaped face with arching eyebrows over big wide-set black eyes. Outside I spot a traditional restaurant, offering the local speciality, *cavarma*: chicken, peppers and tomatoes in a herby sauce. The Bordeaux Pilgrim doesn't tell us anything about where they ate. We're left to speculate whether (like me) they enjoyed the local cuisine, or turned up their nose and longed for home.

We do know, however, that from Sofia the Pilgrim headed to Philippopolis, now Plovdiv. An ancient Thracian city that had been under Roman rule since 46 CE, Plovdiv, like Sofia, was located on the Via Diagonalis or Militaris (of which more in the next chapter). It was the turning-off point for a minor road that connected this route to the more southerly Via Egnatia through the passes across the Rodopi mountains that now divide Bulgaria from northern Greece. I take a cab from my hotel to Sofia station. The driver is young and chatty, with good English and a cousin in Birmingham. I tell him I'm from Manchester, so he starts talking about football, and hooliganism, and in a surprising leap shares that he's a believer in Jesus Christ. Christianity is very present in these cities, as is the subtext of opposition to Islam, though some of the driver's friends are Muslims, and they're reasonable guys. I could imagine him, with his beard and shades, as the trendier sort of vicar, telling his congregation we need peace in the world, and not to beat up fans of the opposing team. He tells me that in Plovdiv I will 'feel the spirit of the old times'.

Two-and-a-half hours later I clamber down from the train, ready to explore Plovdiv. Extensive development of the city's heritage sites in the past decade and a half, leading up to its stint as European City of Culture in 2019, has delivered to impressive effect and I run across my Roman road almost by accident. As I descend steps into an underpass I find myself standing on great slabs of stone, glass-fronted shops to either side, among them a clothes store named 'Simply Irresistible', a shop selling glass trinkets, another with cheap jewellery, others offering watch repairs and second-hand books. Outside a florist are little plants stacked around what looks remarkably like an ancient stone altar. A query later on social media, and it turns out that it is in fact a funerary monument, dating from the second century CE and dedicated to Good Fortune. It commemorates Lucius Crispinus Epagathos, originally from Cappadocia in central Anatolia, who became a citizen of Philippopolis.[20]

Up the steps, at present-day ground level, stretches of Roman street run around the central Post, Telegraph and Telephone building, located next to the old Forum. Their lines are marked out by patterned paving in the modern square, ending where the lower Roman level has been revealed and with it the old road. A young man all in black – fedora, jeans, sleeveless T-shirt, jacket slung over his shoulder – takes the steps down and walks along the Roman pavement, disappearing into a subway beneath a modern dual carriageway. Beyond him lies the Ramada Trimontium, with lines of gold-framed windows, gilt balconies and in Latin cursive a red neon sign for its casino. The name Trimontium references Plovdiv's three hills. At the far end of town, the east gate, once marked by a triumphal arch to Hadrian (of all the emperors Hadrian does seem the most travelled) is now fenced off, the site awaiting restoration.

Plovdiv's original settlements are far older than those of the Romans. They go back millennia, and were situated on a group of volcanic outcrops that remind me of Stirling, in Scotland, where I grew up. In some accounts there are not three, but seven of them, though I suspect that's because, on the Roman example, seven is the correct number of hills for any city, and the calculation is made to fit.[21] The Romans, however, secure in their control of the area, settled not on the hills but at their foot, building a forum, odeon and temples, and a stadium, one of the few in the entire empire. The stadium is now largely buried beneath the main street, but one end survives, has been excavated, and houses a stylish café-bar, while another section can be seen in the basement of fashion store H&M. The Romans did take advantage of the hill to site a theatre, still in use, built into the slopes much like the one in Athens at the Acropolis.

Following the edicts of Serdica in 311 and Milan in 313, which together ended persecution of Christians and extended toleration in the Roman Empire, Plovdiv became an important centre for early Christianity. Its influence is apparent in a striking pair of basilicas, both recently restored. The larger bishop's basilica was beautifully decorated with a mosaic floor (Plovdiv's expertise in mosaic production is apparent in the fact that it's the only place where Greek had a specific verb to describe the process). The two layers of mosaics, the second laid after the first was damaged, perhaps by an earthquake, have been carefully separated and are now displayed showing designs of birds alluding to Christian themes amid the geometric patterns, among them a peacock, parrot and guinea fowl. A little way down the road, a small basilica, once a baptistry, incorporates a cross-shaped baptismal font for full immersion. Beside it are images of a stag drinking water, a metaphor for Christians receiving truth from the gospel. Birds are also present in the decor, especially the Holy Spirit as a dove, though the interpretive panel translates this as 'pigeon'.

From Plovdiv the Bordeaux Pilgrim headed south-east to Constantinople, then travelled via Ankara to Tarsus and Antioch before picking up the Via Maris south. The Pilgrim made few notes, although there is mention of the spot where Diocletian killed Carinus (at the Battle of the Margus, in present-day Serbia), of the tomb of King Hannibal, and the link of Tarsus to the Apostle Paul. The narrative picks up significantly with the Pilgrim's arrival in the Holy Land, where they detail the places visited. Some of the roads of Palestine pre-dated the Romans, but the network had been developed under Hadrian (117–138 CE).[22] The return leg of the journey illustrates an alternative route: from Constantinople the pilgrim travelled via Thessaloniki, on the Via Egnatia, then turned through Pella, 'where Alexander the Great the Macedonian was', south towards Aulon Trejectum. The precise location of this place is not known but Aulon was in the province of Messenia in the south-western Peloponnese.[23] From there, the Pilgrim returned by sea to Brindisi, from where the Via Traiana provided a route through Canosa di Puglia (Canusium) to Benevento before connecting with the Via Appia to Rome.

Some fifty years after the Bordeaux Pilgrim, the account of another Christian traveller, Egeria, confirms the possibilities of travel across the breadth of the Roman Empire. These itineraries are sparse in detail, sometimes barely more than lists of stops, but would help a subsequent pilgrim plan and prepare for a journey. Thought to have been a Spanish nun, perhaps aristocratic, certainly acquainted with monastic life, Egeria probably travelled from somewhere on the Atlantic coast, perhaps Galicia or Aquitaine, to the Holy Land.[24] Although she made her journey in about 381–4, the only copy of her *Travels* dates to the eleventh century. It was most likely made in the monastery at Montecassino, ended up in the hands of a lay fraternity in the Tuscan town of Arezzo, and was only published in the late nineteenth century.[25] While no description of Egeria's western travels survives, the manuscript details her efforts to reach Mount Sinai, which involved a journey south along the eastern shore of the Gulf of Suez:

> At one time you are so close that the animals' feet are in the water, then you are a hundred or two hundred yards from the shore, and sometimes you are half a mile from the sea and going through desert.[26]

The party made use of staging posts to replenish their supplies of water as well as to stop overnight. The writer observed, however, that the locals had an advantage in travelling: in the desert, where there was 'no road whatsoever', their camels were able to follow direction marks even by night. Arriving finally at Clysma, the Roman Red Sea port for trade with India (located at the northern end of the Gulf of Suez), Egeria and her companions 'had to have a long rest, as the way through the desert had been so sandy'.[27] Sand, however, was not the only difficulty that the pilgrims encountered. They were provided by the Roman authorities with a military escort 'through the danger areas'. These were evidently located off the state highway, since once the party regained that road, they were able to dismiss the soldiers who had accompanied them from fort to fort.[28]

The records of Theophanes of Hermopolis give us a further insight into the practicalities of moving around the empire. Now known as Al Ashmunin, Hermopolis was located in the Nile valley about 300 km south of Cairo, and Theophanes, an imperial administrator, travelled through Egypt and north along the Mediterranean coast to Antioch (now Antakya in Turkey, close to the border with Syria). In the fourth century, Antioch was one of the empire's largest cities, and at this point more significant than Constantinople.[29] This Via Maris, or road of the sea, was a key thoroughfare in Roman times,[30] but a part of it runs through what's now the Gaza Strip, and has long been inaccessible to tourists. Theophanes' memoranda detail what he and his party ate: in the city of Athribis (about 40 km north of Cairo) he bought 'meat, eggs, two varieties of vegetables and *loukanika*, or smoked sausages'.[31] Elsewhere, his expenses included olive oil, bread, honey, artichokes and fish; he paid for a bath, and for boots for one of his travelling companions, as well as for a felt cap and soap.[32] The honey in Theophanes' notes reminds me of the hotel buffets in Plovdiv and Thessaloniki, both graced by devices to hold chunks of honeycomb from which honey drips down into a little pot.

The meat Theophanes purchased included pork and goat as well as snails; sometimes he bought firewood, suggesting that the party were doing their own cooking.[33] He also purchased 'snow-water', perhaps a substitute for ice.[34] As a public official he could take advantage of the *cursus publicus*, which would enable him to travel more swiftly than someone lacking that privilege, and the accounts suggest that when it was available he did so.[35] He generally covered between twenty-four and thirty-five Roman miles a day, with a minimum of sixteen and maximum of forty-five; on the final stretch between the port city of Laodicea (Latakia, in modern Syria) he travelled sixty-four miles in a day, apparently with a six-strong mounted escort.[36]

Where might these travellers have stayed? Near Sofia, close to the town of Kostinbrod, is the site of the *mutatio* Scretisca. Consisting of nine rooms around a courtyard, it had space for its own staff as well as travellers, and was probably built in the first quarter of the fourth century, functioning for around fifty years.[37] Recent archaeological work in Turkey has allowed for the detailed reconstruction of an outstanding example of a probable *mansio* on the Via Sebaste, a major military road in southern Anatolia. This survives not just as an outline of bricks, but up to a second storey. Probably built in the late third or fourth century, and laid out around a central courtyard, the building measured about 44 metres by 29 metres, making it at 1,276 square metres almost twice the size of the Scretisca *mutatio*, which was 730 square metres, to be expected given its more substantial functions. The *mansio* had thirteen rooms on the ground floor, including several for animals (perhaps twenty to thirty mounts in total) as well as guard chambers. Accommodation for travellers (with a capacity of approximately twenty) was on the upper floor, accessed via a wooden courtyard staircase. The rooms had windows and tiled floors, though the accommodation was probably quite basic. So far as staffing was concerned, there might have been half a dozen stable hands, along with domestic staff and a small contingent of soldiers.[38]

I find these spots across the former empire, including in England, at Wall in Staffordshire, a little settlement known to the Romans as Letocetum. Its name is one of many across Europe that evoke Roman remains or heritage. In Italy names beginning with 'For' like Forlì (Forum Livii) or Fornovo (Forum Novum) often refer to way stations; the French Fréjus is Forum Julii; place names featuring numbers, like Tor di Quinto, may refer to milestones.[39] Driving from Wroxeter to Wall, I follow green signs marking Watling Street along the A5. This modern road isn't quite the Roman route (it was improved under the direction of Thomas Telford early in the nineteenth century) but it's not far away. The landscape becomes more built up as I cross the M6 and head for Lichfield.

Wall was a way station at the intersection of Watling Street and Icknield Street. Surviving in a field are the remnants of a bathhouse and a hostel, somewhere for travellers to put up and relax. It was sufficiently important to be listed on the Antonine Itinerary, and is a good example of how settlements might grow up around Roman roads and their service facilities. The villagers of Wall are clearly proud of their heritage. They've put up their own Roman milestone to mark the Diamond Jubilee of Queen Elizabeth II. The jubilee is a milestone in its own way, a panel explains. I put 20p into the honesty box for a leaflet and follow the village heritage walk. It takes me up past the Roman way station and along a drove road. I hear the variety of birdsong, spot a black feather dotted with raindrops lying between track ruts in the grass. Walkers here might once have heard the sound of singing, of marching feet, the clatter of cart wheels. Now there's a distant hum from the M6.

It wasn't only human travellers who needed way stations for rest and relaxation. Animals were an essential part of the transport infrastructure. The roads did not dispense with the use of pack-mules – illustrations of which can be seen on Trajan's Column in Rome – but they also allowed for wheeled transport in the form of carts pulled by draft animals. These might well be mules, though oxen were also used for heavier loads.[40] The task of caring for horses was particularly important, and fell to expert 'horse-doctors'. Some of these men were attached to army units, while others were posted to *mansiones* to ensure that the mounts of passing officials were cared for. The Theodosian Code required that they be fed and clothed by the state.[41] The horse doctor Theomnestos took a midwinter journey over the Julian Alps with the Emperor Licinius, in about the year 312. (These are the mountains between Italy and Slovenia, perhaps named for a road begun under Julius Caesar; like Fréjus, the Friuli region of Italy here gets its name from a town called Forum Julii.) As they began their ascent into the Alps, they were hit by a 'sudden and heavy snowstorm'. Soldiers froze to death on their horses, their mounts continuing as long as they could, 'bearing the soldier's corpse, the corpse still clutching its weapon and the reins, remaining rigid and still somehow united to the horse'. Some horses themselves froze stiff. Only the fast-riding couriers, whose exertion kept them warm, were safe. Among the mounts to suffer was a horse belonging to Theomnestos. As soon as he could, he got the mount inside a small stable, and lit a fire of 'smokeless wood' around him. He force-fed the animal with bread dipped in spiced wine, and applied a restorative potion, to good effect: the horse survived, and Theomnestos' cure, a mix of spices, salts, fats and oil, as well as pigeon dung, was later included in a compilation of veterinary handbooks.[42]

Travel across desert terrain likewise posed particular challenges. The Via Hadriana in Egypt, linking the Red Sea port of Berenike and Antinoöpolis on the Nile (now El-Shaikh Ebada), was equipped with cisterns to collect rainwater and with deep wells to ensure access to water.[43] Military routes beyond the Euphrates and into Mesopotamia in the far east of the empire were similarly provided.[44] Cornelius Nepos described how the Greek general Eumenes opted for a short desert route as opposed to a well-supplied but circuitous one, hoping his manoeuvre would remain secret.

> With that end in view, he ordered the greatest possible number of bladders as well as leathern bags to be procured, then forage, and finally

> cooked food for ten days, wishing to make the fewest possible campfires. He concealed his proposed route from everyone.[45]

The further east we travel in Syria, however, the less evidence we have for the Roman road network. The roads were often beaten into hard earth, though there are some paved roads, for example at Ufacıklı, a road junction in southern Turkey, about 100 km inland from the Mediterranean, and further east at Diyarbakìr on the banks of the Tigris. Beyond the Peutinger Map and Antonine Itinerary there are few visual or written sources. From the fourth century CE onwards there is no evidence of milestones east of the Euphrates, though this does not rule out trade continuing along the roads.[46] On the other hand, fewer sites in these parts of the world have been excavated than in western Europe, and there may well be more to find.[47]

Some pilgrims turned their hands to providing accommodation for those who followed. Among them were Saints Paula and Jerome. Paula (347–404), daughter of a Roman senator, was widowed in her thirties, and embarked on a life of asceticism and celibacy. She became acquainted with Jerome, who was hoping for patronage from the growing numbers of well-off and well-connected Christians, and the pair embarked on extensive travels through the Holy Land, later described by Jerome in his *Epitaph on Paula*. Having made the journey to Seleucia (on the coast of Anatolia) by sea, Paula, taking a social step down from the days when she was 'ferried by eunuchs' (presumably in a litter), now travelled 'seated on a donkey'.[48] Jerome's description of this trip is not, on his own account, complete, focusing only on those locations mentioned in scripture, though he does indulge in a brief reference to Andromeda being tied to a rock near Joppa. His Christian sites included 'the sands of Tyre, in which Paul had knelt', the house of Philip, the site of Dorcas' resurrection, Arimathea, home of Joseph, and Nicopolis (Emmaus). Paula later ascended Mount Zion, and visited Bethlehem, where she saw Rachel's tomb by the roadside. Travelling to Gaza, she took 'the old road', and also visited Nazareth and Cana.[49] Taking the decision to settle permanently in Bethlehem, Paula had a pilgrim hostel constructed, apparently inspired by the Christmas story in which Mary and Joseph fail to find lodging.[50] This provided free accommodation to those who needed it, subsidised both by Paula's personal wealth and by donations from those pilgrims who could pay. It was such a success that in 398 Jerome lamented they were 'overwhelmed'; five years later he reported that his guests included 'monks from India, Persia and Ethiopia',[51] testimony to the extent of travel networks in this period.

Other churchmen, meanwhile, headed north from Rome. Among them was Augustine, a Roman monk, who in 595 was chosen to lead a mission to England, arriving in Canterbury in 597. The main source for Augustine's mission, Bede's *Ecclesiastical History*, does not detail his journey, but a series of letters from Pope Gregory the Great suggest that he avoided the Lombard-controlled north of Italy by taking ship to France. At this stage, it seems that Augustine and his companions returned to Rome, rather than (in Bede's words) 'going to a barbarous, fierce and unbelieving nation whose language they did not even understand'. However, they were persuaded to continue, and most likely proceeded up the Rhône, via Arles, Vienne and Lyons, before heading west to Tours and then north to cross the Channel.[52] Roads from Rome mattered as much as roads to Rome.

These Christian journeys, however, were significant for another reason. As travel to Rome developed through the centuries, the stories of pilgrims, and the journey of Paul in particular, provided travellers with an alternative or complementary script for their own experience on the roads. This script was more ambivalent about the Romans, and more engaged with the lives of those from distant provinces. A traveller on the Via Appia did not have to emphasise the genius of the ancients: he could, if he chose, walk with the Apostle Paul.

PART 2

Saints and Soldiers, 500–1450

4
Byzantium and the Via Egnatia

In the middle of the sixth century, Arthelais, a young Byzantine noblewoman, set out on a dangerous journey from Constantinople. Arthelais had taken a vow of chastity, but when her beauty caught the eye of the imperial ministers, the emperor demanded that her father Lucius, a proconsul, hand her over. To avoid a forced marriage – so the hagiographer of this future saint tells us – Arthelais fled west to Italy to seek the protection of her uncle Narses, a famed Byzantine general who had risen from the ranks of the court eunuchs to lead the empire's greatest military campaigns.[1]

By the time of Arthelais' journey, the Roman Empire was no longer the force it had been, and that had consequences for the state of the roads. Byzantium (the Latinisation of its Greek name Byzantion) had been made the capital city of the Roman Empire in 330 during the reign of Constantine the Great, after whom it was renamed Constantinople. The division of the empire was formalised in 395, but by the final quarter of the fifth century the western part of the Roman Empire controlled little territory outside Italy. The empire's road network, ironically, eased the task of first raiders, then invaders. A well-connected but inadequately defended Roman province offered rich pickings.[2] The last person who can meaningfully be described as a western emperor, Romulus Augustulus, a child ruler, was deposed in 476 by Odoacer, who himself was murdered in 493 by Theodoric the Great, leader of the Ostrogoths. With the support of the Byzantine emperors, Theodoric ruled for thirty years, basing his court not in Rome but on the Adriatic coast, in Ravenna. Of all the sites in Italy, it's Ravenna that best conveys the splendour of this period of Byzantine rule, the glitter and grandeur of its art. Its churches, mausoleums and baptistery together constitute a World Heritage Site: the mosaics in Galla Placidia's mausoleum that trick the viewer into thinking the walls are covered in rich carpet, which might be soft to the touch; the beautiful image of the Baptism of Christ in the Neonian baptistery; the virgins and martyrs in Sant'Apollinare; the mosaics of the Emperor Justinian I (r. 527–565) and Empress Theodora, her pearls and fabric gleaming from the walls. It was this Justinian who, according to the legend, was scheming to marry off Arthelais.

It was also this Justinian who after the death of Theodoric seized the opportunity to invade Italy and take back the territory that had once been ruled by his western counterparts. In 535, his general Belisarius, who had already enjoyed victory in Africa, began assembling troops to attack from the south in a campaign echoes of which would be heard 1,400 years on. Landing first in Sicily (in parallel with a separate attack on Ostrogothic territory on the Dalmatian coast), Belisarius took control of the island, only to have to pause his campaign to deal with a rebellion back in Carthage. By the end of 536, however, his troops had seized both Naples – thanks to some innovative siege-breaking in which soldiers used an aqueduct for access to the city – and Rome. 'Belisarius', wrote Procopius in his *History of the Wars*, 'led his army from Naples by the Latin Way'.[3]

En route, they would have passed a new monastery at Montecassino, where around the year 530 the future St Benedict had taken over a hilltop formerly occupied by a Roman temple. (If the name sounds familiar, that's because this will be the site of an important battle in the Second World War.) Montecassino lay on the Via Latina, later known as the Via Casilina and now roughly speaking the SR6, which ran south through Lazio via the wide Liri valley, on the opposite side of the Aurunci Mountains to the Via Appia, further away from the sea. It was more suited than the relatively narrow Appia to moving a large force. Yet even in the sixth century, Procopius was impressed by the state of the Appian Way: 'after the passage of so long a time, and after being traversed by many waggons and all kinds of animals every day, [its paving stones] have neither separated at all at the joints, nor has any one of the stones been worn out or reduced in thickness,—nay, they have not even lost any of their polish.'[4]

In Rome, Belisarius benefited from the desertion of many Gothic troops once they realised the local population was against them. Further north other towns surrendered to the Byzantines, and by 538 the Byzantines were in control of the Via Flaminia. Despite various attempts by the Goths to regain the upper hand, they were eventually defeated by Narses, as was a putative invasion by the Franks and Alamanni. The church of Santi Apostoli, built during the reign of Pope Pelagius I (r. 556–561), celebrated the general's victory. If anyone was in a position to protect Arthelais from the emperor, it was this uncle.

The authors of medieval saints' lives did not aim for historical precision, so I proceed with Arthelais' story on the basis of what might have been, rather than what certainly happened. The essentials of the tale – a young woman taking risks to flee an unwanted marriage – seem plausible enough. From the limited information we have, by far her most likely route west was the Via Egnatia. This road was named for Gnaeus Egnatius. A milestone identified in 1974 and now in the museum at Thessaloniki, tells us he was the son of Gaius, Proconsul of Macedonia,[5] but beyond that there is little detail about his life. Dating to the 140s or 130s BCE, the Via Egnatia was the first Roman road built outside Italy, pre-dating those in Spain.[6] Cicero called it the 'military road',[7] which gives an indication of its purpose. Its milestones were inscribed in both Latin and Greek, making Roman power visible to both travellers and Greek-reading locals.[8] It was one of two major 'imperial' roads that connected Constantinople with the west, the other being the more northerly Military or Diagonal Road (Via Militaris or Via Diagonalis), which linked the major centres of Carnuntum (near Vienna) and Constantinople via the cities of Belgrade, Niš, Sofia and Plovdiv, crossing the mountainous territory of the Balkans. Like many Roman routes, it is probably better understood as a collection of roads: indeed, the inscription from which it gets its name refers not to a single road but to multiple ones.[9] In the eastern Roman provinces, roads had been built over an earlier Hellenistic network that was more haphazard than its newer western counterpart, albeit still extensive. They were typically wide (over 6.5 m), though if they were paved, it was not with the large flags of the familiar image, but with smaller stones that made for a less even ride or drive.[10]

Arthelais' journey cannot have been comfortable. Despite Procopius' praise for the Via Appia, further east road maintenance was patchy, and the Via Egnatia became all but impassable in wet weather. Over the course of the fourth and fifth centuries, wheeled transport became less and less practical; pack animals took its place.[11] While the exact process of the roads' decline is a matter of debate among the experts, one theory is that from the later sixth century attempts to maintain the routes for vehicles were largely abandoned: instead they were kept up for mounted or pedestrian travellers, with steps constructed in more mountainous areas.[12] There's general agreement, however, that the quality of public roads did deteriorate. Although diplomatic travellers were still using the Via Egnatia in 519 and 534, both Malchos of Philadelphia (in the fifth century) and Procopius (in the sixth) complained of the state of the Via Egnatia, while the laws of the Codex Theodosianus similarly suggest the roads were in a poor way.[13] Inscriptions show that some repairs were undertaken, for example to the Via Egnatia under Justinian I, but these seem to have been piecemeal rather than the product of long-term planning, and after Justinian there is no evidence for significant repair projects.[14] Among the factors in the roads' decline was periodic raiding, both in the Balkans and Anatolia, that put pressure on governmental structures.[15] If the local authority was barely functioning, there was little chance of road repairs.

Still, Arthelais would have known the Milyon Tasi, Constantinople's Golden Milestone. Like what passes for the remnants of the Roman equivalent, albeit taller, it's now an unprepossessing piece of stone, inscriptions no longer visible, not even distinguished by an explanatory panel. If the Milyon hadn't been labelled on Google Maps I never would have found it. Across the street hundreds of tourists are queuing for the Hagia Sofia, and a few dozen yards down it another queue has formed for the Basilica Cistern. Mosaics, gold and frescoes, and the giant sideways head of Medusa are far more glamorous than a grey, chipped piece of stone. But for the comparison to Rome and the meeting point of roads it's important.

I follow Arthelais from Istanbul along the Via Egnatia, one section at a time – like her, leaving in the middle of the night, though my father has not supplied an escort of 400 armed men. The first leg of my trip, to Thessaloniki, involves an overnight coach. Istanbul bus station's bays are organised in a massive oval: as an indication of the size, my coach firm occupies numbers 137 and 138. All roads lead to Istanbul. At 10 p.m. we're off. Jason at Crazy Holidays Greece has got me a front seat on the bus. I can see the sprawl of Istanbul, and the ribbon of building that runs beside the road. Now, as in the past, good transport links favour development. The queues at the border between Turkey and Greece, I suspect, do not, but there's no choice but to park up and wait.

You know what they don't mention in ancient itineraries, or indeed in the hagiographies of Arthelais? Borders. For most of the existence of these Roman roads there were no border crossings. That's not to say travel was completely unregulated – there were wartime restrictions, and health restrictions – but today's routine checks have only been around since the early twentieth century. We're required to remove our bags while the coach is searched, which didn't happen coming from Bulgaria. A Greek passenger, expensive clothes, returning from a shopping trip with her daughter, tells me the problem is that Turkey has been sending migrants across to Greece. She understates it. News websites are reporting a horrific story of almost a hundred refugees stripped of their clothes and forced to cross the river between the two countries in rubber dinghies.[16] Our stop is revealing of border police priorities. They care to search the coach for people sneaking over the border, but not to search the suitcases for undeclared designer outfits or indeed illegal drugs. Today's young woman fleeing a forced marriage faces barriers that Arthelais did not. Repacked and passports stamped, it's about two in the morning. I glimpse the word EGNATIA on a road sign, then at the toll 'Egnatia Pass', the tag allowing drivers a clear way. This is the Egnatia motorway. We're off. I fall asleep.

We arrive in Thessaloniki early, and I walk down the Via Egnatia (not the motorway this time, something very close to the old road). It's dark enough that cars still have their headlights on, but I'm facing east, and the deep blue sky is slowly turning orange. My hotel is on this street. It's the Imperial Plus, an appropriate name, and to my enormous relief they let me check in six hours early. A few hours' sleep and I'm off to explore. By the time of Arthelais' arrival here, the city had been thoroughly Christianised, with the construction of a new church to the city's patron, Demetrius, in the early fifth century as well as much improved walls, which helped it fend off multiple attacks in the coming centuries.[17] The feast of St Demetrius, which fell in late October, coinciding with the harvest, became the date for a regular trade fair, known as the Demetria.[18] Arthelais and her entourage would have been able to purchase supplies here. Thessaloniki is certainly bustling. One street on my wanderings is filled with Chinese import-export firms. I walk down the Odos Egnatia, as it's called here, to see one monument that certainly dates back to Arthelais' time, the Arch of Galerius. Built in brick, its marble friezes show the tetrarch's victory over the Persians in 298 CE. The remains of later Byzantine walls with alternating layers of stone and brick lead up the hill, while back towards the hotel is a roadside fountain, its ruins including square Roman columns decorated with twisting leaves.

I don't have long here. The following day I set out from Thessaloniki on the coach to Durrës. It's only about 270 miles, but it takes ten hours, once you factor in the wait at the border (again). Like the ancient Via Egnatia, which varied from ten Roman feet wide (2.96 m) to just six feet (1.77 m) in less hospitable territory,[19] this one narrows as it leaves Greece for Albania, where only a single carriageway weaves through the mountains. The Greek exit signs read EXODOS, which feels very biblical. The driver has his mobile in one hand, a fag between his lips and folk music on the speakers. We're briefly along the coast and then turn inland, passing the turn-off at Vergina to the tombs of the kings of Macedon, among them Philip II, father of Alexander the Great. The road curves up, terraced into the hillside through a spectacular pass and a series of tunnels, the longest of them 855 metres, followed by a breathtaking view from a concrete bridge spanning a gorge, a tiny cloud lilting between the file of wooded hills. This is the sort of landscape described by Apuleius in his *Metamorphoses*, when he heads to his ancestral home of Thessaly on 'steep mountain tracks and slippery valley roads, damp places in the meadows and cloddy paths through the fields'.[20] Though this is called the Egnatia motorway, the old Via Egnatia didn't come this way, but took a more northerly route through Edessa.

The hills with their red soil get scrubbier and stonier as we approach the crossing into Albania. This bus, it turns out, is part-funded by the European Regional Development Fund, in a project to improve international transport links. Most of the passengers are olive and fruit pickers coming home after a stint working in Greece. Not far after the border, in the small town of Bilisht, we pass a black marble monument featuring the flags of Albania and the USA. Online, I learn it's a memorial to the victims of communism. During the forty years of Enver Hoxha's rule, Albania had the most repressive of all the Stalinist regimes. Religion, travel and private property were banned, and those judged enemies of the regime faced prison, exile or execution. A little further on, a lake comes into view over the brow of the hill. We make a twisting descent to softly rippling blue. This is Lake Ohrid, bordered by both Albania and North Macedonia. The old Via Egnatia ran round its other side.

We see horses with pack saddles, and in the street people selling fruit and vegetables. By the side of the road is an overgrown railway track. The driver's assistant, a recent law graduate in a seasonal job who speaks excellent English, explains to me that the railway stopped running in the 1990s. After the fall of the Hoxha regime, Albania slipped into virtual anarchy for a while, its citizens' finances destroyed by a giant Ponzi scheme as new banks set up without regulation. Now parts of the railway have been stolen, and buses are the only public transport option. The decline of these roads 1,500 years ago finds a curious echo in the present.

Arthelais made her journey not to Durrës but to another port, Vlöre, seventy-five miles to the south. By this point she had lost her initial military escort, and was kidnapped by robbers. Her devoted servants, however, headed off to pray and give alms at the church of St Eulalia. After several days and the intervention of Jesus (disguised as a poor man), some demons who set upon the kidnappers, and an angel who slew Arthelais' jailer, she was freed from captivity. No doubt happy to leave Vlöre behind, she and the eunuchs took ship for Italy.

Durrës is a port city on the Adriatic coast, once a Roman army colony.[21] I walk here down the Via Egnatia, locally signposted as Rruga Egnatia. It's a busy shopping street, with factory outlets for

Italian brands, cafés, greengrocers, insurance brokers, and a shop selling safes in a little hint that it's more secure to keep your cash at home than risk it in investments. On a nearby street there's a Traiana café, the name evoking the Emperor Trajan and his Via Traiana, while there's an Egnatia travel agency at the port. The next morning I head out to explore. The amphitheatre at Durrës is not so well kept as some I've seen. A mound of grass fills what should be the arena, but its presence is nonetheless a reminder of just how many European states retain the relics of the Roman Empire. My Cold War childhood taught me Rome was part of the West, but these past few weeks of travel have made clear just how much Roman heritage is in fact in the countries of the former Eastern bloc. Buried beneath housing for centuries and initially excavated between 1966 and 1970,[22] the amphitheatre would have held 12,000 spectators. Beneath its seats, off a corridor, is a tiny chapel with a pair of sixth-century mosaics showing St Stephen, alongside Mary in the guise of a Byzantine empress, with two angels and two further saints, Sofia and Ireni. Durrës, like many of the cities on these roads, has had many rulers: the Romans, their successors in Byzantium, the Normans, and later the Venetians (1390s to 1501) and the Ottomans, before the town (as it then was) played an important role in the Albanian liberation movement that proclaimed independence in 1912. Besides the amphitheatre, the Roman past is apparent in columns on the seafront and one of the central streets, amid the palm trees that seem compulsory for beach resorts.

I'm taking the ferry across the Adriatic to the port of Bari, to pick up Arthelais' route in Italy. The young woman on hotel reception doesn't know which gate foot passengers need. 'I've never taken a cruise,' she says. That must be true of many people, historically, along these roads: there might be passing travellers, but they themselves stay still. I wonder how far Arthelais had been from home before she had to flee. For most of the year this ferry runs only overnight. I treat myself to an outside cabin and buy myself a miniature bottle of red wine from the bar, which I'm delighted to find is called the Bar Egnatia. It's a much more comfortable night than the Thessaloniki bus. Once in Bari, I have a lovely walk past sparkling sea and fishing boats. On that same seafront, stepping forward from a line of columns collected from various sites, is a milestone. Originally located on the Via Traiana, it marked the 128th mile of that road, commemorating the fact that Trajan had built it at his own expense.[23] I leave my case at the hotel and retrace my steps towards the Cattedrale di San Sabino before it closes for the traditional southern long lunch and siesta. The church is not the main historical attraction here. No: I'm here to see a road. Downstairs from the cathedral, a small piece of the Via Traiana, perhaps, though that's not certain, has been uncovered in a corner of the excavations. Perhaps even Arthelais travelled this road. A deep rut cuts through its stones, made by centuries of wheeled traffic, testimony to thousands of past journeys. I may have crossed the sea to get here, but I'm still on Roman roads.

Like the eastern roads, those in the west were also affected by ongoing conflict as the Gothic Wars saw one northern ruler after another seek to conquer Roman territory. Sidonius, a fifth-century bishop, complained that the roads were 'rendered insecure by the commotions of people' and that couriers typically experienced 'a great deal of difficulty' in the course of interrogation by over-zealous public guards.[24] There was evidently concern over security, and there were problems with maintenance too. The Appian Way was not consistently repaired: during the reign of Theodoric the section leading up to Terracina known as the Decenovium became impassable as the canal beside it flooded.[25] Driving round Terracina in heavy rain it's easy to see why: water streams down from the steep cliffs and if drains aren't kept clear, flooding is the end result. Even today, the canal is tinted muddy brown. Rainwater's pooling on the roads, spraying up as vehicles drive through, and an aquaplaning vehicle can block a road for hours.

Inaccessible roads also compromised sea routes: while sailing was often swifter, it was only viable if connecting roads stayed open. One that did not was the Via Aquitania that led from Bordeaux, on the Atlantic coast, via Toulouse to the Mediterranean port of Narbonne. After the fifth century, it appears to have fallen out of use as a major thoroughfare.[26] That left travellers from Britain to Rome reliant on the Channel crossing from Dover, and then an overland route along the Via Agrippa via Amiens, Dijon and Lyons, from where they could follow the Rhône south to Marseilles, then either pick up a ship to an Italian port, or take the Via Julia Augusta along the Ligurian coast to

Genoa.[27] This was probably the route taken on his first trip to Rome by Wilfrid, a Northumbrian bishop whose *Life*, like that of Arthelais, features the dangers of travel. When he returned to Rome in 679, however, Wilfrid, who was involved in a dispute about his bishopric, feared that enemies might set him up for attack on the more obvious road. These fears were not unfounded. A prior traveller, Winfrid, also a bishop, had been mistaken for Wilfrid:

> He fell into the hands of these same enemies, as though into the jaws of a lion. He was immediately captured and robbed of all his money. Many of his companions were slain and the holy bishop was left naked and in the utmost straits of misery.[28]

Wilfrid opted instead for the Great St Bernard Pass, another Roman route.[29] The choice of road could, in certain contexts, be a matter of life or death. Seventh-century travellers also probably had the option of the more southerly Mont Cenis Pass, accessed via an easterly route from Lyons leading through Chambéry, Maurienne, Modane and then across the pass to Susa. A reorganisation of local bishoprics in 574, linking key points along the route, suggests it may by then have been in use.[30]

Whatever their dangers, the functioning roads remained essential links for trading. Writing around the year 527, Cassiodorus described a fair held 'in Marcelliana', a location on the Via Popilia between Naples and Reggio Calabria near modern Padula. (The Via Popilia left the Via Appia at Capua, continuing towards the Straits of Messina while the Appia turned inland to cross to the Adriatic coast.) Marcelliana was mentioned as a way station in the Antonine Itinerary and had connections across the south of the peninsula, its annual fair attracting traders from across southern Italy.[31] Trade continued internationally, too. The sixth-century burial site at Sutton Hoo in Suffolk includes remnants of Middle Eastern bitumen as well as French coins, Syrian cloaks, and a Byzantine bronze bucket. For part of their journey, at least, they surely passed along a Roman road.

Safely arrived in Italy, perhaps via Brindisi or Bari (a shorter crossing), or perhaps sailing all the way, Arthelais came to the town of Siponto. There, she heard of the nearby sanctuary at Monte Sant'Angelo in

Gargano, on the spur of Italy's boot and near the main route east to Byzantium and the Holy Land. On the side of this steep hill, a cave-church was dedicated to the archangel Michael. Initially a local shrine, it began to attract visitors from far across the sea. Its location near the port of Bari made it an obvious stop-off point for longer-distance pilgrims.[32] Arthelais set out to give thanks.

I join her trail at Siponto, taking the train north from Bari, past olive groves and grapevines, close to the sea at first, through a series of towns whose names I know only as titles of Italian aristocracy (next stop, Bisceglie: Lucrezia Borgia's second husband, murdered). The train turns inland towards Foggia. There I take the first of two buses east towards the Gargano National Park. This journey is a pain by public transport, but eventually our suitcases are loaded into the luggage compartment and we leave for Manfredonia, passing through more flat agricultural land. The Gargano hills rise with drama to the left. We pass a firefighter beating out a wildfire. Cactuses. The sea again, to my right. Banks of solar panels by a factory. Just outside Manfredonia lies an old church, and beside it the outline of a ghostly second structure, made in metal wire. An art intervention by Edoardo Tresoldi, it recreates a building that Arthelais herself might have seen: the ancient basilica that existed 600 years before the current Romanesque church of Santa Maria Maggiore.[33] At Manfredonia we wait again for the Monte Sant'Angelo connection. A bus that looks very much like ours powers past without stopping. My fellow passengers look after it in disbelief. One runs and slaps the back. That couldn't have been it, surely? It would have stopped. I bring up the stop on Google Maps. There's meant to be another, two minutes later. And sure enough, a little late, a bus arrives. Another moment of panic when it doesn't take the turn-off for Monte Sant'Angelo, but I soon understand why: it's going the long way round, and with its hair pin bends even the long way round is barely navigable for a full-size bus. The driver has a pale wooden rosary hanging from the rearview mirror. I suppose serious pilgrims trust that God will protect them.

Some people opt to walk – there's a route marked all the way to Jerusalem – but most pilgrims here have arrived in comfortable coach parties, rather than braving local buses. San Michele itself, behind the pretty facade, is one long, loud queue down the stairs as we wait for

Mass to finish so we can get into the cave. Probably a Roman cult site, the cave became associated with St Michael in the sixth century, though only under the Angevin rulers in the fourteenth was the staircase connecting the cave with the town centre built. The gold archangel which has pride of place in the devotional museum is from the first half of the eleventh century. The cave itself is so crowded and busy – despite the attendants' pleas for quiet – that it's hard to feel the atmosphere as we circle the side chapels around the altar beneath the low stone ceiling. Some people are trying to pray. Others are taking not-so-surreptitious selfies. Here, according to her legend, Arthelais prostrated herself before the altar. I doubt there would be space today, though her donation of thirty gold coins would, I'm sure, be welcome. The earlier crypt, calm and tranquil, provides a contrast to the bustle. It's now a museum, home to graffiti that records travellers from the north, including a handful of English pilgrims. It's remarkable to see, thirteen centuries on, names carved in runic letters into stone. Herraed, emphasised by its enclosure in a rectangle, stands out, but there are also Hereberehct, Wigfus and Leofwini.[34] Further along is a medieval selfie: a half-finished face cut into stone. The eyes are there, and the hair, and the beginning of a sash across the shoulder, but the nose and mouth are not. Maybe some official stopped the carver part-way through. There are many outlines of hands down the staircase to the cave, and sometimes today's pilgrims place their own hands over them, as if to absorb the essence of the church. There are many more names to spot, from the sixteenth to the twentieth century, and in earlier times graffiti seems to have been widely tolerated.[35] Inscriptions ensured that pilgrims remained spiritually present in a holy place long after their physical departure.[36] Today, however, signs in three languages (Italian, English, Polish) insist that we do not add our own.

Having made her offerings at San Michele, Arthelais returned to Siponto to find her uncle Narses, and the pair travelled on via the town of Lucera to Benevento. There Arthelais was responsible for many, though unspecified, miracles. Her life, however, was short: she died of a fever a few months after her sixteenth birthday. Narses, in contrast, lived well into old age, dying in his eighties or nineties, having spent his later years as Dux Italiae before his dismissal by the new Emperor Justin II in 568 after accusations of abuse of power.[37] Narses' successors, however, lacked the skill or luck to hold all the territory he had gained. In 568, led by Alboin, the Lombards (originally from northern Germany) invaded Italy. By 572 they had made Pavia their capital, controlling the north of the peninsula, from the region of Liguria around Genoa across to Friuli at the north end of the Adriatic. Securing roads once again became vital to sustaining power. The Lombard conquest of Spoleto after 571 enabled them to block the Via Flaminia, the major road connecting Rome and Ravenna.

This proved a particular problem for what remained of Byzantine territory in Italy, now governed by an official called the exarch on behalf of the emperor in Byzantium. Ravenna was the capital of this exarchate (later the term came to mean only Ravenna and its immediate surroundings), which also incorporated the duchies of Venice and Istria on the Adriatic coast and of the 'Pentapolis', so named because it included five cities: Rimini, the terminus of the Via Flaminia, and (in order down the coast) Pesaro, Fano, Senigallia and Ancona. To these the exarch could add Rome and Naples plus Perugia, which had initially fallen to the Lombards but was back in Byzantine control after 598. With the Lombards in control of the middle section of the Via Flaminia, an alternative route through the Byzantine corridor was needed. The exarch and his officials turned instead to a minor Roman route, the Via Amerina.[38] Departing from the Via Cassia just north of Baccano, it crossed the Tiber at Orte, then followed the river valley through Umbria via Todi to Perugia. Travellers then had two options to reach the secure section of the Flaminia: either via Gubbio, or via Gualdo Tadino, which the Byzantines retook in July 599. As important as the road were the new fortifications now built along its route, not least over the mountain pass between Perugia and Fossombrone.[39] The Umbrian cities were politically fragmented, but despite the challenges this posed, a route between Rome and Ravenna was kept open.[40]

Late in the eighth century, however, the road again became a target as fighting picked up following conflict over the election of Pope Adrian I. In 772, a Lombard army laid siege to both Rome and the towns along the Byzantine corridor. Hadrian dispatched a messenger to

Charles, king of the Franks, requesting aid against the Lombard king Desiderius. With the roads blocked, this messenger was obliged to take the sea route to Marseilles. At stake for Desiderius was an agreement made some decades earlier that allowed him to cross papal territory to reach the central duchy of Spoleto: this link was essential to maintaining the loyalty of Spoleto and Benevento to the Lombards. That was not all. Were Hadrian to achieve all that he wanted, Desiderius would have to return earlier conquests too, losing out on vital segments of the Via Emilia as well as the Via Flaminia.[41] In the end it was even worse for Desiderius. Not only did he lose his road connections, he lost his kingdom. Charles – who became known as Charlemagne, or Charles the Great – defeated the Lombards and from 774 the whole of north and central Italy was ruled by the Franks and the Church. There was now, in effect, a second Roman emperor.[42] There was also an easy road from Ravenna to Rome.[43]

With Charlemagne in power, Europe's north–south travel axis grew in importance. His empire stretched across the territories that are now France, Germany and northern Italy, as well as through the Low Countries, Austria and Switzerland. The Carolingian period saw multiple imperial visits to Rome, demanding corresponding improvement of transport facilities. There are more than thirty documented visits by Carolingian kings south: some in the company of armies, some not, and increasingly sophisticated infrastructure developed to support them.[44] Like the ancient Romans, Charlemagne saw the power of roads. His most politically significant trip was that of November 800, when he travelled to Rome in the company of Pope Leo III. Leo had fled to Charlemagne's court after being attacked by political rivals, who had tried to blind him and tear out his tongue, leaving him for dead. Leo's reliance on Charlemagne put him at a disadvantage, but he restored his position by crowning him Emperor of the Romans, thus establishing himself as maker of emperors. This was controversial, because there was already a Roman empress, Irene, ruling from Constantinople. Irene, however, was a woman, which in the period was sufficient in the eyes of some to disqualify her. She was also arguably a usurper. Initially regent for her son, Constantine VI, she secured his betrothal to Charlemagne's daughter Rotrud, before making an abrupt switch of alliances. When relations between Irene and Constantine broke down, she had the young man blinded (a common punishment for treasonous conduct) and secured sole control of the empire. She revisited the possibility of an alliance with Charlemagne, in which he would have retained power in the west and she in the east, but after five years in power Irene was deposed in a coup, and for several centuries the two empires asserted rival claims to the name 'Roman'.[45]

Charlemagne, his relatives and successors had a substantial impact on the road network. The Mont Cenis Pass was certainly operational by the reign of Charlemagne's co-ruler and successor Louis the Pious (r. 813–840), who funded a hospice at the monastery of Novalesa there.[46] (In this period hospices and hospitals were institutions providing accommodation, as in the modern hostel.) Louis' uncle Carloman, who abandoned secular power in favour of the religious life, established a monastery dedicated to San Silvestro (St Sylvester), an early Bishop of Rome, and located on Mount Soratte. This isolated ridge was a well-known landmark and lay to the east of the Via Cassia, a convenient site for pilgrims. One of Horace's *Odes* depicts it in winter: 'Do you see how Soracte stands there shining with its blanket of deep snow, how the straining woods no longer support their burden, and the streams have been halted by the sharp grip of ice?'[47] His readers were invited to pile logs on the fire and pour some wine, and it's easy to imagine travellers at an inn doing the same. The Royal Frankish Annals record that Carloman also visited Montecassino, a pilgrim destination then as now, where he became a monk.[48] These were not only sites for devotion, but by providing hospitality to visitors took on at least part of the role of the ancient way stations.

The closest I get to the Mont Cenis Pass is on a train that takes me from Nîmes to Valence and then north to Chambéry to cross the Alps. It skirts the foothills, passing sharp cliff drops as we begin the stretch north; sometimes rocky, sometimes wooded, pine higher, deciduous lower; glimpses behind of snow-clad mountains proper. It's a long way north to meet this pass, but just as past travellers gambled on which route might be easier and took the advice of local guides, so I've checked the SNCF website, which has sent me north via Grenoble to change, then south-east through the mountains to Turin. From Chambéry the train heads straight into a tunnel. So much for a view. We emerge and the person next to me has shut the blind. Fair enough: it's sunny, she's reading on a screen and I don't want to be rude, but I'd quite like to look out of the window. There's a ten-minute delay because of a train with a fault in front. I head for the bar just as we head back into a tunnel, and my credit card doesn't work because there's no reception. Neither of my credit cards. Slight panic that they've all been stopped, which would not be good, but rather than my coffee get cold, the barista lets me drink it until online service resumes, which happens once we get out of the mountains.

There's always been an industry of small shops and eating places along the roads, and there were other ways to profit too. One important Carolingian route ran via Chur (now in eastern Switzerland). Travellers would head south from Zürich and at the Walensee pick up a royal boat along the lake, the road transport supplemented, where convenient, by inland water. These ferries were expected to turn a profit of £8 a year. From Chur several routes led south: if one was blocked, others might still be navigable. Archaeological research at Luni (near the coast in southern Liguria) also suggests that in some cases ancient roads were being resurfaced.[49] Beyond the need for maintenance, however, there were security risks if the passes fell into the wrong hands. The emperors took care to ensure that they did not, granting the Valtellina (the Adda river valley, now close to the Italian–Swiss border) to the monks of the prestigious monastery of St Denis in Paris. On the Bavarian side of the Brenner Pass (further east, on the road connecting Trento and Innsbruck) imperial client households were required to provide the emperor with mounted couriers, rather in the manner of the *cursus publicus*.[50] Further evidence for the revival of older practices lies in the fact that in 787 Carolingian officials were permitted at least during winter to 'requisition shelter'.[51] Increasingly, Carolingian travellers acquired access to a reliable network of inns. On the route through the Rhaetian Alps (the range stretching from eastern Switzerland through the Austrian Tyrol and into Trentino-Alto Adige and Lombardy) these allowed for stages averaging 26 km.[52] After centuries of conflict, the Carolingian Renaissance was also something of a rebirth for the roads.

5

Pilgrims and the Via Francigena

Even prior to Charlemagne's campaigns, the need to cross from Lombard to Byzantine territory did not entirely deter travel to Rome. In northern Europe, conversions to Christianity were creating more potential pilgrims, and not only wealthy ones. In his *History of the Lombards*, Paul the Deacon wrote:

> Many of the English race, noble and commoner, men and women, leaders and ordinary people, were accustomed to come from Britain to Rome, stirred by divine love.[1]

With the rise of pilgrimage came new guidebooks, improved infrastructure, and increasingly detailed travellers' tales.

English pilgrims would not have been entirely unfamiliar with the Roman past. Although it is hard to say how widely used the old Roman roads were in early medieval Britain, or how well their history was understood, they are repeatedly mentioned in legal documents from the seventh to tenth centuries, making clear that they were recognisable landmarks. In the ninth century, when Alfred the Great of Wessex and Guthrum, Viking ruler of East Anglia, made peace, they used Watling Street – the Roman road from Kent to Wroxeter in Shropshire – as an effective boundary between their territories.[2] Some infrastructure was clearly out of use, such as the 'brokene strate' at Liddington in Wiltshire, or the broken bridge (*pons fractus*) that gave Pontefract in Yorkshire its name.[3] On the other hand, some Roman salt roads, connecting production areas with consumers and, importantly, transporting a commodity that might be taxed, seem to have survived.[4] Not much is certain about early medieval England, but perhaps we can rely on taxes.

In Rome, the presence of English pilgrims is confirmed by graffiti in the catacombs of Commodilla (located south of the city centre, off the Via Ostiense).[5] The *Anglo-Saxon Chronicle* details the visits of several kings who abdicated and then made a late-in-life pilgrimage to Rome: Caedwalla, king of Wessex, baptised there by Pope Sergius in 688; Cenred of Mercia and the East Saxon king Offa in 709; Ina of Wessex in 728 (or 726). All these men died in Rome, and Caedwalla's epitaph recalls some of the motivation for his journey: to 'look upon Peter and Peter's see, take nourishment from the pure waters of his font, and, by drinking, take up that splendid brightness, from which a life-giving brilliance flows everywhere'.[6] Ina's stay coincided with the foundation of a *schola*, which provided a centre for pilgrims arriving from the English kingdoms. Referred to as the Burgus Saxonum, it gave its name to the area near the Vatican now known as the Borgo. Its location was also memorialised in Rome by the presence of the hospital at Santo Spirito in Sassia, the name 'Sassia' alluding to its Saxon heritage.[7]

Travel to Rome was somewhat complicated by the Umayyad conquest of Iberia in 711–18, and concerns over continuing Muslim expansion. In 738, Boniface, a bishop, wrote from Germany to the English abbess Bugga that she 'would do better to wait until the rebellious assaults and threats of the Saracens who have recently appeared about Rome should have subsided'.[8] Some pilgrims, however, evidently thought Rome worth the risky journey. In about 787 a deaf and mute English traveller was reputedly healed after visiting the shrine of St Benedict at Montecassino, finding himself able to speak both Latin and English.[9] Safety and comfort, moreover, were not fundamental to the pilgrim experience. Walking up to twenty miles a day (perhaps riding a little faster), the travel time from England to Rome was estimated at sixteen weeks, or almost four months. The pilgrim could, however, comfort him- or herself that any hardships were an *imitatio Christi* – an imitation of Christ – central to which was suffering.[10]

By the middle of the ninth century, royal visitors to Rome had Charlemagne as a model, and we begin to see records of their travel in the places where they stopped along the way. At the monastery of San Salvatore in Brescia, east of Milan (now part of a group of Lombard

World Heritage Sites), the West Saxon ruler Alfred's name is recorded twice in the *Liber Vitae*, which noted names of visitors.[11] Welsh and Irish kings made the journey too. Cyngen ap Cadell, king of Powys, was there in 854, Hywel in 886 and Hywel Dda, king of Dyfed (and later Gwynedd) went in 928. An unnamed Irish king travelled to Rome in 848, as did Sihtric, king of Dublin, in 1028.[12] By this time practices of pilgrimage had changed. Kings were no longer retiring, handing over their realms and then heading to Rome, where they might well spend the remainder of their lives. The new pilgrimages had a much stronger element of political power-play – indicating Rome's wider significance – and kings were more likely to return home.[13]

Ecclesiastical travellers from England (who may have been pilgrims, or on business, or both) are recorded at a number of Alpine stops including Sankt Gallen, Reichenau and Pfäfers in the first half of the tenth century.[14] Elite women went to Rome too, among them Queen Frithogitha of Wessex in 737; Queen Ethelswith, sister of Aelfred of Wessex, set out on pilgrimage in 888, but died in Pavia, where she was buried.[15] In Pavia today, the nearest one gets to the spaces that Ethelswith and her predecessors might have inhabited is the crypt of the church of San Giovanni Domnarum (St John of the Ladies), a Lombard establishment said to have been founded in 654 by Queen Gundeberga in the period when Pavia was the Lombards' capital city. Its name probably refers to the ladies of her court.[16] The upper church is rather worn baroque, but down some steps past signs reading LEAVE OPEN and SWITCH OFF THE CRYPT LIGHTS is a little vault with fragments of fresco. These are twelfth-century, but I suspect the columns, which don't match and have probably been recycled from another site, may be earlier. The most recent research, however, suggests that Ethelswith was buried in the convent of San Felice, founded by a later queen, Ansa, who also endowed accommodation for pilgrims to Rome and Monte Sant'Angelo.[17] The building is now home to the local university's Faculty of Economics,[18] and I wander round the corner to see if it's possible to view, but there's no indication that it's open. On the side someone has spray painted FEMINISM AND REVOLUTION, with the woman symbol and a hammer and sickle. I wonder what the queen would have made of that.

*

Once safely arrived in Rome, what might these pilgrims do? A list of sights compiled in the first half of the seventh century offers clues. The *Notitia Ecclesiarum Urbis Romae*, the first text of its kind, provides readers with an introduction to key Christian locations outside the city walls, including churches and martyrs' tombs. A slightly later text, the *De locis sanctis martyrum quae sunt foris civitatis Romae*, added information about churches within the walls.[19] These were exclusively guides to Christian sites, but a series of itineraries, perhaps datable to the time around Charlemagne's coronation, and certainly to the century between 757 and 855, show that travellers acquired other interests too.[20] These guides are the first to combine descriptions of Rome's Christian sites with details of its pagan monuments.[21] They reflect a revival of interest in ancient Rome, and especially its later Christian period, during the Carolingian Renaissance. Armed with these guidebooks, pilgrims could not only make their devotions but also copy inscriptions, and take notes on the once-great empire.[22] Some of the recommended routes led tourists out from the city along the roads dotted with the tombs of early martyrs. Itinerary XII includes a description 'of martyr tombs outside the walls along via Portuensis, via Aurelia, via Salaria, via Pinciana'. Itinerary XI winds around the sites south of the city including the basilica of San Paolo, and the church of San Sebastiano on the Via Appia.[23] They do not, yet, say much about the roads themselves, but provide the foundations for writers who will.

Alongside the new guidebooks, this period also saw some relocations and reworking of city heritage. With many of the catacombs falling into disrepair, important relics were moved instead into the city churches. The *Liber Pontificalis* (Book of the Popes) records the restorations undertaken by Pope Nicholas I in the middle of the ninth century: at San Sebastiano, for example, he commissioned 'improved construction' and established a monastery.[24] These early interventions were arguably the first steps towards creating the monumental zone around the Appia that we see today.

As the rule of the Franks created relative stability for pilgrims, a new route to Rome became established from the north. According to his biographer Odo, second abbot of Cluny, Count Gerald of Aurillac (died *c.*909), founder of the monastery of Saint Pierre at Aurillac in the Auvergne, central France, made seven trips to Rome. Odo was mainly interested in his subject's miracles, and the reference to seven journeys may be more symbolic than literal – the equivalent of Plovdiv's seven hills – but in among the description are important details of a new road to Rome: the Via Francigena.[25] First mentioned in the year 876 as the Via Francisca,[26] the road's name means literally the route of the Franks. Like the naming of the consular roads, it made a statement. The Francigena led from Pavia via Piacenza, Lucca and Siena and then south to Rome, hence its later name Romea Strata or Strata Romana. It replaced on the one hand the Via Aurelia, close to the coast and vulnerable to flooding and pirate attacks, and on the other those parts of the Via Cassia earlier abandoned as too close to the territory of the Byzantine exarchs or otherwise no longer passable.[27] (Some sections of the Cassia were incorporated.) This was, in fact, not a single road but, like other roads that we've encountered, it included variations that changed over centuries of use.[28] Those towns and cities on its route, like San Gimignano and Siena, however, undoubtedly benefited.[29] That said, Odo's account confirms that even high-status travellers could not rely on accommodation at every stage of the route: Gerald's party at least sometimes stayed in tents.[30]

The itinerary of Archbishop Sigeric of Canterbury, drawn up early in the 990s, when he travelled there to receive his pallium from Pope John XV, provides the first full list of way stations on the medieval road from England to Rome.[31] If there was ever an account of his travel *to* Rome it is lost, because the diary picks up with his arrival, describing his stay in the city and then his return. His party's accommodation was most likely the Schola Saxonum, which they used as a base to tour churches and sites, first outside the walls, and then in the city centre.[32] The document is rare evidence – in fact, the sole surviving list of Roman churches between the eighth and twelfth centuries – for what a visitor to Rome might choose to see.[33] On his homeward journey, Sigeric took the Via Cassia, stopping overnight a little way outside Rome at San Giovanni in Nono, close to La Storta (the name, sharing an origin with the English *tortuous*, refers to the twists in the road). He continued north to Lake Bolsena and Viterbo.[34]

By the time of Sigeric's journey, Viterbo was already growing as a Christian centre. It's a medieval walled town, streets paved with *sampietrini* weaving up and down its hills, and it's here that I begin my own journey on the Via Francigena, taking a bus from Viterbo to Montefiascone, which as the name suggests is located on a mount. At the top is a papal fortress dating back to the twelfth century from where I gaze across the gleaming waters of Lago di Bolsena in the north and back towards Viterbo in the south. The views aren't just spectacular, they're strategically important: you wouldn't miss an advancing army from up here. It's ninety-five per cent downhill to Viterbo, beginning with a drag through the industrial outskirts, past a supermarket promising mortadella for €6.90 a kilo. I head onto a track by some electricity pylons, recalling the complaints of nineteenth-century travellers that pylons ruin the view. There's plenty of view to enjoy, from the pink flowers by the hedgerows to the olive groves and, to my surprise, the kiwi fruit, which grow on vines rather like grapes. Little lizards scurry away from their sunbathing as I pass. Not so charming are the flies, and the road isn't straight, but for a long stretch it does have the Roman pavement of the Via Cassia. Along the way red and white signs indicate the Via Francigena, occasionally varying to the Romea Strata, a little pilgrim on them pointing the way, sometimes waving a European flag (this is an accredited Council of Europe cultural route). The image includes the traditional attributes of a pilgrim, especially the 'scrip and staff', the latter being the long stick that helped with walking distances, and the former a bag to carry their possessions.[35] There isn't much on the way, bar one 'pilgrim house' offering accommodation, and a single drinking fountain, both nearish Montefiascone. I'm glad I brought my water bottle.

At the viewpoint of Sosta Marina, previous travellers have adorned the picnic table with graffiti. We have the basic: 'Imre was here, 26.4.22.' The pensive, from Matteo: 'If the eyes are the mirror of the soul, nature is the mirror of life.' The commercial: 'Go to Porca Vacca in Viterbio [*sic*]', followed by a smiley face. This last is a burger bar and steakhouse with an online rating of 4.4, so it isn't terrible advice. Many ancient travellers made their own mark on the landscape: some still survive in the rock shelters of Egypt's Eastern Desert.[36] Even a basic inscription such as 'X was here' prompts later travellers to ask who X was, and why he had ended up so far from home. Graffiti artists today tend to be more reticent about leaving their names, but sometimes they do: on the Via Francigena, at San Michele, and – as tags – beside track after railway track.

I look up to the mountains behind Viterbo with their distinctive three peaks and ridge between. Milestones were one means of finding the way, but landmarks were also important. I pass a white statue of Mary, draped in rosary beads; a Padre Pio candle left beside her, and a present gift-wrapped. On a rock someone has painted in blue letters 'St Mary of the Cammino, pray for us'. The more Christianity took hold along the Roman roads, the more these new elements spread. Here's a fun piece of trivia: the word 'trivia' means 'three ways' and refers to the noticeboards placed at junctions of three roads. At the English church of St Michael in Herefordshire, a small Roman altar can be found, dedicated by a man named Beccicus (his name is not a usual Latin one so he may have been a local) to the God of the three ways.[37] If trivia was still posted at junctions, it was now accompanied instead by tiny saints' sanctuaries. It's quiet. I pass a few other walkers, and a few more cyclists: you need imagination to see this as a busy thoroughfare with carts passing, and litters, as well as riders and walkers. There were baths nearby: the Aquae Passeris mentioned on the Peutinger Map are just off this route, and several Renaissance artists sketched the Terme del Bacucco.[38] In the distance I can see a domed brick building that might just be a bathhouse, but it's in the wrong place for the baths marked on the map. In any case, there's plenty of advertising for the spa facilities to tourists in Viterbo. 'Let's reinforce our immune defences with a bath,' proposed one billboard on the way to the bus stop. I would try the public hot springs here, but last time I did, our van got broken into and three colleagues' stuff – clothes included – got nicked, so I'm wary.

From the eleventh century, English royal pilgrimage to Rome picked up again. King Cnut travelled to Rome in 1027 for the coronation of the Emperor Conrad by Pope John XIX. This was as much a political journey as a religious one, however, because Cnut was clearly there to negotiate and, moreover, his daughter went on to marry Conrad's son in 1036.[39] A thirteenth-century Norse account describes his founding of hospitals 'all along the route' and the gifts he made to support poor pilgrims making the journey.[40] During his discussions with Conrad, Cnut raised the issue of tolls on the roads to Rome. Back in 796, Charlemagne had warned Offa, king of the Mercians, that some commercial travellers were evading tolls by pretending to be pilgrims.[41] Cnut, however, took a different view, arguing that 'both merchants and others who travel to say their prayers, should be allowed to go and return from Rome without any hindrance of barriers and toll-collectors, in firm peace and secure in a just law'.[42] Now, it was agreed, everyone travelling to Rome should enjoy free passage. Whether that always worked in practice is, of course, another question.

As the geographical reach of Christianity expanded, so did the range of travellers. Niklas of Munkathvera, an Icelandic pilgrim, made his way to Rome probably in 1154, about 150 years after the conversion of his homeland. He travelled first to Norway, perhaps to the Arctic port of Bergen, before heading south via Denmark and Germany to Switzerland, where he picked up the Great St Bernard Pass. Once in Italy he could make his way south to cross the Po at Piacenza.[43] South of that city, he may have stopped at 'Eric's hospice', which had been founded by Eric I Svendsson, king of Denmark (r. 1095–1103), another indication of the reach of pilgrimage to Rome.[44] At Bolsena Niklas likely visited the relics of St Christina, which are referred to in his itinerary. Among them was the mark of her footprints in a stone that had supposedly been tied around her neck to drown her (today, it is incorporated into an altar). Niklas then picked up the Via Cassia via Viterbo to arrive in Rome from Monte Mario.[45]

Today Monte Mario is a nature reserve, one of the few large green spaces accessible from central Rome. Henry James visited in the late nineteenth century, praising 'the finest old ilex-walk in Italy . . . all vaulted grey-green shade, with blue Campagna stretches in the interstices'.[46] Now a notice on its gates warns me to beware of wild boar. A paved path snakes up through a pine wood, beginning not far from the Stadio Olimpico, where on the afternoon I make the walk Lazio are playing Juventus.

Niklas' account of Rome brings together details of its Christian monuments and their relics with an account of pagan sites. He knew both of 'that place that is called *Catacumbas*' and of 'that hall that King Diocletian owned'.[47] Here he differed from Sigeric, whose Roman itinerary focused strictly on the Christian monuments. As we've seen, Niklas was not the first to do so, but evidently the contrast between pilgrims who concentrated on Christian sites and those who ranged more widely continued. It was a distinction that would shape travel through the centuries.

From the twelfth century onwards, travellers to Rome began to leave more detailed accounts of their journeys. The sparsely annotated lists of earlier centuries gave way to more descriptive narrative, and we hear from a greater variety of people with their own individual and sometimes idiosyncratic tales of travelling to Rome. Among them is a rabbi, Benjamin of Tudela, who in the middle of the twelfth century made his way from Zaragoza – in what is now Spain – to the eastern Mediterranean. His motivations are something of a mystery: his preoccupations suggest that he was not only a pilgrim and may have been a merchant. His notes on a pearl fishery are suggestive in that regard, as are his interests in port access, but we should not rule out that he simply enjoyed travel on its own merits, and liked meeting fellow Jews around the Mediterranean.[48] Benjamin travelled first down the Ebro river to Tortosa, then via Tarragona and Barcelona, at that time an important Jewish cultural centre. From there, he followed the Mediterranean coast to Gerona, Narbonne, Montpellier and finally to Arles,[49] his route close to that shown a millennium before on the Vicarello cups.

From Arles, near the mouth of the Rhône, Benjamin proceeded to Marseilles, from where it was possible to sail to Genoa, avoiding an Alpine crossing or the coast road that was prone to flooding. He then headed south via Pisa and Lucca to Rome, where he found a community of 'about 200 Jews', who, he observed, 'occupy an honourable position and pay no tribute'. Some of them, in fact, were in the service of Pope Alexander III. Like many Christian travellers, Benjamin took an interest in both the Christian and pagan buildings of Rome, but he also sought out locations with significance for Jewish history. Outside Rome, he noted the presence of a palace 'said to be of Titus'.[50] Titus was of note because of his defeat of a Jewish rebellion and the destruction of the Second Temple. Benjamin also took an interest in relics brought to Rome from Jerusalem, including 'two bronze columns taken from the Temple [in Jerusalem], the handiwork of King Solomon', now in the Lateran.[51]

From Rome, Benjamin travelled south to Capua, we may assume on the Via Appia, noting that the city's 'water is bad and the country is fever-stricken'.[52] Long before modern understandings of malaria, it was acknowledged as a practical threat. In Pozzuoli Benjamin noted the presence of hot springs known for their curative powers, as well as one particular spring that he claimed 'issues forth from beneath the ground containing the oil that is called petroleum'.[53] (This is probably a reference to the sulphuric springs still found in the area today.) Benjamin also saw at least one of the Roman tunnels in the area, though he was exaggerating when he said that from Pozzuoli 'a man can travel fifteen miles along a road under the mountains'. He attributed this work to Romulus, founder of Rome.[54] If there was general awareness that these were ancient sites, knowledge of the specifics could be somewhat hazy.

The Crypta Neapolitana is in fact about 700 metres long, and was designed by the engineer Lucius Cocceius Auctus in about 37 BCE on the commission of Augustus' leading general Agrippa.[55] One of four known tunnels in the area, it connected the major port of Pozzuoli with the city of Naples, cutting beneath hills that previously had to be traversed by a difficult path. Its presence is marked in the names of the modern city quarters of Fuorigrotta (meaning 'outside the tunnel') and Piedigrotta ('at the foot of the tunnel'). It became a popular tourist site on the later Grand Tour, with distinguished visitors including Mozart.[56] Inaccessible to the public at present, the entrances are still visible. On the Fuorigrotta side, towards Pozzuoli, a high narrow arch stretches up into the rock at the end of a cul-de-sac, apartment blocks on either side. Standing outside the tunnel's entrance, I feel a cool draught from the chilly air inside. No such luck at the other end: the entrance on the Naples side is in a park that's closing as I arrive (it hadn't occurred to me that anyone would lock up a public park at 3 p.m. on Saturday, but there you go). I decide one tunnel entrance will look much like the other, and head down the hill to the marina front, where I have a beer and fight the pigeons to keep my snacks. This is yachting territory, with some flash examples in the harbour, and some flash people in Helly Hansen kit, and I'm pleasantly surprised not to be ripped off at a reasonable €4 including table service, not bad for a view of Vesuvius.

Benjamin's motivation for the attribution of the tunnel to Romulus becomes clear when he explains that the founder of Rome 'was prompted to this by fear of King David and Joab his general'.[57] In other words it was a response to the threat posed by Jewish rulers. Making his way down via Naples, Amalfi and Benevento, he crossed to the Adriatic coast, visiting several cities before embarking at Otranto, almost at the tip of Italy's heel, for Corfu.[58] Benjamin did not opt for the Via Egnatia, preferring sea travel to Constantinople, stopping off at ports along the coast.

There was an alternative route between Spain and the eastern Mediterranean. In the first two centuries CE, the Romans had constructed a coastal highway from Alexandria to Tangiers, linking the multiple centres of the North African coast, from which ships criss-crossed the Mediterranean. Ludolph von Suchem, a German priest writing in the fourteenth century, explained that Muslims 'who dwell in Spain and Arragon pass along this road when they would visit the courts of their prophet Mahomet'. This route, however, was not an option for Christians, 'for these two kingdoms of Morocco and Granada are exceedingly powerful and rich, and are inhabited by Saracens who care naught for the Soldan [of Egypt], and are ever at odds with the [Christian] King of Spain, and ever help the King of Algarve, who is a Saracen, and whose kingdom lies on the borders of Spain'.[59] A fifteenth-century Burgundian writer likewise ruled it out: besides the Holy Land being 2,500 miles from Gibraltar, the road was 'extremely dangerous, on account of the fortified castles near which you must march, the risk of wanting provision, the desert you must pass through, and Egypt'.[60] (He didn't specify what it was about Egypt: presumably his readers knew that the crusaders had clashed with the Mamluk Sultans.) Whether the route would have been an option for Benjamin is unclear, but he did not choose it.

Indeed, while the North African road was clearly known to

medieval Christian writers, the extent of Rome's empire south of the Mediterranean seems to have fallen out of later European memory – or been deliberately forgotten as Rome's heritage came to be claimed for the modern West. There was considerable scepticism, for example, when eighteenth-century Scottish explorer James Bruce published sketches of the spectacular remains of a grid-plan town at Timgad (Thamugadi) in Algeria, probably in fact the work of an accompanying Bolognese artist, Luigi Balugani. Only a century on, when the British consul in Algiers decided to look for himself, publishing a book of *Travels in the Footsteps of Bruce in Algeria and Tunis*, was Bruce's tale confirmed.[61] Today, the security situation in Libya means the full route is impassable for tourists: the remarkable Roman site at Leptis Magna is out of reach. But the western half of the road is now reopening to visitors, from Sala Colonia, Rome's last outpost in the west, through Caracalla's triumphal arch at Volubilis in Morocco, to the Colosseum of El Jem and the many Roman towns of Tunisia.

Benjamin did not travel at an easy time for western Christianity. Concerns about the safety of pilgrims were such that – according to the contemporary historian William of Malmesbury – Pope Calixtus II advised the English that they might be better off travelling to St David's, at the south-western tip of Wales, instead. Two St David's pilgrimages were ruled to equal one to Rome.[62] The period 1159–78 saw the election of two anti-popes, rival claimants to St Peter's throne. On the other hand, the twelfth century saw a further renaissance of interest in the ancient past, and those travellers who did make it to Rome were clearly paying attention to the pagan sites. They might have consulted the *Mirabilia Urbis Romae* (Wonders of the City of Rome), compiled in about 1140 by a canon of St Peter's, which provided ample information on the pre-Christian monuments.[63] A visit to these locations was perceived to have educational value, and the canon's guide was followed in the late twelfth or early thirteenth century by a *Narratio de Mirabilibus Urbis Romae* (Narration of the Wonders of the City of Rome). This was composed by an English visitor, Gregory, whom one scholar has described as 'the first Romantic traveller to Rome'.[64] Gregory had a literary style, cared about art, and encouraged his readers to look over the cityscape 'from a view'.[65] He is perhaps the earliest writer to highlight the significance of this first impression:

> So I reckon the panorama of the whole city is exceptionally wonderful. There is such a crop of towers, so many palatial buildings that no man can count them. As soon as I saw it from the first slope of the hill from afar, my amazed mind recalled that speech of Caesar's, uttered after he had conquered the Gauls, flown across the Alps and was greatly 'admiring . . . the walls of Rome' when he asked 'Home of the gods, have men abandoned you without a fight? What city will they then defend?'[66]

This was a speech described in an ancient epic poem, Lucan's *Civil War*, which in the original refers to a journey from the south, along the Via Appia, past Lake Nemi and through the Alban Hills.[67] Travelling from England, Gregory is more likely to have entered the city over Monte Mario or on the Via Cassia. Either way, however, to appreciate the view required a stop on the road and this moment became incorporated into the script for travel to Rome, to be repeated down the centuries. There is evidence for other travellers' antiquarian interests, too: in the 1140s a Bishop of Winchester was spotted buying statues.[68] If engagement with the roads was still mainly practical, visitors were now walking them – and pausing on them – to see the ancient sites.

The routes, meanwhile, were shifting. The Via Francigena got significantly less use after the thirteenth century, when the preferred road north from Rome moved closer to its present-day route, via Florence and Bologna, partly in recognition of Florence's growing commercial importance.[69] There had been a Roman route between the two, but it was not a major one. The foundation of Bologna's university in 1088 provided a new draw, and the city's location at the crossroads of multiple routes in northern Italy led to the development of numerous inns on the road network nearby.[70] From mid-thirteenth-century city records, we know that in every settlement of more than thirty hearths in the district, there was a tavernkeeper to sell refreshments, both to locals and to outsiders.[71] These inns were regulated by local officials known as *massari*, and were required to have on hand facilities for shoeing horses.[72] It was in the city's interests to ensure visitors were well catered for, and the Comune (council) of Bologna regulated the location of inns, restricting building too close to the city itself, and securing its own income by banning construction near its own lodging facilities.[73] The largest number of inns were to be found on the road to Florence, but the smaller routes also counted significant numbers: five in the direction of Pistoia, seven towards Modena, and four each towards Imola and Ravenna.[74] In Lucca, situated on the Via Francigena but also between Florence and the coast on the old Via Cassia, there were eighty-two *alberghi* in 1332, with a total of 423 beds.[75]

For much of the fourteenth century, however, travel to Rome was disrupted by the absence of the papal court. Although pilgrimage continued, conflict between the papacy and the king of France led first to seven decades of papal rule from the southern French city of Avignon, and then to an outright schism, during which one pope ruled from Rome and another (the anti-pope) remained in Avignon. For a while it was far from clear that the roads of western Christendom led to Rome. The papal court had already been itinerant during the twelfth and thirteenth centuries, spending more than half the period between 1198 and 1304 away from Rome; six popes did not make it to the city at all.[76] Between 1309 and 1376 any travellers who sought audience with the Pope, or simply had business to do at the papal court, would make their way instead to Avignon. A chronicle recorded that in 1347 'people from other provinces were refusing to visit Rome, due to the fact that they might get robbed on the road'.[77] After the return of a pope to Rome in 1378 (despite the rival still in Avignon), the old incentives to visit on business returned.

Among the most prominent travellers of this period – on account of the unique recollections she left – is Margery Kempe, who made the journey to Rome and Jerusalem in 1413–15. Female pilgrims were not universally welcome in the city; in fact, they were banned from visiting certain sites. Chapels forbidden to women included those of St John the Baptist at the Lateran, and of St Leo and the Holy Cross in St Peter's. Pero Tafur, a Spanish pilgrim, described the exclusion of women from the chapel of the Sancta Sanctorum, while Nikolaus Muffel, a German observer, complained about a woman who had menstruated there, bloodying the sacred marble steps. Fears about such incidents – and a wider belief that menstruating women were unclean – may have lain behind the purported concern for women's safety.[78]

Male writers had long complained about the immorality of women on the roads to Rome. St Boniface thought women should be banned from going on pilgrimage, complaining in a letter of 747 to the Archbishop of Cambridge (probably an error for Canterbury) that 'in almost all Lombard French and Gallic cities there is at least one adulteress or prostitute belonging to the people of England'.[79] While he may have been exaggerating, there is no shortage of evidence for the sex industry operating along the Roman roads. A life of the sixth-century saint Theodore of Sykeon, for example, tells us that he was the son of a courtesan named Mary and an imperial messenger named Cosmas who stayed in the inn kept by Mary, her mother and sister, in a village on the imperial highway about 100 km west of Ankara.[80] Half a millennium before, Strabo had described some of the entertainments available to travellers in Egypt:

> Eleusis is a settlement near both Alexandria and Nicopolis, is situated on the Canobic Canal itself, and has lodging places and commanding views for those who wish to engage in revelry, both men and women, and is a beginning, as it were of the 'Canobic' life and the shamelessness there current.[81]

Pliny the Elder, meanwhile, had a broader observation to make: 'Along what other path, if not the road, is vice so widespread? Along what other path have ivories, gold, and precious stones become so commonplace?'[82] While travel could demonstrate religious devotion, there were equally concerns that the roads were a space for less than desirable behaviour. Seven centuries on, Felix Fabri, a Swiss pilgrim of the fifteenth century, also noted the brothels to be found along the route, observing that the 'keepers of houses of ill-fame . . . for the most part are Germans'.[83] Even as I take the bus down Monte Sant'Angelo, at the bottom of the hill, a woman sits on a plastic chair by the roadside, red bag by her feet, sheer black tights, while the Grand Hotel Savoia offers me a free 'Love Kit basic' from reception, or for €25 a 'Love Kit deluxe'. The convention in pilgrim accounts, however, was to skim over such detail, and indeed to skim over detail of the journey more generally. Pilgrims emphasised their religiosity: though they used the ancient roads, they were more concerned about their destination. Fabri, travelling through Venice on his way to the Holy Land, wrote down 'only the holy and honourable wanderings which we made in the city'. Those made 'out of curiosity, or worse motives . . . albeit they were made also' he left out of his report.[84] (This may, however, explain how he knew about the brothel-keepers.) A fifteenth-century Italian pilgrim to Jerusalem, Santo Brasca, was likewise hostile to *curiositas*:

> A man should undertake this voyage solely with the intention of visiting, contemplating and adoring the most Holy Mysteries . . . and not with the intention of seeing the world, or from ambition, or to be able to say 'I have been there' or 'I have seen that' in order to be exalted by his fellow men.[85]

The type he had in mind was probably the anonymous French traveller of 1480, who observed of a Cypriot temple of Venus that it was 'famous throughout the world, as much for the sumptuous edifice as for the superstitions observed there'.[86] Yet the existence of guidebooks shows that religious travellers might take an interest in pagan remains, though in their own narratives stories of saints generally took precedence over those of ancient Romans.

Margery Kempe is a fine example of this approach, her observations on her experience of travel entering into her account only so far as they affected her efforts to be a pilgrim.[87] Born in about 1373 in King's Lynn (then Bishop's Lynn), she was the daughter of the town mayor, a background that gave her the financial wherewithal to travel: long-distance pilgrimage was not cheap from the point of view of either time or money. Kempe married, had fourteen children, and then settled on a life of chastity and pilgrimage.[88] Her book was produced in collaboration with several others including a priest and the scribe, Salthouse, of the surviving manuscript.[89] Setting out from Yarmouth, Kempe went by sea to the port of Zierikzee, between Rotterdam and Antwerp in what is now the Netherlands. From there she headed south to Constance, on the Rhine, where she made the acquaintance of 'an English friar, a master of divinity and the Pope's legate, who was in that city'.[90] Such individuals were a vital resource for travellers: they could serve as sources of local information and advice. In this case, however, the friar was asked to do rather more. Kempe's overt religiosity, including repeated crying and a refusal to eat meat, had got her fellow travellers' backs up, and they abandoned her to his care. They later took her back, on condition that she would 'not talk of the Gospel where we are, but you will sit and make merry, like us, at all meals',[91] before relations broke down for a second time.[92] We only have one side of the story here, but it does convey the tensions between those pilgrims with deep, almost mystical, religious conviction, and those who were in it for adventure and good times.

I'm not religious at all, but I could see where Margery was coming from as I stood in the queue for the pilgrim church of San Michele in Monte Sant'Angelo. There were signs up asking for silence, and no photographs and no mobile phones, but they were generally ignored, as visitors pushed and jostled down the stairs to get into the cave church with little respect for personal space. They may have been there for parish days out, but the lunch seemed as important as the spirituality – if not more so. On the street outside shopkeepers competed to sell them souvenirs. I passed at least three different stalls with bags of chestnuts, one man roasting there and then, tossing his pan over a brazier.

Kempe went on to Rome via Assisi, presumably, although she doesn't say, on the Via Flaminia, which from Venice would have been the most likely choice. A possible companion for this leg of the journey was a hunchbacked man named Richard. He was concerned, however, that he might be unable to protect her:

> I fear that my enemies will rob me, and perhaps take you away from me and rape you; and therefore I dare not escort you, for I would not, for a hundred pounds, have you suffer any disgrace while you were with me.[93]

This was, for women travellers, a real threat – there is, for example, a recorded case of a noble French widow being trafficked into prostitution, albeit briefly, after being separated from a group of pilgrims.[94] The case of Kempe and Richard points to the distinct experience of both disabled and women travellers, who might have particular fears about their treatment on the roads. (Only once in my three months of travel for this book did I feel the need to invent a boyfriend, but as a forty-something woman I now get much less hassle than I did in my twenties.) Kempe made it to Assisi, home to the dramatically sited basilica of St Francis, apparently without incident. Though the town was not on the Via Flaminia, it was close enough to be accessible;[95] and there she joined the party of a Florentine gentlewoman for the final leg to Rome 'so as to be kept safe from the danger of thieves'.[96] Perhaps there was also a degree of solidarity here between the women.[97] Kempe's former travelling companions, however, were not so supportive. On her arrival in Rome (a trip that would have taken her from Assisi down the remainder of the Via Flaminia), Kempe stayed at the hospice of St Thomas which – after several centuries during which the English had been without a national hostel – had succeeded the Schola Saxonum as the English pilgrim hospital in Rome. The arrangement, however, did not last, because one of her party 'spoke so badly of this creature and slandered her name so much' that the hospital officials kicked her out.[98]

Yet while we learn relatively more about travel experiences from these later pilgrims, for the majority, the roads remained a matter of getting from A to B. If their symbolic role as an expression of Roman power attracted interest that is only occasionally reflected in the written sources. Gregory's fascination with the view was an exception. Within a few decades of Kempe's journey, however, that would change.

6

Crusaders and the Via Militaris

Roads were never solely about devotion or sightseeing. They continued to have a military role, which becomes apparent in the course of the crusades. Beginning in the late eleventh century, the crusades were perceived by participants and advocates as armed pilgrimages.[1] The city of Jerusalem that they sought to capture for Christianity had once been within the Roman Empire, and as we know there was a choice of routes to reach it. 'Whosoever would journey to the Holy Land,' wrote Ludolph von Suchem, in about 1350, 'must go thither either by land or by sea. If he would go by land, I have heard from some who know it well that the best way is through Hungary, Bulgaria and the kingdom of Thrace, but they say that the road is a very tedious one.'[2] If in and around Rome there was slow but growing interest in the ancient past, so far as the crusaders were concerned the roads mattered for their practical function. There were eight big crusades (and many smaller ones) between 1095 and 1291, but those intended to recover the Holy Land from Muslim rule are the most significant in terms of understanding long-distance travel and the fate of the Roman road network a millennium or more after its original construction. The crusaders' accounts not only tell us about the physical roads to the east, but also illuminate the contest over transport links that had emerged in the borderlands between the Byzantine Empire and its western competitors, and occasionally reveal something of how their heritage was understood.

Participants in the First Crusade (1096–9) took one of three main routes, all close to historic Roman roads. Two ancient routes in particular were important: the Via Egnatia, which as we have seen led from Durrës east to Thessaloniki and then to Constantinople, and the

Via Militaris, leading south-east from Carnuntum via Belgrade and Sofia. (This road is also referred to as the Via Diagonalis but for convenience I will stick to simply Militaris from here on.) The gradual loss of the Balkans from Byzantine to Slavic control through the seventh century made for further disruption of land travel between Constantinople and Rome. The Via Militaris had already been subject to attacks by 'Huns' in 552, when they prevented an army from passing through Philippopolis (Plovdiv).[3] By 700 most travellers were opting instead to go by sea.[4] During the eighth and ninth centuries, diplomatic sources suggest a preference for almost any other route over the Via Militaris: the coast, the Egnatia, or the roads that continued along the Danube towards the Black Sea.[5] That said, some complaints seem to be over-egged. In the sixth century General Komentiolos allegedly struggled to find the Via Militaris, but a tenth-century text on imperial administration provided not only details of the route but an estimated speed of travel to reach it: eight days from Thessaloniki to Belgrade.[6] Even at this relatively late stage, some sense of the *cursus publicus* remained, with an obligation on local communities for its maintenance, even if in practice what they were maintaining was now a beaten track and not a paved road.[7]

In fact, there is perhaps a stronger case for thinking that the Via Militaris remained in service. Linking as it did the major cities of the Balkans with the Danube and northern Italy, this was a key trade route.[8] Unlike the Via Egnatia, there was no alternative coastal option. Despite the ongoing conflict, in 784, the Byzantine Empress Irene made a journey through Thrace, the region to the west of Constantinople, now split between modern Turkey, Greece and Bulgaria. That she could make this trip, and with a substantial entourage, shows that roads in this area must have been reasonably passable. A few years later, attendance by bishops at a Council in Nicaea (100 km south-east of Constantinople as the crow flies, though a much longer trip overland) was much improved from councils of a century before, further evidence that more people felt able to travel.[9] Those who might have taken the Egnatia had as an alternative the maritime route, skirting from port to port around the coast of Greece, but this came with its own risks, from both weather and pirates.[10] In the middle of the ninth century, however, a land route between Constantinople and

Rome came back into more regular use. By this time the Bulgars controlled a corridor stretching from Plovdiv to the Adriatic coast. When envoys of the king of the Bulgars came to the court of Pope Nicholas I, papal officials realised that 'through their kingdom, an easy, overland route to the land of the Greeks [Constantinople] lay open to our envoys'.[11] It seems that both sides seized on the option, with five journeys documented in just six years.[12] Diplomacy could make a remarkable difference to transport links.

In the principal crusading sources, however, only one of these two main roads is recognised as Roman: the Via Egnatia, described in the anonymous *Gesta Francorum* (*Deeds of the Franks*) as 'the old Roman road'.[13] That this was the author's perception of the Via Egnatia is notable, as is the description of the Via Militaris. Not named in this account, the route is explained instead as 'the road which Charlemagne, the wondrous king of Francia, once had constructed all the way to Constantinople'.[14] This account most likely drew on an earlier story that grew up around a mythical journey of Charlemagne to the Holy Land. There's no evidence that he ever made the trip, but a tenth-century version of the legend, written by a monk at Mount Soratte, describes him at the shrine of Monte Sant'Angelo receiving a blessing from Pope Leo before his departure.[15]

This, however, is myth rather than fact, nor do the sources suggest he was involved in improvements to the Via Militaris. As we have seen, evidence from diplomatic accounts of Charlemagne's time suggests that those on embassy preferred to travel by sea, or failing that then other roads.[16] Why might the writers have credited Charlemagne in this way? Perhaps the Via Militaris had fewer standing milestones or monuments to mark it out as Roman to observers. Perhaps among this group of educated scribes – more likely than most to have access to the ancient texts – the concept of the Roman road retained enough symbolic power that they thought road building a good way to associate Charlemagne with his ancient predecessors. However the description came about, here is an example of an early myth – one of those memories of the imagination – attaching to a Roman road a millennium on from its construction.

More important than Charlemagne in ensuring access to the Via Militaris was the changing religio-political climate in the Balkans and central Europe. The Bulgarian Empire, which had become a significant challenger – and sometime ally – to its Byzantine neighbour from the seventh century, fell to the Byzantines in 1018. King Stephen of Hungary, who ruled that kingdom from about 1000 until his death in 1038, committed to establishing Christianity in his realm, which helped consolidate the road as an option for pilgrims – and then crusaders – to the Holy Land.[17] On the other hand, in the background of the crusades lay the Great Schism of 1054, in which the eastern and western Christian churches had split: the Byzantine emperors were by no means reliable allies to the western princes. The First Crusade succeeded in capturing Jerusalem, but that city was lost in 1187 to an army led by Saladin. The fourth failed even to reach the Holy Land, ending in 1204 with the sack of Constantinople by crusader armies, and until 1261 its rule by the 'Latins' or Franks.

Thus the First and Second Crusades (1096–9 and 1147–9) saw armies travelling overland from western Europe to Byzantium. The leaders of these troops came from England (Richard the Lionheart), France, Flanders, and the German lands. Even at the far ends of these territories, the roads on which they started their 2,000-mile journeys might well have had Roman roots. By the thirteenth century the British road network was a mix of Roman and post-Roman, and would stay that way until the advent of the motor car. Britain's roads had, however, declined in quality in the previous centuries, and with the exception of some city streets they were unmetalled. Wheeled transport became impractical: people rode, or walked, and pack animals bore goods.[18] From France and Flanders soldiers marched south through Italy, crossing the Adriatic from Brindisi or Bari to Durrës and heading east along the Via Egnatia. Soldiers from the German lands could take a more easterly route, heading south along the Danube towards what is now Belgrade, then joining the Via Militaris east to Byzantium.[19] Sea travel was already deployed during the Second Crusade, in which a fleet of Anglo-Norman, German and Flemish ships sailed via the Iberian peninsula, and from the Third Crusade (1189–92) onwards, the use of ships grew. Though expensive, they allowed for a smaller and more disciplined force, and gave the invaders the advantage of surprise. The Holy Roman Emperor Frederick I Barbarossa, however, still led his armies south from Regensburg on the land route.[20]

Some crusaders had better knowledge of the Balkans than others. Advice from former pilgrims to Jerusalem, and the books written to guide them, would have helped plan logistics. Such planning was vital: the greatest threat to these soldier-pilgrims' lives was not in battle but from disease and starvation. It is estimated that half of those who set out on the First Crusade lost their lives.[21] While it was feasible to transport some supplies by cart (one advantage of land over sea routes), the terrain made it difficult.[22] For part of the journey goods could be floated down the Danube, but further along the way purchases could not be avoided. Market towns such as Niš (in modern Serbia, near the former Roman settlement of Mediana), thus became important stops.[23] Crusaders, however, also relied on foraging and – where permission from local rulers was not forthcoming, or in enemy territory – on raiding to seize what they could find.[24] Walter Sans Avoir, a French lord, 'crossed through Germany and approached the Kingdom of Hungary, which is surrounded on all sides with great lakes and marshes; nor could he approach except along narrow paths which are gateways to the Kingdom'. Initially he found King Kaloman supportive in supplying the crusade, but at Belgrade there was no such welcome: the ruler refused to hold a market and violence between crusaders and citizens broke out.[25] The troops of Raymond of Toulouse, travelling the Via Egnatia, sacked the town of Roussa and faced retaliation from the Greeks, while crusaders responded to a dispute over supplies at Kastoria by simply stealing livestock.[26] It cannot have been easy to live beside these roads.

In some cases, violence was targeted. The First Crusade is notorious for its participants' attacks on the Rhineland Jews. In 1096, in cities from Mainz to Cologne, Regensburg and Prague, Jews were forced by crusaders to choose between baptism as Christians or death. A twelfth-century Hebrew chronicle recorded crusaders' determination to 'avenge' themselves on the Jews 'whose forefathers murdered and crucified [their Messiah] for no reason'.[27] With 'blows of sword, death and destruction' they murdered the people who had hoped to find protection in the archbishop's fortified palace. Some of them chose to kill each other rather than wait for the crusaders.[28] Whether the massacres were predominantly a matter of looting, a means to fund the army, or ideologically motivated, with an aim of forced baptism parallel to the crusaders' desire to recover the Holy Land, has been a matter of debate among historians.[29] They are often seen as a turning point in European Jewish history, the beginning of centuries of persecution. In relation to travel, they remind us that while travellers often portray themselves as – and indeed are – victims of violence, they may equally be perpetrators, and when they are, they don't often admit it. The antisemitic violence of the eleventh century was recorded by Jewish writers. Most Christian chroniclers made minimal reference to the massacres, if they mentioned them at all. Other more individual instances of violence on the ancient roads – when travellers raided local food stores, trashed tavern rooms, harassed or assaulted serving staff – were almost certainly not written down.

Having travelled down the Rhine, the pilgrims of the First Crusade settled on their different routes. Godfrey, Duke of Lorraine, opted to go overland through Hungary.[30] Bohemond, a prince of Apulia who had served in earlier campaigns in the region, briefly capturing Durrës and parts of northern Greece, dipped into his own resources to fund an Adriatic crossing.[31] Those who travelled via southern Italy had the option of a stop in Rome with its numerous shrines,[32] or indeed in Bari. Landing well to the south of Durrës at Avlona (now Vlöre), Bohemond avoided the Via Egnatia for the first leg of his journey, leading his army on a more southerly route across what is now Albania, and picking up the main road only at Edessa (now in Greece).[33] A third route also came into play during the First Crusade. This took crusaders from northern Italy down the eastern Adriatic coast (present-day Croatia) to join the Via Egnatia. The choice of Raymond of Toulouse and his followers, this avoided the crossing from Bari to Durrës.[34] There was good reason: the risks of even this short crossing are evidenced by several shipwrecks. One, in 1097, saw the loss of 400 men, while Hugh of Vermandois, younger brother of King Philip I of France, was shipwrecked and washed up on Byzantine territory: not the most auspicious moment for a commander.[35]

Sea crossings precluded the transport of carts,[36] which may have been a factor in Raymond's decision to march. The road he took was, both literally and metaphorically, a rocky one. Raymond d'Aguilers, who claimed to have accompanied Raymond of Toulouse as a chaplain,[37] gave a vivid description of the 'forsaken land, both inaccessible and mountainous, where for three weeks we saw neither wild beasts nor birds'. He complained that the 'barbarous and ignorant natives would neither trade with us nor provide guides' and that they attacked the weakest members of the crusade.[38]

Beyond the crusade context, other travellers also give away important details about their cultural attitudes to those around them on the road. The Byzantine official Gregory Antiochos, for example, observed the Bulgarian dislike of fish with distaste, while Mesarites, a churchman, was sickened by a smoke-filled inn and repulsed by his drunken servant's greedy midnight feasting.[39] You do notice drinking habits, travelling. In a restaurant in Turin, I ordered a *quarto* (quarter-litre, 250 ml) of white wine to accompany my three-course dinner. I thought this was pretty restrained, compared to British drinking habits. Across the room, one man ordered a half-litre of white to himself, while the woman with him got a quarter of red; this pair (accompanied by their child) were, however, outdone by the bearded man in denim shorts and an Oregon Ducks shirt, who ordered an entire bottle of white to himself. Maybe the Ducks had just lost.

If outsiders sometimes looked on with disdain, from the locals' point of view, their knowledge of the countryside was a considerable asset as they resisted the presence of this crusading army: they knew the 'rugged mountains and dense forests' and were not hampered by heavy armour inappropriate for the terrain. 'Our soldiers', reported Raymond, 'could neither fight them in the open nor avoid skirmishes with them.'[40] For almost forty days, he claimed – more likely a symbolic allusion to Christ's forty days in the wilderness than to an actual duration – 'we journeyed in this land at times encountering such clouds of fog we could almost touch these vapours'. That they succeeded in this leg 'without losses from starvation or open conflict' was, in his view, attributable to 'God's mercy' as well to the efforts of the commanders.[41] Writing much later, in the early fourteenth century, on the prospects for a crusade, Marino Sanudo Torsello was firmly of the view that 'there should be no going by land'. As for the success of Peter the Hermit and Godfrey of Bouillon on the Via Militaris during the First Crusade, he wrote: 'I reply that their mission was not subject to human forethought and strength but was directed with divine assistance and concluded with celestial grace.'[42]

Compared to the Roman roads in Italy or indeed Britain, those in the Balkans are far less well researched, to the point that debates remain about their precise routes, although there is a consensus on the general picture, not least because the geography of the area left few practicable options. (The mountainous terrain continued to challenge road builders even in the twentieth century.[43]) The Via Militaris, for example, once past Belgrade, almost certainly led south along the eastern valley of the Morava river the 120 Roman miles to Niš (the Roman Naissus, birthplace of the Emperor Constantine).[44] These were the borderlands of three different realms – the Byzantine Empire and the kingdoms of Bulgaria and Serbia – and there is reason to think that from the mid-eleventh century the Byzantines deliberately allowed the road between the Danube and Niš to fall into disrepair. According to the chronicler William of Tyre, they effectively depopulated the region, meaning there were no locals with an incentive to maintain the route. 'Consequently,' wrote William, 'since the whole country is covered with woods and shrubby growth, no one, however desirous, can enter there, for the Greeks place greater confidence in the hindrances afforded by difficult roads and the defenses of thorny brambles than in their own forces.'[45] This 'Bulgarian Forest' of tall oak trees, stretching across what is now part of Serbia, formed a strategic natural defence.[46]

I do not directly have to contend with the Bulgarian Forest. I do have to deal with the fact that, thanks to a combination of Covid restrictions and track repairs, all international trains to and from Belgrade remain suspended, the railway authorities doing a job nearly as impressive as the eleventh-century Byzantines in preventing anyone travelling through the country. My attempt to go from Vienna to Belgrade and Niš is thwarted, and I have to make a detour. There is, however, an alternative night train. The guard at Vienna ticks me off his passenger list. I find my sleeper compartment and stretch out on the white sheets of the lower bunk. In a Formica cupboard is a washbasin supplied with soap, a towel and sachets of shoe polish. A glimpse of red light on the water as my train crosses the Danube at Budapest and we head off, away from the route of the Via Militaris, and instead to Bucharest, where I'll catch a day train back to Sofia and join the road's south-eastern stretch. This is somewhat frustrating, but my journey could have been much worse: if I'd travelled two days earlier I'd have been caught in chaos on the German railways, prompted by an IT incident allegedly caused by Russian saboteurs cutting the communication cables. A millennium on, the rules of war are still the same: attack the enemy's transport networks.

Although I'm on a detour from the ancient route, the wooded hills make it easy to imagine what pilgrims and crusaders were contending with. This river valley is surely vulnerable to attack from above; all the more so the stretch between Brasov and Bucharest, where the train curves between the Carpathian mountains. Ridge succeeds tree-lined ridge of foothills, dense lines of pine concealing who-knows-what. Behind them clouds top yet higher peaks. We pass a station called Alba Iulia, surely Roman, I think, and yes, it was once a Roman *castrum*, Apulum. Despite the name, Romania itself was not entirely a Roman province. Some of its modern territory formed part of Roman Dacia, but there's a debate about whether or not Romanised locals stayed in the area north of the Danube after the empire's withdrawal, or whether they were largely forced south of the river.[47]

One of the richest sources for the troubles the crusaders encountered in the Bulgarian Forest is the anonymous *History of the Expedition of Frederick Barbarossa*. (Frederick was the Holy Roman Emperor, though he styled himself 'Roman Emperor and always Augustus': from the tenth century this title was granted by the popes to the kings of Germany.)[48] Possibly from Passau, the *History*'s compiler put together a variety of sources to create a vivid account of the Third Crusade.[49] The plan had been for co-operation with the Byzantine emperor, whose representatives promised them 'escort on a good road, the best possible market preparations and free passage across the sea'.[50] That the road is named first is perhaps an indication of its importance. As the *History* explains, however, the 'poison of the snake was on [the Greeks'] lips' and they failed to do what they had promised.[51] Instead, the Duke of Branchevo (presumably Branjevo, in present-day Bosnia) 'led us away from the public road of Bulgaria, or as they say the beaten track, into other places; and furthermore the road by which he took us was rocky and not a main one', which left them vulnerable to attack.[52] Some Hungarian pilgrims, who were familiar with the area, formed a vanguard to scout for a route, with some success. But in 'that most lengthy forest of Bulgaria' the crusaders were repeatedly ambushed. Stragglers and foraging servants were targeted by the attackers' poisoned arrows, and people were 'murdered wholesale during the daytime'.[53] (The chronicler evidently did not see this as reasonable resistance to the arrival of a foreign army.) Hunger was another threat, especially for poorer pilgrims who could not carry additional supplies. Where the crusaders managed to capture attackers, they were hanged, in some cases ignominiously 'by their feet, as wolves are hung'.[54] It is no surprise that under the circumstances, the promised markets were withdrawn, which in turn increased the crusaders' need to forage, and made them more vulnerable still. The Byzantines further 'ordered the road junctions to be blocked with trees that had been cut down and covered with huge rocks, and he instructed that certain ancient fortifications in the passes, ruined with age, which served as a protection and defence for all Bulgaria, should be strengthened by renewing the towers and bastions'.[55] Their men took advantage of the mountainous area to attack from high up the mountain slopes, though the crusaders fought back. It is perhaps not surprising that Frederick described the plain of Circuviz, location of the city of Thrace (now Plovdiv), at the end of the 'laborious crossing of Bulgaria', as 'filled with all sorts of good things'.[56]

As I'm not marching an army through their country, my encounters with the locals are rather more positive. In Bucharest, the hotel manager welcomes me and my British accent – he spent some time in London, and his English teacher advised him to watch *Fawlty Towers* for the practice. I'm not sure that's a great recommendation for a future hotel manager but this establishment is, in fact, very well run. He tells me I have a BBC accent, which I do, on account of occasionally working for the actual BBC. The next morning I navigate buying some snacks at the station and set off on the train to Ruse, and thence to Sofia. I have a reservation but the guard has decided to abolish reservations so he can keep half-a-dozen seats to himself for 'his office'. Makes no difference to me, but some passengers are unimpressed. A couple of other chaps turn up to join him. There's obviously a system of buying reservations on the train here. We run late, and a few nervous tourists ask about the connection to Sofia, at which the guard flips a hand and says 'no problem', to their sceptical gaze. When we do hit the connecting station, Ruse, just after the long bridge over the Danube, there's a passport check and the efficient young woman in charge, faced with the same question, says firmly in English, 'You can wait for me over there, the train for Sofia is not leaving until I say so.' There follows a roll-call of names and nationalities while we retrieve our passports: France, Germany, the US, Argentina. Ms Bulgarian border cop, showing creativity, has stamped mine sideways. The connecting train leaves a good forty minutes late to curve back west towards Sofia. The signs on the stations are in Bulgarian (which uses a Cyrillic alphabet that a long-ago Russian evening class and a couple of visits to Greece help me through) and French: 'Dames' and 'Salle d'Attente', a legacy (so far as I can tell from internet searching) of the fact that it was fashionable to look west after Bulgaria gained its independence from the Ottoman Empire, a process that began with autonomy in 1878 and was formalised thirty years later. BBC English and fashionable French: the modern replacements for the ancient common language, Latin.

The train judders to a stop, tilting more than I would like. I look up from my book. We're in a pass, about 80 km north of Sofia. Passengers hang out of the windows to try to see what's happening. There's some anxious chatter, but the German students in my compartment speak enough Romanian to translate for me. We've hit a cow. The locals aren't panicking and an inspection later, we head on to the next station. I don't know how the cow looks, and decide that I don't want to. There's no damage that will stop us getting to Sofia. From now on, in my journey, whenever I spot a herd of cows I also check the robustness of the road barriers.

I have my few days in Sofia, then out of the city and the train enters a wide valley. Writing in the twelfth century, Odo of Deuil, who accompanied Louis VII, king of France on the Second Crusade, spoke of this part of Bulgaria as 'a wide, rich and pleasant plain'. He reckoned it took four days to travel from Niš to Sofia, about the same again from Sofia to Plovdiv and Plovdiv to Edirne, and then five days to Constantinople.[57] This was an average of 43 km per day (27 miles), which suggests relatively straightforward passage. For all the crusaders' complaints, they barely register in the local history section of the Sofia museum: perhaps a loutish bunch of foreigners tipping up for a few weeks then leaving again don't deserve a mention.

This is, by and large, flat territory. It wouldn't be a difficult hike. Now, it's agricultural land. There are a few rises and falls, but it's definitely no more than 'moderate' in the hiking guide stakes. The main problem, I suspect, is that the land is boggy: I wouldn't want to cross some of these fields after heavy rain. A raised, and drained, road ought to deal with that, but there was no guarantee of maintenance in the period of depopulation. An hour away from Plovdiv, and we hit hills again, the train curving along a wooded hillside, across bridges that might all too easily be damaged. This is one of those stretches where the road and railway have to run tight beside one another. After the ease of the Sofia plain this must have led to sighs.

Here as in the past there are local transport connections. A narrow-gauge train leads up south into the Rodopi mountains, linking Septemvri, on the main line, with Dobrinishte. Past the interchange, the plain opens out, wide and flat, following the line of the Maritsa river, which runs close to the line of the old road between Plovdiv and Edirne, the only hills far distant, once again the main risk bog, not attack from above. I can see why travellers on foot or cart or horseback felt relief at their arrival here. There was perhaps less relief for the locals, however, who for some centuries had found themselves at the border between the Byzantine Empire and the Bulgarian Kingdom. As insecurity increased, the Roman sites at the foot of Plovdiv's hills were largely abandoned and the population retreated to the walled hilltop town. Its fortifications can still be seen in part, below nineteenth-century wood-framed houses, and beside the one surviving medieval gate, Hisar Kapia. Other fortresses in the area became important too. That of Asen, originally Thracian, lies to the south of Plovdiv on a clifftop beside the Asenitsa river, a tributary of the Maritsa. Rebuilt under Justinian, it was seized in 1204 by crusaders led by Renier du Trit, who held out for thirteen months (according to a tourist website, or in the words of one chronicler, 'a long time') under siege by the forces of Tsar Kaloyan. Today, travellers can also hike the nearby Roman road.[58]

For all that the crusaders found the minor roads dangerous, they were an essential part of transport infrastructure. A few years after the Third Crusade, in 1203, Archbishop Basil of Trnovo (Veliko Tarnovo, in north-central modern Bulgaria) made a journey to Durrës for discussions about relations between his eastern Church and that of Rome.[59] The experience did not end well: Basil met a papal representative, probably Walter of Brienne, Count of Lecce and Prince of Taranto, but was then arrested by the Byzantine authorities and held for eight days before being released.[60] A reconstruction of Basil's likely route proposed by twentieth-century scholar James Ross Sweeney, however, illustrates the continuity of roads over many centuries in this region, and also the importance of the smaller ones. There was no major road connecting Trnovo with Durrës, but the former was near the ancient town of Nicopolis ad Istrum from which a Roman road led west to Lovech. This in turn connected to the Etropole Pass which led south over the Balkan mountains to Sofia. At Sofia, Basil would have crossed the route of the Via Militaris, but rather than take this road, he would instead have headed south-west via Kyustendil and then south to Bitola (now in North Macedonia), the intersection with the Via Egnatia.[61] It took him thirty days to travel a route that was 469 miles long, but only fifteen days to return. In other words, he covered over fifteen miles a day on the way out but more than thirty on the way back. This may have been the consequence of a larger party on the initial leg taking longer stops,[62] but even so it gives an indication of the very wide range of journey times, and, moreover, that by this time the speeds achievable on these routes were not far off those of ancient Romans.

I make my way from Plovdiv to Istanbul on a route that more or less follows the ancient Via Militaris. There is a train, but only overnight, and I want to see the view so I resign myself to seven hours on the coach. The driver loads my suitcase in. He's rocking a blue-and-white checked jacket and company tie (blue squares, red embroidery) and his well-trimmed grey moustache reminds me of a 1980s game show host. No one can make the passenger numbers add up, so there's a full ticket check before we leave to drive across the wide Plovdiv plain.

It's mid-October and some fields are newly ploughed, stubble glistening in sunlight on the soil, while others seemingly lie fallow. We cross the Maritsa river: I read online that the earliest bridge across it dates to Roman times, another expression of imperial power. At Haskovo we pause, and the driver gives out little cakes flavoured with vanilla. The sun is just visible now behind pale slate clouds and the terrain is hillier. A little way short of the Turkish border we make a longer stop at Mustafa Market, and from the quantity of booze being brought onto the bus in black carrier bags I deduce that Bulgaria has a favourable tax rate. In fact, it has the lowest tax on spirits of any EU country, while in Turkey the AKP (Justice and Development Party) has been systematically increasing alcohol taxes since it came to power in 2002, the most recent rise increasing prices by thirty per cent. Mustafa Market is, incidentally, the first off-licence I've encountered with a prayer-room.

The country beyond isn't empty, exactly: I spot a van, a tractor, a building with a corrugated roof, but it's slow, and still. A road sign marks the turn-off for Greece: here the Maritsa river becomes the border, and another sign indicates that nearby we'll find the 'Ancient Road Via Diagonalis'. That's in English: clearly, Roman heritage is perceived to have international appeal. Not far away, in fact, is Castris Rubis, a Roman fort and way station marked on the Peutinger Map. A local wine company has adopted the name Castra Rubra, and produces a Via Diagonalis Red (Merlot and Cabernet Sauvignon, plus a Bulgarian cross of Syrah and Nebbiolo called Rubin, and local grape Mavrud). The border with Turkey is marked by massive Bulgarian and EU flags. We sit and wait. A couple of cyclists pass, a Norwegian flag on their trailer. It's a very dull wait. Did the Romans get to Norway? No, it turns out, but there were trade links. We get off the bus and file slowly through the checks, passports stamped, passengers smoking hasty cigarettes before we have to board again. Just beyond the border is a mosque with a pair of minarets, its white plaster stained – with exhaust fumes? We stop again, for a check of the Turkish passengers' ID cards by some police labelled *jandarmes*, like the French. And then we carry on.

It's dead flat for a while, the land mostly agricultural, some bits of scrub, not too many hills. We pause again for cigarette and toilet breaks. The service station Wi-Fi password is 14531453, a reference to the year the Ottomans conquered Constantinople – such a good date in Turkish memory that the IT guy used it twice. Eventually we see the sea: the Sea of Marmara, that divides the Mediterranean from the Black Sea. When we finally arrive in Istanbul, it's half past five, dark, and raining. Once upon a time, travellers on the Via Militaris arrived in imperial style at the Golden Gate. In fact, this last stretch of the old road was probably kept in good condition precisely for use in triumphal entrances.[63] I tip up at Istanbul's central bus station with less sense of power and authority and more sense that the local council needs to get on top of these traffic jams. I make a dash to the metro, taking the wrong stairs at first, hauling my suitcase back up several flights when someone points out my mistake. The city's largely invisible as I cross underground to Pera, historically the quarter where European traders were obliged to live. A floodlit mosque breaks the darkness when the train emerges briefly on a bridge over the Golden Horn.

From Byzantium the old roads led south through Galatia to Antakya (near the ancient site of Antioch) then along the eastern coast of the Mediterranean. These routes had their own challenges. The road that French crusaders followed from Lopadian (now Uluabat) to Edremit (both in modern Turkey), along the south coast of the Sea of Marmara, to reach the Mediterranean was so far in a state of disrepair that it was easy to get lost. Still, it was better for supplies than the alternative, more easily passable, hill route. In such circumstances, guides and scouts were indispensable.[64] The anonymous author of the *Gesta* recounted how in order to secure a route for the crusaders to Nicaea, Duke Godfrey 'sent ahead three thousand men, with axes and swords, and told them to go and cut and widen the road for our pilgrims'. They marked the route with 'crosses made of iron and wood',[65] a Christian equivalent, perhaps, to the Roman milestones that had once asserted political power, and one that intentionally or not evoked the image of ancient roadside crucifixions.

In the Holy Land itself, crusaders also made use of a road network developed from earlier Roman roads. These were not necessarily the safest options. For the twenty-seven miles from Tyre to Acre the coast road occupied a slender strip of land between mountainside and sea, and at one point not even that, requiring an ascent onto steep paths. They were highly vulnerable to attack.[66] (That geography adds some context to the present-day closure of the Tyre to Acre route.) The sources are silent on the specifics of the approach of the First Crusade to Jerusalem from Ramla (a town just south-west of modern Tel Aviv) in 1099. The armies had three possible options but it seems most likely that they took a southern route from Emmaus, which was the most heavily used; this had been built in the early Arab period parallel to an earlier Roman-Byzantine route. There were alternative approaches, but the evidence from the remainder of the journey is that in most cases they opted for major routes rather than risk unmarked or less marked paths where, as on the southern coast of the Sea of Marmara, there was a risk of getting lost.[67] There's evidence that the Franks did use a more northerly option: a Roman road that ran via Bayt Ghur and Mons Gaudii (just as there was a Mons Gaudii in Rome from which pilgrims might look down joyfully at the city, so there was one in Jerusalem and also in Santiago de Compostela). However, it seems unlikely that this was a First Crusade route.[68]

After the crusaders seized the city, the road network was modified substantially, in light of an expected rise in traffic.[69] Military orders, including the Knights Templar and Hospitallers, fortified roads in and out of Jerusalem. Control of a road could be lucrative. While in theory pilgrims here, as in western Europe, were not required to pay tolls, those who could afford to make the trip could often also afford substantial services en route and indeed to make donations to their hosts.[70] Travel accounts from the period confirm that at least some roads were relatively well maintained. John Phokas (or perhaps John Doukas), who travelled to the Holy Land in the late twelfth century, noted that:

> From Samaria to the Holy City is reckoned eighty-four stadia; the road is all paved with stone, and, albeit the whole of that region is dry and waterless, yet it abounds with vineyards and trees.[71]

Elsewhere, however, the roads were less accommodating. Phokas also travelled to the monastery of Choziba, which lies a few kilometres east of Jerusalem, north-west of the Dead Sea:

> After this comes a long, narrow, and very rough road, leading to the back of the wilderness, before you come to which you see in the midst of it two mountains, between which the road to Jericho passes: on this road there is no stone pavement, but, nevertheless, the outline of it can be faintly traced; but, at the present day, all the neighbouring country abounds with springs of water for the use of the monasteries which have been founded in the wilderness, for the land, having been divided and parcelled out among these holy monasteries, has become well wooded and full of vines; so that the monks have built towers upon their fields, and reap rich harvests from them.[72]

It is notable that Phokas does not refer to the cisterns and wells that existed on at least some desert roads in ancient times. Nor does Marino Sanudo, in his fourteenth-century observations on the roads south from Jerusalem to Cairo: 'good road, with water and plenty of grass . . . road leads over sand . . . road all over sand . . . much sand, plenty of grass land, good water and a market.'[73] The roads were evidently still passable, if perhaps not with the ease that ancient travellers had enjoyed.

To the north, in the remaining parts of the Byzantine Empire, some Roman-style road management persisted. An account from 1299 describes poor travel conditions in winter on the road between Skopje and Constantinople, but attests to the expectation that those living along the route would provide accommodation for official travellers, in return for certain tax and service exemptions.[74] On the other hand, between the beginning of Latin rule in 1204 and the Ottoman conquest in 1453 the Via Egnatia does not seem to have functioned as a long-distance route.[75] In practice, what mattered to most local people were not the trunk roads but the secondary routes that facilitated their own travel to market and, when necessary, to administrative centres.[76] Still, almost a millennium on from the shift of the empire's capital to the east, while the paving of the Roman roads might now be badly worn, their routes had proven remarkably resilient.

PART 3

Proofs of Roman Greatness, 1450–1800

7
The Renaissance of the roads

The popes were hardly swift to settle their differences after the Avignon schism – at one point three men claimed the role! – but by the middle of the fifteenth century they were established back in Rome. Italy's location at the heart of the Mediterranean trade routes made it one of the richest parts of Europe, and that wealth underpinned a new Italian Renaissance. With the Renaissance came a conscious movement to rediscover and promote Rome's antiquities: the ancient pagan heritage alongside the Christian churches. On the roads as elsewhere there were efforts to recreate the Roman past – at least as these Renaissance men imagined it – and for the first time we start to see efforts to analyse and protect their heritage.

Presiding over this restored Rome were a series of popes. The first, Martin V, who ruled from 1417, was one of the Colonna, a leading baronial family of Rome. He was succeeded by Eugenius IV, a Venetian, who ruled from 1431 to 1447 but faced a rebellion in the city and spent the majority of his papacy in Florence. It fell to Eugenius' successor, Nicholas V, to stabilise the popes back in Rome, which he did with considerable success. In 1452 he presided over the coronation in St Peter's of the Holy Roman Emperor Frederick II. Meanwhile, more systematic study of the monuments and structures of the ancient world began. One of the first people to write about this history was Poggio Bracciolini, a Florentine scholar known for his identification of multiple classical texts in the monastic libraries of western Europe. His work *De varietate fortune* (On the variety of fortune), circulated in manuscript from 1447, included a description of the tomb of Caecilia Metella on the Via Appia at the second intact milestone; he cited Pliny on the walls of Rome and the gates leading out from the city, which he tried to match to those of his own day.[1]

This was a period of restoration and renovation for Rome's infrastructure. The men directly responsible for the maintenance of the roads were the *maestri di strade e degli edifici* (masters of the streets and buildings). This office was recorded as early as 1227 and its holders were responsible for urban planning decisions, not least concerning the city's ancient structures. In 1425 Martin V made the *maestri* answerable to the Pope rather than to the civic magistrates, an indication of his interest in the fate of the city's historic sites and ruins.[2] The popes of this period likewise took an interest in the Pontine Marshes – not least because properly reclaimed agricultural land was more profitable than uncultivated swamp. Their efforts at improvement are recorded in the names of two rivers in the area: the Rio Martino after Martin, and the Rio Sisto, for a later sixteenth-century pope, Sixtus V.[3] Indeed, the Rio Martino can be seen on a 1515 drawing by Leonardo da Vinci, one of the bird's-eye views he had pioneered a decade earlier. Leonardo was known for his interest in water and waterworks and had previously been involved in an abortive military plan to divert the Arno river. His map shows the series of rivers running down from the Aurunci Mountains to the wooded marshland. Cutting across, clearly labelled, is the Via Appia.[4]

Over the course of the fifteenth century, urban planners worked to redevelop Rome's road network, sometimes in line with the historic structure (as in the case of the three roads that met at Ponte Sant'Angelo: the Via del Pellegrino, Via Papalis and Via Recta), sometimes clearing areas for new roads (like the Via Alessandrina leading to St Peter's).[5] Nicholas V required that any excavations be approved by the papal chamberlain, one of the Vatican's most senior officials.[6] By the end of the century, under Pope Alexander VI (Rodrigo Borgia, who ruled from 1492 to 1503), the city conservators (Rome's senior civic leaders) were formally responsible for 'investigating and inflicting the most severe punishment against all those who destroy ancient things'.[7] Isabella d'Este, Marchioness of Mantua and a prominent collector, observed that on account of the conservators' interest, it was 'necessary to use art to bring [antiquities] out of Rome'.[8] Whether this referred to promises of diplomatic favour or something more underhand is hard to say, given the blurred line between legitimate tips and more dubious bribery in the period. The more conservative attitude towards the display of pagan sculpture that followed the Council of Trent (1545–63) led to the sale of some collections held by prominent churchmen, including to the ruling families of Florence, Ferrara and Mantua.[9] Still, Rome and its remains stayed an important – perhaps the single most important – stopping point on travellers' itineraries.

At the Campo de' Fiori, the historic flower market that now sells all manner of produce and souvenirs and is surrounded by tourist-trap bars, I find a surprising reference to Renaissance road improvement. On a terracotta wall, between two shuttered windows, a plaque marks Alexander VI's commitment to urban regeneration. 'After the Mole Adriana [Castel Sant'Angelo] had been restored,' it reads, 'he ordered the widening of the city's narrow streets.' It's not what the Borgias are usually remembered for, but it probably made a bigger difference to the average Roman than any of the murderous intriguing. It's a short walk from there to Via Giulia, the project of Alexander's rival and successor Julius II, who like the Roman consuls named a road after himself. Flanked by walls draped in greenery, and at one point traversed by an arch, if the Via Giulia once served to project papal power, its *sampietrini* now conjure a romantic image of Rome's history.

One of the travellers most conscious of the interplay between ancient and modern was Enea Silvio Piccolomini. Prior to his election in 1458 as Pope Pius II, Piccolomini had travelled extensively through the lands of the old Roman Empire on diplomatic missions and as private secretary to various cardinals, and late in his life he wrote of those encounters with Europe's past. As Pope, however, he was also contending with new political dynamics in the east. There the Ottoman Empire had gradually expanded to control much of the territory around the remaining lands of the Byzantine Empire. Five years before Pius' election, the troops of Mehmet II had succeeded in conquering its last bastion, Constantinople, and in the coming years the Ottomans would extend their reach into the eastern Mediterranean and along the North African coast. Along the Via Militaris, they conquered Belgrade in 1520 and briefly besieged Vienna in 1529. While trade through Constantinople continued, the predominant method of transport between that city and Italy was by sea, with the Venetian state protecting shipping convoys east. The Roman routes remained in place, but with Islam now the principal religion in Constantinople, and the Roman successor state the loser to the Ottomans, the Via Egnatia was no longer a route between two capitals of an empire, but between two hostile powers. On the other hand, there was now only one city that claimed the heritage of the Roman Empire, and that was Rome itself.

It was in this context that Pius II became an important thinker in the development of a European or Western identity, established in opposition to the eastern Ottomans. In his early work, Pius had often used the concept of the Roman Empire when he wanted to convey a 'sense of a larger community', but subsequently he came up with an alternative: the adjective 'European'.[10] As he underscored the extent of Europe's ancient heritage in his *Commentaries*, he was simultaneously constructing a superior identity for those living in the western half of the old empire. Over centuries, as these ideas were refined, and Europe's new empires rose and fell, questions of who belonged to the West and who did not, and who were the true heirs of the Romans, would be crucial.

Unlike most medieval travel writing, Pius' commentaries deal extensively with history. The town of Perugia, near Assisi, was 'one of the twelve cities of Etruria and renowned in antiquity'.[11] The Colosseum makes an appearance, as does the Arch of Constantine.[12] He noted that the Ponte Nomentano, which crossed the Aniene river a little way north of Rome, was a 'famous work of Narses',[13] the Byzantine general who had played an important role in Justinian I's reconquest of Rome, and who according to the legend was the uncle of St Arthelais. Narses' connection to the bridge is not historically certain, but it had definitely been restored by Pius' predecessor Nicholas V and possibly by the eighth-century pope Adrian I.[14] Other trips included one down the Tiber to Ostia, in the company of four cardinals: 'The extensive ruins', he wrote, 'show that [the city] was once large. It lay about a mile from the sea. Ruined porticoes, prostrate columns, and fragments of statues are still visible.'[15]

On another occasion, during extended efforts to secure peace with Alfonso I of Naples, Pius took the opportunity to visit key sites in the south, including 'Baiae, Cumae and the ruins of ancient cities, Salerno, Amalfi, and the venerable tombs of the Apostles Andrew and

Matthew, where the holy bodies are said to exude the famous manna'.[16] Here he blends references to Christian relics and pagan sites in a manner characteristic of the Italian Renaissance. Like those of his ancient predecessors, Pius' journeys were measured against the physical markers of the roadside, testimony to their continued use. When he took the Via Tiburtina to Tivoli he was met by the populace 'at the second milestone'.[17] On the Via Appia, he noted, the pavement was still visible, and Nature, 'who is superior to any art', had enhanced the road's beauty still further with shady filbert trees. There were, moreover, 'ancient ruins on the mountains to the left at the foot of which are the remains of old buildings called Bovillae. It is said to be the spot where Milo killed Clodius.'[18] This was the famous case of Cicero, with which Pius, a Renaissance humanist schooled in classical literature, was of course familiar. This is far more precise engagement with the ancient works than we see in earlier periods. Returning to Rome on the Appia, Pius (now Pope, and following the style of Julius Caesar by describing himself in the third person) recorded his intervention to protect the ancient road and its retaining wall:

> Here a man was digging out the pavement and destroying the road, breaking up the great rocks into small pieces to build a house near Nemi. The Pope sharply rebuked him and instructed Prince Colonna, the owner of Nemi, not to allow the public road, which was the Pope's responsibility, to be touched thereafter.[19]

Pius was not entirely consistent in his attitude towards Roman heritage, and incorporated marble from a variety of ancient sites into his own building projects, including at St Peter's (not today's domed basilica, but its predecessor). Marble from the Colosseum was used to restore its front steps, and Roman columns from the Portico of Octavia were to be built into the Loggia of Benediction that Pius commissioned for its facade. Further marble for the project was dredged up from the Tiber delta. 'Wherever you dig,' wrote Pius, 'you find pieces of marble, statues and huge columns.'[20] Subsequently, however, he banned the destruction, removal or reuse of ancient ruins in Rome and the surrounding countryside on pain of excommunication, though he reserved the right to grant dispensations.[21]

Pius' travels were not restricted to the Italian peninsula, nor to pagan sites: pilgrimage remained a constant. Prior to his election as Pope, the young Enea Silvio Piccolomini had travelled to Scotland on a diplomatic mission, although as the English king refused him a safe-conduct he was obliged to do so via ship from Sluys, in the Low Countries near Bruges. 'Violent gales' forced the ship towards Norway but after twelve days they finally made land in Scotland. Piccolomini made a barefoot pilgrimage to the shrine of St Mary at Whitekirk, twenty-five miles east of Edinburgh.[22] The name Whitekirk comes from the fact that the old church of St Mary was whitewashed. That building, however, does not survive. It was burned down by suffragettes in 1914, and the subsequent restoration has a red sandstone facade. A panel outside tells me that in 1413 more than 15,000 pilgrims travelled here. Stone from the hostel that once housed them can be found reused in at least one village home today. The holy well that pilgrims hoped would heal their ills later dried up, and in any case pilgrimage dwindled with the Reformation a century later.

The dangers of travel had not disappeared. Back in the fifteenth century, having struggled to persuade King James to commit to war against England, Piccolomini departed, opting to travel by road instead of again risking the ship. Lacking a safe-conduct, he travelled in disguise south from Berwick-upon-Tweed, a journey he narrated in high colour, ranging from an encounter with peasants who had 'never seen wine or white bread', to an offer from two young women 'to sleep with him, as was the custom of the country' when one night he was forced to lodge in a stable.[23] I receive no such exciting propositions while in Berwick, but I do enjoy some excellent fish and chips, and a pleasant walk around the walls (in this case, Elizabethan, not Roman). Pius assured his readers he had turned down the offer, and been rewarded for his restraint when a disturbance outside in the night proved to be not Scottish robbers but friends.

Piccolomini continued down the Roman route past Newcastle, 'which is said to have been built by Caesar' (modern scholarship attributes the founding of the colony to Hadrian). At Durham he noted the tomb of the Venerable Bede.[24] Bede's remains are still in Durham Cathedral, though the shrine Piccolomini would have seen was destroyed during the Reformation. Northern England now has a much more substantial offer of Roman sites for the visitor than it did in Piccolomini's time. I can head off to visit, say, the Roman town of Corbridge, located at the junction of ancient routes Stanegate and Dere Street. There in the museum I can examine the archaeological finds, among them the tombstone of Palmyran standard-bearer Barates, and the remnants of military equipment like the spiked caltrops that would be scattered in the ground to stop a cavalry advance. A lavish silver serving tray from Ephesus (in fact a replica: the original is now in the British Museum) gives an impression of more elite lifestyles. Piccolomini, on the other hand, saw the British past through its towns and cathedrals. Only in the 1530s, when Henry VIII commissioned the first survey of antiquities, would the island's Roman history begin to be more systematically catalogued.

At York, 'a large and populous city', Piccolomini observed 'a cathedral notable in the whole world for its size and architecture and for a very brilliant chapel whose glass walls are held together by very slender columns'.[25] This Lady Chapel, at the east end of the Minster, was relatively new. Completed in 1408, its spectacular stained glass window, the largest in medieval Europe, survives to this day. Like so many ecclesiastical centres, York had been a Roman city too: as Eboracum it was a provincial capital. The intersection of York's Roman past with its Christian heritage is embodied in the figure of Constantine the Great, who happened to be here when he was proclaimed emperor in 306. He's commemorated with a statue outside the Minster. 'His recognition of the civil liberties of his Christian subjects and his own conversion to the Faith, established the religious foundations of Western Christendom,' reads a plaque on the railings nearby. Also in this cluster of monuments is a Roman column, found during excavations at the Minster in the 1960s, while one of the main streets of present-day York, Stonegate, takes its name, according to a notice on the wall, from 'the fact that it was a Roman stone-paved street', the Via Praetoria of the old Roman fortress.

Between the lines of Pius' narrative, we also find occasional tales of those he encountered or who served him on his travels. Someone – presumably not the future pope – had to break open the ice on a winter journey from Ferrara to the Reno river; someone had to carry him in a chair across the frozen river; his attendants, on that occasion, 'had to walk'. Stranded in the darkness, 'they were forced at some inconvenience to pass the night in any peasants' huts they could find'.[26] The view of the peasants on this arrangement is lost to history, but the story points to the fact that elite travel was only possible thanks to the efforts of maintenance workers, litter-bearers and those who made up beds and stables for the night.

The last year of Pius' rule, 1464, saw the establishment of Italy's first printing press, at Subiaco, which lies east of Tivoli further along the Aniene river. Printing enabled much wider circulation of texts and indeed maps. In 1492, Erhard Etzlaub, an instrument maker and surveyor, published a map showing the 'Rom Weg', or road to Rome. Probably intended for German pilgrims heading to Italy for the jubilee of 1500, it showed several routes over the Alps as well as highlighting the shrine to St Mary at Loreto.[27] Alongside maps, printing also facilitated the production of itineraries. No longer did guidebooks have to be copied and circulated by hand. By 1500, multiple compilations and translations of guidance for pilgrims were available to purchasers in Europe.[28] These works were complemented by more detailed studies of Italian antiquities. Leandro Alberti's exhaustive *Descrittione di Tutta Italia* (Description of All Italy), published in Bologna in 1550, drew on numerous ancient sources in its description of the roads of the peninsula and the monuments that might be observed to either side of them. Alberti had undertaken careful investigation, noting for example that the inscription mentioning Vespasian at the Furlo tunnel was badly worn away.[29] He also provided important testimony to the present state of the roads. At Terracina, he wrote, the Via Appia was 'in large part ruined' as a consequence of the Pontine Marshes flooding, but beside it many tombs were still visible, 'some whole, some half-ruined, some only foundations'.[30] An earlier account, from Isabella d'Este in 1514, suggests that there were also problems with the roads further south: returning from Naples to Rome in December, she proposed if the weather were fine to 'go by sea at least as far as Gaeta in order not to take the bad roads we took in coming here'.[31]

In parallel to books like Alberti's, the sixteenth century likewise saw growing interest in the artistic representation of the ancient past. Besides Leonardo's mapping of the Via Appia, many other

Italian artists drew Roman ruins, and the sketches of Martin van Heemskerck, a Netherlandish artist who travelled to Italy in the 1530s, also provide an important early visual record of Rome's antiquities. Guidebooks such as Ulisse Aldrovandi's 1556 *Delle statue antiche* (On ancient statues) advised visitors on which antiquities to see. Many of these were held in private collections and relied on the owners' good will for access, but this could be negotiated by local guides, whose services are clearly documented from the 1470s onwards.[32] In the context of this wider appetite, some scholars took particular interest in the roads, among them the Spanish royal chronicler Juan Ginés de Sepúlveda (1491–1573), who spent an extended period living in Rome and became a prominent figure in debates over Spain's imperial policy. In 1543, he accompanied Maria of Portugal on her journey to marry the future Philip II of Spain. As they travelled the Roman road from Mérida to Salamanca, Sepúlveda transcribed a series of inscriptions from Roman milestones, measuring the distance between them, and sent a report of his investigations to the bridegroom.[33] An unusual wedding gift, perhaps, but one that would assure the prince of his land's imperial heritage. As the modern powers of Europe built their own empires, they had good reason to study the empires of the past. In 1575, Sepúlveda's work would be followed by Ambrosio de Morales' *The Antiquities of the Cities of Spain*, the first book in the kingdom to draw together both textual sources and observation of its ancient remains.[34]

Around Rome itself the landscape of the roads changed as the luminaries of the papal court sought to emulate the villa life of the ancients. The earliest surviving example of a Renaissance Roman villa is a *casino* (little house) on the Via Appia which features an attractive loggia and is now used for city functions. Sometimes linked to Cardinal Bessarion, who had accompanied the Byzantine emperor to a Council of the eastern and western churches held in Florence/Ferrara in 1438/39, it was in fact more likely restored for summer use by a Giovanni Battista Zeno, who succeeded Bessarion as Bishop of Tusculum in 1475. Zeno's coat of arms, not Bessarion's, is to be found in the decor.[35] A letter of 1444 from the humanist scholar Flavio Biondo to the Marquis Leonello d'Este of Ferrara notes the rich hunting that might be found in this area between the 'most famous' Via Appia and Via Latina,[36] once again testimony to Renaissance interest in, and awareness of, the roads.

Villa construction really took off, however, in the middle of the sixteenth century, after the land wars that had scorched the Italian peninsula in its early decades began to cool. There had been building in that time, of course, but the popes had preferred to restore apartments in the fortified Castel Sant'Angelo (as did Clement VII and Paul III), or commission improvements to Rome's fortifications, like the fortress constructed to a design by Antonio da Sangallo at the Porta Ardeatina.[37] Sometimes evidence of the winners and losers in those wars is to be found on the roads. By the early sixteenth century the Kingdom of Naples, which stretched across southern Italy, was under Spanish rule. In 1568, just past Terracina on the Via Appia, the Spanish viceroy erected the 'Tower of the Epitaph' to mark the boundary between Naples and the Papal States.[38]

Implicit in the reconstruction of villa life was a need for reliable infrastructure to get to and from these country homes, or as an estate agent might put it, excellent transport links. Pope Pius V's *vigna*, Casaletto (meaning little farmhouse or cottage), was off the Via Aurelia Antica.[39] Cardinal Ippolito d'Este (a younger son of Lucrezia Borgia and Alfonso d'Este, Duke of Ferrara) headed out along the Via Tiburtina to Tivoli, where his architects developed the Villa d'Este with its gardens full of fountains on a complex scheme tying into local antiquities including the Emperor Hadrian's villa in the valley below. Nearby was another Roman villa, that of Horace. The foundations of this property, situated on a hillside with spectacular views across a deep valley to the town centre, were built over in the ninth century and the subsequent building has variously been a monastery and a private home. In 1878 it was purchased by Frederick Searle, and is now available to rent through the Landmark Trust.[40] I stayed there with a student group – thanks to their educational visit scheme – in 2018, one more connection of present-day travel with the past. Beneath the modern rooms, an ancient nymphaeum is still visible.

In some cases architects and patrons – both ancient and Renaissance – positively valued a view of the roads. From the Gianicolo hill (located in Trastevere, across the Tiber from Rome's centre), visitors could look south to the Alban Hills, or north to the Flaminia and Salaria: thus Martial (Marcus Valerius Martialis) praised the view from the villa of Julius Martialis, where a millennium and a half later a senior official at the court of Pope Leo X commissioned the Villa Lante.[41] A few decades on, in the 1550s, Pope Julius III purchased substantial landholdings, including an existing vineyard, along the Via Flaminia in order to build the Villa Giulia, now home to Rome's Etruscan Museum. Beside this splendid residence, complete in classical style with a nymphaeum, Julius commissioned a church on the Via Flaminia, dedicated to St Andrew in memory of the spot where Cardinal Bessarion had paused while bringing the saint's relics from Patras (in the Peloponnese, where the local rulers anticipated an Ottoman invasion) to Rome. In autumn 1552, races were held on the Flaminia, including one in which stonemasons working on the church competed with the staff of the papal vineyard. The villa became a useful lodging place for distinguished visitors to Rome, among them Cosimo de' Medici, Duke of Florence, who stayed there in 1560.[42] Its location just outside the city walls gave them space to dress and prepare for a grand formal entrance. Other popes and cardinals followed Julius' example. Pius IV had his own *palazzetto* erected on the Via Flaminia (alongside a public fountain that still survives, though online reviews advise against drinking the water).[43] In a 1565 description of Rome's ancient heritage, Bernardo Gamucci (about whom we know little except that he came from San Gimignano) observed: 'The Via Flaminia has been so embellished in our time as far as the Ponte Molle with walls, palaces, and beautiful gardens, all about, that I doubt that the proud Romans ever saw it in such beauty.'[44] English ambassador Thomas North, who saw the Villa Giulia shortly after Julius III's death, thought it 'of such an excellent building and hath such a notable commodity in it, all of white marble, so curiously wrought, so replenished with strange fruits, and furnished with antiquities that be daily dug up in old Rome, and some found in the river of Tiber, in such sort that it doth far exceed all the buildings that ever I saw except the Charterhouse beside Pavia'.[45]

The Charterhouse to which North referred (in Italian, Certosa) was a well-established stopping-off point for dignitaries on the road to Rome, and can still be visited. I see it on the morning of Friday,

9 September 2022. England is in mourning for the death of Queen Elizabeth II. In North's day, such news would have taken a fortnight to arrive, perhaps ten days with a fair Channel crossing. I, on the other hand, have heard it via my phone on a train, the busy 1344 *regionale* from Genoa towards Milan the previous day. The only thing that stops the flow of news are the multiple tunnels through the western Apennines that cut off my access to the internet. I check in to a B&B in Pavia. The host explains that Pavia follows the usual layout of a Roman town, with two main streets at right angles. The B&B is just off one of these, and occupies the surviving floors of a medieval tower. The duomo is just across the square, and at one point this building housed the cathedral works department. My room is at the top, and though the window doesn't open onto the piazza, it does have a marvellous view across red-tiled rooftops to the hills that my train crossed coming up from Genoa.

Mourning in England means a hiatus in strike action on the post and on the trains. There is, however, still a train strike in Italy, and after watching one train to Certosa get cancelled I opt instead for the bus, up a road so straight it might be Roman, though Wikipedia tells me that in fact it follows a medieval route some way to the west of the original. There's a canal to either side and turning off I spot a lock, a rare sight in Italy. The monastery lies a good fifteen-minute walk down a long tree-lined avenue off the main road (leading east, so it's probably closer to the old Roman route). Founded at the turn of the fourteenth to fifteenth century, the building is spectacular, overwhelmingly so, facade clad in marble and peopled with statues, the largest cloister I've ever seen, roses growing around it, a beautiful marquetry choir, frescoes and the stunning marble tombs of the rulers of Milan (down to perfect details such as Beatrice d'Este's platform shoes, which would have kept her feet out of the mud). Not much has changed, in fact, since North described it:

> Five miles from Pavia, we were brought to La Certosa di Pavia, where the lords dined, and were greatly feasted. It is the goodliest and best built house of all Europe. It was founded by Gian Galeazzo Visconti, [1st] Duke of Milan who lieth there interred in a tomb of white marble; the 2 coffins and the table of the altar are all of ivory, with such

> workmanship that it is a spectacle to all Lombardye. There is a cloister 40 foot quadrant; the doors, desks, and stools be so garnished with such notable histories, all of cut work, of divers kinds of woods, that no man possibly can paint them out more finely and lively.[46]

One new addition is the small museum that now occupies what were once rich guest apartments, providing hospitality for visitors on the road to Rome, but also a space to pause in their travels and engage in religious devotion.

Such stays were commonplace, not only for diplomats but also during royal visits, while the roads into Rome became a space for theatrical entries into the city. Featuring temporary arches, living tableaux, parades, music and crowds, these were splendid occasions. In Rome the papal masters of ceremonies carefully organised welcoming parties along the roads, stretching out past posting inns and chapels in strict ritualised fashion. The size of a visitor's entourage was an indicator of his status. Among those to make a 'kind of triumphal progress' through Rome was Pope Pius II, who while facing down a conspiracy in 1460 went from a monastery at the Porta del Popolo (on the site, Pius said, of Nero's murder), 'through the city to St Peter's amid extraordinary acclamation from the populace. Houses all along his way were decorated, the squares were covered with carpets, and all the streets were strewn with flowers and grass.'[47] From Pope Alexander VI onwards, the ceremony of the *possesso*, with which a new pope took office, increasingly deployed classicising elements, mimicking the ancient triumph both through the incorporation of actual Roman remains and through the addition of temporary structures in idealised classical style.[48]

Many entries were staged from the north, and this was the route for which the papal master of ceremonies kept official guidance in his handbook for dealing with ambassadors to Rome. Visitors would enter over Monte Mario, above which the Emperor Constantine had seen a vision of the Holy Cross the night prior to his battle with his pagan rival Maxentius. Taking the descent today this Via Trionfale route still passes the little church of San Lazaro (once the site of Rome's leper colony), rather inauspiciously tucked into a side street, though with a more modern sensibility there's then the opportunity to pause at a popular ice-cream shop, or to enjoy a meal at the Trattoria del Falcone, its name echoing that of an old *vigna* where travellers sometimes dined before a formal entry to the city. Some celebrated entries, however, proceeded from the south, such as that of Charles V, Holy Roman Emperor, in 1536, following his victories in North Africa, and that of Marcantonio Colonna in 1571, after the Battle of Lepanto. These successes against the Ottoman Empire and its allies provided opportunities for Renaissance commanders to draw parallels with the victories of the Roman Empire in Africa and Asia Minor, in particular those of Scipio Africanus, and – albeit temporarily – revived some sense of a Mediterranean-focused Roman Empire.[49] Charles' entry was preceded by significant demolitions that in theory at least would allow the emperor to follow a historic route of ancient processions.[50] Although we now know that there was no such standard route,[51] the Renaissance 'recreation' involved a tour of city sites, both Christian and pagan: the emperor was greeted by cardinals at the church of Domine Quo Vadis,[52] made his way up the Via Appia and entered Rome via the Porta San Sebastiano; he then went via the Forum and thence to the Vatican. In what would be one of many such interventions through the centuries, areas around the Septizodium and the Arch of Constantine were cleared to put the ancient landmarks on effective display.[53]

Besides the symbolic power of the newly embellished Roman roads, some practical elements of the ancient network were re-emerging. Among them were new postal services. Unlike the unified imperial *cursus publicus*, however, these were run on national lines. They were gradually formalised. Louis XI, king of France (r. 1461–1483), began a process of passport inspection for foreign couriers travelling through his realm, allowing messengers of allies to obtain horses from the local postmasters. Spain and England had national masters of post in place by 1505 and 1512 respectively.[54] Printed itineraries listing the post-houses were available in northern Italy by the middle of the sixteenth century, and soon spread more widely. One early seventeenth-century itinerary, that of Franciscus Schottus, was popular enough that it was referred to in an Italian phrase-book for English travellers.[55] Meanwhile, the developing postal network enabled circulation of news: the

Fuggerzeitungen newsletters associated with the Fugger company and family, but probably not written exclusively for them, clearly spread along these routes.[56]

There was not, however, straightforward progress. Between 1494 and 1559, the Italian Wars – essentially a conflict between France and Spain for hegemony on the Italian peninsula – affected patterns of travel, as did the weather. The choice of Alpine pass, for example, would depend on the prevailing political alliances. Travelling the Via Flaminia from Pesaro, on the Adriatic coast, to Rome via the shrine of Loreto in 1525, Isabella d'Este 'found the road difficult and longer than expected'; her anxieties about the trip were exacerbated when on reaching Terni she heard from a Venetian courier that the king of France had been captured (at the Battle of Pavia), and that 'the roads to Rome were wrecked'. Thanks to the efforts of her ambassador, however, she made a safe entry to the city, with a number of gentlemen gathering to greet her in 'a beautiful cavalcade'.[57] People making journeys during wartime were often concerned they might be spied upon, and indeed local rulers used their control of the post routes to check on hostile powers, identifying foreign travellers and disseminating information about their presence through their intelligence networks. Those seeking to evade checks could do so by avoiding the main routes, but that could be dangerous. More commonly, couriers travelling with secret information would carry an anodyne letter for public presentation, and memorise or at least encipher the confidential message.[58]

Routes, moreover, changed over time, year by year and decade by decade, as is apparent from updates to the many printed postal itineraries.[59] All being well, in 1529, a professional courier changing horses regularly could get from London to Rome in just over two weeks, though most travellers took significantly longer.[60] By comparison, an estimate for the same route 1,500 years before gives the journey time by horse relay at just over nine days.[61] To be fair to the couriers of 1529, they were travelling close to areas of conflict, which might well have made for delays. The general picture, however, is that the sixteenth-century post was only just matching its ancient counterpart. Yet if travel times were much the same, thanks to print, by this time European readers had access to much fuller histories of the Roman roads.

8

Explorers, spies and priests

If the sixteenth century saw the revival of villa life and a developing system of postal routes, it also saw new division. The Reformation split the Church once again, with inevitable impact on the dynamics and the narratives of travel to Rome. The city was no longer the centre of western Christendom but the centre of one Christian church – albeit one with growing global influence on the back of European imperial expansion. A different group of people arrived in Rome: exiled Catholics, travelling not so much because they wanted to, but because they had no choice. Their stories are reflected in the fabric of the roads. Walking down the Via Appia, I see one monument associated with a prominent figure in the English break from Rome, Cardinal Reginald Pole. This tiny oratory, its roof topped in terracotta tiles, is located just past the church of Domine Quo Vadis. One story claims it marks the spot where Pole evaded an attempt to kill him.[1] King Henry VIII had indeed sent assassins after Pole, not only because of Pole's loyalty to the Pope in the aftermath of Henry's break with Rome, but because the Pole family were descended from Plantagenets and thus had a claim to the English throne. In fact, Pole and the would-be assassins spent their time up north near Venice and the Via Appia story is more likely a classical allusion to the murder of Cicero on the same road. Myths aside, the oratory is important to the story of English relations with Rome. It was commissioned by the cardinal in the 1530s, probably around the time that Pole and his supporters had taken over the English Hospital in Rome from the remaining loyalists to Henry (the king's excommunication was published in 1538). Placed as it was beside a church linked to St Peter, it made a statement about the continuing vitality of English Catholicism.[2]

The rise of Protestantism did not prevent engagement with Italy: there were, of course, many Italian states beyond the Papal ones, and the ancient past was outside the realm of Christian division. When travellers like William Thomas, whose *Historie of Italie* was published in 1549, visited Rome, they were often critical (if intrigued) by the papal court, but enthusiastic about the monuments. Thomas, for example, conceded that the Via Giulia of Julius II was 'fair builded', but observed that it was 'inhabited with none other but courtesans'.[3] However, while Thomas considered the ancient aqueducts, he did not discuss the roads as roads, except to observe that some small 'decayed or decaying' pyramids might be seen on the Flaminia, Salaria and Appia.[4] A member of Parliament during the reign of Edward VI (1547–53), Thomas was a key player in Sir Thomas Wyatt's rebellion against Edward's Catholic successor Mary, for which he was executed.

Mary's reign saw the re-establishment of English diplomatic relations with Rome, in the context of which she dispatched Thomas North as ambassador to the papal court. We met North in the previous chapter, observing the Villa Giulia, but in general he had less to say about antiquities than Thomas, reflecting instead on issues of diplomatic significance such as town defences and travel viability as well as his party's treatment by their various hosts. He did, however, refer on two occasions to the exploits of Hannibal of Carthage, citing on Mont Cenis 'the way that was cut out of the rock by Hannibal when he entered in to Italy'.[5] North, who is known for his translation of Plutarch's *Parallel Lives*, may have been familiar with the ancient sources for Hannibal's journey. He noted the site of a battle between the Africans and Romans between Fano and Fossombrone, and also (incorrectly) attributed the Furlo tunnel to this period, writing that it was 'made by man's hand for Hannibal to bring his army that way against Scipio Africanus'.[6] The point here – as with Charlemagne's mythical road to Constantinople – is that credit for a road was a way to communicate a ruler's achievement.

Wider interest in the road network is evident from the publication in 1552 of Charles Estienne's *Guide des chemins de France*, a survey of that kingdom's roads. Presented largely in list form, much like the old itineraries (Estienne referred explicitly to the Antonine Itinerary), it incorporated information on the major ancient monuments, including the amphitheatres at Arles and Nîmes, as well as practical details about journey times and posthouses.[7] Now, in the twenty-first century, maps live in my phone, automatically linked to the reviews of thousands of travellers, who in turn can read my own thoughts on the places that I've been to. When I first travelled to Italy, though, in 1999, it was with a *Lonely Planet*, or perhaps a *Rough Guide*, a book that shaped my journey through hotel recommendations, and notes on where to eat and what to see. Even in the age of phones, what often makes the difference to a trip is advice from other travellers, or local residents. A former colleague, for example, messages with restaurant tips for Rimini. Standing in a station toilet queue, I assure a highly groomed American eyeing the squat-style toilets that if she waits a moment, one of the more familiar sit-down ones will come vacant. In Ravenna some tourists at the next table tell us that the *piade* (local flatbreads) are good; I send my visiting friend off to Bologna with instructions to try the rival ice-cream shops and to walk up the hill beneath the portico to the church of San Luca.

Among the people who made their way to post-Reformation Rome were the young men who came from England to study – illegally – for the priesthood. Seven hundred and fifty arrivals are recorded between 1598 and 1685, as the English pilgrim hospital was reinvented as a seminary.[8] The English College is situated on Via Monserrato, not far from Piazza Farnese and the Campo de' Fiori, and continues to fulfil its 400-year-old educational function. Back in the 1570s, however, with priests banned from England amid fears of conspiracy to overthrow Elizabeth I, it was now no longer a welcoming source of homely hospitality but rumoured to be a hotbed of spies. Enter Anthony Munday, who took up residence there early in 1579. At the age of eighteen he had decided to travel to Rome, on account (as he explained it) of his 'desire to see strange countries, as also affecting to learn the language'.[9] He seems to have been bored with life as a printer's apprentice; certainly travel abroad for education was not uncommon for young men in Tudor England, and while it had become more awkward following the break with Rome, all things Italian were popular at the court of Elizabeth I.[10]

Munday quit the College before four months were up, but not before he had gathered sufficient material for a book. After first publishing a sexed-up account of the arrest of Edmund Campion, a Jesuit priest who arrived in England with others from the English College, in 1582 Munday decided to capitalise on his knowledge of the College with *The English Roman Life*. This entertaining narrative combined tales of gap-year high jinks with the sort of anti-Catholic exposé that was proving very saleable in England. The work, which as one critic puts it 'hovers between history and fiction', was unusual among Munday's wider literary output in going to reprint in his lifetime.[11] Munday travelled between two flare-ups of the French Wars of Religion, which posed its own challenges. Up until 1578 travellers from England to Rome had typically opted for a more easterly route through the Netherlands and Germany, then over the Gotthard Pass. By the time of Munday's trip, however, it was feasible, if not without risks, to travel via Paris and Lyons.[12] Crossing to Boulogne, he wrote, 'from thence we travelled to Amiens, in no small danger, standing to the mercy of despoiling soldiers who went robbing and killing through the country'.[13]

Today the route south from Paris involves a TGV. I have a seat on the top deck, the better to gaze out at the passing fields and woodland. I'm watching this journey on fast-forward, a time-lapse camera version of the old post road. Cows sit in a field flicking their tails. The occasional river crossing, or cutting, the landscape hillier as we head south, now and again a village, red-tiled rooftops, a church tower or spire: one has a walled cemetery outside its bounds. To my left, in the distance, are the Alps. Wind turbines dot the landscape. No religious war and yet conflict is not entirely absent from our lives. Today, 31 August 2022, Russia has closed the Nord Stream gas pipeline to Europe.

In the sixteenth century, closer to the war zones there were more obvious risks. In 1527, troops loyal to the Holy Roman Emperor kidnapped Thomas Wyatt, then an agent of the English Crown.[14] Even properly contracted commanders were no respecters of diplomatic status, and in any case ideas of diplomatic immunity were in their infancy. In the early decades of the sixteenth century, both a French ambassador's entourage and a Spanish cardinal acting as papal legate were attacked on the roads to Rome.[15] In the aftermath of conflict, demobilisation was typically chaotic, often leaving soldiers wherever the campaign had finished without the resources to return home. For all the efforts of the town captains to police the post routes the economic crisis of the later sixteenth century exacerbated problems, and the danger of the road increased with the proliferation of handguns. Munday and his companion Thomas Nowell found themselves robbed of their possessions and they were forced to turn for support to exiled English Catholics living along the way, first an old English priest in Amiens, Master Woodward, who put them up at his expense.[16] Woodward gave them an introduction to a Doctor Allen at Reims (later Cardinal William Allen, then running a seminary for English exiles), though they had to sell their cloaks to fund the onward journey.[17] In Paris they got an introduction to the English ambassador, who encouraged them to turn back: this they ignored, making their way south via first Lyons, then Milan, 'where in the Cardinal Borromeo's Palace we found the lodging of a Welshman named Doctor Robert Griffin, a man there had in good account, and confessor to the aforesaid cardinal'.[18] Griffin likewise arranged lodgings, and it is clear from Munday's account that there was a network of English exiles who supported their fellow countrymen. Following the post route via Bologna, Florence and then the Via Chiantigiana to Siena,[19] Munday and Nowell arrived in Rome, where they found accommodation at the English College.

Despite his tendentious anti-Catholicism, Munday gives a fair account – that can be corroborated with other sources – of daily life at the seminary, from its location 'not far from the Castel Sant'Angelo' to the trestle beds and coverlets.[20] The food was 'fine and delicate', including five-course meals with an antipasto, 'pottage' in the Italian style, two meat courses, one 'boiled meat, as kid, mutton, chicken, and suchlike', and one 'roasted meat, of the daintiest provision that they can get, and sometimes stewed and baked meat'. The final course was 'sometime cheese, sometime preserved conceits, sometime figs, almonds and raisins, a lemon and sugar, a pomegranate, or some such sweet gear: for they know that Englishmen loveth sweetmeats'.[21] In part this underlines an impression of Catholic wealth and luxury, but it also tells us something about the type of food that relatively well-heeled travellers might have enjoyed during a visit to the city.

All this was combined, however, with reports on the treasonous comments of the priests: one at the College described Elizabeth I, at least according to Munday, as a 'proud usurping Jezebel', and hoped 'ere long the dogs shall tear her flesh, and those that be her props and upholders'.[22] Munday's account of the seminary day incorporates an extended and salacious description of flagellation, in which one priest advises that should Munday care to try it, he 'should not find any pain in it but rather a pleasure'. Munday politely declined, or so he tells us.[23] In their spare time, the College students walked in the vineyard or played games, or visited the seven churches of Rome, and here Munday's account acquires more of the conventional flavour of a pilgrim or tourist guide, listing St Peter's, St Paul's, the Lateran, Santa Maria Maggiore, Santa Croce, San Lorenzo, San Sebastiano and their highlights, suitably qualified with a critique of relics, 'whereby the Pope deceiveth a number, and hath good gains, to the maintenance of his pomp'.[24]

Munday further provided a dramatic description of the visitor's experience exploring the catacombs of Santa Priscilla that lay north of the city next to what is now the park of Villa Ada. 'When they go into this vault,' he wrote, 'they tie the end of the line at the going in, and so go on by the line, else they might chance to lose themselves, and so miss of their ever coming out again; or else if they have not a line, they take chalk with them, and make figures at every turning, that at their coming again (being guided by torchlight, for candles will go out with the damp in the vault) they may make account till they get forth; but this is not so ready a way as by the line.'[25] Beyond Rome, he explained, pilgrims often made their way to Santiago or Loreto, to the Franciscan complex at Montefalco, north of Rome on the way to Perugia, or to Turin to see the famous shroud.[26] All this offers clues to typical tourist trajectories of the period, but Munday is also notable for his focus on Christian sites to the exclusion of any classical heritage. (He did, however, take a brief detour to the Jewish ghetto, established in 1555 in the context of wider antisemitic persecution.)[27] If Munday was familiar with the work of, say, Alberti, he was not engaging with it in this piece of writing.

We do, however, hear from Munday of one notable transport development. Describing the great 'noise and hurly-burly' of the Roman Carnival, he explained that:

> The gentlemen will attire themselves in divers forms of apparel, some like women, other like Turks, and every one almost in a contrary order of disguising; and either they be on horseback, or in coaches, none of them on foot, for the people that stand on the ground to see this pastime are in very great danger of their lives, by reason of the running of coaches and great horses, as never in all my life did I see the like stir.[28]

Documented from the thirteenth century, and initially used primarily by women, coaches became increasingly popular with the wealthy. By the sixteenth century, they were widely used as an alternative to horseback or the litter, including by men, and in their various forms came to dominate elite long-distance travel.[29]

In Rome at much the same time as Munday was the French essayist Michel de Montaigne, whose travel journal is not only a classic of its genre, but complements both Munday and the earlier Alberti with its detailed commentary on the Roman roads. Unlike the others, Montaigne was not writing for publication (the journal was eventually printed in the late eighteenth century), which gives the writing a different character. Importantly, it illustrates how interest in the ancient roads fitted into wider experiences of travel. Montaigne was concerned with both contemporary mores and with the ancient precedents. Travelling initially through Germany and Switzerland, he observed that 'the practice of bathing here [Baden, in Switzerland, on the Limmat river] is of high antiquity and is remarked by Tacitus, who searched to the utmost to find the chief spring, but could get no knowledge thereof'.[30] He lamented the locals' lack of familiarity with the ancient monuments. They were told nothing at all about a local 'portion of some column' by the side of the high road, but Montaigne spotted 'a Latin inscription, which I was not able to decipher fully, but . . . seemed to be a simple dedication to the Emperors Nerva and Trajan'.[31] (This sounds to me like a milestone.) Further along his route, he stayed in the 'Standard of Cologne', a posthouse at Markdorf, 'which is kept here for the Emperor's route into Italy', an observation emphasising how infrastructure catered to rulers' needs.[32] He rather regretted not bringing a cook, who might have learnt the local recipes, and likewise lamented not hiring a German valet or finding a German travelling companion: he 'felt it very irksome to be always at the mercy of a blockhead of a guide'.[33]

Still, despite the lack of a guide and his reliance on Sebastian Münster's *Cosmographia* (a geographical treatise of very limited use for travel tips), Montaigne still contrived to find some information about roads. In a monastery at Isny he found an inscription 'telling how the Emperors Pertinax and Antonius Verus had repaired all the roads and bridges for a distance of eleven thousand paces around Campidonium, that is to say, Kempten, whither we were bound for the night'.[34] Montaigne doesn't tell us how it made its way to the monastery, nor whether it was preserved for its historic interest or simply used – like so much *spolia* – as building material. Despite the rather mundane nature of this inscription, Montaigne decided to investigate, an indication of the growing interest in the ancient world and its material remains, but concluded that 'having inspected all the roads about Kempten, we could find no repairs worthy of such artificers, and there was not a single bridge. We certainly remarked that a way had been cut through some of the hills, but this work was not of prime importance.'[35]

Heading south to Italy, Montaigne obtained a 'bulletin of health' at Trent, to confirm he was not infectious with the plague; he had this confirmed at Rovere and used the document to gain access to Verona, 'not that there was any talk of danger of the plague, but this is always done by custom or by way of tricking wayfarers out of a few coins'.[36] I felt some sympathy with Montaigne when, returning from my first trip to Rome for research on this book, I was stung by a change in the rules for coronavirus testing, which left me £20 out of pocket. Montaigne was far from the only tourist to find such certificates necessary: a century and a half later, in 1722, an English traveller, Edward Wright, 'shuffled his cards right' and came up with a cunning scheme to obtain two sets of documentation from Ravenna, 'one to certify that we were well, the other that we were sick; the former on account of their fear of the Plague, to get us entrance to their Cities, and the other (it being Lent) to get us some *Grasso* (flesh-meat) in the Inns'.[37] While I avoided all but two days of quarantine, historically it was common in Italy, especially during outbreaks of plague.[38]

In Verona, Montaigne visited the Arena, 'the grandest building he had ever seen'.[39] In Ferrara, he noted the practice of obliging visitors to register with the magistrate; at Scarperia, crossing the Apennines, he found innkeepers competing for visitors' business.[40] Florence came as a disappointment. 'I cannot tell why this city should be termed "beautiful", as it were by privilege,' he wrote. 'Beautiful it is, but no more so than Bologna, and little more than Ferrara, while it falls far short of Venice.'[41] From Florence he headed south to Rome via Siena. He was impressed with the infrastructure:

> Lodging on this road is of the best, inasmuch as it is the great post road. They charge five giulios for the hire of a horse, and two for the post, and they make the same terms if the horses are hired for two or three posts, or for several days, in which case the hirer has no trouble about the horses; for, from one place to another, the innkeepers take charge of those belonging to their neighbours, and, moreover, they will make a contract under which you may be supplied with a fresh horse elsewhere on the road in case one of your own should fail.[42]

On the day of his departure for Rome, Montaigne and his party set out three hours before dawn, 'so keenly was M. De Montaigne set on seeing the Roman plain by day'. This was unusually early for Italy, which was, he observed, 'a good country for lazy folk, seeing the hour of rising was so late'.[43] Here the Roman roads make an appearance:

> After the fifteenth milestone we caught sight of the city of Rome: then we lost it for some long time . . . We came upon some portions of road, elevated and paved with large stones, having about them a certain look of antiquity.[44]

In Rome, Montaigne lodged initially at the Bear, on the corner of Via di Monte Brianzo and Via dell'Orso (the latter name translates as 'street of the bear'), then moved to an apartment opposite the church of Santa Lucia della Tinta;[45] and did the requisite exploring of the city, including its ancient monuments and churches; he had an audience with the Pope.[46] He headed west to the coast and Ostia, observing that the Via Ostiense 'abounds in vestiges of its ancient splendour, such as causeways and ruins of aqueducts; moreover, all along it is set with mighty ruins, and for two-thirds of its length it is still paved with those large black squares of stone which they used formerly as pavement'.[47] He even obtained for himself the title of Roman citizen: 'now altogether a vain one, nevertheless I felt much pleasure from the possession of the same'.[48]

Leaving Rome for Loreto, Montaigne took the Via Flaminia, along which were situated 'rare antiquities about which nought is known'; crossing the Tiber at Orte, he observed the ruins of a bridge built under the Emperor Augustus between the countries of the Sabines and Faliscii.[49] Montaigne admired the improvements to the road, and noted that the Pope had named it Via Boncompagna after his own family name: this was customary in Italy and Germany and followed, of course, the example of the Via Appia. Montaigne thought it 'an excellent stimulus to urge on men of that temper which recks little of the public weal to execute some useful work, from the hope of gaining fame and reputation thereby'.[50] He passed further road repairs en route to Arezzo, and was impressed by the quality of highway maintenance in Tuscany.[51] He visited the baths near Lucca (Bagni di Lucca), where he put to the test 'a certain appliance called a *Doccia*, which is composed of a number of tubes, through which hot water is turned on to various parts of the body and notably the head'.[52] After further trips to Florence, Pisa, the baths at Viterbo and then Rome, he turned back to the north, enjoyed a stay at the *Posta* in Piacenza – the 'best inn in all Italy, after the one at Verona' – and crossed over the Alps.[53]

For the most part the travellers whose lives are recorded are those of the middle and upper class, but there were migrants to Rome from across the social spectrum, some of whom appear in Montaigne's journal in a tragic event. The story centres on the church of San Giovanni a Porta Latina: the church of St John at the Latin Gate, that is, the gate in Rome's walls that led out to the Via Latina. This was the ancient road south through Lazio, the land of the Latins, that the straighter Via Appia had replaced almost two millennia before. At the time of Montaigne's visit it lay amid orchards and vineyards on the sometimes dangerous fringes of Rome. The church itself was rather neglected. It should have had a cleric in charge, but the cardinal responsible does not seem to have appointed one, and it was in effect managed by a Portuguese man, Marco Pinto, who may have been a sort of caretaker. San Giovanni had become a location for regular meetings of a group of men who had sex with men. As is so often the case with histories of sexuality, we know about this only because eleven of the men were arrested and tried – in this case after planning a same-sex wedding. Eight were burned at the stake. From the surviving trial notes (some documents were apparently burned 'to erase all memory of them')[54] we can see not only the lively community that prevailed, but also fragments of their histories as travellers to Rome.

Of the eight, six were Spaniards (three Castilian, two Aragonese/ Catalan, one Andalusian, though these distinctions do not seem to have mattered much in Italy). One was Portuguese, and another was from what is now Montenegro, but was then under Venetian rule.[55] This last man, known as Baldassare or Battista, worked as a ferryman on the Tiber. He had come to Italy from Flanders, where one of his co-accused had been an innkeeper. This co-accused, Robles, was alleged to be on the run from a Flemish charge of sodomy.[56] Some of the men on trial had links to the national churches that supported pilgrims and other travellers to Rome: San Giacomo degli Spagnoli (St James of the Spanish) on Piazza Navona, and San Giuliano dei Fiamminghi (St Julian of the Flemings) on Via del Sudario.[57] Had Munday wished (or had his publisher allowed him) he might have produced a still more scandalous account of the pilgrim hospitals than his *English Roman Life*. The story of these men, however, also raises another possibility about why travellers might make this famous journey: because they'd heard of such a subculture. Protestant propaganda made ample allusion to sexual deviance in Catholic Italy, from William Thomas' comments on Rome's courtesans and the 'pageboys' of Pier Luigi Farnese (son of Pope Paul III), to Julius III's notorious appointment of a young adopted 'nephew' to the cardinalate. A popular Puritan book of the seventeenth century observed that it was Julius' 'custome . . . to promote none to Ecclesiasticall livings save only his buggerers'.[58] If that put off some readers, it perhaps encouraged others.

More and more young Europeans went off to explore. The *Itinerary* of Fynes Moryson, a Cambridge fellow and son of an MP, describes his travels in Europe and the Middle East while in his late twenties in the 1590s. Published in 1617, like Montaigne's journal it provides rich detail of the practicalities of undertaking a journey. At Ancona, for example, he hired a *vetturino* to obtain horses and fodder for the travel to Rome. Literally meaning 'little driver', the *vetturino* not only drove but acted as a guide and tour fixer, and Moryson is one of the earliest writers to employ what became a motif of travel writing on Italy: comment on the *vetturino*'s cheating ways, in this case attempting to evade his commitment to pay for clients' food and to charge them extra for river crossings.[59] I have no doubt that *vetturini* could tell equally hair-raising tales about their clients, but more importantly for our purposes, Moryson provided an extensive description of the roads from Rome, drawing on the work of Leandro Alberti (the Frier Leander, in his words), which in the eighty years following its publication had gone through eleven editions in Italian alone.[60] Among these roads, wrote Moryson:

> The most famous is the way of Appius, called the Queene of waies . . . It begins at the Gate of Saint Sebastian, and is paved to Capua, and then devided into two waies, that on the left hand leading to Brundusium, and that on the right hand leading to Pozzoli and to Cuma, having stately Pallaces on all sides, and it hath the name of Appius Claudius the Censor.

Alongside the other major routes, Moryson also mentioned the 'no lesse famous' Flaminian Way.[61] By the time of his journey, printed guidebooks were widely available, but works like Moryson's both shaped the experience of those making their own journeys and brought the history of the ancient roads to readers far away from Italy who might never personally travel.

There remained reason to be cautious about such travel. When in 1608, Thomas Coryat set out from Odcombe in Somerset to make his way south through the continent, he chose to see Venice but not Rome. There was considerable anxiety in English political circles at the time about journeys to the latter. King James VI and I complained that travel was used as an excuse to 'flock to Rome, out of vanity and curiosity to see the Antiquities of that City', whereupon men might become corrupted by the influence of Catholicism, and 'return again into their Countries, both averse to Religion, and ill-affected to Our State and Government'.[62] Many English writers preferred instead to praise the republic of Venice as the inheritor of Rome's better values.[63]

Following Henry VIII's break with Rome, Venice had become the base for English diplomacy in Italy: formal relations between the UK and the Vatican had to wait until the twentieth century.

Coryat's narrative, as one might expect in those circumstances, focuses far more heavily on the ancient empire's history than on the Catholic churches. Crossing to Boulogne, he noted that the watch tower, on a clear day 'easily to be seen from Dover Castle', was said to have been founded by Julius Caesar.[64] Travelling south in a cart which 'according to the fashion of the country . . . had three hoops over it that were covered in a sheet of coarse canvas', he passed through the dangerous forest of Veronne, where he was advised to keep his sword in hand, to arrive at Amiens. There he encountered his first pilgrim travelling to Rome, 'a very simple fellow, who spake so bad Latin that a country Scholler in England should be whipped for speaking the like'.[65] He likewise found Paris unimpressive, noting that in Latin it was called Lutetia, 'from the Latin word Lutum, which signifieth durt [*sic*], because many of the streets are the durtiest, and so consequently the most stinking of all that ever I saw in any citie in my life'.[66] On the other hand, he did notice its 'very auncient [*sic*] stone wals that were built by Julius Caesar'.[67] This is not confirmed by the archaeology: it seems that Caesar was simply the go-to assumption when crediting northern fortifications.

Today, the ancient remains of Paris, such as they are, lie across the river in – or rather beneath – the Latin Quarter. The rue Saint-Jacques and the boulevard Saint-Michel were once central roads of the Roman settlement of Lutetia. The rue Saint-Jacques gives the best impression, leading straight up from the river to the Montagne Sainte-Geneviève, hardly a mountain but certainly a steep walk. The biggest visible part of Roman Paris is the Arènes de Lutèce: the amphitheatre. Not much of the stone looks Roman and it's only of modest size, though that's not surprising given that the settlement it catered to had only about 8,000 inhabitants. A runner's doing stretches, and some kids have taken over the arena for a ball game. Outdoor exercise seems popular here: I've seen yoga in the Tuileries and tango in the sculpture park. Beside the amphitheatre a pretty garden flowers beside a reconstructed nymphaeum, water bubbling into its lily pond. There's more Roman water in a well beneath the place de la Sorbonne, though you'd have to know to spot it, and the same with the line of Roman wall that's marked across the rue de la Colombe. The most striking remains are at the Museum of the Middle Ages, built into the imposing ruins of a Roman bathhouse, part converted into exhibition space, part conserved, part left open to the air. Nearby the exterior of the Panthéon borrows from its Roman ancestor.

At Lyons, Coryat noted the city's ancient origin: 'founded by a worthy Roman Gentleman Munatius Plancus, a scholar of Cicero's, and an excellent Orator'.[68] (This comes from ancient sources.) He also observed the ruins of the amphitheatre, 'wherein those constant servants of Jesus Christ willingly suffered many intolerable and bitter tortures for his sake'.[69] With that comment, he shows some of the ambivalence of early modern Europeans towards that ancient past: while the Romans may have been great builders, they were nonetheless pagans and persecutors. Coryat's narrative was also designed to entertain his readers with curious tales of the world abroad. He made sure to include plenty of gossip: for example, the Earl of Essex had once stayed at the Three Kings in Lyons. (The earl, a favourite of Elizabeth I, fell from grace to be executed as a rebel.) Coryat was intrigued – in a way that today comes across as rather racist – by the Turks he met in the entourage of a former French ambassador to Constantinople, one of them a jester, the other a scholar. Arriving in Italy he, like Montaigne before him, encountered the system of bills of health that proved a traveller was 'free from all manner of contagious sickenesse' on his departure from the previous city.[70] He saw travellers carried in chairs over the Alps[71] and was entertained by the company of one 'merry Italian'. This Antonio claimed descent from the famous Mark Antony, which may come across as eccentric, but implausible genealogies were all the rage among the Italian upper classes at the time. Antonio cheered the party with his motto: 'Be merry, for the Devil is dead'.[72] However, Coryat was also keen to learn, and to substantiate his claims. Throughout his journey he referred back to the ancient authorities: 'that excellent historiographer Cornelius Tacitus', Livy, and Suetonius.[73] In Padua he visited Livy's house to see the collection of antiquities, and defended it against claims that it wasn't, in fact, Livy's: an early debate on the importance of authentic heritage.[74] Not for Coryat spurious tales of Charlemagne's mythical road or implausible attribution of the Furlo tunnel to Hannibal, even if he was a little quick to credit Caesar with the walls of Paris.

Coryat's narrative, in fact, sits at a turning point in the history of travel literature. While earlier readers had enjoyed invention and even fantasy, now far greater importance was accorded to accuracy. Written works helped to inform not only other travellers but also governments – whose diplomatic relations were also becoming more systematic in this period. As one modern critic observes, especially in the context of growing imperial and colonial projects, 'knowledge about foreign cultures became an instrument of power'.[75] It also shaped ideas back at home about what was significant in the history and geography of Europe. Travellers like Coryat and Montaigne and in 1615 George Sandys with *A Relation of a Journey* played an important part in developing a secular rationale for travel that replaced the old – and for Protestants problematic – reasons for pilgrimage to Rome. Indeed, Sandys decided to focus on lesser-known parts of Italy: the 'lesse remote' sites of the north were already 'daily survaide and exactly narrated'.[76] (This became something of a trope as travel writers sought to emphasise their novelty: a century later, Joseph Addison would decide to 'say nothing of the Via Flaminia, which has been spoken of by most of the Voyage-Writers that have pass'd it'.)[77] No longer was travel a matter of religious devotion, or at least that was not the only option: there was a more scientific, information-gathering approach to surveying neighbouring states.[78] In 1632, Nicolas Sanson's *Carte Géographique des Postes* became the first printed postal map, and in the following decade a map was produced to complement the 1552 *Guide des chemins de France*.[79] A painting by Matteo Bolognini, dated 1647, shows the English traveller John Bargrave, with flowing hair and white collar and cuffs beneath dark overgarments, alongside two companions, inspecting a large if somewhat imprecisely rendered map of Italy.[80] Bargrave points to Italy and Rome. Representations of this journey had moved from the textual itinerary to the visual. The Roman roads were, quite literally, on the map.

9
Royal refugees

In the seventeenth and eighteenth centuries the roads to Rome continued to draw antiquarian interest, but they also became escape routes. Exiled Catholics created their own ways of seeing Roman history, along with new tales of travel for new readerships. While some of them were enthusiasts for Rome's treasures, others presented rather different narratives, shaped by both religious conflict and imperial expansion.

In 1607, the so-called 'flight of the earls' saw a group of prominent Irish noblemen, among them Hugh O'Neill, Earl of Tyrone and Rory O'Donnell, last king of Tyrconnell, leave their home country amid murky circumstances. Having come to terms after defeat in the Nine Years' War, they were accused of treasonous rebellion against the English, although as ever the story is far more nuanced than the old competing narratives of either absolute innocence or all-out treachery would suggest.[1] The broader context was the long-running English expansion into Ireland under the Tudor monarchs, which the earls had unsuccessfully resisted, and which would soon be followed by the 'Plantation of Ulster' with Scottish Protestant settlers. Initially intending to travel to Spain, the earls and their party were forced by poor weather to cut their sea voyage short in France, and after several further mishaps made their way to Rome, where they hoped to see the Pope. Along the way, Tadhg Ó Cianáin, whose family had a long history as chroniclers, produced the first travel narrative in the Irish language and, importantly, one that focused less on Roman achievement and more on Roman persecution.[2]

Ó Cianáin's story is one of perils. The earls left the Low Countries for Rome on 28 February 1608, when the Alps would have still been covered in snow. Crossing via the Gotthard Pass, they lost a horse at Devil's Bridge and with it £120 of O'Neill's money. The roads over the mountains, Ó Cianáin observed, 'were neither excellent nor such as would be level enough for riding on wild, spirited, untamed horses, but as they descended from the mountain they were icy, stony, narrow and rugged until they reached a town called Airolo' at the south end of the pass (now best known as a ski resort).[3] Further down the Ticino valley, the town of Bellinzona was 'fine, fortified', and equipped with 'three strong castles ... which maintain supremacy and command over the town and all the country in the neighbourhood of the road'.[4] These passes had strategic importance.

The party travelled down the Via Emilia by way of Piacenza, Parma and Bologna across to the Adriatic coast and visited the shrine at Loreto, before taking the Via Flaminia back across the peninsula to Rome. Ó Cianáin, who devoted an extensive part of his narrative to Loreto, noted the risks of the journey there: 'But many heretics and robbers, as it was situated in a lonely dark waste, and as pilgrims went to and from it, used to go to rob and murder near it.'[5] From Loreto to Rome took six days (including a short detour to Assisi), these visits to the shrines already revealing something of the party's priorities. On their arrival in Rome on 29 April, the party was greeted at Ponte Molle by the Archbishop of Armagh.[6]

Once in Rome, Ó Cianáin's Christian emphasis continues: in some ways his account has more in common with earlier pilgrimage accounts than with Coryat or Montaigne.[7] He describes the papal blessing, and the traditional tour of Rome's pilgrim churches; by far the most prominent ancient figure is the first Christian emperor, Constantine. Ancient Rome comes into the story only so far as it comes into the churches. At the Lateran, for example:

> There are four very fine columns before the great high altar, made of brass and brightly gilt on the outside, and filled in the interior with holy clay brought from Jerusalem to that place. It was Augustus the Emperor who built these columns for the success which he had upon the sea. Others say they were neptunes. Situated under the high altar is the oratory which John of the Bosom* had, at which he worshipped Almighty God when he was imprisoned by the Romans.[8]

* 'John of the Bosom', the term used here for St John the Evangelist, is a reference to the Gospel of John 13:23: 'Now there was leaning on Jesus' bosom one of his disciples, whom Jesus loved.'

Though Ó Cianáin noted the Roman origins of Santa Maria Rotonda (the Pantheon),[9] when the earls visited the catacombs of San Callisto the emphasis was once again on persecution:

> In that cemetery there were buried one hundred and seventy-four thousand martyrs. In that cave the apostles and disciples of the Lord used to remain to avoid and escape the pagans. Eighteen Popes were buried in it after having been put to death as noble, great and glorious martyrs by unbelieving heretics.[10]

If Coryat had briefly noted the more brutal side of Roman history in his description of Lyons, Ó Cianáin went further in highlighting those elements of the Christian narrative of ancient Rome in which the Roman authorities were the oppressors. It is not surprising to find this in the context of a narrative of people fleeing a hostile foreign power, set on expanding its interests in their home country, nor that the achievements of the Romans highlighted by other travellers make no appearance here. Although the group wandered down the Appian Way, perhaps visiting what is now the Grotto di Egeria, the road is not mentioned by name; when they took a trip out to Ostia, once again it was simply 'to make holiday and take a change of air'.[11] Ó Cianáin and the people whose story he told certainly travelled the Roman roads, and no doubt found them useful, if sometimes hazardous. They engaged far more strongly, however, with the histories of those persecuted by the ancient rulers.

The journey to Rome featured not only in the first Irish travel narrative but also in the first published African autobiography. The narrative of Ṣägga Krəstos, who travelled through France and Italy in the 1630s, includes an account of his extended stay in Rome, where he tried to convince the Pope that he was the heir of the Ethiopian Emperor Yaʿəqob.[12] Inconsistency in the dates means that cannot have been true, but Ṣägga Krəstos was clearly educated enough to pull off the deception and multiple European rulers, who had their own interest in improving relations with the Horn of Africa, were either fooled or despite their suspicions decided it was worth indulging him. He made his way first to Cairo from Sinnār, hundreds of miles to the south in the Nile valley. This was not an easy journey: in the Egyptian desert his camels 'sank into the sand' and 'could hardly cover ten miles in twenty-four hours'.[13] Even the expansive Roman road network had not reached this distance. Ṣägga Krəstos then travelled overland to Jerusalem and Nazareth (from Cairo to Jerusalem was easier at only fifteen days, though there were some difficulties with customs duties). The next leg was by ship, via Crete, Zante and Corfu. From Otranto, on the heel of Italy, Ṣägga Krəstos took the road to Naples – a route that must have been a variation on the Via Appia or Via Traiana – and then headed north to Rome. He subsequently went to Venice via Rimini – the Via Flaminia – across northern Italy to Turin (the Via Emilia) and over the Alps to Lyons and Paris.[14] The account gives few details of the journey, beyond its sponsorship by generous local rulers, who variously provided an entourage of 'many noblemen' and an 'expensive and luxuriously harnessed horse', which suggests the latter part was comparatively comfortable (and that not everyone chose coaches). The expectations for seventeenth-century royal hospitality were lavish in the extreme, so if there was even a possibility that Ṣägga Krəstos was who he claimed, he could expect to make his journey in some style.

While the majority of visitors to Rome were Europeans and white (a term first codified in its modern racial sense in the seventeenth century), the case of Ṣägga Krəstos illustrates that there were some exceptions. Indeed, since the twelfth century the monastery of Santo Stefano, now within the walls of the Vatican, had provided a base for travellers from Christian Africa to Rome.[15] One such man was Yoḥannəs, born in Cyprus to exiled Ethiopian parents, who became the second Black bishop in the Roman Catholic Church. He arrived in Rome in about 1525, when he was sixteen, but his father died shortly afterwards and Yoḥannəs then undertook a pilgrimage to Santiago in the company of one or more of the Ethiopian friars from Santo Stefano. (This community numbered about thirty at the time.)[16] Christians from Turkey, Syria and Iraq (to give their modern names) came for meetings with a series of popes, and occasionally for longer-term visits.[17] From the sixteenth century travellers from the Americas came too. A poem describes the voyage of Nahua visitors to Europe; from Spain they were sent to Rome, to the 'Pope's long house, where stands the multi-hued crypt'.[18] While none of these people wrote the kind of memoirs that tell us what they made of the roads to Rome, they were certainly present on them. Meanwhile, the growing trade in enslaved Africans created new routes by which Black people arrived in the city. Among them was the artist Juan de Pareja, enslaved in the service of Diego Velázquez. In 1649, while in Rome, Velázquez painted Pareja's portrait; he was freed the following year and went on to make an independent career as a painter.[19]

A few years later, Queen Christina of Sweden joined the elite circles of Rome following her abdication. Christina had succeeded at the age of five and been sole ruler of the realm from her eighteenth birthday in 1644, but decided not to marry, recommending instead that her cousin should succeed. Controversy over this choice, as well as her leanings towards Catholicism and her financial extravagance, provided the backdrop for her abdication in 1654, following which she converted in secret, and went on to relocate to Rome. A 1656 account of her travel, written by Galeazzo Gualdo Priorato, author of several (mostly military) histories and biographies, was swiftly translated into English. It provides rich detail not only of how royalty and nobility might now make their journeys, but also of how such grand events were stage managed, and the ways that current ceremony engaged with the ancient past.

Departing from Brussels on 22 September 1655, Christina travelled with an entourage of fifty, plus a thirty-strong guard, three coaches and four baggage wagons. This did not include the staff of the noblemen and women who accompanied her, who must have raised the party's numbers to well over a hundred.[20] Christina made her way first to Lorraine, 'a great City encompass'd with strong and ancient walls',[21] and then Cologne (a former Roman colony, which takes its name from the Latin *colonia*). There she was visited by two exiled royals: Charles II, king of Scotland (later to be king of England too) and his brother the Duke of Gloucester.[22] From Cologne she continued south and east to Augsburg, but had to wait to receive coaches suitable for crossing the 'streight [narrow] wayes of the mountains of Tyrol, where she could not possibly pass with her own'.[23] Besides these smaller coaches, she was in possession of a 'very stately litter', in which she made her entrance to Innsbruck.[24]

Through Priorato's account, we learn not only that the queen deployed multiple types of transport as appropriate to the occasion, but also that as she made her stately way, couriers were dashing back and forth along the roads to ensure that preparations were made for her next arrival. There is intriguing detail of the infrastructure: at Bolzano, on the far side of the Alps from Innsbruck over the Brenner Pass, 'the clear river *Adice* [Adige] made navigable, carries with a rapid current all the Merchandize sent into *Italy*, from those noble Faires, which are usually kept foure times a year'.[25] (This river links Merano, Bolzano, Trento and Verona before running into the Adriatic.) Along the Po for fifteen miles from Ficarolo to Ferrara, Priorato noted, the banks of the river had been made 'very strong, as a fence against its dangerous inundations'.[26] When Christina eventually crossed, she was provided with an elaborate personal barge but others used a bridge 'made of 46 great and thick barques' that allowed coaches to pass four abreast.[27] Whether or not this was intended to allude to the ancient examples across the Bay of Naples, it could certainly be read that way.

Priorato did not write much about the ancient past: he was more interested in the noble families Christina met en route and the pilgrimage elements of her journey (like the Irish earls, she visited the shrine at Loreto). He did, however, note that Bologna lay 'in the midst of the Emilian way', and that the walls of Fano were 'partly antique' and the city 'famous for the Temple of Fortune . . . and for the remains of the Arch of Augustus'.[28] On occasion, such arches, whether ancient or more modern recreations, were decorated especially for Christina's visit. That was the case with the Arch of Pio at Macerata, a commission of the late Cardinal Carlo Emmanuel Pio (who died in 1641): this was 'beautified with Pictures, Figures, Mottos, *Hieroglyphicks*, and Inscriptions, in the praise and honour of her Majesties arrivall', while at the cathedral a further arch was erected to mark the occasion.[29] Sometimes less well-known antiquities attracted Priorato's attention: the 'renowned gate' at Foligno, for example, 'out of which the citizens expelled the Lombards'.[30] At Spoleto an 'ancient gate of the city' was decorated with two inscriptions, one in honour of the queen, and one 'alluding to the place where *Haniball of Carthage* after the battail won at *Thrasymenus*, desiring to advance towards

Rome, was put to flight, whereupon the same gate retains to this day the name of the gate of the flight'.[31] The monuments of the ancient past were integrated into this modern royal journey, and while Priorato's treatment of the roads consists of passing mentions, that arguably indicates the way they were experienced: quietly present in the background but nonetheless essential to the setting. As with Charles V's entry to Rome, they were a stage set on which royal actors could perform.

As the presence of Charles II and his brother on Christina's itinerary makes clear, the mid-century conflicts of the British Isles often provided good reason to leave the country. John Bargrave, whom we saw inspecting his map, had lost his Cambridge fellowship for his royalist associations.[32] Later in the century, during the civil wars in the British Isles, some exiles joined them. Sir John Denham, an Anglo-Irish poet, tried to look on the bright side in writing of their experience:

At Paris, at Rome,
At the Hague they are at home;
The good fellow is nowhere a stranger.[33]

John Raymond, standing alongside Bargrave with the map, wrote an account of his travels in Italy, which was published in 1648. He took a roundabout route to join the Via Appia, leaving Rome initially on the Via Latina before joining the road south at the Tres Tabernae, which he noted as the site 'where the Brethren met Saint *Paul*'.[34] Raymond's text is notable for the combination of Christian references with detailed recording of inscriptions. Of the Via Appia, he observed that it was 'compacted of such solid stones, that after so long a succession of time, neither the continuall passage of foote or horse, nor the injurie of weather, hath yet consum'd any part of it, unless that which past through the *Pomptine Fennes*, which the water hath overflowde, the rest is very entire and firme'.[35] (Sixtus V's interventions in the Pontine Marshes had evidently made limited difference.) Not all visitors were so thorough in their descriptions, however: writing in his journal, the English traveller Banaster Maynard recorded his trip from Rome to Naples solely by the stops, making no explicit mention of the Via Appia.[36]

It fell to another English traveller of the Interregnum to set the tone for future descriptions of the Roman roads. Richard Lassels, educated at the English seminary in Douai and later Latin secretary to Cardinal Richelieu, pioneered the idea of a tour to educate young aristocrats. He made his journey to Italy as the tutor of Lady Whetenell, a Catholic with connections to the English convent in Louvain and the driving force behind a trip to Rome for the 1650 jubilee, on which she was accompanied by her husband as well as Lassels. Lady Whetenell died after giving birth to a stillborn child during the trip; two decades later, Lassels' account of the journey, written for her widower, was published.[37] It's notable as the source of the term 'Grand Tour',[38] but also established for English readers an influential image of the roads, as Lassels observed the Via Appia:

> This Cawsey [causeway] is one of the greatest Proofs of the *Romans* Greatness and Riches. For it was five days Journey long, beginning at *Rome* and reaching through the Kingdom of *Naples* to *Brundusium*. It was as broad as two Carts might easily meet upon it and pass: It was all of great black Flint Stones, each one as big as two Men can carry, and laid so close together, that they have held together these 1800 years, and seem, as *Procopius* saith ingeniously to be rather *Congeniti* than *Congesti*, born together, than laid together. The frequent passing of Horses and Mules (for so many Years) upon this Cawsey, have made it both so smooth and shining, that when the Sun shines upon it, you may see it glister two Miles-off, like a Silver Highway.[39]

Lassels helpfully provided his references: Procopius on the Gothic Wars, plus Plutarch's life of Gracchus. Here we move beyond Pius II's appreciation of the roads' beauty and Montaigne's observation that the roads had a sense of antiquity, to a firm statement that the roads were proof of greatness. Combined with the poetic image of the glistening highway, this ancient idea was thus newly emphasised for a modern readership.

The Grand Tour became a rite of passage for young aristocratic men (and some women) from across Europe, especially though not only from the north. Recent research has identified that Italy was far from the only popular destination,[40] but it certainly offered a unique opportunity for education in classical civilisation, though certain of the tourists' activities were more educational than others. Some were accompanied by tutors and it was common to commission portraits from artists like Pompeo Batoni in Rome or Rosalba Carriera in Venice,[41] who made careers from this work. Tourists had a choice of routes: for example, a British traveller might head south via Paris, with a visit to the court at Versailles, then to Lyons and via the Roman sites of the Rhône valley to Avignon before crossing the Alps into north-western Italy, visiting Turin, Milan and Florence. There were, however, also potential routes through Germany. Once arrived in Italy they might take the main post route or a detour to Arezzo and Perugia, picking up the Via Flaminia at Terni to head south to Rome and Naples. On their return, options included a circular route up along the Via Flaminia to the Adriatic coast and Venice, from there either crossing the Brenner Pass for Germany and the Low Countries, or taking the Via Emilia through Bologna, Modena, Parma and Piacenza, to head home through France.

At this early stage, Grand Tourists were a tiny elite of the British population. One estimate places the numbers abroad at around 15–20,000 a year: assuming no one went twice in an adult life, that still would mean fewer than ten per cent of Britons ever went abroad, and of course some people did travel more often.[42] In the fourteenth century pilgrims from Aragon had flocked to Rome in the summer,[43] but the typical itinerary for a nine-month Grand Tour began in October. Travellers spent the first few months in northern Italy, the coolest months in the south and then returned north. This, incidentally, enabled them to avoid malaria season: while the relation to mosquitoes was not understood (*malaria* takes its name from the Italian for 'bad air', assumed to be the cause), guides warned of seasonal risk and from the mid-seventeenth century travellers tended to avoid Rome in the summer. Northern visitors, who had not acquired the same immunity as locals, were particularly vulnerable.[44]

As a guide to what to see, travellers could consult the writings of Coryat and his predecessors, but for those who cared to project a learned image, a new text soon became essential: Joseph Addison's *Remarks on Several Parts of Italy*, published in 1705. Addison's approach to the history of the roads differs from Lassels', but between them they demonstrate the fundamentals on which many later stories would be built. While Lassels had cited Procopius and Plutarch as historical sources, Addison instead turned to literature:

> The greatest Pleasure I took in my Journey from *Rome* to *Naples* was in seeing the Fields, Towns, and Rivers that have been describ'd by so many *Classic* Authors, and have been the Scenes of so many great Actions; for this whole Road is extreamly barren of Curiosities. It is worth while to have an Eye on *Horace*'s Voyage to *Brundisi*, when one passes this way; for by comparing his several Stages, and the Road he took, with those that are observ'd at present, we may have some Idea of the Changes that have been made in the Face of this Country since his Time. If we may guess at the common Trevelling of Persons of Quality, among the ancient *Romans*, from this Poet's Description of his Voyage, we may conclude they seldom went above Fourteen Miles a Day over the *Appian* Way, which was more us'd by the Noble *Romans* than any other in *Italy*, as it led to *Naples*, *Baïae*, and the most delightful Parts of the Nation.

Addison concludes his account agreeing with Horace, who had observed that the Appia was more suited than the alternative route for the tardy traveller (*Minus est gravis Appia tardis*), with a dig at the state of the roads: 'It is indeed very disagreeable to be carry'd in haste over this Pavement.' He provided a second poetic source too, that of Lucan, travelling in the opposite direction, from Anxur (Terracina, here going by the pre-Roman Volscian name) to Rome. This was, Addison observed, 'not indeed the ordinary Way at present, nor is it mark'd out by the same Places in both Poets'. He understood that the roads had changed. It is notable, too, that Addison's translation of Lucan picks out (as had Gregory in the twelfth century) the importance of Caesar's first impression of Rome from the Alban Hills:

> He now had conquer'd *Anxur*'s steep Ascent,
> And to *Pontina*'s wat'ry Marshes went,
> A long Canal the muddy Fenn divides,
> And with a clear unsully'd Current glides;
> *Diana*'s woody Realms he next invades,
> And crossing through the consecrated Shades
> Ascends high *Alba*, whence with new Delight
> He sees the City rising to his Sight.[45]

With Addison to hand, tourists could immediately cite a relevant story. This was a handy textbook for tutors swotting up on their literary notes, but also a script for the uncertain traveller who wanted guidance on how to think and feel: delight at the sight of Rome; pleasure in sharing the campagna with the authors of the classics.[46] When James Boswell, best known for his biography of Samuel Johnson, did the Grand Tour in 1765, he took with him both Addison's *Remarks* and Charles-Nicolas Cochin's 1758 *Voyage d'Italie*, which was particularly strong on art history.[47] While this may have made for fascinating journeys, in the wrong hands it could also become tedious, as Lady Morgan, author of her own book on Italy, observed a century later. 'The "gentle dulness" that "ever loves a joke",' she complained, 'loves classical topography also, and repeats its criticisms with an oracular authority, as though all its citations were as original as they are erudite.'[48] I suspect Lady Morgan had been subjected to what we now call mansplaining.

Her comments, however, also prompt me to think about the process of writing as a traveller myself. How far do I care to refer back to the literature? What am I looking for? As you probably realised from the opening chapters, I've roamed far beyond the route of the Grand Tour as I've travelled through Spain and eastern Europe. Which leads me to an important point: the 'Roman roads' as they're described by northern travellers are a subset of the whole. The Appia is queen; the Flaminia her second; the Emilia, connecting the Flaminia to the Alpine passes, may get a mention, but there was a clear hierarchy and beyond Italy the roads got significantly less attention.

That is not to say that the rest of the empire was ignored entirely. From the sixteenth century onwards there was clear interest in antiquities across the western countries, whether Juan Ginés de Sepúlveda transcribing Spanish milestones, Henry VIII (as we will see) commissioning reports on antiquities, or Francis I hoping to restore the arena in Nîmes. Where there were fewer direct survivals, alternatives were invented. In Vienna, as I wander around the Meidling district, I find myself walking down a street called Tivoligasse, German for Via Tiburtina. It leads towards the grounds of Schloss Schönbrunn, summer residence of the Habsburg rulers of the Holy Roman Empire. Remodelled under Empress Maria Theresa in the middle of the eighteenth century, its vast gardens are dotted with classicising sculptures, including an enormous statue of Neptune, as if the designer was determined to outdo the originals in size if not in class. Some fabulously kitsch fake Roman ruins, in multicoloured stone with collapsing pedestals and half-pilasters, surround a lily pond. In the city centre, there's still more. Karlskirche, the eighteenth-century imperial church, was completed in 1737 on the commission of the Emperor Charles VI and dedicated to a St Charles (San Carlo Borromeo). It has a high green dome and lavish Corinthian capitals on its pilasters, but the highlight of its facade is not one but two giant columns after the fashion of the Emperor Trajan's. Before it the local children are more impressed with a street artist blowing bubbles to entertain them, while Saturday strollers chat and kiss and pose amid the potted palms around the water feature. So is the architecture of empires old and new embedded in Europe's urban landscapes.

Further east, the situation was less straightforward. Some travellers to Constantinople were aware that they followed a Roman route. Ogier Ghiselin de Busbecq, ambassador of Ferdinand, king of the Romans (a title used by the Holy Roman Emperor-elect), travelled in 1555–6, not long after publication of Alberti's lists of Italian antiquities. He observed near the Serbian town of Niš, on the banks of the Nishava river, 'where there remained traces of a Roman road, a small marble column still standing with an inscription in Latin, but so mutilated as to be illegible'.[49] His Turkish escort pointed out to him in the distance the site of Trajan's bridge over the Danube at Severin (this must however have been eighty miles away, and only the piles remained).[50] Further on into the area around Ankara, the situation was the same again: 'in the Turkish cemeteries we often came upon columns and ancient slabs of fine marble, on which were remains of Greek and Latin inscriptions, but so mutilated as to be illegible.'[51] In Constantinople itself, he noted 'remarkable remains of ancient monuments, though one cannot help wondering why so few have survived'.[52] It was a good question, and Busbecq was not the only western traveller to wonder. In the 1540s French antiquarian Pierre Gilles, visiting on the commission of King Francis I (then newly allied with the Ottomans), lamented local 'carelessness and contempt of every thing that is curious'.[53]

Similar absences were also noted a century and a half later, in a letter of 1717, written from Adrianople (Edirne) on the Via Militaris. Lady Mary Wortley Montagu, travelling with her husband who like Busbecq was an ambassador to Constantinople, had taken the road from Belgrade, observing that the 'desert woods of Servia are the common refuge of thieves, who rob, fifty in a company, [so] that we had need of all our guards to secure us'.[54] She spent much of her letter discussing what she had learned about the branches of Islam from discussions with a scholar in that city, but acknowledged that her correspondent would expect some notes on the antiquities. Here, however, like Busbecq, she was rather disappointed:

> There are few remains of ancient Greece. We passed near the piece of an arch, which is commonly called Trajan's Gate, as supposing he made it to shut up the passage over the mountains between Sophia and Philipopolis. But I rather believe it the remains of some triumphal arch (though I could not see any inscription); for if that passage had been shut up, there are many others that would serve for the march of an army; and, notwithstanding the story of Baldwin Earl of Flanders being overthrown in these straits, after he won Constantinople, I don't fancy the Germans would find themselves stopped by them. It is true, the road is now made (with great industry) as commodious as possible, for the march of the Turkish army; there is not one ditch or puddle between this place and Belgrade that has not a large strong bridge of planks built over it; but the precipices were not so terrible as I had heard them represented.[55]

The gate aside (and evidently Wortley Montagu is sceptical about the Trajan story), her historical point of reference is not ancient Rome but the crusades. In so far as she notices the roads, it is because the Ottomans have improved them for their armies. They had besieged Vienna in 1683 and been defeated, but their ability to mount a repeat attack would no doubt have been on diplomats' minds. Wortley Montagu does not, however, mention the Roman origins.

In fact, there is a wider reason for this absence. It was not that the Ottomans were lacking curiosity, rather that they had defeated the remnant of the Roman Empire's only true successor state. They referred to the inhabitants of the Eastern Roman Empire and beyond as the Rûm, meaning Romans (the term 'Byzantine' was not used in the Middle Ages). The conquerors had no interest in glorifying the losers' achievements and the view that Constantinople should be 'thoroughly Islamised' gained ground with the accession of Mehmet's son Bayezid II. Over the course of a century and a half, both Christian churches and secular monuments were replaced.[56] When the Ottomans did engage with the existing infrastructure, it was on practical terms. Besides the famous conversion of the Hagia Sofia to a mosque, they restored 'ancient aqueducts [to] give Constantinople a proper water supply' and either improved the Via Militaris or took stone from it to develop new roads for their armies.[57] As I found when looking for the Milyon, wandering the streets of Istanbul today it takes a determined effort to spot the Roman heritage. Where late Roman or Byzantine sites have been made accessible to visitors that is a twentieth-century development, following the establishment of modern Turkey as a secular state: the Chora Church, for example, where Christian frescoes had been plastered over, became a museum in 1945, while the Basilica Cistern was largely drained to allow general tourism in the 1980s.[58] In short, while the western powers were embracing the symbolic value of their Roman pasts, the Ottomans were doing quite the opposite. The consequence is, however, that it's all too easy to think of the ancient empire as more western than it really was.

The growing interest in the roads of the western empire was reflected not only in travellers' accounts but in other types of document too. Over Christmas 2022, I was visiting my mother in Scotland. It was that stage of the holidays when we were casting round for entertainment, and we ended up looking over some old maps of Stirling, where I went to high school and she still lives. Marked on one, dated 1896, was the line of a Roman road – not a route that was still in use then – but one significant enough for the mapmakers to include it. Mapping the antiquities of Britain, in fact, dates back at least to the reign of Henry VIII, when between 1534 and 1542 John Leland served as the King's Antiquary, travelling the realm to investigate its ancient past. (Not coincidentally, this was the period immediately following Henry's break with Rome, enacted by an Act of Parliament that declared 'this realm of England is an empire'.) Leland's work was followed in 1586 by William Camden's *Britannia*, whose book was perhaps the first to make a genealogical link between present-day

Britons and their Roman ancestors: ''tis easy to believe that the Britains and Romans, by a mutual *engrafting* for so many years together, have grown up into one Nation.'[59] Interest in Britain's Roman past continued: in 1658, William Burton published a commentary on the Antonine Itinerary, and Camden was published in an expanded edition, translated from Latin into English in 1695.[60] By comparison to southern Europe, ancient monuments were few and far between, but Roman roads could perhaps compensate for lack of spectacle. There was considerable excitement when sometime after 1736 Francis Drake, an archaeologist, learned from the Earl of Burlington's head gardener that his patron's lands might be the site of an ancient road:

> Being at Londesborough last week, I prevailed with Lord Burlington to dig for the Roman causeway in his park ... At about 19 inches deep, through a very fine soil, by the side of the canal, the workmen came to the stratum, and bared the whole breadth of it, which measures 24 foot. This is the broadest Roman road I ever mett with, and on it is plainly to be seen the impressions of wheel carriages. Most certainly this was the great military way, mentioned in the first Iter, from York to Praetorium, one way, and crosse the Humber to Lincoln the other ... My lord proposes to lay bare as much of this road as is in his territorys.[61]

Burlington – Richard Boyle, the third earl, best known as a patron of Palladian architecture and of a series of important classicising buildings – clearly appreciated the symbolic value of a Roman road on his property. As important public works with evident benefit to society, the roads fitted the values of a British aristocracy that following the so-called 'Glorious' Revolution liked to portray itself as heirs to the senatorial class of the Roman Republic in terms of civic virtue and defence of liberty.[62]

As Lady Mary Wortley Montagu was travelling, one of the most famous exiles in Europe was about to relocate to Rome. This was James Francis Edward Stuart of England, the so-called 'Old Pretender', grandson of Charles I. James' father (James II) had been exiled in the revolution of 1688–9, replaced by the more certainly Protestant Queen Mary and her husband William of Orange. The younger James, a baby at the time and widely rumoured to have been exchanged at birth, spent the first years of his exile in Paris and Lorraine, but following the unsuccessful Jacobite rising he moved to papal territory and from 1718 until his death in 1766 lived principally in Rome. There, his court became an attraction on the Grand Tour, if one to be approached with caution, lest a visitor be spotted by spies.

Today, Palazzo del Re – the king's palace – isn't looking particularly grand. Patchy orange plaster stretches up five floors, if you include the mezzanine; beside the front door the columns have Ionic capitals but need a good scrub. Around the corner, near what was once the main entrance, there's a pizza shop; the ground floor houses an Abruzzese restaurant and beside it a Mailboxes Etc. That's as close as you'll get to confidential messages, but 300 years ago clandestine visits were commonplace. In 1724, a secret staircase was constructed to allow discreet access to the king's apartments in his palace (located on Via di San Marcello, with a side entrance onto Piazza dei Santi Apostoli), though this did not prevent reports on visitors reaching the court in England: in December that year, for example, two masked men were said to have been led up those stairs. Engravings sold in Rome deliberately misidentified the royal palace as the Palazzo Muti, so that purchasers could not be accused of harbouring Jacobite sympathies.[63]

Across Via di San Marcello is a site of unexpected significance. I've come to the Antica Birreria Peroni for a spot of lunch, but once inside, a local history printed on paper placemats informs me that this was once the location of stables for the imperial post. Even when I'm not trying, I find tales of the roads in Rome. Not only that, it was the place where the Emperor Maxentius (a noted persecutor of Christians, defeated by Constantine) enslaved Pope Marcellus I, who for nine months was given an unspecified 'degrading task', presumably mucking out the stables. Later, the place became a depository for ice and beer, and now it's adorned with little red pennants, slogans about how beer is good for you, and frescoes of putti drinking beer and playing sport. I get out my notebook and start writing. The waiter asks me if I'm doing my homework. I tell him I'm a writer, and he introduces himself and tells me to record that I met a good-looking guy called Lenin (he's not joking about the name: it's printed on the sleeve of his red T-shirt). The menu is printed in Italian on A4 paper, and the place is full of locals, which I take as a good sign. Lenin claims to be personally responsible for the tiramisu, which is also excellent.

Living in Rome is always a bit like this: a casual stop in the city centre and you've three layers of tales about the past. The city's history is mutable. You can take up the papal past, or the pagan one, or the tales of persecution. Like our travellers, you can tell your own stories. Yet even as you do that, those who've gone before have given you a set of motifs, of images, with which to begin your adaptation. As the Grand Tour developed, more and more travellers from the north and west of Europe made use of them.

10
The Grand Tour

The Old Pretender's presence in Rome did not preclude many young British aristocrats from taking their Grand Tour. The books and letters of those who did tell us not only about these travellers' practical experience of the roads, but also more about what the roads meant to them. The writer Thomas Gray went to Italy in 1738 with Horace Walpole, a friend from Eton and son of the then prime minister. Both were in their early twenties. As Gray arrived in Rome on the Via Flaminia, his initial impressions were positive: descending 'Mount Viterbo', he spotted the dome of St Peter's – constructed under Michelangelo's supervision and since the later sixteenth century a dominant feature of Rome's skyline. A little way further on he 'began to enter on an old Roman pavement'.[1] When in the twelfth century Gregory had highlighted this importance of a view in his *Wonders of the City of Rome*, his emphasis had been rather a novelty (though a religious idea of joy at the sight of Rome was implied in Monte Mario's alternative name, Mons Gaudii). Now the pause for a view joined the standard repertoire of travellers' accounts. In 1814, Samuel Rogers noted in his diary that he had been 'told between the 15th and 16th milestone to prepare for a sight of Rome' (though he mistakenly thought he was on the Appian Way). Charlotte Anne Eaton, whose account of her travels was published in 1820, recorded her *vetturino* making the same stop.[2]

Crossing the Tiber, Gray found the entrance to Rome 'prodigiously striking':

> It is by a noble gate [the Porta del Popolo], designed by Michael Angelo and adorned with statues; this brings you into a large square, in the

> midst of which is a vast obelisk of granite . . . as high as my expectation was raised, I confess, the magnificence of this city infinitely surpasses it.[3]

Gray observed but did not join the Young Pretender – James' son, Charles Edward Stuart, 'Bonnie Prince Charlie' – at a shooting match in the Borghese Gardens; he took trips out from Rome, including to the Villa d'Este at Tivoli, where the fountains failed to impress him ('half the river Teverone', he wrote, 'pisses into two thousand several chamber-pots'). Later he went south to Herculaneum and Vesuvius, taking the Via Appia, which he thought 'somewhat tiresome'.[4]

Gray's verdict might come as a surprise, but despite the historical and imaginative importance of Roman roads, travellers of the eighteenth century generally agreed that they did not make for a comfortable journey. Charles de Brosses, a French nobleman who wrote extensively about the ancient past, blamed the 'wretched peasants of the surrounding villages', who had 'scaled [the Via Appia] like a carp'.[5] Thomas Nugent, author of a book on the Grand Tour, thought the Appia less than ideal for modern transport: 'The hardness and smoothness of this old pavement renders the road very troublesome, especially to the horses who often lose their shoes.'[6] Anna Riggs Miller observed similar problems on the Via Flaminia.[7] She was, moreover, alarmed on her journey from Rome to Naples to find – as many had found before her – just past Terracina 'the road (if I may so express myself) lying through the sea'. Her party was obliged to travel with water rising 'above the floor of the carriage'.[8] Nor did James Boswell enjoy his journey in the heat: he was 'sick and fear'd fever' en route.[9] On the other hand, modern roads might not be much better. The Marquis de Mirabeau compared them unfavourably to their ancient counterparts: the latter had been 'built for eternity, while a typical French road could be wrecked within a year by a moderate-sized colony of moles'.[10]

Riggs Miller spent nine months in France, Switzerland and Italy, and her *Letters from Italy* were issued anonymously in 1776, the first such published work by a woman.[11] They give a vivid insight into both the quality and the danger of the roads. Writing from Viterbo, she described two 'bad accidents' that had befallen her party, though she also noted the prospect of improvements:

> The post-master, who had himself rode as postilion to the Roman courier, was killed on a mountain by falling from his horse; and in another part of the road, the best horse belonging to the post-master of *Aquapendente* was swallowed in a slough, where he expired, they not being able to get him out. However, bad as this road is at present, it is now better than ever it has been; for just before the Emperor was expected, the Pope and the King of Naples agreed to repair the roads in their respective dominions: we are told, that on the Neapolitan side it is much better.[12]

It was relatively rare to credit modern restoration for the state of the roads: many writers preferred instead to imply that their quality was such that the ancient stones had simply stayed intact. Tobias Smollett picked out the Via Flaminia as his route into Rome, 'well paved, like a modern street', telling readers that the city 'notwithstanding all the calamities it has undergone, still maintains an august and imperial appearance'.[13] There was something of a tension between promising readers that in Italy they might have access to an authentic past while at the same time that the roads were – or would soon be – maintained to modern standards.

Although there is no doubt that Gray and Riggs Miller went on their tours, the same cannot be said for every writer who published on their experience of travel. Nugent is one of the more doubtful.[14] Born in Ireland, he spent much of his life in London where he made a career as an author and translator, publishing a French–English dictionary. *The Grand Tour* came out in 1749 when he was in his forties and was one of the pioneering volumes of the modern guidebook type.[15] Still, even if Nugent cobbled together his guidance from the work of others, it stands as a useful introduction to the kind of advice given to tourists in the period. His third volume, on Italy, was packed with practical tips. Travellers, for example, were advised to take 'a light quilt, a pillow, a coverlet, and two very fine bed-cloths', although if that was 'troublesome' they should at least 'travel with sheets, and upon coming to an indifferent inn, where the bed may happen to look suspicious, you may call for fresh straw and lay a clean sheet over it'.[16] He discussed transport options: the type of coach available, whether or not to change horses. He considered it 'requisite to have a skilful antiquarian at *Rome*, which saves a person a great deal of trouble by directing him to the several remains of antiquity that are particularly worthy of a traveller's notice'.[17]

Furthermore, Nugent had plenty to say about the road network and its remains that would have created an impression for his readers. Describing the crossing of the Tiber just north of Civita Castellana, Nugent explained that it consisted of 'a stately bridge, raised, as appears by the inscription, by Sixtus V and Clement VIII out of the ruins of a magnificent bridge built here by Augustus, by which the Via Flaminia was continued'.[18] (Sixtus' interventions in the Roman landscape during the later sixteenth century were not without controversy. On the Via Appia, the tomb of Caecilia Metella faced demolition, and was only saved after city officials objected.[19]) Continuing south to Rome, Nugent arrived at Castelnuovo di Porto, a small town dominated by the imposing Rocca of the Colonna barons, where 'you will find an inscription shewing that the Via Flaminia, which appears so intire and beautiful all this road, was not long ago buried under the earth which covered it by degrees'.[20] This implied that there had been some restoration, but Nugent did not say so directly: the Grand Tour was all about antiquity. 'All the way,' he wrote, 'you see a great number of ancient ruins, the melancholy remains of the Roman magnificence'; crossing the Ponte Milvio to arrive in Rome, 'you meet with a paved way, the ancient *Via Flaminia*, which leads you for two miles between pleasant gardens and houses to the famous city of Rome'.[21] The villas of two centuries before were now an established feature to be remarked upon. Nugent, in fact, included an extended passage entitled 'Of the Roman Highways', which is worth quoting in full for the insight it gives into perceptions of the surviving roads (his dates are given from the foundation of Rome rather than the birth of Christ):

> Before we take our leave of *Rome* and its neighbourhood, it will not be amiss to mention a word or two concerning the ancient *Roman* highways, whereof there are still very considerable remains. The chief of them were *Via Flaminia* and *Via Appia*; though there was scarce a city that had not a way paved to it, on which travellers and carriages might pass with ease in the depth of winter. The *Via Flaminia*, so called from the consul *Flaminius* that projected it, led to *Rimini*, and was begun to

be paved in the year of *Rome*, 533. The emperor *Vespasian* carried it afterwards over the *Apennine*, as far as the *Adriatic* sea, extending about 200 miles. A great part of this road is still intire; it is paved with broad flints and pebbles, having on each side a border of stone, and in that border at every second or third pace, a stone standing above the level of the border. The *Via Appia*, the noblest of all the rest, which took its name from blind *Appius* the senator who directed the work, led from the *Porta Capena* or *Appia* to *Capua* and *Brundusium*, extending upwards of 350 miles. It was paved in the year of *Rome* 442, and from thence several other roads were branched out to the cities in the south-west parts of *Italy*. This road is still in a good condition in many places between *Rome* and *Naples*. It is twelve feet broad, made of huge stones, most of them blue, generally a foot and a half large on all sides. The strength of this cause-way appears in its long duration, for it has lasted above nineteen hundred years, and in a great many places is as intire for several miles as when it was first made. The cart-wheels have in some parts made ruts, which at the most are not above three or four inches deep. In fine considering that this pavement has been trod upon for so many ages by an innumerable succession of passengers, horses, coaches, waggons, and chariots, it is a subject of astonishment it should have remained so intire down to our time.[22]

De Brosses concurred with Nugent on the Appia's splendours: it was 'the greatest, most beautiful and most estimable monument that remains to us from antiquity', first-ranked among 'everything the Romans had ever done'. The only ancient achievements to match it, he claimed, were the canals and irrigation systems of Egypt, Chaldea and China. In the modern world, the sole comparable feat was the 150-mile-long Canal de Languedoc (now the Canal du Midi), built in the seventeenth century to connect the Mediterranean and Atlantic, which enabled ships to avoid the Strait of Gibraltar.[23]

Other writers lamented the loss of Roman roads that could no longer be travelled. Tobias Smollett, who made his Grand Tour in 1763–65, was evidently familiar with the ancient sources. Travelling through the south of France, he commented:

What pity it is, they cannot restore the celebrated *Via Aurelia*, mentioned in the Itinerarium of Antoninus, which extended from Rome by

> the way of Genoa, and through this country as far as Arles upon the Rhone. It was said to have been made by the emperor Marcus Aurelius; and some of the vestiges of it are still to be seen in Provence.[24]

Mariana Starke, whose *Letters from Italy* were published in 1800, likewise observed that it 'seems extraordinary [that] the old Roman road over the Maritime Alps is no longer discoverable'.[25] For the lack of restoration Smollett blamed the Genoese nobility, 'all merchants', who:

> from a low, selfish, and absurd policy, take all methods to keep their subjects of the Riviera in poverty and dependence. With this view, they carefully avoid all steps towards rendering that country accessible by land; and at the same time discourage their trade by sea, lest it should interfere with the commerce of their capital, in which they themselves are personally concerned.[26]

Starke and Smollett here deploy a common trope in Grand Tour writing of disdain for present-day Italians and respect for ancient ones, but disputes over who should bear the cost of road maintenance are hardly new. Ancient Roman town leaders had valued good quality transport links, not just because of the prospect of contracts but also because voters cared about the state of the roads, something that local politicians will tell you has changed little in 2,000 years.[27] This was a prominent enough political issue that under Tiberius there was an 'outcry that numbers of roads throughout Italy were broken and impracticable owing to the rascality of the contractors and the remissness of the magistrates'.[28] There followed multiple prosecutions for corruption, and some of the culprits received significant fines, though Claudius (the next-but-one emperor, who came to power in 41 CE) apparently gave some refunds.[29]

Indeed, similar complaints about the sad state of Italy's infrastructure may be found in the newspapers today. Walking through Genoa I look up to the current Via Aurelia, the Strada Statale (state road) 1. Occupying a flyover around the old port, it's built in concrete and metal and looks disturbingly past its best. Not far away, in 2018, forty-three people were killed in the infamous collapse of the Morandi Bridge, constructed in the 1960s and at the time of the disaster known to be in need of urgent maintenance. More pleasurable to look at are the facades of baroque palaces, a medieval gate, and a relocated twelfth-century cloister.

It was a rare Grand Tour that passed without laments over hospitality and transport, especially concerning the unsprung Italian coaches; as borders between the Italian states became more formalised, passengers frequently had to obtain passports in advance and wait for tedious customs checks.[30] From his published *Travels through France and Italy*, Tobias Smollett appears to have been a frequent complainer. Like Nugent, Smollett was rumoured not to have done all his own research, at Turin at least remaining in his room and taking 'his information from his valet de place'.[31] 'My personal adventures on the road,' wrote Smollett, 'were such as will not bear a recital. They consisted of petty disputes with landladies, post-masters, and postillions.'[32] Some decades later, Nikolai Gogol, in a fragment of writing on Rome, would criticise this attitude. He appreciated the Italians, who 'could not be perverted even by the incursions of foreigners, who debauch inactive nations and engender in the taverns and along the roads a despised class of people by whom the traveler often judges the people as a whole'.[33] From a historian's point of view, the reluctance of Grand Tourists to narrate their encounters with the people who made their travel possible is frustrating, and there's still relatively little research on their lives: while servants' journals exist, only now in the twenty-first century are they being published.[34]

Just as travellers and innkeepers, and servants and employers, had differing experiences on the roads, so did men and women. From Moryson onwards, male writers often complained about the *vetturino* system: William Hazlitt, a journalist, wrote: 'Let no one who can help it, and who travels for pleasure, travel by a vetturino.'[35] Women, however, were frequently more positive about his role.[36] Elisa von der Recke, for example, thought her *vetturini* superior to German drivers; 'traveling through Italy is infinitely easier and more pleasant than traveling in Germany: the roads are superb; those traveling with the post [coach] are quickly served and cleared in the post stations';[37] while Fanny Lewald noted that her drivers not only took care of the luggage but also made sure her party was booked into the best hotels.[38]

Between the lines of Riggs Miller's account is also reference to the duties required of those living nearby the roads, which recalls the ancient obligations placed on residents. Near Turin, she explained:

> The road was not very safe neither [*sic*], as there was a banditti who lay concealed in a forest not far removed. Armed peasants were ordered by the magistrates to patrol, four or five in a company, in their turns, between one village and another, in order to assist travellers, in case of necessity; and as the road lies through both the king of Sardinia's territories and the Milanese, it is a convenient circumstance that these villains sometimes avail themselves of, to escape into the one or the other state, when they play on the borders of both.[39]

We're left to speculate on what the peasants made of the magistrates' instruction. Peasants landed with unpleasant tasks also feature in Laurence Sterne's 1768 book *A Sentimental Journey Through France and Italy*. Something of a riposte to Smollett (the pair had met and disliked one another), and written in the form of a novel, it features its protagonist's own troubles on the roads:

> Let the way-worn traveller vent his complaints upon the sudden turns and dangers of your roads—your rocks—your precipices—the difficulties of getting up—the horrors of getting down—mountains impracticable—and cataracts, which roll down great stones from their summits, and block his road up.—The peasants had been all day at work in removing a fragment of this kind between St Michael and Madane; and by the time my Voiturin got to the place, it wanted full two hours of completing before a passage could any how be gain'd: there was nothing to do but wait with patience.[40]

While Sterne waited, it was 'the peasants' doing the hard work.

While in its early stages the Tour had primarily been an educational experience for young men, across the eighteenth century at least a third of the best-documented travellers to Italy were women.[41] After Riggs Miller, other women writers followed, notably Hester Piozzi, with her *Observations and Reflections* (1789), and Lady Morgan (née Sydney Owenson, an established novelist and travel writer) who published a book entitled *Italy* in 1821, while notable German authors included Friederike Brun, Elisa von der Recke and Therese von Artner. Many earlier writers, among them Fynes Moryson, had been opposed to women's travel, though for obvious reasons significant numbers of young English Catholic women had been educated in convents abroad.[42] John Moore, whose *A View of Society and Manners in Italy* was published in 1781, observed that:

> Ladies, who have remained some time at Rome and Florence, particularly those who affect a taste for virtù,* acquire an intrepidity and a cool minuteness, in examining and criticising naked figures, which is unknown to those who have never crossed the alps.[43]

His concern for the effect on women's morals has an echo of the language of a millennium before, when St Boniface was complaining about Englishwomen working in the pilgrim route brothels. Some things are very slow to change.

Riggs Miller and Piozzi provide important testimony to the ways travellers perceived the roads and their sites. Miller's party took a trip from Naples to Pozzuoli through what she called the Grotto di Pausilippe but from the description of the location must be the Crypta Neapolitana (the only tunnel in Posillipo is the Grotta di Sejano, which doesn't lead to Naples). 'This grotto,' she wrote, 'is of very ancient date; the best antiquarians attribute it to one Marcus Cocceius, a Roman'; she added in a footnote that: 'The common people are persuaded it was effected by the power of magic, and attribute it to Virgil, whom they universally believe to have been a sorcerer.' Enlarged and paved in the sixteenth century, it was lit via 'two perforations in the vault' which, however, were inadequate on windy days, obliging travellers to use torches instead.[44] Here Riggs Miller contrasts the expertise of the 'best antiquarians' with local superstition, hinting at the inferiority of the 'common people'.

Piozzi took this further, portraying her local guide suspended outside normal time:

> That an odd jumble of past and present days, past and present ideas of dignity, events and even manner of portioning out their time, still

* In this context, *virtù* refers to the fine arts.

> confuse their heads, may be observed in every conversation with them; and when a few weeks ago we revisited, in company of some newly-arrived English friends, the old baths of Baiae, Locrine lake, &c. Tobias, who rowed us over, bid us observe the Appian way under the water, where indeed it appears quite clearly, even to the tracks of wheels on its old pavement made of very large stones; and seeing me perhaps particularly attentive, 'Yes, Madam,' said he, 'I do assure you, that *Don* Horace and *Don* Virgil, of whom we hear such a deal, used to come from Rome to their country-seats here in a day, over this very road, which is now overflowed as you see it, by repeated earthquakes, but which was then so good and so unbroken, that if they rose early in the morning they could easily gallop hither against the *Ave Maria*.'[45]

The case of Tobias highlights the role of local guides in shaping visitors' understandings of the roads. I wonder, though, whether in eliding past and present Tobias was playing up to tourists' expectations in much the same way that until the mayor imposed a ban modern 'gladiators' used to pose for the crowds outside the Colosseum. Piozzi wanted an ancient tour experience: Tobias delivered. (Research suggests that this often happens today when Western tourists turn up to an 'authentic traditional village' somewhere in the Global South.)[46] Italian writers took up the theme of ancient presence too: in his *Notti romane* (Roman Nights), Alessandro Verri placed himself among the tombs of the Via Appia in the company of ghosts, including that of Cicero.[47] The same elision that might be read as peasant superstition could, elsewhere, be a literary device.

A generation later, in 1800, Mariana Starke's *Letters from Italy* became essential reading for their detailed advice on routes and prices. So much was Starke's a standard work that in Stendhal's *Charterhouse of Parma* a character insists on consulting it.[48] A follow-up book, *Travels on the Continent*, published by John Murray, went into seven editions, while her single-volume *Information and Directions for Travellers on the Continent* became a model for future guidebooks.[49] The daughter of a former British governor of Fort St George in Madras (now Chennai), Starke spent an extended period travelling with family in Europe, nursing both her sister and mother, and her highly practical guide was framed by that experience.[50] She made particular effort to cater to the needs of families and invalids who needed to be conscious of their health. Her advice shows concern for the state of Rome's drains, and the quality of the air; the Campidoglio museum, Starke warned, was 'very cold', and the historic prison at San Pietro in Vincoli 'cold and damp'.[51] Hers is an early example of a book providing ratings for key sights, using exclamation marks in place of the stars that we are now accustomed to. Thus the Sistine Chapel ceiling and *The Last Judgement* get !!!!!, Raphael's fresco *The School of Athens* !!!!, and Constantine's victory over Maxentius (also in the Vatican's Raphael Rooms, though by his assistant Giulio Romano) !!!.[52] She was open-minded about travellers' possible motives for a trip to Rome, observing that:

> every body may find amusement; for whether it be our wish to dive deep into classical knowledge, whether arts and sciences are our pursuit, or whether we merely seek for new ideas and new objects, the end cannot fail to be obtained in this most interesting of Cities.[53]

She was not, however, overly impressed by the city's fabric: Rome's streets were 'ill-paved and dirty; while ruins of immense edifices, which continually meet the eyes, give an impression of melancholy to every thinking Spectator'.[54] She had, nonetheless, numerous recommendations for essential viewing, including the 'master-piece of modern genius' that was St Peter's, as well as out-of-town trips to Tivoli, Palestrina and Frascati.[55] At Tivoli, her recommended sights included Horace's villa.

All these travellers required accommodation and as the Grand Tour developed, so did an infrastructure catering not only to the needs of pilgrims and traders but also to a new type of demand. Tourists typically required longer-term accommodation, and had more of an interest in enjoying their journey in clean and comfortable circumstances than the rider simply looking for somewhere basic to pause overnight. Certain areas of cities became popular with these travellers: the Faubourg Saint-Germain in Paris, for example, or the Piazza di Spagna in Rome. In a precursor to Airbnb, families of fading fortune in the larger Italian cities found that letting furnished apartments to tourists could prove lucrative.[56] Today, several hotels in Rome claim distant heritage. Among the oldest is the fifteenth-century Albergo del Sole, across the piazza from the Pantheon (known to pilgrims as the church of Santa Maria Rotonda, or St Mary in the Round). Many of the convents that offered medieval travellers accommodation still do, and some in grander style than others: painted ceilings and a roof terrace with a view grace the Casa di Santa Brigida, run by Swedish nuns, just off the Campo de' Fiori. (St Bridget, who had already made a pilgrimage to Santiago, relocated to Rome in 1349, following her husband's death, and later made her own pilgrimage to the Holy Land.)[57] In his 1749 guide to the Tour, Thomas Nugent recommended three Roman inns: the Scudo d'Oro, the Lion d'Oro, and La Cerena by name, as well as 'several public houses for the reception of particular nations', a cautious reference to the hostelries linked to the (Catholic) pilgrim hospitals. 'But those who intend to make any stay,' he added, 'had better hire furnished apartments, which are very reasonable; for you may be accommodated with a *Palazzo*, as they call it, or a handsome furnished house, for about six guineas a month'.[58] Mariana Starke, in her 1800 guide, reckoned that 'The best Hotels at Rome are Margariti's, Sarmiento's and Pio's', while in the 1770s Anna Riggs Miller praised Vanini's in Florence, which along with Schneiderff's was one of the best-rated inns: its keepers had 'an honourable honesty, a rare quality in hosts'.[59]

That insidious implication of Riggs Miller that the majority of hosts were trying to cheat tourists continues in popular discourse. It is, to be fair, pretty easy to be caught out by unexpected rules if you haven't paid close attention to the guidebook. The classic Italian miscommunication involves table service. I go up to the bar, ask for a coffee and brioche, and the barista asks if I'd like to sit outside, without mentioning that the convention here is that outside is table service only, there's a charge for that, and your breakfast will cost quite a bit more than the €2.60 you'd pay to eat it standing up. If you don't know the rules you probably will feel cheated, even though it's in the small print of the menu pinned up behind the bar.

For the early Grand Tourists, few in number and high in class, there was a further option for information: the British Embassy. Some long-standing envoys hosted social events where visitors could mingle with locals of suitable standing. These included Horace Mann in Florence (1738–86) and William Hamilton in Naples

(1764–1800).[60] Elsewhere along the various routes to Rome upmarket hotels were established to cater to the needs of travellers. Among the oldest surviving establishments is the Royal Victoria Hotel in Pisa. Opened in 1837 and developed from an old city inn, its founder was an Italian who studied in London, began helping wealthy travellers with their accommodation requirements, and realised there was a market for an attractive city residence as an alternative to renting private villas.[61]

Starke travelled south from Rome to see the sights around Naples, including the excavations at Pompeii, which had been firmly identified in 1763. There she saw 'an excavated Street, supposed to be the Appian-way'.[62] In fact, the Via Appia turns inland further north, but (like Samuel Rogers' confusion) this only underlines the Appia's grip on the cultural imagination. Several decades later, James Fenimore Cooper made the same mistake.[63] On the road from Rome itself Starke had been more taken by the process of draining the Pontine Marshes, which had been begun by Appius Claudius but completed only after centuries under the 'present Pontiff' (Pius VI, who ruled 1775–1799), whose road was 'justly esteemed one of the best in Europe: and so wise are the precautions he has taken to purify the air, that no danger is to be apprehended from it now, except during the prevalence of very hot weather'.[64] Yet in Pompeii she was struck by the parallels between past and present:

> To visit it even now is absolutely to live with the ancient Romans: and when we see houses, shops, furniture, fountains, streets, carriages, and implements of husbandry, exactly similar to those of the present day, we are apt to conclude that customs and manners have undergone but little variation for the last two thousand years.[65]

The immersive experience that Pompeii offered has a parallel with Piozzi's interest in the shifting bounds of past and present, and underlines that travellers were not necessarily in search of an educational engagement as much as an emotional one.

Perhaps these parallels were on Starke's mind when she later travelled north on the Via Flaminia to Perugia, crossing the bridge at Narni 'supposed to have been built by Augustus'.[66] This bridge was a key attraction on the Grand Tour, especially for landscape artists, and in 1826 was painted by Jean-Baptiste-Camille Corot. Rather than the road, I take the train to see this iconic sight of the Via Flaminia. The Bridge of Augustus is located in Narni Amelia, about an hour out of Rome. My train is a *regionale veloce*, a fast regional, which means it isn't fast at all, taking four-and-a-quarter hours to reach its final destination, Ancona. On the positive side, the fare to Narni is only €6.25 each way. First stop is Roma Tiburtina, on the road to Tivoli, then out of the city we head for Orte, past the staples of the Roman view: pines, poplars and graffiti. Orte is also a motorway junction and service station, from which the road to Spoleto leaves the modern Autostrada del Sole. This is the Tiber valley. The river's to our left, motorway to the right and mountains beyond. The houses thin out as we leave the suburbs, past olive groves and into wooded countryside, leaves yellowing.

Narni itself has the characteristic layout of an Umbrian town: railway station at the bottom of the hill, in 'Narni Scalo', which means roughly 'Narni Calling-Point', and walled town above on the hilltop. I walk away from the cluster of shops around the station, through a street of square, squat houses in traditional earth colours, and down through a small industrial area, beneath the railway through a graffitied concrete underpass. Among the trackside graffiti is a spray-painted slogan in English: 'No Farmer, No Food, Modi Kutta'. 'Kutta' is the Hindi word for 'dog', and this is a reference to the Indian farmers' protests of 2021 against laws introduced by Narendra Modi's government that farmers argued would leave them worse-off. Indian agriculture might seem a world away from the Grand Tour, but it was at precisely the same time that global trade in commodities such as tea, coffee, tobacco and sugar was expanding, and at least some of the Grand Tourists, and the painters listed on the interpretive panels that dot the site at Narni, were probably wearing Indian-grown cotton, or dining in rooms decorated with *chinoiserie*. A sign advertises bikes to hire. The firm's called 'Grand Tour Rando'.

The bridges come into view. There are three. A single monumental arch remains of the ancient one, no longer passable. High above, cars pass on the modern concrete that stretches between the hills across the river valley. Lower down a third bridge carries pipes and a back street. I sit on a stone to write these words: the stone is probably a part of the old Roman bridge. Three sections have fallen at angles in this little park. There's a QR code on a nearby sign. Snap it and you can view all this by drone. Birds call from the trees. Leaves fall through the view.

It's a killer climb for the calves to reach the charming town centre at the top (unlike the more famous Orvieto, there's no funicular here). Such is the atmosphere of the imposing buildings and twisting roads that the main square is being set up as a film set. Around the hilltop city, the medieval walls are still in evidence. Extended in the fourteenth century, they cut across the line of the Via Flaminia. I enter the old town first through the Porta Polella, part of those fourteenth-century walls, and make my way along a snaking road to the Porta Nova. Nova means 'new', but this gate was new in the sixteenth century, after the sack of 1527 forced the abandonment of the land further down the slope. The stones are tidily cut around the arches, and more rugged in the twenty-foot walls beside. They might have impressed Starke, who was writing in the aftermath of Napoleon's campaigns in Italy. She made a point of commenting on Hannibal's campaigns in the area around Perugia, adding a summary of his key stops, and observing:

> It is impossible to view the country between Passignano and Ossaia, without feeling the highest admiration of the military skill of Hannibal, who contrived, on an Enemy's ground, to draw that enemy into a narrow, swampy, and uncommonly foggy plain, where no army, however numerous, however brave, could long have defended itself: for on three sides are heights which were possessed by the Troops of Carthage; and, on the other, a vast unfordable lake.[67]

Starke, one scholar argues, 'helped shape a more efficient Grand Tour for the emerging British civil servant class that viewed itself as the true heirs to the Roman Empire'.[68] She was far from the only visitor to have such connections. This was, after all, when Britain was building an empire. William Beckford, whose family fortune came from sugar plantations in Jamaica worked by enslaved labourers, took his Grand Tour in 1782. An outsider to English high society, for Beckford the

Tour was an opportunity to exchange his family wealth for the cultural polish that might enable him to be welcomed by the metropolitan elite.[69] Like many travellers, he opted for an early start on the final day of his journey to Rome:

> We set out in the dark. Morning dawned over the Lago di Vico; its waters, of a deep ultramarine blue, and its surrounding forests catching the rays of the rising sun. It was in vain I looked for the cupola of St. Peter's upon descending the mountains beyond Viterbo. Nothing but a sea of vapours was visible. At length, they rolled away; and the spacious plains began to show themselves, in which the most warlike of nations reared their seat of empire. On the left, afar off, rises the rugged chain of Apennines, and on the other side, a shining expanse of ocean terminates the view. It was upon this vast surface so many illustrious actions were performed, and I know not where a mighty people could have chosen a grander theatre. Here was space for the march of armies, and verge enough for encampments: levels for martial games, and room for that variety of roads and causeways that led from the Capital to Ostia. How many triumphant legions have trodden these pavements! how many captive kings! What throngs of cars and chariots once glittered on their surface! savage animals dragged from the interior of Africa; and the ambassadors of Indian princes, followed by their exotic train, hastening to implore the favour of the senate! During many ages, this eminence commanded almost every day such illustrious scenes; but all are vanished: the splendid tumult is passed away: silence and desolation remain.[70]

Beckford's description of the roads is unusual in its global scope. His Romans are conquerors of the world, and while nothing here is entirely inauthentic, the ambassadors of Indian princes could equally be visiting the British Empire of Beckford's present day. As for vanished empires, just six years before this Tour, England had lost its North American colonies, which were now the United States.

Earlier Grand Tour accounts had also hinted at developments in imperial thinking. After a dramatic crossing of the Alps, Thomas Gray and Horace Walpole had arrived in the Po valley, the broad glacial plain of northern Italy that sits between the Alps and the Apennines. (Nowadays it is the route of the trains from Venice or Bologna to

Milan.) Musing on the ruined aqueducts he passed, Gray composed Latin verse on the plains' imagined history. 'We passed the famous plains', Gray began in English, then switched to Latin to tell the story of 'Roman woes' at the Battle of Trebia, the river even now running red where in ancient times the 'sons of Ausonia' (a poetic term for Italy) had been put to flight by the 'Moorish cavalry, the dark-skinned battalions' of Hannibal and the Carthaginians.[71] This characterisation of the Carthaginians reflected the developing concepts of race in eighteenth-century Europe. Yet it was not only the North Africans whom Gray categorised by the colour of their skin. His description of the local people in Naples has a definite racialising overtone, reflecting the ambivalence in northern European thought about the extent to which Mediterranean people were entirely white:

> The common sort are a jolly lively kind of animals, more industrious than Italians usually are; they work till evening, then take their lute or guitar (for they all play) and walk about the city, or upon the sea-shore with it, to enjoy the fresco. One sees their little brown children jumping about stark-naked, and the bigger ones dancing with castanets, while others play on the cymbal to them.[72]

Indeed, it was not only a prejudice of northern Europeans: Italians from the north of the peninsula could also express significant prejudice against southerners. Luigi Farini, prime minister of Italy in the 1860s and born near Ravenna, observed of the south:

> But, my friend, what places they are down here, in Molise and Terra di Lavoro! What barbarism! It's not Italy at all! This is Africa: the Bedouins are the flower of civic virtue compared with these peasants.[73]

For Mariana Starke, though, such concepts began even close to Rome: 'The Master of the inn at Tivoli is worthy and civil; the Natives of the country, generally speaking, savage.'[74]

Yet if contemporary Italians, certainly the 'common sort', were perceived by these middle- and upper-class British travellers as inferior, sometimes in racialised ways, their ancient predecessors were a fount of civilisation. Samuel Johnson, considering a journey to Italy, observed to Boswell that on the shores of the Mediterranean 'were the four great Empires of the world; the Assyrian, the Persian, the

Grecian, and the Roman.—All our religion, almost all our law, almost all our arts, almost all that sets us above savages, has come to us from the shores of the Mediterranean.'[75] The roads, too, fell comfortably into this way of thinking. Even Lady Morgan, a republican and Irish radical, could agree: 'The art of road-making ranks high in the means of civilization.'[76] Praise for the infrastructure of the Roman Empire had a subtext: praise for that of modern empires. Yet for this to work involved a sleight of hand: those who had once been colonised by the Romans had to identify with them. Camden provided it with the metaphor of engrafting, and after all, with a few qualifications one could just about argue that the new European empires were simply doing for others what the Romans had once done for us.

PART 4

First Roads, and Afterwards Railways, 1800–1900

11
Napoleon

On 22 September 1792, Mariana Starke arrived with her party in Nice, then within the kingdom of Piedmont-Sardinia. She was somewhat alarmed to find 'almost every lodging-house without the walls occupied by Piedmontese soldiers', but this daughter of a military governor was the sort of individual for whom the description 'formidable character' might have been invented. She booked into a city hotel and as the prospect of French invasion grew and 'almost every remaining Person of rank who had strength to walk, fled into the Alps', waited out the threat under the protection of the town's Commandant. Disguised as a servant, lest she be mistaken for an aristocrat, she got her family and friends evacuated alongside the British consul and his household and sailed on to Genoa.[1] Over the course of two-and-a-half decades, the French Revolution and then the Napoleonic Wars changed the dynamics of European politics and of travel across the continent. The roads still led in many ways to Rome, but as Napoleon made himself a Caesar, that city gained a rival: Paris.

Mariana Starke's extended stay in Europe coincided almost precisely with Napoleon's campaigns. 'You will think us very unfortunate,' she told her readers, 'in having just reached Nice to see it captured', but this was a point on which she and her publisher could capitalise. She was not only in Nice for that French conquest, but in Florence four years later when Napoleon entered the city and in Rome for the twelve months running up to the entry of French troops in February 1798. (One starts to suspect this was not accidental.) Hostile to Roman Catholicism, she admired Napoleon despite disapproving of his apparent atheism, and had ample praise for his 'most rapid and brilliant conquests ever gained in so short a period, either by ancient or modern Warriors'.[2]

Napoleon had been made commander of the French Revolutionary Army of Italy in 1796 and over the next two years his armies overthrew the centuries-old republics of Venice, Genoa and Lucca before marching on Rome. In September 1797, Napoleon wrote from Passariano (north-east of Venice, near Udine), to tell his brother that 'The Directory [the French government] does not intend to allow the petty intrigues of the Italian princes to recommence.'[3] He went on to set out his concerns about a possible coalition between Naples, Rome and Florence: 'the alliance of the rats against the cat'.[4] In Rome, Pope Pius VI, almost eighty years old, was not expected to live long, and Napoleon issued instructions in the case of a potential conclave: his brother should 'alarm the Cardinals by threatening that I shall in that event march instantly on Rome'.[5]

In fact, it was another four months before the troops entered, 10 February 1798, and Pius VI was still alive. Their commander, General Berthier, made a grand entrance from the north, as so many Grand Tourists had done before, only this time with a substantial military entourage. His speech from the Capitoline was peppered with references to the heroes of Rome's ancient republic.[6] Pope Pius VI was deported to France, and spent the last eighteen months of his life in exile. In his place a Roman Republic was established: a French puppet regime that opponents called the *repubblica per ridere*, loosely translated as the 'ridiculous republic'. This struggled on for about eighteen months,[7] but its defeat did not prevent Napoleon seizing power in France in the coup of 18 Brumaire (9–10 November 1799). Adopting the ancient Roman title of First Consul (from 1802 First Consul for Life), he came to style himself as a new Caesar, and in 1804 proclaimed himself Emperor of the French. Rome mattered to Napoleon and so – as we will see – did its roads.

Roads also mattered, however, to Napoleon's adversary. Pope Pius VI (Giovanni Angelo Braschi) had been elected in 1775, more than two decades before the French invasion. He steered a moderate line between admirers and opponents of the Jesuits and among his early international initiatives was the establishment of the first Roman

Catholic bishopric in the newly formed United States of America (the diocese of Baltimore). Closer to home, his long tenure gave him time to develop major infrastructure projects, including a revived attempt to drain the Pontine Marshes and restore the Via Appia. Pius ordered the renovation of the Decenovium canal beside the road and commissioned a posthouse at the site of the old way station known as 'Ad Medias' (so named for its location halfway along).[8] This Casale di Mesa, its large entrance arch allowing access for carriages, is still visible on the road beside the remains of a Roman mausoleum. Inside, the Bar Antica Posta provides passing travellers with refreshments. Pius gave himself personal credit for this project, and according to the nineteenth-century historian Ferdinand Gregorovius, renamed the road the 'Linea Pia',[9] a name that has not, however, stuck. Further to the north there was also new building. Describing a recently constructed road over the Alps, opened in 1785, Mariana Starke noted that it 'may certainly vie with, if it does not surpass any ancient Roman road in point of magnificence'.[10]

John Chetwode Eustace, an Anglo-Irish priest who acted as tutor to three young men on a Grand Tour in 1802, had much praise for Pius' works when he wrote up his travels (and given the politics perhaps also a reluctance to give Napoleon credit). The restored Via Appia was an 'excellent road'; it was 'shaded by double rows of elms and poplars', today often replaced by Roman pines. At Tor Tre Ponti, travellers could admire 'several milliary [mile] stones, columns, &c.' excavated during the works.[11] Elsewhere Chetwode Eustace noted even quite obscure Roman roads, such as the Via Posthumia, linking Cremona and Mantua; he knew that the Via Emilia had been 'made by Marcus Emilius Lepidus, about one hundred and eighty-seven years before the Christian aera'.[12] This was information that could be found in the writings of Livy and confirmed by inscriptions, and illustrates the level of detail available to those Grand Tourists with a serious interest in Rome's past.

The French Revolution, with its suppression of the Catholic Church in France and confiscation of Church holdings – as well as the seizure of the Avignon territory of the Papal States – proved Pius' major challenge. In the first wave of French invasions in 1796, smaller papal cities including Ancona (a key Adriatic port) and the pilgrim destination of Loreto were occupied. Pius made peace with the French in February the following year, but it did not last. Following the invasion of Rome in 1798 (which was unopposed), Pius was taken prisoner. His initial exile in the luxurious surroundings of the Certosa di Pavia ended when the French declared war on Tuscany, and he was escorted north to Valence, a town on the Rhône midway between Avignon and Lyons. There he died on 29 August 1799, at that point the longest-reigning pope in history.

With Rome out of the question as a location for the papal election, the cardinals convened three months later at the monastery of San Giorgio, which lies on an island in the Venetian lagoon. This was the first and last conclave to be held outside Rome since the Avignon schism. The discussions were not swift, and it took the cardinals until March to compromise on Cardinal Barnaba Chiaramonti. He was crowned on the 14th of that month with a papier-mâché tiara, because the French had held on to the real thing. He made his way first by ship to Pesaro and then across Italy on the route of the ancient Via Flaminia. Following Napoleon's victory over Austrian forces at the Battle of Marengo (near the northern town of Alessandria, in Piedmont), the French came to terms with Pius VII, and he was restored to rule in Rome. In 1804 he oversaw Napoleon's coronation, but Napoleon did not make the journey south, and instead had the Pope attend him in Paris. Nor, on that occasion, did the Pope, as per tradition, crown the emperor. Napoleon crowned himself.[13]

Napoleon's engagement with the ancient past of Rome and its empire functioned largely through archaeology, new infrastructure projects, and the creation in Paris of triumphal routes that echoed those of the Eternal City. He made the most of the surviving antiquities of Paris – including the baths now in the Musée de Cluny – to re-imagine the city as a new Rome, or even an improvement. Perhaps about 1809, Napoleon was said to have stood by the side of the Louvre and declared his intention to build a celebratory route for triumphs:

> This is where I will build an imperial road. It will begin here and extend to the Barrière du Trône; the road will be one hundred feet wide and

> lined with a gallery of trees. The rue impériale must be the most beautiful road in the universe.[14]

Although this plan never came to pass, there's plenty of other evidence in Paris for Napoleon's interest – and also to demonstrate that such classical inspiration had precedents. Paris pre-dated the Romans, and as Lutetia Parisiorum had been Caesar's headquarters during his campaigns in Gaul in the 50s BCE. Legend had it that Paris took its name from the instigator of the Trojan Wars:[15] while the etymological research does not support this, the existence of the story is another indication of the significance of classical heritage in European culture. Walking down the boulevard Magenta from the Gare du Nord I catch a glimpse of an arch at the end of rue Faubourg Saint-Martin, the Porte Saint-Martin. Commissioned in 1674 under Louis XIV, it shows the king in the images of Mars, Hercules and Fame, and is one of several classicising monuments to him. Louis also established a French academy in Rome, while the artist Piranesi, famed for his engravings recording Rome's antiquities, attracted many French students.[16] In the sixteenth century, art historian Giorgio Vasari had compared Fontainebleau under Francis I and Paris under Henri IV to Rome, while we have already seen the precedent for reconstructing ancient triumphs in the case of Francis' contemporary and rival, the Holy Roman Emperor Charles V.[17] Napoleon, however, had declared an empire, which demanded ever more spectacular architecture. His monuments borrowed not only from models in Rome (the arches of Titus, Severus and Constantine, as well as Trajan's Column) but also from examples in France itself, emphasising the country's long links to the historic empire. The Trophée des Alpes, located at Turbie near Monte Carlo, may be compared with Napoleon's Colonne de la Grande Armée at Wimille (Boulogne), while the Arc d'Orange provided a model for the Arc du Carrousel in Paris. (This wasn't only a Parisian project: classicising sculpture, including arches, was commissioned for Italian cities too.[18])

I'm familiar with the name Carrousel, from the shopping centre that sits below the Louvre. This time I make a point of looking for the arch above it. I must have walked past it last time I was here, but it merges into the other decorative structures that garnish the Tuileries, the classicising statues and the lines of trees. I pay €2.20 for a *noisette* (macchiato) from an artisan catering van and €1.50 to use the Carrousel superloos that sell coloured toilet paper. I'm not sure it's the impression Napoleon intended. Much further south, in Orange, a short train ride from Avignon, I try for the original. You get a better sense of the Napoleonic look here. The arch was built up with battlements in the medieval period but restored from 1807 – the Napoleonic regime was restaging monuments long before the Fascists got there. From then on it has sat in a circle of avenues, rather than above a road in use. Located on the Via Agrippa, the name used for various roads leading out of Lyons, the arch marks the Roman conquest of Gaul, and was dedicated to the Emperor Tiberius (though he may not have been the original dedicatee). Its carvings show scenes of combat, prisoners, and the abandoned weapons of the defeated armies. Yet while the Arc d'Orange celebrated the Roman triumph over the barbarian French, on the Arc du Carrousel the French were now the victors in their European wars.[19]

The best-known of the Napoleonic monuments is of course the Arc de Triomphe, influenced by the Arch of Titus in the Forum and commissioned in 1806 to celebrate Napoleon's victory at the Battle of Austerlitz. The emperor did not live to see its completion, but it was intended to occupy a key spot on a triumphal route through Paris, mimicking the ceremonies of ancient Rome.[20] To reach it, I walk through the Tuileries, through gardens made for Catherine de' Medici, an Italian heiress who became queen of France. Past the chestnut and linden trees stands a gold-tipped obelisk, first noted by the French during Napoleon's campaign in Egypt and formally presented by the Ottoman governor some thirty years later in an exchange of diplomatic gifts. Beyond, a tree-lined boulevard stretches a mile uphill to the Arc de Triomphe. That's a proper parade route, though between designer shops and navy-suited office workers out for lunch, armies and conflict seem very far away. That is, until on the side of a newsstand I spot a magazine advertising its interview with Volodymyr Zelensky, a reminder that expansionist warfare remains an issue in the present day. Napoleon's urban remodelling has not gone without criticism.[21] A monument in the place Vendôme, designed on the model of Trajan's Column and topped by a statue of Napoleon, was toppled during the Paris Commune of 1871. It was described by the artist Gustave Courbet (president of the Commune's art commission) as 'a monument devoid of all artistic value, tending to perpetuate the ideas of war and conquest of the past imperial dynasty, which are reproved by a republican nation's sentiment'.[22]

Even in Napoleon's own time, writers were linking the seizure of art to wider imperial projects. In 1801, Catherine Wilmot, whose *An Irish Peer on the Continent* described her travels in the company of Lady Mount Cashel, observed of the Musée Central des Arts at the Louvre that 'As well as being the Sanctuary for French, Dutch, and German Masterpieces of genius it is possess'd of the plunder of Italy.'[23] She compared the pillage of Italian art to French attempts to conquer Ireland, and sarcastically observed to a general of that country that:

> had their philanthropic undertaking prosper'd as happily in Ireland as it did across the Alps, I should expect by this time to see our little Island hung up as a curiosity in the Louvre among the Italian trophies.[24]

Despite her general admiration for Napoleon, Mariana Starke was also concerned by his removal of art works from Italy, although she reassured her readers that plenty remained. She did not wish them to 'conclude that all her choicest works of genius are destroyed, or removed to Paris'.[25] She reported, in fact, on the Pope's efforts to protect the 'treasures of Loreto', describing:

> droves of mules and horses proceeding towards the Castle of St Angelo, at the gates of which fortress stood carriages guarded by cannon, and laden, as the Soldiers said, with the treasures of Loretto, which his Holiness was going to send to Terracina.[26]

Located on a hilly outcrop and surrounded by the Pontine Marshes, Terracina was easy to defend. Despite the Pope's precautions, however, the removal to Paris of numerous artworks, among them Veronese's *Marriage Feast at Cana* (which was never returned), along with antiquities such as the *Laocoön* and *Apollo Belvedere* (which were), gave the city new importance as a tourist destination. Even before Napoleon's coup, a 1797 engraving dedicated to the Republican government approvingly showed a convoy transporting art out of Rome, while a song composed for a triumphal entry in 1798 included the line 'Rome is no longer in Rome, it is all in Paris'.[27]

Ironically, the plunder of so many artworks from the Vatican prompted Pope Pius VII to toughen up on the export of antiquities from Rome, and indeed to sponsor new excavations. The sculptor Antonio Canova took responsibility for multiple projects, including the restoration of antiquities on the Via Appia. While there had been over a hundred excavations on the road between 1775 and 1780,[28] Canova created a model for treating remains in situ rather than transporting them elsewhere for display. His pioneering interventions included the restoration of the tomb of Servilius Quartus, at the fourth milestone, undertaken during 1807–8 and still visible, in which he pieced together parts of the original with fragments gathered nearby, creating a sort of memorial wall.[29] That said, the conservation of the road's monuments was a long process and discussions about the need for urgent work, including on the Grotto of Egeria,[30] extended over several years.

In 1809, however, Napoleon forced Pius VII into exile and went on to name his own infant son the king of Rome. There were ambitious plans to rebuild Rome as a new imperial capital. The opening up of the Forum area, especially the space immediately surrounding Trajan's Column, dates to this period. It saw the excavation of the road leading through the Forum, the Via Sacra, in case Napoleon might need to celebrate a triumph. The occasion, however, did not arise: within a few years the emperor's fortunes had turned, and in fact he never visited Rome. It was in this period, too, that the idea of an archaeological park in Rome was first touted, although again it would take almost a century to come to fruition. The proposed scheme for an avenue to link the Colosseum and Campidoglio would also have to wait more than a century, and for a new, ambitious dictator.[31]

In a volume of 1815, English traveller Henry Coxe (a pseudonym for John Millard) had considerable praise for the 'various improvements and alterations made by the *French* at Rome'. He reported 'upon the authority of a gentleman, many years a resident in that capital', that the area around the Colosseum had been cleared, as had the surroundings of the Temples of Vesta and of Fortuna Virilis, of Concord and of Jupiter Tonans. These now had 'a majestic appearance', as did the arches of Titus and Severus. Moreover, the operation had functioned as something of a public works project, affording a 'daily allowance of a small sum of money and a portion of soup' to the workforce.[32] (In the previous century, Hester Piozzi had also regarded road construction as a good employment opportunity for the 'vagabonds' she observed begging at Loreto. She could not imagine that they could truly be distressed, 'when their sovereign provides them with employment on the beautiful new road he is making, and insists on them being well paid, who are found willing to work'.)[33] The opinion of the Roman workforce on the outcome of their labour is sadly not recorded. At least in this instance they were getting paid: at other times gangs of prisoners were deployed on the work.[34]

Canova also attracted the attention of Napoleon, who eventually succeeded in obtaining the services of the sculptor. Canova initially (and ironically) made the state of the roads an excuse for his refusal, ultimately negotiating very good terms for a brief stint of work in Paris.[35] Canova was among those who deployed ancient comparisons in praise of Napoleon's works, claiming to have told the emperor that his 'magnificent roads' were 'truly worthy of the ancient Romans'. In response, said Napoleon, 'Next year . . . the *Cornice* road will be completed, by which you may travel from Paris to Genoa without crossing the snow'.[36] Tobias Smollett's hopes for a revival of the old Via Aurelia were to be satisfied.

I pick up this route at Avignon, taking the railway towards Nice, via Arles and Marseilles, past the Etang de Berre, a lagoon that at first I mistake for the Mediterranean. On the road beside the train someone is out in a vintage car. The aircon on the train is chilly and for the first time on this trip I dig a cardigan out of my suitcase. Through a tunnel and as the train pulls into L'Estaque on the outskirts of Marseilles the Mediterranean opens out to our right. Cruise ships cram into the harbour. I change for a slow train from Marseilles to Nice, riding on the upper deck. Past some lush allotments, out through sprawling suburbs, past some apartments that are perhaps l'Unité de l'Habitation, though looking later at the map I realise they can't be. Generic brutalism, then. The train slides through cuttings and tunnels. This isn't the easiest landscape for a straight road. Pine trees, scrub, little vineyards tucked into the valleys, houses in shades of baked earth, and once again the Med, the railway skirting the edges of blue bays. We arrive at the industrial outskirts of Toulon. For a long time the train runs inland, but past Fréjus and Saint-Raphaël the line curves with the coast, gleaming sea to our right, close enough to spot the bathers and the bright beach umbrellas. A speedboat crosses Cannes harbour. The railway's right on the front here. Past the airport, likewise on the seafront, and we're into Nice.

Birthplace of Garibaldi and stopping-off point of Mariana Starke, Nice, as Nikaia, was founded as a Greek/Phocaean colony around 350 BCE; it has some modest Roman remains, but it's best known as a fashionable nineteenth-century English resort. Its palm-lined seafront is named the Promenade des Anglais for the tourists who came here for a break from the British weather. I wander through a busy flea market into the old quarter and enjoy lunch at Chez Palmyre on a communal table, chatting to another single diner, a gallerist from Frankfurt who's taking a day off after the opening of an exhibition at the Cap de l'Ail. Back on the train, the route is squeezed between the cliffs and sea, on embankments and in tunnels. It's packed with tourists skipping from town to town along the Côte d'Azur. This is the most English my travel has been. I hear sun-seeking students arguing over the Tory leadership (this was the day of Liz Truss' short-lived victory). The train tunnels beneath Monaco–Monte Carlo (there's a location for a heist plot) and emerges beside a bay speckled with sailing boats: Roquebrune-Cap-Martin. The hills are high enough here that they peek up into low cloud.

You get a sense of the challenges of cutting this road: the terraces and bridges and tunnels; the hair-raising bends around the rock. Cornice is too decorous a name for it. I can understand why the sea felt safer. Sheer cliffs, scrubby trees, orderly terracing. It's striking in the sunshine but can't be fun in a storm. There hasn't been much rain, though. The river we cross on the Italian side of Ventimiglia is dry. So is another at Imperia, and another. Only at Albenga does one look healthier. There are tunnels en route, lots of them. Grey stones on the beaches: this line too runs close to the sea. The mountains retreat for a while from the shore here. Big, fat-leaved succulents grow on the trackside, and still the palms. Just before we reach Pietra Ligure

I spot a tiny cemetery built into the cliffs. Even death here requires engineering.

The Cornice road was not the only one to be developed under Napoleon. Even half a century on, his works on the Mont Cenis Pass, further to the north, were still attracting praise. It was, wrote the memoirist Elpis Melena, recording her own crossing, 'an object of admiration and wonderment, as a monument of the imperial engineer, Napoleon'.[37] Besides drawing inspiration from the ancient past, Napoleon's works also made reference to more recent rulers: a road beside the Rhine, for example, was named the 'route of Charlemagne'.[38] (Napoleon's brother, Lucien Bonaparte, wrote an epic poem called *Charlemagne*, published in Paris, 1814.)[39] If Charlemagne had overseen improvements to infrastructure, however, and Charles V used roads as a stage set, Napoleon went significantly further. News of his road improvements made the British press. In March 1813, the *Liverpool Mercury* reported on the 'great beneficial labour' that was the drainage of the Pontine Marshes. Originally planned – in the correspondent's version at least – by Julius Caesar, it had now been achieved:

> by the command of Bonaparte under the direction of some celebrated French engineers; who has in this made Caesar an example to him of benefit to mankind: well were it for Europe if he would confine himself to the imitation of what was good and really great in the conduct of Caesar!

That wrote out several earlier improvement schemes sponsored by the popes, probably a product of the British correspondent's conventional anti-Catholicism. Napoleon, the report continued, had thus brought 'salubrity and safety to the most famous portion of Italy'. In the early nineteenth century the significance of the marshes as a habitat for malarial mosquitoes was still not understood, and it was thought to be the removal of 'vapours' from the 'stagnant pools and foul morasses' that would lead to a reduction in 'various epidemic disorders'. Yet even if accounts of cause and effect were somewhat askew, the benefits were unquestionable.[40]

That said, the enthusiasm of the reporting did not always reflect the facts. In Naples, for example, the Napoleonic regime benefited from works begun under the previous, Bourbon rulers. These were incremental additions, rather than a project started from scratch.[41] A new General Directorate of Bridges and Roads was established to oversee improvements in the provinces, but tax revenues had a habit of going astray: in one instance the staggering sum of 180,000 ducats intended for road repairs south of Naples failed to reach the target projects.[42] (This could have funded a workforce of several thousand for a year.)[43] Banditry continued to be a problem, as English travellers complained in 1815. When Lord Holland, Mr Orde and their families were planning a trip from Rome to Naples, the king of Naples offered either a frigate for their travel by sea, or an escort of gendarmes. A report in the *Caledonian Mercury* observed (again with a measure of anti-Catholicism):

> It is certainly disgraceful to the Papal Government, that no traveller can with safety pursue his way through the Ecclesiastical States; and that robberies are committed, not only during the night, but even in broad day, by hordes of thieves, who attack almost every carriage that ventures from Florence to Rome, or through the Pontine Marshes to Naples.[44]

In 1815, traveller Henry Coxe offered readers of his *Picture of Italy* what he promised was the first English description of the new road over the Alps. There had been a pass at Simplon for centuries, but the upgraded version allowed for the transport of artillery, and besides was a far more comfortable experience for the tourist:

> This wonderful monument of human labour and ingenuity, which may justly claim the admiration of the world extending from Geneva to Milan, was constructed by order of BONAPARTE, under the direction of M. CEARD, on whom it confers immortal honour. In the course of this grand route, more than forty bridges of various forms are thrown from one wild chasm to another—numerous galleries or subterranean passages are not only cut through the solid rock, but through the *solid glaciers* also—those 'thrilling regions of thick-ribbed ice'—and if to these we add the aqueducts which have been built—the walls that support and flank the whole of the route—together with the

> innumerous works of art which must necessarily enter into and form a part of this more than Herculean work—we are at a loss which most to admire, the genius which contrived, or the skill which executed, so stupendous a work. More than 30,000 men were constantly employed in this undertaking, which was finished in 1805, after three years incessant labour.[45]

The Simplon Pass here has not only an implicit parallel with ancient roads, but in the reference to the demigod Hercules almost surpasses human achievement. Coxe was not the only one to write in such enthusiastic terms. Samuel Rogers recorded his experience of the Simplon in his travel journal: 'an object for wonder . . . we could not but wonder at the boldness that planned, & the genius & industry that executed it'.[46]

Given the dangers of Alpine travel, the establishment of a new and reliable route was unquestionably welcome. The anonymous author of a book on travel published in 1839 described an accident alleged to have befallen Napoleon as he made his way across the Alps in 1800 prior to the improvements. Crossing the Great St Bernard Pass, 'In a dangerous part of the way, near the termination of the Forest of Saint-Pierre, he slipped from off his mule, but was saved from falling over by his guide . . . who . . . caught hold of him by his coat. The guide was rewarded with a present of a thousand francs.'[47] The painting by David of *Bonaparte Crossing the St Bernard Pass* (1800–1801) gives a rather more triumphant view of proceedings, showing the emperor instead on a white horse, and beneath him inscriptions evoking the prior crossings of Charlemagne and Hannibal.[48] The allusion to Hannibal here illustrates the flexibility of narratives around the Roman roads. As we saw, Hannibal was credited with constructing a road for his troops' descent, but on the other hand he was fighting the Romans. Just as British connoisseurs of Roman heritage found ways to situate themselves as heirs of the Romans as much as of the colonised Britons, so Napoleon could alternately emulate the Roman emperors' triumphs and pick up the mantle of a rival.

More tales of life on the road come from François-René de Chateaubriand, who in 1803–4 was briefly a secretary to the French Embassy in Rome. He was not always an enthusiast for the restoration of ancient sites, as least as he saw them proceeding in Herculaneum and Pompeii,[49] but in his *Voyage en Italie* he reflected on the ease of travel even prior to the road improvements. His chapter on a trip to Naples provides a memorable description:

> Behold the personages, the equipages, the things and objects which one encounters pell-mell upon the roads of Italy: English and the Russians, who travel at great expence in good berlins, with all the customs and all the prejudices of their respective countries; Italian families, journeying in old calashes, in order to repair economically to the vintage; monks on foot, leading perhaps by the bridle a restive mule, laden with relics; labourers driving carts drawn by large oxen, and bearing a little image of the Virgin at the top of a staff, supported on the pole or beam; country-women veiled, or with the hair fantastically braided, wearing a short petticoat of glaring colour, boddices open at the bosom and laced with ribbons.[50]

Arriving in Naples, he noted, you enter the city 'almost without seeing it, by a very deep road. (You can no longer, if you would, follow the old route. Under the last French domination, another entrance was opened, and a beautiful road has been traced round the hill of Pausylippo [Posillipo].)'[51] Yet he also conveyed a sense of loss. Outside Rome, the countryside was desolate, the old empire and its riches gone:

> You see here and there some remains of Roman roads, in places where nobody ever passes, and some dried-up tracks of winter torrents, which, at a distance, have themselves the appearance of large frequented roads, but which are in reality the beds of waters that formerly rushed onward with impetuosity, though, like the Roman nation itself, they have now passed away. It is with difficulty you discover any trees; but on every side are beheld the ruins of aqueducts and tombs, which may be termed the forests and indigenous plants of this land – composed as it is of mortal dust and the wrecks of empires. I have often thought I beheld rich crops in a plain, but on approaching found that my eye had been deceived by withered grass. Under this barren herbage traces of an ancient culture may occasionally be discovered. Here are no birds, no labourers, no lowing of cattle, no villages. A few miserably managed

> farms appear amidst the general nakedness of the country, but the windows and doors of each habitation are closed. Neither smoke, noise, nor inhabitant issues from them. A sort of savage, in tattered garments, pale and emaciated by fever, guards these melancholy dwellings, like the spectres that defend the entrance of abandoned castles in our gothic legends. It may therefore be said, that no nation has dared to take possession of the country once inhabited by the masters of the world, and that you see these plains as they were left by the ploughshare of Cincinnatus, or the last Roman team.[52]

The language of the British Grand Tourists was not exclusive. We find it here too in the French: 'the wrecks of empire', the 'sort of savage' that guards it, the Romans as 'masters of the world'. Even absent an explicit effort to compare empires ancient and modern, the language does the job. Moreover, in evoking that sense of ruin, dust and debris, and with that eye for landscape, Chateaubriand became a model for the new Romantic writers.

12
The Romantics

In 1790, William Wordsworth, then aged twenty, took a hike over the Simplon Pass, following the old Stockalper trail.[1] This was prior to the construction of Napoleon's new road, and the route – which can still be walked – led Wordsworth through a dramatic landscape that he later described in a poem:

> —Brook and road
> Were fellow-travellers in this gloomy Pass,
> And with them did we journey several hours
> At a slow step. The immeasurable height
> Of woods decaying, never to be decayed,
> The stationary blasts of waterfalls,
> And in the narrow rent, at every turn,
> Winds thwarting winds bewildered and forlorn,
> The torrents shooting from the clear blue sky,
> The rocks that muttered close upon our ears,
> Black drizzling crags that spake by the wayside
> As if a voice were in them, the sick sight
> And giddy prospect of the raving stream,
> The unfettered clouds and region of the heavens,
> Tumult and peace, the darkness and the light—
> Were all like workings of one mind, the features
> Of the same face, blossoms upon one tree,
> Characters of the great Apocalypse,
> The types and symbols of Eternity,
> Of first and last, and midst, and without end.[2]

While previous travellers to Italy had been at pains to avoid thwarting winds and shooting torrents, Wordsworth and his fellow Romantics introduced a new set of narratives to the road to Rome. It was not so much that the route changed, but that travellers' reflections did, as they placed far greater emphasis on the natural world and on the setting of the roads in the landscape, amid skies and streams, crags and cascades, which had been of marginal interest to earlier tourists eager to get on to the next stop.[3]

I make my own trip through the Simplon Pass in November 2021. I've been at a conference in Switzerland and mention to my host that I'm taking the train.

'It's mostly a tunnel,' he says, and my face must have fallen, because he adds, 'but you will get a view of the mountains either side'.

The Eurocity 57 takes just over three hours to reach Milan. The scenery out of Bern is a mix of modern buildings and the old medieval-imitation-baroque that got the city its UNESCO listing. Bern's second station is called Wankdorf, the sort of name a British tourist is obliged to snap and post on Facebook with an apology for childish humour. There are more elevated views to enjoy, though: we pass forests in full colour, rich reds and copper leaves on what I think is silver birch, every shade of autumn, pines holding their deep green, other trees fading red; others still clad in falling mist and almost monochrome. The train announcements cycle through the languages. '*Nächste Halt*'. '*Prossima fermata*'. Next stop. At the station in Thun two young men in camouflage fatigues are sitting on a bench. In Switzerland military service (or a civilian alternative) is compulsory for men: 300 days is the norm, generally over ten years, sometimes concentrated into one. A flash of blue sky over Thun, then the grey settles in with a rain shower. The lake to my left has melded into cloud, just a glimpse of houses on the far-side slopes. The next stop, Spiez, has connections for Interlaken, which, as its name suggests, sits between this lake and the next, and then we turn away into a tunnel. Out and it's proper chalet territory: wooden houses and a little more sun on the hillsides. Out again to blue skies, sunshine and snow-topped mountains. Next stop Visp. This time 'next stop' and '*prossima fermata*' are accompanied by '*prochain arrêt*'. Perhaps more people speak French in Visp. Brig, the last stop in Switzerland, gets a French announcement too.

The Guardia della Finanza come round for a customs check. This is my third trip to Europe since Brexit and the first time I've remembered I should pay attention to the new customs rules. I'm flicking through them on my phone but the officer takes one look at my British passport and says that's fine. He asks the well-dressed woman across the aisle how much shopping she's done, and whether she's exceeded any customs limits. They have a bit of banter about how shopping is better in Milan in any case, and he moves on. On my return trip through Domodossola, first stop in Italian territory, I spot graffiti on a trackside building reading 'Love Trains, Hate Borders'.

The skies are very grey now, a pale misty grey, rain streaming across train windows as we follow the valley down. I catch a glimpse of a big stone inscription set into a cutting, but we're moving too fast to read the words. The valley widens out alongside Lago Maggiore, the great lake of the Italian lakes, which seems to stretch for ever. In fact it's about twenty-five kilometres in this section, though the other arm of its waters reaches as far again north to Locarno. We leave the lake behind and hit the plain north of Milan. A muster of white storks stands in a field beside the railway line, one taking off as we pass.

The pioneer of the Romantic vision of Rome was Johann Wolfgang von Goethe, one of the hundreds of German literary travellers who made the journey south between 1452 and 1870.[4] Goethe visited Italy between 1786 and 1788 when he was in his late thirties, meeting various prominent figures including the artist Angelica Kaufmann and Emma, soon to be Lady Hamilton, though only much later, in 1816, did Goethe publish his account of this *Italian Journey*. While writers like Mariana Starke had focused on practical tips for their readers, Goethe's journey had a far stronger sense of aesthetic experience. In the history of travel writing, this marked a division of what had previously been one genre into two: on the one hand the guidebook, on the other the personal essay or memoir. In part, this was a gendered distinction: it was far easier for Goethe to wander off the beaten path or even travel in disguise than it was for Starke (even bearing in mind she had ample experience of travel and life abroad).[5] Goethe's response to the antiquities of the Appian Way, and the Colosseum, gives a flavour of the approach:

> Yesterday I visited the nymph Egeria, and then the Hippodrome of Caracalla, the ruined tombs along the Via Appia, and the tomb of Metella, which is the first to give one a true idea of what solid masonry really is. These men worked for eternity—all causes of decay were calculated, except the rage of the spoiler, which nothing can resist. Right heartily did I wish you had been there. The remains of the principal aqueduct are highly venerable. How beautiful and grand a design, to supply a whole people with water by so vast a structure! In the evening we came upon the Coliseum, when it was already twilight. When one looks at it, all else seems little; the edifice is so vast, that one cannot hold the image of it in one's soul—in memory we think it smaller, and then return to it again to find it every time greater than before.[6]

Both Wordsworth and Goethe in these passages, observing very different sections of the roads to Rome, set them in the context of eternity. They do so in different ways: for Wordsworth the types and symbols of eternity are to be found in the natural surroundings of the pass, while Goethe emphasises the Romans' work as in its own way eternal, at least up to a point. Surveying the wider city, Goethe lamented the loss of the old Rome in the face of its modern adaptations:

> It must, in truth, be confessed, that it is a sad and melancholy business to prick and track out ancient Rome in new Rome; however, it must be done, and we may hope at least for an incalculable gratification. We meet with traces both of majesty and ruin, which alike surpass all conception; what the barbarians spared, the builders of new Rome made havoc of.[7]

Goethe's observations of the city echoed his approach to the countryside:

> Wherever one goes and casts a look around, the eye is at once struck with some landscape,—forms of every kind and style; palaces and ruins, gardens and statuary, distant views of villas, cottages and stables, triumphal arches and columns, often crowding so close together, that they might all be sketched on a single sheet of paper.[8]

Here the ruins of Rome are no longer specific but have merged into a landscape of forms to be admired thanks to the traveller's good aesthetic taste. More prosaically, Goethe observed that 'by the evening one is quite weary and exhausted with the day's seeing and admiring',[9] a sentiment that will be familiar to many visitors to Rome. Yet not all Goethe's travels as recounted in the published book are quite what they seem. He told a tale of getting lost in Venice, but in fact he bought a map beforehand. He was, in fact, rather keen on Italian classicism. He was also, much like our previous writers, suspicious of the 'exotic', disdainful of a proffered view from Sicily of the African coast, and in general focused on Rome as the 'cradle of European civilization'.[10]

Goethe's approach to the landscape was not universally admired, but it was undoubtedly a point of reference. His visit to Terracina is commemorated by two plaques in the loggia of the square marking first its 175th anniversary and then its 200th. I hear plenty of German tourists round here: perhaps it pays to make the connection. An association grew up, too, between Goethe and the area around Piazza Montanara, near the Forum. Here, at the Osteria della Campanella, he is supposed to have encountered a young woman called Faustina, with whom he had an affair and who is mentioned in his *Roman Elegies*.[11] The area was home to multiple artisans' workshops as well as taverns, and nineteenth-century woodcuts show off its lively flea market and street life.[12]

By the time Goethe's travels were published, Napoleon had been defeated, and Pope Pius VII was back in Rome.[13] The end of the wars enabled the return of tourism, which had been significantly disrupted. Despite popular hostility to a military foe, as we have seen, many British travellers had warm words for the improvements to Italian infrastructure achieved under Napoleon. Moreover, while the *Caledonian Mercury* had lamented the papal failure to tackle banditry, Henry Coxe credited the French with addressing that problem:

> The great improvements made in the condition of the *Inns*, are not the only advantages derived from the French in Italy. The dissolution of the monasteries and religious houses, and the appropriation of their magnificent, but long neglected libraries to purposes of useful instruction; the making of new roads, and clearing the old ones from banditti; the use of reverberators for lighting the cities and principal towns; and the

> wise regulations of the police, which have almost effectually sheathed the *stiletto*, and rendered assassination of rare occurrence;—these, and a thousand other minor advantages (not to mention the preservation and discovery of many fine vestiges of antiquity), will be long felt and acknowledged in Italy.[14]

Even Lady Morgan was an admirer. While previous writers – she cited Evelyn, Addison, Lalande, Eustace, 'and an hundred others of inferior note' – liked to make a point of showing off their knowledge about which of the modern roads matched an ancient route, she was more concerned for comfort:[15]

> To those, however, who tremble for the springs of light carriages, and shudder at dislocated joints, *Roman pavements—read*, better than they *tread*; and it is much more gracious to such gothic travellers, to learn, at starting, that the road they are about to pass was made under the consulate of Napoleon Bonaparte, than under that of *Lepidus* and *Flaminius*. The road to Parma, however, unites the two-fold advantage, classic and gothic. It is precisely the track opened by the Roman Consuls, and is rendered smooth as a bowling-green by the French government.[16]

For all the romance of ruins, there was something to be said for modernisation.

Protestant tourism became easier, too, following the death of the Young Pretender in 1788. British visitors no longer needed to be anxious about being seen in the company of the papal court. Hugh Williams observed:

> We have often met his holiness taking his favourite walk near the Coliseum. His morning dress is a scarlet mantle, a scarlet hat, with a very broad brim, edged with gold, scarlet stockings and shoes. When he is met by the Romans, they invariably fall on their knees and he gives them his blessing. The British stand, and take off their hats, and their bows are graciously returned.[17]

In contrast to the years when British visitors carefully omitted any contact with Catholicism from private letters and published work, here the Pope is no longer the threat he was in the period of religious conflict. After the French Revolution and the numerous Napoleonic suppressions (the Certosa di Pavia, noted Catherine Wilmot, had been reduced from 500 to just twenty-five monks),[18] he had become a part of the city's picturesque landscape.

Some British writers retained a more critical tone. In the 1820s, William Hazlitt, by that point a well-established journalist, sent letters back from his tour to be serialised in the *Morning Chronicle*; they were published in 1826 as a book.[19] Hazlitt, from a family of radical religious dissenters, was particularly sceptical of pilgrims, observing that their numbers in Rome were far diminished from those of a century ago: they were 'either knaves or fools' while the 'Popish religion' was a 'convenient cloak for crime, an embroidered robe for virtue', a theme which he kept up at considerable length in his column.[20]

Meanwhile, other newspaper coverage whetted tourist appetites for a return to the continent. The *Scots Magazine* published a column called 'Letter from Italy', while the *Sussex Advertiser* of 4 December 1815 reported that:

> There has lately been found upon the Appian way, near Rome, an ancient sundial, cut upon marble, with the names of the quarters of the heavens in Greek. It is exactly calculated for the latitude of Rome; and from circumstances, it is concluded to have been the discus belonging to Herodes Atticus, and described by Vitruvius.[21]

Two hundred and eight years on, as I made my own journey, the newspapers were still reporting discoveries on the Via Appia, in the latest case a winery at the Villa of the Quintilii.[22] British writers also reassured readers of the improved law and order situation. Hugh Williams, whose *Travels in Italy* was published in 1820, explained that down the Via Appia troops were 'stationed at short intervals; and though one dragoon was shot by the robbers a short time since, the road may now be regarded as perfectly free from danger'.[23]

Occasional instances of violence might even become part of the attraction. Catherine Wilmot's narrative echoes another literary trend – for the Gothic – as she describes the risk of 'horrid robbery and murder' on the roads, the 'fear of stillettos', the 'horror of Desperadoes'.[24] A 'Letter from Italy', part of the regular column in the *Scots Magazine*, offers a fine example:

> As we approached Rome from Baccano, we saw on the way side five or six long upright poles, at the tops of which were suspended the legs and arms of assassins; the curved fingers seemed still to grasp the murderous knife. These horrible objects, shrunk and blackened by the sun, disturb that train of poetical and pleasing thoughts which must pass through almost every mind on approaching Rome,—the greatest theatre on which human power and magnificence were ever displayed.[25]

The author had also enjoyed (if that is the right word) seeing the so-called 'tomb of Nero', located north from the Ponte Milvio on the Via Cassia.

> I scrambled up the bank to take a hasty look of this curious monument, inclosing the dust of one of the most execrable monsters that ever disgraced the human species; the inscription is almost obliterated. I had not time to decypher it, but contented myself with looking at the ruinous fabric, and reflecting for a moment on the dark deeds and frightful character of the man to whom it was erected.

While the Roman roads had their standard repertoire of references, they were simultaneously spaces to which a traveller could apply imagination. That said, some travellers were more sceptical. Samuel Rogers noted merely that he had 'passed an antient sarcophagus on the right, commonly called Nero's tomb',[26] phrasing that does not suggest complete confidence in the attribution. However, he was writing a private journal, not delivering colourful copy for magazine readers.

I take the 223 bus up the Via Cassia from Euclide to look for Nero's tomb. One of my fellow passengers wears a striking tattoo of Jesus across most of his lower arm. Another has a street sign on his skin: Piazza della Libertà. Liberty Square. Off the bus, and I find the monument survives, and beside it a milestone marking the fifth mile of the Via Cassia. The place has, however, been absorbed into the urban sprawl of Rome, and the low-rise apartment blocks, red-brick, shutters, shades and greenery on their balconies, clog any potential vista. I try to set aside the mental image of the twenty-four-hour supermarket, the 'magnificent' furniture store, the tobacconist, driving school, ironmonger and pizzeria that sit across the road from the monument. Someone has torn down enough of the fence that I get a moderately clear shot of the inscribed stone. Beside it, now, is a monument to Italian troops killed on the Russian front in the Second World War.

If the Romantics were less directly engaged with the roads than some, they did have a remarkable impact on the dynamics of subsequent travel to Rome, as sites associated with poets and writers became destinations in a new sort of secular pilgrimage. Wandering through the Borghese Gardens, I encounter a statue of Goethe, an extravagant eccentricity, surrounded by a series of figures alluding to his works, among them Faust and Iphigenia. A Roman pine stands to one side (Wordsworth wrote a poem to those). Byron is commemorated with a statue here, too: he should be holding a book but half of it's been broken off and it now looks more like a sandwich. We're not far from the top of the Via Veneto with Harry's Bar, the Hard Rock Café and a string of hotels. Down the hill from the gardens are Rome's famous 'Spanish Steps' and beside them is the Keats-Shelley House. In this building, no. 26 Piazza di Spagna, John Keats died of tuberculosis in 1821, aged twenty-five. He had travelled to Italy with a friend, Joseph Severn, in the hope that the warmer climate might improve his health, but they arrived only in November, had to quarantine due to a cholera outbreak, and the effort proved in vain. James Clark, a Scottish doctor in Rome, found the new arrivals rooms in this house, which was located in a popular and picturesque area for foreigners. In 1906 the property was purchased by the Keats-Shelley Memorial Association, which now maintains it for visitors.[27] Shelley did not live there: his residence in Rome is commemorated by a plaque at no. 375 Via del Corso, the city's main shopping street. The sign is barely visible unless you happen to look up, which puts you at serious risk of bumping into a fellow pedestrian. Shelley also stayed at no. 65 Via Sestina, but that goes without a plaque altogether.[28]

I visit the Keats-Shelley House to see the relics. That's how they're labelled. Modern pilgrims climb up the steps from the ground floor to view a vase that once belonged to Shelley, and an alabaster urn containing a fragment of his jawbone, one of the few parts of his body that survived his cremation on the Viareggio beach.[29] We step into Keats' bedroom to see the striped mattress and bolsters of a narrow bed, to peer from the window down to the piazza. Here, during his last illness, he thought he was living a 'posthumous existence'.[30]

Others travelled south too: Coleridge had visited Rome, a decade and a half earlier, only to be forced to leave in 1805, when Napoleon ordered the British out.[31] Lord Byron lived for seven years in Italy between Venice, Ravenna, Pisa and Genoa, and featured key Roman sites, including the Colosseum, in his *Childe Harold's Pilgrimage*, in which he evoked the image of modern travellers treading in the dust of heroes. That motif also appears in Samuel Rogers' poem *Italy* (1822), in which the poet looks back on a childhood 'glowing with Roman story' but in which he had never imagined would actually 'live to tread the Appian'.[32] One reason for the roads' grip on the imagination is that we can still share that embodied experience, that we can walk in the footsteps of the ancients.

Byron did not, however, live long-term in Rome. He stayed briefly in April–May 1817 (post was sent c/o 66 Piazza di Spagna, very near the Keats-Shelley House), but travelled on from Italy to Greece where he died in the Greek war of independence.[33] He is nonetheless commemorated in the city. Today a Lord Byron hotel sits just north of Villa Giulia in a back street of the uphill and upmarket quarter of Parioli, where automated gates beside the tree-lined streets slide open for luxury cars to tuck into villa basements. Above the hotel's iron gate is the motto: 'Life is a journey, and to travel is to live twice.' Those aren't Byron's words, but are attributed to Omar Khayyam, a Persian polymath of the eleventh and twelfth centuries. Whether or not the attribution is correct, they give a good sense of how these journeys have been sold over the centuries.

Goethe's house, as with Shelley's on the Corso, is now a small museum. Goethe, too, liked a view, moving to a second-floor room from which he could see the Pincio hill.[34] It may be in the room now displayed as his bedroom that his fellow resident, the artist Johann Heinrich Wilhelm Tischbein, painted his watercolour of *Goethe at the window*. During their stay, Tischbein also produced his more famous work, *Goethe in the Roman campagna*, a two-metre-wide canvas that gives a visual summation of the Romantic approach to Rome and its surroundings. Goethe is reclining in the countryside, around him fragments of ruined architecture that allude not only to Rome but also to

Greece and Egypt. The background hints at the landscape of the Via Appia, incorporating the tomb of Caecilia Metella and the ruined aqueduct.

Tischbein was far from the only artist of the Romantic period to depict the landscapes of Rome. In 1819, J. M. W. Turner sketched a view of the city from Monte Mario.[35] They followed earlier painters whose landscapes incorporated the roads to Rome, from Claude Lorrain in the mid-seventeenth century to William Marlow's eighteenth-century watercolour of a post house near Florence and Thomas Jones' view of the Via Appia as it traversed the Alban Hills, a place he called the 'Magick Land'.[36] Indeed, such was the trend that the location had appeared, complete with the tomb of Caecilia Metella, a 'solitary pine' and the requisite ruins, in William Beckford's 1780 parody *Biographical Memoirs of Extraordinary Painters*.[37]

Today, Keats' tomb is one of the prime attractions of the Cimitero Acattolico, or 'Non-Catholic Cemetery'. Percy Shelley described the 'English burying place' in a letter of December 1818: 'a green slope near the walls ... the most beautiful and solemn cemetery I ever beheld'.[38] I take the metro across town to the stop at Piramide, named for the ancient pyramid of Gaius Cestius built *c.*18–12 BCE and now squashed into a busy road junction. Located to the south of the city centre near the station for Ostia, the cemetery is the burial place for numerous distinguished travellers to Rome. In near view of the pyramid is Keats' grave, marked as that of a 'young English poet' with the epitaph 'Here lies one whose Name was Writ in Water'. Beside him is buried his 'devoted friend and death-bed companion' Joseph Severn. This is one of those phrases that leads the modern viewer to wonder if they were in fact a couple, but in this case it seems not. After Keats' death, Severn made a successful career as an artist, and towards the end of his life became Consul to Rome during the turbulent first years of Italian unification. He died in 1879. Tucked behind his grave is a memorial to a son who died in infancy: on it is noted that Wordsworth was present at his baptism in Rome. I roam the lines of graves. Shelley's lies beneath a tower: 'Nothing of him that doth fade, But doth suffer a sea-change, Into something rich and strange,' reads the epitaph. The Shelleys' son William, who died at the age of just three

1 & 2. Across the former Roman Empire are monuments – large and small – to its road network. The Arch of Augustus in Rimini (*above*) marks the end of the Via Flaminia. A milestone (*below left*) from Ephesus is inscribed with the name of roadbuilder and consul Manius Aquillius, in both Latin and Greek.

3. Echoing a milestone's shape, this silver Vicarello cup is engraved with an early travel itinerary (probably first century CE), listing stops on the road between Cádiz and Rome.

4. Travel brought with it dangers. This votive plaque, from the third century CE, features an inscription thanking the goddess Caelestis for a safe journey, and return, indicated by the direction of the feet.

5. The Peutinger Map draws together multiple itineraries to show the road network in a schematic layout, with Rome at the centre. It survives only in this thirteenth-century copy. The fourth-century original may have decorated an imperial palace.

6. People often feared violence on the roads, depicted here in one of Simon Marmion's illuminations for William of Tyre's history of the crusades.

7. The Bible contains many travel narratives. Duccio's fourteenth-century painting of Christ on the road to Emmaus shows a stone-paved street.

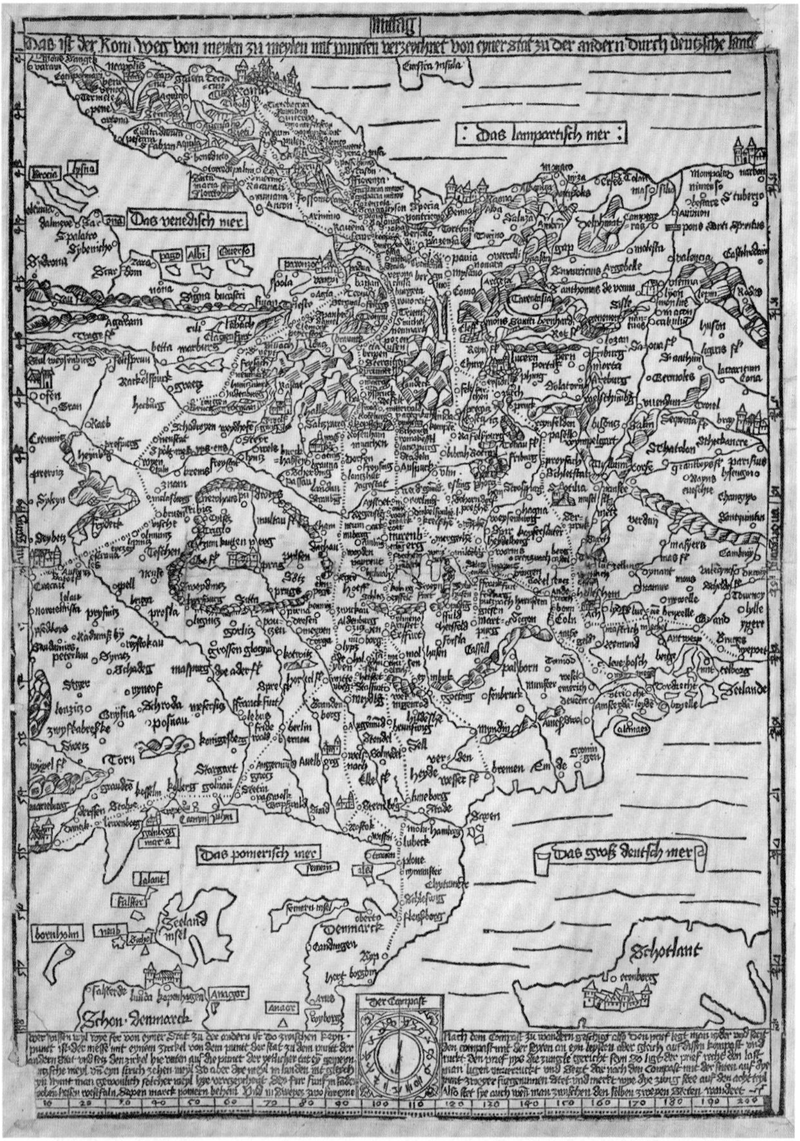

8. Erhard Etzlaub's wood-cut map shows the way to Rome through Germany. It was probably produced for German pilgrims travelling to Italy for the 1500 jubilee declared by Pope Alexander VI.

9 & 10. The development of the Grand Tour brought new business to posting inns, which provided food, accommodation and fresh horses. Travellers sought out ancient sites like the Crypta Neapolitana (*below left*), connecting Naples and Pozzuoli. These became popular subjects for artwork, which could provide a reminder of imperial grandeur back at home.

11. The Napoleonic Wars (1803–15) interrupted travel, but Napoleon also initiated road improvements, including across the Alps.

12. Travellers to Rome would often stop outside the city to enjoy views like this one, painted by André Giroux in 1831.

13. By the nineteenth century the Ordnance Survey in Britain was routinely recording ancient sites. The characteristic straight line of Fosse Way in Gloucestershire is captured in this aerial photograph. The presence of such heritage enabled the builders of Britain's modern empire to identify themselves with the Romans.

LA DOMENICA DEL CORRIERE

	NEL REGNO	ESTERO
Anno	L. 15,-	L. 40,-
Semestre	» 8,-	» 21,-

Per le inserzioni rivolgersi all'Amministrazione del *Corriere della Sera* - Via Solferino, 28 - Milano.

Si pubblica a Milano ogni settimana

Supplemento illustrato del "Corriere della Sera"

Uffici del giornale:
Via Solferino, 28 - Milano

Per tutti gli articoli e illustrazioni è riservata la proprietà letteraria e artistica, secondo le leggi e i trattati internazionali.

Anno XXXVII — N. 9 3 Marzo 1935 - Anno XIII Centesimi 30 la copia

Il Duce vibra il primo colpo di piccone per liberare l'area destinata alla Mole Littoria che, fra quattro anni, di fronte alle glorie monumentali dell'Urbe, simboleggerà la potenza dell'Italia fascista. (Disegno di A. Beltrame)

14. This Sunday supplement cover of Mussolini with a pickaxe conveyed his personal commitment to Rome's urban transformation and in particular the new triumphal route through the Forum, opened in 1932, which offered an ancient backdrop to the modern Fascist motorcade.

15 & 16. Motor transport changed the experience of travel. Aldous Huxley scribbled this postcard of his 1924 tour through Europe for his son Matthew. The glamour of *Roman Holiday* (1953) replaced the images of destruction that had accompanied reports of the Second World War, attracting a new wave of tourists to Rome.

or four, is buried behind Keats, and elsewhere I find markers for the English writer John Addington Symonds, and Goethe's son August. India's first ambassador to Italy, Dewan Ram Lall, who died in 1949, is memorialised here, although his ashes were scattered into the Ganges. So is Antonio Gramsci, founding member of the Italian Communist Party, whose death in 1937 followed more than a decade of imprisonment by the Fascist regime.

The year of Keats' death, which also saw the death of Napoleon, was the year in which Lady Morgan's *Italy* was published. As we have seen, she praised the civilising nature of road-making, but she had more than that to say on the subject of the roads. While most commentary focused on their ancient origins, she drew a link between roads and Christianity, again highlighting the variety of narratives that might be built around their fabric:

> The art of road-making ranks high in the means of civilization; and its utility, better felt than understood in the dark ages, was sufficiently appreciated to render it an object of monopoly to the Church. To build a bridge, or clear a forest, were deeds of salvation for the next world, as for this; and royal and noble sinners very literally paved their way to heaven, and reached the gates of paradise by causeways made on earth. St Benedict laid the basis of his own canonization with the first stone of the famous bridge of Avignon; which, says Pope Nicholas the Fifth, was raised by the inspiration of the Holy Ghost. The *Frères Pontifs* by dint of brick and mortar built up a reputation which rendered their order the most opulent as well as the most revered of their day.

There is no historical evidence for the existence of an organisation called the 'Frères Pontifs' (in English the 'Bridge-Building Brothers'). In the nineteenth century, however, and indeed into the twentieth it was widely believed that a religious order founded late in the twelfth century had been responsible for the construction of bridges along the pilgrim routes.[39] Following another popular etymological theory, Morgan went on to link the title of Pontifex Maximus, used both by Roman emperors and subsequently by the popes, with the concept of 'chief bridge-builder'.

> But if there is one, by whom this significant epithet is merited more than by all others, it is he who made roads, cleared forests, and built bridges, from the Alps to the Pontine marshes.[40]

Her interest here in the medieval past reflects the fact that the Romantics had heralded a greater appreciation of this period of history, which was more easily accommodated in the aesthetic mode of viewing than in the earlier, more classically focused tours.

Among the travellers who enjoyed Italy in the 1840s was Mary Shelley, who returned with her son Percy Florence Shelley two decades after her husband's death. By this time Rome had featured in her dystopian novel, *The Last Man*, in which the protagonist, believing himself the final survivor of a disastrous plague, makes the city his destination. More happily, Shelley published an account of her travels, *Rambles in Germany and Italy*, in 1844, describing a charming carriage ride down the Via Aurelia from Civitavecchia, where they had landed:

> The road for some miles bordered the sea. The shore is varied by little bays, inlets, and promontories—every five miles is a watch-tower,—the Maremma is spread around, deadly in its influence on man, but in appearance, a wild, verdant, varied pasture land, with here and there a grove of trees, and broken into hill and dale: the waves sparkled on our right; the land stretched out pleasant to the eye on the left; mountains showed themselves on the horizon. No one can look on this country as merely so much earth—every clod is a sacred relic—every stone is an object of curiosity—every name we hear satisfies some desire or awakens some cherished association. And thus, in a sort of trance of delight, we were whirled along, till the old walls appeared. We entered by the Janiculum, and skirted the Place of St Peter's; then the pleasant spell was snapped, as we had to turn our thoughts to custom-houses, hotels, and all the worry of arrival.[41]

Although the built environment is present here, the landscape also features strongly: it isn't only the stones that evoke curiosity, but 'every clod' of earth. Charles Dickens, who likewise travelled to Italy in the 1840s, was equally an admirer of the seaside routes:

> There is nothing in Italy, more beautiful to me, than the coast-road between Genoa and Spezzia. On one side: sometimes far below, sometimes nearly on a level between the road, and often skirted by broken rocks of many shapes: there is the free blue sea . . . on the other side, are lofty hills, ravines besprinkled with white cottages, patches of dark olive woods, country churches with their light open towers, and country houses gaily painted.[42]

Dickens was disappointed, however, with his first sight of Rome:

> It looked like – I am half afraid to write the word – LONDON!!! There it lay, under a thick cloud, with innumerable towers, and steeples, and roofs of houses, rising up into the sky, and high above them all, one Dome. I swear, that keenly as I felt the seeming absurdity of the comparison, it was so like London, at that distance, that if you could have shown it me, in a glass, I should have taken it for nothing else.[43]

It is perhaps inevitable that opinions of Rome were mixed. Nikolai Gogol (or in the Ukrainian of his birthplace Mykola Hohol), who spent much of the decade 1837 to 1847 there and like Goethe is commemorated with a statue in the Borghese Gardens, tended to be more enthusiastic. Travel was important to Gogol's creative process. 'I put much hope into being on the road,' he wrote. 'When I am on the road content usually comes to mind and develops in my head; I have worked out almost all of my subjects while on the road.'[44] This resonates. I'm writing more on my travels, away from the routines of everyday life. There's no tidying to do here, no DIY projects to contemplate. I'm not tempted to reorganise my desk. Gogol did not write a straightforward narrative of his journeys but did leave a fifty-page fragment. 'Rome' tells the story of a young prince on his travels, first from Rome to Paris, then after he becomes disillusioned with that city, back again. The return journey is similar to Gogol's own.[45] Gorgeously written, it includes the conventional scenery of the Grand Tour – the view of St Peter's as the prince approaches the city, the ancient ruins that he now comes to appreciate, but also the medieval, Renaissance and modern buildings: 'he found everything equally beautiful . . . He liked the way they merged into one.'[46] He goes out to see the landscape, travelling on what must be the Via Appia, though it isn't named, and concludes with the stunning view of Rome at sunset, now routinely photographed from the terraces of the Borghese Gardens.

The experience of travel, however, was soon to change. The length of tours to Italy was already shrinking. While sixteenth-century travellers had often come for years, effectively as long-term students, by the 1830s the average length of a tour had dropped to four months. The growing numbers of middle-class tourists did not have the wealth to sustain extended trips.[47] In 1844, moreover, Wordsworth had reason to revisit his poem on the Simplon Pass. In England, plans were afoot to build a railway through the Lake District, and Wordsworth pointed to the impact of Napoleon's new road to make his case against it:

> Though the road and torrent continued to run parallel to each other, their fellowship was put an end to. The stream had dwindled into comparative insignificance, so much had Art interfered with and taken the lead of Nature; and although the utility of the new work, as facilitating the intercourse of great nations, was readily acquiesced in, and the workmanship, in some places, could not but excite admiration, it was impossible to suppress regret for what had vanished for ever.[48]

Even more so than Napoleon's roads, the railways were about to transform the experience of travel to Rome.

13
The Americans

Following Napoleon's defeat, it had fallen to successor governments to continue road improvements, not least the new route along the Ligurian coast, finished in the 1820s.[1] American author George Palmer Putnam, who toured Europe in 1836, noted the presence of these roads in his guide *The Tourist in Europe: Or, A Concise Summary of the Various Routes, Objects of Interest, &c*, published in New York two years later. He praised the new Via Mala, which crossed the Splugen Pass to Como: 'excellent, through mountain-passes of the utmost sublimity'.[2] He enjoyed the 'fine mountain drive, replete with the richest scenery' between Turin and Genoa,[3] and enthused over the 'stupendous' Simplon Pass:

> full of Nature's wildest looks and her sweetest smiles, you are conveyed in char à-banc containing four persons, and built so low that you descend when you please. The road into Italy is very sublime, and will be enhanced even by a due portion of, not fear perhaps, but something very like it.[4]

Visiting artists, amateur and professional, looked out for spots on these routes where they could sketch and paint new views.[5]

Palmer Putnam was one of a growing number of travellers to Rome from North America, a trip that by the middle of the nineteenth century had become de rigueur for educated Americans.[6] Back in 1775, Ralph Izard and his wife Alice De Lancey had had their portrait painted by a fellow American, John Singleton Copley. Izard was appointed Commissioner to Tuscany by the Continental Congress, a post that he held from 1776 to 1779.[7] The painting, which may have been shown at the Royal Academy in London, portrays the couple in

Rome, the Colosseum in the background, a composition redolent of the aristocratic European Grand Tour. Engagement with the ancient past was important in constructing the United States' new ruling class, a process in which the awkward fact of the Roman rulers' multi-ethnic heritage was frequently glossed over.[8]

The development of rail travel made the American tour significantly easier. By mid-century steamships were crossing the Atlantic, and indeed these tourists no longer had to rely on the old Roman roads, but might even have taken the railway through the Lake District to which Wordsworth had so vigorously objected. Among the favoured tours was one that began in England. Arriving at the Liverpool docks, which had prospered on imports of slave-grown cotton, the Americans started with the nearby city of Chester, perhaps followed by a trip north to Scotland or the Lake District to see the country of Scott or Wordsworth, before returning south to England to cross to the continent on some approximation of the Roman routes. In his *Transatlantic Sketches* (1875), Henry James described Chester: boasting Roman walls, the town was 'so rare and complete a specimen of an antique town' that others 'suffer a trifle by comparison'.[9] Although it was possible to sail directly to the Mediterranean, Grant Allen, whose book on *The European Tour* was published in 1899, emphasised the advantages of what by then was the 'good old plan of coming *first to Liverpool or Southampton*'. That way, the tourist would start off with the 'relatively familiar' architecture of England and France, and, via the Low Countries and Rhine, Venice and Florence, 'proceed by degrees from the known to the unknown', completing the journey with visits to Rome, Athens and Egypt.[10]

An 1858 painting by Albert Bierstadt shows a pair of American tourists in Rome, one of them clutching a red travel guide as they make their way through a scenic fish market close to the area around Piazza Montanara that had so fascinated Goethe. The artist has elided past and present by showing the locals in the pose of well-known ancient sculptures.[11] From its characteristic colour, the guide the tourist is clutching is almost certainly one of John Murray's, which had become the standard, and was regularly updated. A *Daily Telegraph* correspondent was most frustrated in 1866 to find that the edition he was sold by an English bookseller in Florence was almost three years out of date.[12] The guide included an extensive section on the Via Appia, listed in the 1853 edition as 'one of the most interesting excursions from Rome', suited both for the 'casual visitor' and the 'antiquarian traveller', although the latter might need 'several visits'.[13] These guidebooks reflected extensive archaeological activity by people such as Luigi Canina (1795–1856), probably the single most significant figure in this period in the archaeological exploration of the Via Appia. In 1830 Canina produced a topographical plan of ancient Rome, and as work continued to document and present the remains lining the route, new discoveries included in 1849 the catacombs of San Callisto.[14] Murray's guide likewise recommended a trip to Tivoli, to which 'the road follows the Via Tiburtina, and in some parts traverses the ancient pavement, formed of large blocks of lava'.[15] At Monte Cavi (or Monte Cavo, the dominant peak of the Alban Hills to Rome's south), there was an excellent possibility to observe a road close to its original state:

> The pavement of this ancient road is nearly perfect; the kerb-stones are entire throughout the greater part of the ascent, and the central curve, for which the Roman roads were remarkable, is still visible. Many of the large polygonal blocks of which it is composed bear the letters V. N., supposed to signify 'Via Numinis'.[16]

The references kept coming: the modern road to Naples 'follows the Via Labicana', while on a trip to Ardea, 'about 22 m[iles] from Rome: the road follows the Via Ardeatina, which is still perfect in many parts'.[17] The author regretted that Via Laurentina was now impracticable to travel owing to the trees that had 'so encroached on it in many places that the immense polygonal blocks have been displaced by their roots'.[18] Tourists were thereby encouraged to situate themselves in the footsteps of the ancients, and provided with authoritative information about the roads on which they travelled. That said, the guide did not neglect the modernisations, referring for example to the 'new road recently constructed by the Tuscan government from Civita Vecchia to Leghorn'.[19] Such advice was important in developing tourism along these improved roads.[20]

My own journey to Rome begins not far from those Americans, in Manchester. The 'chester' is a clue to its Roman past. Common to many English place names, it comes from the Latin word *castrum*, for fort, and the military outpost in turn gives its name to Castlefield, one of the gentrified parts of town, its ancient history represented by a reconstructed gate and the foundations of a handful of buildings. Unlike the marching legionary, however, I take a train. It's faster, though not as fast as usual: it's a public holiday and train drivers are refusing to work overtime in a dispute over pay and working practices, so the timetable has been slashed. I'd been worried about having to sit on my suitcase in a packed corridor, but I needn't have been: Manchester isn't awake at 0835 on the Monday after Pride weekend, and the carriage is less than a quarter full. It's been a hot summer, 2022, another record-breaking heat, and as I take the train south at the end of August the green and pleasant land has an exhausted tinge of drying yellow. In London, the Eurostar's delayed: in the end it leaves about twenty minutes late. I haven't taken this train since they built the UK high-speed section, and it zips between concrete, in and out of tunnels, across the flat Kent countryside and into the Channel Tunnel. Out and up and we're into France. Not far off Kent, and yet the pylons are squatter; the cars drive on the right. We're travelling at 297 km per hour, the screen tells me.

American journeys to Rome were framed not only by the advice of Murray and other guidebook authors. Literary texts like *Corinne* and *Childe Harold*, as well as Samuel Rogers' poem *Italy*, and the works of Starke, Lady Morgan and Beckford, were also widely read.[21] Among the American travellers were multiple novelists, including Nathaniel Hawthorne, Herman Melville and Mark Twain, who found inspiration in their walks through the city and along its roads. Hawthorne travelled to Rome largely on the initiative of his wife, Sophia Peabody Hawthorne, partly in the hope of improving her health, partly for her interest in its history (as a teenager, she had read *Corinne*).[22] Peabody Hawthorne wrote her own *Notes in England and Italy* and like so many travellers before, she valued the contact with Rome's tangible remains:

> We wandered about, and walked along the true Appian pavement, lately laid bare by Pio Nono [Pope Pius IX],—composed of large flat stones, more than a foot long and wide. Whose chariots and horses have passed this way? What legions have stepped on these very

> identical stones, with their worn traces, in which I plant my own foot? . . . What way in all the earth is so rich in memories as this?—and I actually step upon it, without any doubt.[23]

While Peabody Hawthorne distinguished her own experience from that of the past, Margaret Fuller, travelling in 1848, observed that this took time: 'as one becomes domesticated here, ancient and modern Rome, at first so jumbled together, begin to separate'.[24] Melville chose a different script, less involved, more cynical, alluding to St Paul in his ironic description of a tomb topped by olive trees as 'sown in corruption, raised in olives'. The Grotto of Egeria did not impress him: 'Nothing very beautiful or at all striking about it.' Still, even he found something to like: the church of San Paolo fuori le Mura (St Paul Outside the Walls) was 'magnificent'.[25]

Nathaniel Hawthorne's *The Marble Faun*, a romantic and sometimes fantastical tale of Italy, itself became a significant influence on fellow Americans' perceptions. Roads were not a particular emphasis of the novel, but no book set on the peninsula could escape them entirely. His protagonist Donatello, travelling through Italy, knelt 'not only at the crosses . . . but at each of the many shrines'.[26] As the travellers crossed the Tuscan hills, the roads and bridges were ever present, and with them the memory of ancient Rome:

> Their road wound on among the hills, which rose steep and lofty from the scanty level space that lay between them . . . A stone bridge bestrode it, the ponderous arches of which were upheld and rendered indestructible by the weight of the very stones that threatened to crush them down. Old Roman toil was perceptible in the foundations of that massive bridge; the first weight that it ever bore was that of an army of the Republic.[27]

Inevitably, as a romance set in Italy, *The Marble Faun* incorporates a scene on the Via Appia, 'this ancient and famous road . . . as desolate and disagreeable as most of the other Roman avenues'. Here it is the tombs that offer much of the atmosphere, conjuring the pointlessness of memory. 'Except in one or two doubtful instances,' wrote Hawthorne, 'these mountainous sepulchral edifices have not availed to keep so much as the bare name of an individual or a family from oblivion'.[28] (The description in Hawthorne's personal notebooks is similar, likewise referring to a 'desolate and dreary avenue'.)[29] Yet even negative representations acknowledged the roads' cultural significance. They could not be ignored.

Mark Twain, whose book *Innocents Abroad* takes gentle aim at American travellers, also listed the Appian Way beside domes, hills, ruins, mountains, columns, temples (and of course Rome's great sewer, the Cloaca Maxima, which now partly drained had become something of a tourist attraction) among the city's compulsory sights:

> The Appian Way is here yet, and looking much as it did, perhaps, when the triumphal processions of the Emperors moved over it in other days bringing fettered princes from the confines of the earth. We can not see the long array of chariots and mail-clad men laden with the spoils of conquest, but we can imagine the pageant, after a fashion.[30]

Twain here sums up the attraction of the Appia as a space for imagination. Whether one was after a vaguely Gothic aura of the dead, or a more imperial allusion, a writer could set it on the roads.

Through the course of the nineteenth century, travellers gained a growing choice of rail. Italy's first railway was the Napoli–Portici line, opened in 1839 and linking the royal residence in Naples to the seaside, much as centuries before roads had ensured convenient access for the emperors from Rome to the coastal resorts. Stretches of the Milan–Venice line were opened through the 1840s, the viaduct crossing the lagoon in 1846. These were followed in 1853 by a line linking Turin and Genoa. This was sponsored through the political process by Camillo di Cavour, then prime minister of Sardinia and a key figure in the unification movement.[31] These technologies not only changed tourism – they helped make a nation. Effective new railways needed political unity: it was hardly practicable for trains to stop for seven different customs checks between Lucca and Bologna. There were many motivating factors for the unsuccessful First War of Italian Independence in 1848–9, but one of them was the frustration of businessmen with the failure of the Austrian rulers (who had followed Napoleon) to take seriously the prospects for constructing new rail connections across Italy.[32]

Among the leaders of the 1848–9 uprising was Giuseppe Garibaldi.

He had been born in Nice in 1807, now in France but at the time of his birth the subject of a tussle between the French emperors and the kings of Sardinia. Sentenced to death for his part in an uprising in Piedmont, he escaped to South America, where he learnt guerrilla warfare in Brazil and Uruguay. Global travel was no longer just a possibility but increasingly normal, and Garibaldi returned to Europe to fight in the First War of Italian Independence, part of a Europe-wide wave of uprisings. This campaign, and that of 1860, illustrate the importance of roads and who controls them. Today at the entrance to the Furlo tunnel, built two millennia before, a plaque marks the resistance of Italian troops to Austrians attempting to march down the Via Flaminia to relieve the Papal States. Erected in 1911 to mark the fiftieth anniversary of the beginnings of Italian unification, it commemorates the efforts of Colonel Luigi Pianciani and his troops in closing and fortifying the pass. Still on the Flaminia but much closer to Rome, I find another commemorative inscription at the Ponte Milvio, this time marking the mining of the bridge on Garibaldi's orders by a 'maniple' of soldiers (the term alludes to a tactical unit of the ancient Roman army), thus delaying foreign occupation of the city. The Via Appia and Via Casilina were also key routes for troop movements from the south.[33] Important, too, were guerrilla tactics in which Garibaldi's army avoided the principal roads to Rome, on one occasion taking instead a 'mule-track' over the hilly territory between Tivoli (on one of the radial routes out of Rome, the Via Tiburtina) and Monte Rotondo (on the next radial route round, the Via Salaria). 'It was,' wrote the later historian G. M. Trevelyan, 'an operation of the most dangerous kind, for if the French had got wind of his return westward they could have poured out from Rome along any of those roads with great rapidity, and so taken his column in flank.'[34]

Following the failure of the 1848–9 uprising, however, Garibaldi found himself fleeing the Austrian authorities, a story most notable here for his need to stay off the busy highways. Finding himself between Ravenna and Venice, he and a wounded companion 'Leggero' (Battista Colliolo) succeeded in hiding with the help of local supporters, although it took them two weeks to cross the Apennines. One night in late August they ran into the major road between Florence and Bologna. At risk of being recognised, one of Garibaldi's companions went for help, but still had not returned at dawn, when 'light exposed the two fugitives lingering on the high road patrolled by Austrian and Tuscan troops. No longer daring to wait . . . they chartered a tumble-down country cart and the sorry jade that drew it, and drove southwards up the pass, meeting numerous Austrian columns on the way.'[35] They were not discovered, however, and made it to the sea at Cala Martina, taking a boat to Elba and then to La Spezia, from where Garibaldi could journey overland, perhaps on the modernised Via Aurelia that Dickens had praised, perhaps by necessity avoiding it, to safety within Sardinian territory at Chiavari, south-east of Genoa.[36]

Forced into exile, Garibaldi travelled to New York and eventually found employment captaining a merchant ship, sailing from Peru to China, back to the United States and then to London and Tyneside. Returning to Italy in 1854, he initially avoided politics, but returned to military service at the outbreak of the Second Italian War of Independence in 1859. Uprisings in Sicily presented an opportunity, and he sailed for the island in the company of his famous thousand men, in Italian the *mille*. (Visitors to Italy will notice that almost every city has a Via or Viale dei Mille.) Having conquered Sicily, Garibaldi and his troops made the march north between August and October of 1860, finally defeating the remnants of the Bourbon army at the Battle of the Volturno.[37] The Volturno river flows into the Tyrrhenian Sea north of Naples, on its way passing close by the royal palace at Reggio di Caserta. The outcome of a battle for Naples was initially unclear but the arrival from the north of the Piedmontese army settled it. W. G. Clark, a tutor at Trinity College, Cambridge, whose account of his trip was published in 1861, saw Garibaldi's troops in Naples:

> In the streets at intervals we found bodies of the Garibaldians with piled arms, sitting or lying on heaps of straw strewn on the shady side; some sleeping, some smoking, some mending their clothes, some cheapening figs . . . all apparently in high spirits and good health, more like 'jolly beggars' than a regular army. A barricade of boughs is placed across the brick arch of Roman work which formed the gate of old Capua and is on the road to the new—distant about two miles.[38]

On 26 October 1860, Garibaldi handed over his southern gains to King Vittorio Emanuele II of Sardinia. This much-mythologised meeting took place at Teano, around twenty kilometres to the north of Capua and according to the ancient geographer Strabo the most important town on the Via Latina, which runs south-east from Rome. (The medieval name for this road, still maintained today, is the Via Casilina, from the Latin name for Capua, to which it led.) Today there are two rival monuments to the meeting. I drive down the E24 from Rome, the Autostrada del Sole, to see them. This motorway is the main route down the Italian peninsula, connecting Milan and Naples. South of Rome it occupies the same valley as the Casilina, the wide Liri, easier geography for the construction of a multi-lane highway than the Via Appia with its marshes and tight turns against the coast. The overhead signage offers reminders of the Roman roads: where Pliny the Younger advised visitors to turn off at the fourteenth milestone, today drivers are told that roadworks await at the 628th kilometre. Teano gives its name to a service area; so does Casilina.

The rival monuments are not far off the main road. One, the Taverna della Catena in the *comune* of Vairano, was a posting inn established in the eighteenth century, and would at least have offered the meeting parties refreshments. Now, although there's a small square brick memorial outside, and the Italian flag flies proudly, the building itself looks rather dilapidated. A few kilometres away, in a more romantic countryside setting, the alternative monument consists of a column more in the shape of a milestone, and beneath it a plinth with a quote from Garibaldi: '*Saluto il Re d'Italia*' – I salute the king of Italy. This was put up by the neighbouring *comune* of Teano to mark the hundredth anniversary of the meeting. I wonder if both commemorations might be right, that the pair first met out of town, then adjourned to a suitable venue so they could meet properly in accordance with royal protocol, and my suspicions are confirmed by a letter from Luigi Farini, a Piedmontese official prominent in the unification movement (known as the Risorgimento), who describes the pair's encounter 'on the road from Presenzano to Teano':

> Garibaldi went forward at the head of several hundred of his red-shirted men, and shouted '*Long live the King of Italy*'. Then there was a chorus of '*Viva*', and the king affectionately took the hand of the legendary hero. We all rode together to Teano, Garibaldi on the left of the king, the

> rest of us – top generals, ordinary generals, ministers, adjutants, and orderly officers – all mixed up with the red shirts on horse-back, Lombards, Venetians, Englishmen, Piedmontese, Genoese and *Romagnoli*.[39]

As with Napoleon, ancient parallels were central to the myth of Garibaldi. He wrote himself, during that first attempt at independence, that 'Rome has been and will be worthy of its ancient glories'. One US senator claimed that Garibaldi had revived 'the spirit of ancient Rome amid the monuments of her power and glory'.[40] In an epitaph, the poet Giosuè Carducci wrote that not only was Garibaldi 'worthy to be compared to the best of the ancient Romans' but that in some ways his sense of humanity surpassed them.[41]

When, at the beginning of the twentieth century, the Cambridge historian G. M. Trevelyan wrote an account of Garibaldi's campaigns, he set out to follow 'the whole route traversed by Garibaldi's column', writing that 'it would, perhaps, be impossible to find in all Europe a district more enchanting to the eye by its shapes, its colours, its atmosphere, or one more filled with famous towns, rivers and mountains, than the valleys of Tiber, Nar, Clanis, Metaurus and Rubicon, across which they marched. Through this land of old beauty I have followed on foot their track of pain and death, with such a knowledge of where they went, and how they fared each day, as is not often the fortune of pilgrims who trace the steps of heroes.' As he recounted Garibaldi's journeys, Trevelyan constantly placed him in the ancient landscape, and just as Napoleon's contemporaries had compared him to the ancient emperors, so in Trevelyan's mind Garibaldi became Caesar crossing the Rubicon.[42] If for many travellers to Rome the railways were now the first choice of transport, Trevelyan's readers would find a whole new history of Garibaldi and the roads to add to the old.

As the process of unification played out, improvements to the railways were going on apace. In Rome itself, these followed the election in 1846 of the modernising Pope Pius IX (a local joke had it that his predecessor Gregory XVI would have got to heaven more quickly if he'd built a railway). A line was built out to Frascati in 1856 and another to Civitavecchia on the coast three years later.[43] For their central station, Termini, however, the Romans had to wait, amid controversy about its siting over the Baths of Diocletian.[44] (The name of the station, meaning 'little baths', alludes to that location.) Constructed between 1867 and 1870, it provided a single terminus for the various lines into Rome.[45] Crossing the Alps, Henry James observed construction of a railway tunnel on the Gotthard Pass:

> half-way up the Swiss ascent, a group of navvies at work in a gorge beneath the road. They had laid bare a broad surface of granite, and had punched in the centre of it a round, black cavity, of about the dimensions, as it seemed to me, of a soup-plate. This was the embryonic form of the dark mid-channel of the St. Gothard Railway, which is to attain its perfect development some eight years hence.

The Mont Cenis tunnel, through which he himself travelled, he wrote, 'savors strongly of the future'.[46]

Railways now are slow travel, the environmentally friendly option (the app on my phone clocks up how much carbon I'm saving by travelling this way). Back then they seemed fast. It's on the slow train from Vienna to Bucharest that I get the best idea of old-school speed. This line has yet to be upgraded to allow fast trains (a project is in progress), and it takes over nineteen hours – a night and most of a day – to travel the 660 miles between the two, an average of 35 mph. I have a wash-hand basin in my cabin, and there's a shower at the end of the carriage, though it doesn't look as if it's functioning. The bed is comfortable enough, though, and I have lots of time to read, and to enjoy freshly cooked lunch – chicken and potatoes with a delicious dill-topped salad – in the restaurant car.

Along with new travel options, reports on archaeology continued to tempt visitors to Rome. On 22 May 1869, the popular *Illustrated London News* carried a report of the activities of the British Archaeological Society in Rome, noting that the remains of the Thermae of Severus and Commodus had recently been discovered on the opposite side of the Via Appia to those of Caracalla. Readers might also entertain themselves with copies of a lecture on the ancient streets of Rome and the roads in the immediate neighbourhood, which had recently been printed. One did not have to travel to Rome to keep up with its roads.

On the other hand, conflict also meant new building on the roads.

Following Rome's incorporation into the kingdom of Italy, the government ordered the construction of fifteen forts and three batteries on the major routes into the city, including a fort on the Via Appia.[47] Even before the Papal States joined the new kingdom, Rome had been incorporated into the railway network, with a line to Naples completed in 1863.[48] William Dean Howells, American consul in Venice, took the new train, which he described in a book of *Italian Journeys*, first published in 1867.

'Nobody', wrote Howells, 'who cares to travel with decency and comfort can take the second-class cars on the road between Naples and Rome, though these are perfectly good everywhere else in Italy'. This was possibly as much a political point as a practical one, though, for he proceeded to blame the popes: 'The Papal city makes her influence felt for shabbiness and uncleanliness wherever she can, and her management seems to prevail on this railway.' Settling into the first-class cars 'which in themselves were bad', he and his party proceeded north through dreary rain. His account gives a sense of how far agriculture still dominated this area of Italy:

> The land was much grown up with thickets of hazel, and was here and there sparsely wooded with oaks. Under these, hogs were feeding upon the acorns, and the wet swine-herds were steaming over fires built at their roots. In some places the forest was quite dense; in other places it fell entirely away, and left the rocky hill-sides bare, and solitary but for the sheep that nibbled at the scanty grass, and the shepherds that leaned upon their crooks and motionlessly stared at us as we rushed by.

The exception to this rule was their glimpse of the monastery at Montecassino, 'perched aloft on its cliff and looking like a part of the rock on which it was built'.

Howells also gives us a rare observation on the workers of the railway, noting that: 'Here and there repairs were going forward on the railroad, and most of the laborers were women.' (This may be because their male counterparts were away at war, or perhaps this was simply a matter of supplementing a farmer's agricultural wage.) Howells' extensive commentary on the 'spectacular' appearance of these women ('stately grace' . . . 'brave black eyes, such as love to look and be looked at') gives an insight into male travellers' attitudes towards Italian women.[49] I hope Howells had better manners when dealing with his chambermaids.

With the development of railways came the construction of new, convenient hotels. Among them is my accommodation in Genoa: the Grand Hotel Savoia, founded in 1897, sits opposite the Piazza Principe station. Genoa is a long, thin stretch of seafront: a container port, a marina, an airport. The hotel is marble, mosaic, old wood, lots of drapery, a surfeit of pillows (four), bolsters (two, striped satin) and a velvet cushion on the bed. It has proper wooden hangers. They trust the guests. The wardrobe/minibar/safe unit is modern, but the desk looks older, and an antique trunk at the foot of the bed hints at traditional seafaring travel style. One thing you do get in a Grand Hotel (unlike most in Italy) is a proper bath. I put on the obligatory white towelling bathrobe and fill the tub with bubbles. The advertising on the international BBC News website is trailing Sotheby's auction of a 'princely collection' in Paris and telling me that shopping in Istanbul is 'the new cool', alongside continuing bleak news on fuel bills. Upstairs there's a rooftop bar, two jacuzzis, and a view of cruise ships and container cranes. Unlike Naples, Genoa doesn't manage to split out its glamorous marina from the rougher seafront. Step back, though, and think of this hotel with a newly shining railway and it all looks smarter. Along the street, you can look down onto the railway lines and imagine it new, new without the smog hanging over the harbour from the ships, though probably instead with steam and smoke from the trains, perhaps not so different. It's all burning carbon, one way or the other. It's all clogging the pink evening light.

Not all travellers were keen on the new mode of transport. The writer and art critic John Ruskin, who spent extended periods in Italy both before and after the coming of the railways, was a prominent objector. 'Going by railroad,' he wrote, 'I do not consider as travelling at all; it is merely "being sent" to a place, and very little different from becoming a parcel.'[50] This was clearly a favoured metaphor, because he used it more than once.[51] In an echo of Dickens' observations on Rome, he complained that the railway in Venice ruined the view on entering the city:

> We turned the corner of the bastion, where Venice *once* appeared, & behold—the Greenwich railway, only with less arches and more dead wall, entirely cutting off the open sea & half the city, which now looks as nearly as possible like Liverpool.[52]

In the twenty-first century, the Liverpool waterfront is really quite attractive, but in Ruskin's day it had less pleasant connotations (and Ruskin had very particular ideas of good taste). Still, he was not the only traveller to prefer old-fashioned transport. Elpis Melena, whose 1861 memoir combined travel narrative with recollections of her friendship with Garibaldi, likewise complained that:

> The beautiful road that leads from Florence to Pisa, through the vale of the Arno, that garden of Tuscany, over which, in bygone days, the diligence and the vetturino were constantly passing, might now almost be struck out of the map; for where the railroad now makes its appearance the roads become next to useless, and all the poetry and all the enjoyment of travelling vanish, and only the disagreeables remain. The names of the cities and stations through which the hissing engine wings its demoniacal flight, fall only half pronounced upon the tourist's ear. A busy official is forever opening the doors of his ambulatory prison, only to shut them again.[53]

Travellers by train, she feared, were missing out on views of picturesque villages, of which now they got the merest glance from the train window. In some of the railway complaints there's a definite moralising tone of disapproval. W. G. Clark, the Cambridge tutor, was less than impressed by the potential to skimp on actual engagement with the sites:

> We stopped at ... Civita Vecchia ... to enable a party of American gentlemen to pay their visit to Rome, by aid of the new railway. They returned in triumph, having effected their purpose, and spent, as they said, 'fifty minutes, sir, in the E-ternal City!'.[54]

I have to confess to sharing Clark's attitude when, in Italy for the first time and visiting Florence, I heard fellow tourists in my youth hostel deciding on a day trip to Rome. A day trip? To Rome? And that was before the high-speed trains. Rome wasn't built in a day, and it certainly shouldn't be tripped in one. I have some sympathy with the critics of modern trains. Every time I take one of the new fast trains between Bologna and Florence, the Frecce or 'arrows', I experience my own disappointment. Twenty years ago, the trip was an hour of scenic twining through the Apennines. Now there's a tunnel almost all the way.

George Eliot, who made her own journey to Rome by train in 1860, was disappointed by the experience of arriving. In contrast to the dramatic view from the heights of the Via Cassia that had impressed so many earlier tourists, for Eliot there was 'nothing imposing to be seen'.

> The chief object was what I afterwards knew to be one of the aqueducts, but which I then in the vagueness of my conceptions guessed to be the ruins of baths. The railway station where we alighted looked remote and countrified: only three omnibuses and one family carriage were waiting, so that we were obliged to take our chance in one of the omnibuses ... we walked out to look at Rome – not without a rather heavy load of disappointment on our minds from the vision we had had of it from the omnibus windows. A weary length of dirty streets had brought us within sight of the dome of St. Peters which was not impressive ... Not one iota had I seen that corresponded with my preconceptions.[55]

The *Daily Telegraph* correspondent was also unimpressed when, on arriving by train in Rome, the commissionaire of the Hotel d'Angleterre enquired whether he would prefer a cab or an omnibus. 'An omnibus!' he exclaimed, lamenting that 'Rome is no more as she has been'.[56] Olave Potter, author of a book on *The Colour of Rome*, observed that:

> You may very well think of Savonarola when you see a sombre-eyed Dominican frowning in the piazza; for Rome is a city of dreams, where it is easy for the mind to hark back to the past; but your dreaming is apt to be roughly broken when you see him signal to the driver of one of the little red Roman buses.[57]

The artist Yoshio Markino, with whom she collaborated on that book, had likewise been dismayed by the 'hideous electric trams'.[58]

Indeed, as early as 1856, wires were raising eyebrows as visitors on the Via Appia observed the telegraph line that now ran beside the road.[59] Half a century later, the complaints were continuing. In his *Incidents of*

European Travel, Gregory Doyle declared himself 'shocked and almost scandalized to note that modern irreverence had boldly planted ordinary telegraph poles on the last resting places of the famous emperors of ancient Rome'.[60] One visitor, Camilla Crosland, put pen to paper to compose two sonnets on the subject. The first imagines the ancient Romans building tombs, their 'conquering legions' riding the road along with 'captives . . . and caged wild beasts'. In contrast, however:

> To-day, how different is the throng that treads
> The far-famed Appian Way! But still the sky
> Looks down benign, with soft and great blue eye;
> And now the marble mounds, like giant beads,
> Seem hung on beauty's neck; for lo! The threads
> Of fine electric wire pass tremblingly
> Along the sombre rows—make destiny
> To Nations, and show forth their instant deeds!
> Do the great Pagans from their Hades soar
> To know such uses of their ancient tombs,
> And feel the world is shaken to its core
> By throbs of all that in the future looms?
> Past voices speak amid the Present's roar,
> And to the listening ear their murmur comes.[61]

Not all tourists cared, however. After the disappointment of her arrival by train, George Eliot listed 'the drive along the Appian Way to the tomb of Cecilia Metella, and the view from thence of the Campagna bridged by the aqueduct' as one of the Roman experiences she 'most delighted in'.[62] The challenge of reconciling modern electrics with historic authenticity continues to this day. In the medieval district of Viterbo, electric street lamps are framed with the outline of a candle-lit version, the better to convey a sense of the generally old-fashioned. Modern convenience – whether for residents or travellers – comes at a cost.

14
New narratives, old empires

The process of Italian unification coincided with the publication in 1861 of the first Baedeker guide to Italy, not to mention the development of the holidays run by Thomas Cook, whose London shop opened four years later. Henry James, who did the European tour in 1869–70, noted that: 'though, as a fastidious few, we laugh at Mr. Cook, the great *entrepreneur* of travel, with his coupons and his caravans of "personally-conducted" sight-seers, we have all pretty well come to belong to his party in one way or another'[1]. E. M. Forster, whose novel *A Room With A View* was inspired by his own Italian journey, was happy to settle for the standard tourist spots, writing home to friends that 'the orthodox Baedeker-bestarred Italy – which is all I have yet seen – delights me so much that I can well afford to leave the Italian Italy for another time'.[2]

It had taken most of the 1860s to complete the unification of Italy. The first Italian parliament had met in Turin on 18 February 1861. Substantial territories of the Papal States, including the second city of Bologna, had joined the unified kingdom. Rome and Venice, however, remained outside. In 1866 a war broke out between Austria and Prussia, which had direct implications for the new Italian government because since the fall of the Venetian Republic in 1797 Venice and its mainland territories had been under Austrian rule. Italy sided with Prussia and after a referendum viewed with some suspicion for its huge majority in favour of adhering to Italy, Venice joined the new kingdom. That still left Rome, where Garibaldi's troops were again defeated in 1867. In a dry letter, George P. Marsh, American minister in Florence (since 1865 the capital of the unified Italian states), observed that it was hardly the talk of the roads:

> While I have abundant evidence that very deep feeling exists, I did not, in travelling by public conveyance from the Italian border on the Simplon road to Florence, hear from the lips of any person around me a single allusion to the important events now occurring in Italy, except in answer to my inquiries for the latest intelligence.[3]

The defeat was only temporary. Following the withdrawal of the French garrison that had guaranteed the Papal States' continuing independence, in 1870, to only token resistance, Italian troops entered the city. The following year, Rome was for the first time in almost one-and-a-half millennia *Roma capitale*.

Alongside roads and railways, this newly united Italy developed a new and more professional history that informed its visitors. Formally more objective (though in fact with its own biases towards high politics and international relations), this scholarship was part of a wider European trend of history in service of the modern nation state. Even at the time, however, some observers were conscious of the limits of an approach focused too heavily on 'great men'. Among them was Giuseppe Mazzini, one of the leading thinkers of the Risorgimento, who took road building as a metaphor: 'The great men of the earth are but the marking stones on the road of humanity: they are the priests of its religion . . .'[4] The idea of making more of Rome's history was hardly new. For more than a century successive rulers had intervened to preserve parts of the Via Appia.[5] From the tourist point of view, however, scholarly debates about history and archaeology – much as they keep people like me in a job – made interpreting Rome more rather than less complex. As Dory Agazarian observed in a study of Victorian travellers, 'while physical "roads to Rome" were easier to navigate, the imaginative roads were fraught with complications'.[6] Since the eighteenth century, books like Addison's *Remarks on Several Parts of Italy* had helped travellers situate their own visits in relation to ancient voices, but their apparent authenticity could be misleading. Besides straightforward moments of confusion about what was or was not the Via Appia, they often cited texts written centuries after the fact as if they were eyewitness accounts. In response, an 1838 *History of Rome* by Thomas Arnold, headmaster of Rugby School, incorporated the old stories but distinguished them from those with better historical evidence. Being told that 'we don't really know', however, was not necessarily attractive to the visitor hoping for firm facts.[7]

Archaeological projects, which at least promised material evidence, were welcomed by the new Italian government, especially if they could find precedents for the kingdom of Italy. The Lapis Niger shrine, excavated in the Forum at the turn of the nineteenth to the twentieth century, referred to a king, which fitted the national narrative of the new Italian monarchy nicely (though there are debates about exactly what its inscription means).[8] Other archaeological findings, however, were not always so straightforward to incorporate, and for tourists the situation was frankly confusing. In 1854 Frances Elliot, a middle-class English traveller, lamented the need for several guidebooks, and some tourists simply gave up on the facts in favour of fun. If they were enjoying themselves, that was enough.[9] As Grant Allen observed in his later guide: 'I am not writing for people who want to see the Wall of Servius Tullius or the Cloaca Maxima. These things are for specialists; when you are in London, you will not enquire into the Outfall of the Metropolitan Sewers at Barking.'[10]

Alongside the ancient sites, Rome's later history became formalised as part of the attraction. This was no longer only a classical tour. In 1889 Pope Julius III's elaborate Renaissance villa, the Villa Giulia, opened as an Etruscan museum dedicated to the earliest, pre-Roman history of the Italian peninsula. The Keats-Shelley House was developed for those keen on the Romantics. Important works on the Italian Renaissance were published: first, in Switzerland, Jacob Burckhardt's *The Civilisation of the Renaissance in Italy* (1860), followed in England by John Addington Symonds' *The Renaissance in Italy* (1875–86) and the works of Walter Pater and Julia Ady. Botticelli became newly fashionable, and the *Mona Lisa* such a focus for romantic speculation that when in 1911 it was stolen from the Louvre (only reinforcing its fame) Bernard Berenson, doyen of Renaissance art history, declared he was 'glad to be rid of her'.[11] All this was reflected in the guidebooks. It was not only American literary travellers who engaged with the work of their predecessors. In the twentieth century, both W. G. Sebald and Franz Kafka followed Goethe.[12] Like Sophia Peabody Hawthorne, Ibsen consulted *Corinne*.[13] George Eliot had been moved by the graves of Keats and Shelley; Oscar Wilde visited Keats' grave too, and wrote a sonnet about it (and, incidentally, asked his correspondents to address letters via Thomas Cook).[14]

Rome's role as capital of Italy demanded new, national monuments. In 1885, construction of the monument to King Vittorio Emanuele II, the Vittoriano, Altare della Patria, began on the Capitoline hill. Now occupying a full side of the rise, and from 1921 incorporating the tomb of the unknown soldier,[15] the white marble monument, completed only in the 1930s, dominates visitors' arrival at the Forum from the city centre. Its shape and extravagance (or vulgarity, depending on your point of view) have gained it the nicknames of 'typewriter', 'wedding cake' or 'luxury urinal'. Subtle it is not.

This wider range of options made for an eclectic range of narratives of travel to Rome. Many still deployed the traditional motifs, whether of Roman greatness or of the city's Christian past (with more or less explicit reference to persecution). They also harked back to Romantic accounts that were now almost a century old. When Henry James made his Alpine crossing over 'the lovely Scheideck pass, from Grindelwald to Meyringen' the roads were evidently busy, but his description of the traffic owes much to Romanticism:

> It is hardly an exaggeration to say that the road was black with wayfarers. They darkened the slopes like the serried pine forests, they dotted the crags and fretted the sky-line like far-browsing goats, and their great collective hum rose up to heaven like the uproar of a dozen torrents.[16]

Enjoying rides out from Rome, James left the city on the Via Flaminia, 'out of the Porta del Popolo, to where the Ponte Molle, whose single arch sustains a weight of historic tradition, compels the sallow Tiber to flow between its four great-mannered ecclesiastical statues, over the crest of the hill, and along the old posting-road to Florence'.[17] Elpis Melena, whose *Recollections of General Garibaldi* were published in 1861 (and who was no admirer of the railways) praised the recent restoration of the Via Flaminia between Rome and Civita Castellana. This road had fallen into 'entire neglect and disuse,' she wrote, 'since Pius VI formed a post road through Nepi' (in the final quarter of the eighteenth century). The current pope, however (Pius IX), had

had it restored, and it was 'now used by all the vetturini going to Ancona, or to Florence by way of Perugia, as they gain by it the advantage of level ground and a diminution of distance'.[18] Further north, she described a 'capital road, which has been formed on the foundation of the ancient "Via Emilia"'.[19] Elsewhere, other new roads had been opened up, for example, the pass of San Godenzo. Crossing the Apennines, this connected Florence with Rimini and Ravenna.[20] There were new forms of transport, too, as James observed in *Italian Hours*:

> The youth of Rome are ardent cyclists, with a great taste for flashing about in more or less denuded or costumed athletic and romantic bands and guilds, and on our return cityward, toward evening, along the right bank of the river, the road swarmed with the patient wheels and bent backs of these budding *cives Romani* quite to the effect of its finer interest.[21]

The nineteenth century also saw the rise of what we might call a virtual Grand Tour. John Ruskin commissioned copyists to reproduce the best of Italy for the artisans of England's industrial north: if they couldn't travel themselves, they could visit his new museum in Sheffield. The collection is now shown on rotation in Sheffield's art gallery so I don't need to take the roads to Rome: an hour through the Peak District and the copies are in front of me. Of course, there were limits to this experience: no sounds, no smells, no taste, although there is a recipe book in the collection. Rome was not at the centre of Ruskin's early work, and it was only during his later visits (which post-dated unification) that his view of the city changed, a product of his own developing religious ideas, and the change in Rome itself.[22] Still, visiting in Wiltshire he could appreciate the presence of 'a Druid circle—and a British fort—(and tumuli as many as you liked like molehills)—and a Roman Road—and a Dyke of the Belgae—all mixed up together in a sort of Antiquarie's giblet pie'.[23] Indeed, by this time Ruskin and other travellers could rely on proper coverage of antiquities on their Ordnance Survey maps of Britain, although the process by which this had developed was haphazard. Surveyors had initially followed existing county maps, commercially produced, which included ancient features as a matter of interest to their educated customers. Some were more interested in archaeology than others, and the maps for different parts of Britain are inconsistent. Only in 1816 was it made a formal instruction: 'That the remains of ancient Fortifications, Druidical Monuments, vitrified Forts and all Tumuli and Barrows shall be noticed in the Plans whenever they occur.'[24] Even then, Roman roads were not on the official list. By the later nineteenth century, as a large-scale map was produced, archaeological societies were lobbying for (and assisting with) more systematic inclusion of antiquities, and surveyors were required to acquaint themselves with the local history.[25]

Armchair travellers might also have enjoyed the experiences of Dorothea Brooke, a protagonist of George Eliot's *Middlemarch* (published 1871–2), who spends her honeymoon in Rome with her older, intellectual husband. Fast becoming disillusioned with him, Dorothea drives out to the Campagna to escape the overwhelming impact of the city.

> She had been led through the best galleries, had been taken to the chief points of view, had been shown the grandest ruins and the most glorious churches, and she had ended by oftenest choosing to drive out to the Campagna where she could feel alone with the earth and sky, away from the oppressive masquerade of ages, in which her own life too seemed to become a mask with enigmatical costumes.[26]

For Dorothea, a ride that surely takes in one of the Roman roads is thus less a matter of engagement with the city and its past than a flight from it (and its Catholicism) towards nature. The roads here are less symbolic and more simply an escape route.

In contrast, for Sigmund Freud the journey to Rome had heavy cultural significance. Although he eventually travelled to the city seven times, out of twenty-four Italian trips in total, he initially found himself inhibited from visiting.[27] It was not until 1901, a full quarter-century after he had taken his first Italian journey that he went to Rome at all. In the meantime he had published his major work, *The Interpretation of Dreams*, which featured several dreams focused on his imaginings of the city and Italy more generally.[28] One of them involves the image of a telegram, on which is printed an Italian address, perhaps a *Via* or *Villa*. In another, Freud is 'looking out of a railway carriage window at the Tiber and Ponte Sant'Angelo', an impossibility for anyone familiar with the actual lines, but a well-known view in the contemporary art of Rome. In another, Freud looks down at Rome 'half-shrouded in mist' from the top of a hill, a classic first impression of the city. In further analysis, Freud concludes that a reference to asking the way 'was a direct allusion to *Rome*, since it is well-known that all roads lead there'. Later, he identifies himself with Hannibal, the Carthaginian general, who likewise had not seen Rome.[29] Only after working through the meaning of these dreams did Freud feel able to make his own journey.[30]

Yet if Eliot's Protestant Dorothea was disturbed by her experience of Rome, this was also a period in which Catholic travellers reasserted themselves against that strand of Protestant writing which portrayed the city as superstitious and the papacy as corrupt. Handbooks like *The Catholic Pilgrim's Guide to Rome* offered an alternative to the standard guides, emphasising themes of faith and renewal.[31] Such travel had continued in parallel with the more classically oriented Grand Tour. Travelling the Appian Way in 1814, Samuel Rogers had encountered 'two Pilgrims on their way to the Santa Casa in the Church of Loretto. Each with his staff, his flask, & wallet; & a silver cross wrought on his oil-skin. They said they were to get their cockle-shells at Loretto.'[32] To this day, tourists in Rome are presented with the options of the 'standard' and 'Christian' open-top bus tours. These distinctions might seem something of the past, but my own family background is a mix of middle-of-the-road Church of England and more seriously Nonconformist, and even in the 1990s the idea of going to see art in churches was a novelty to twenty-something me.

If some narratives of the roads drew strongly on past tradition, others served new purposes. Among the travellers who made the journey to Rome in those post-unification years was the abolitionist, Frederick Douglass. Like so many American travellers, he crossed the Atlantic to Liverpool, arriving in Rome in January 1887 after an extended stay in Paris. There he met other African-Americans already resident in the city, including Sarah Parker Remond, who twenty years before had qualified as a physician in Florence, and Edmonia Lewis, a sculptor of both African and Native American descent.[33] Parker Remond, who died in Rome in 1894, was buried in the Non-Catholic Cemetery, though the memorial to her is modern, erected only in 2013. While Rome presented some wider opportunities for African-American women at this time than the United States, Lewis still felt constrained to sculpt figures who appeared European.

Black travellers had a variety of experiences on the roads to Rome. In 1851, David F. Dorr, then in his early twenties, had made a journey to Europe, which he described in a book entitled *A Colored Man Round the World*. Dorr, who seems to have passed as white, was enslaved and travelled in the company of his legal owner Cornelius Fellowes, who on Dorr's account treated him like a son, but who later failed to free Dorr as he had promised.[34] It was after Dorr's escape that he published his travel book, in which he made his slave status very clear, while simultaneously presenting himself as a gentleman of leisure, including on the Roman roads.[35] Having 'left Rome in its decay of tyrannical monuments,' Dorr headed down the Appian Way towards Naples in the company of E. G. Squires, 'the author of a book of discoveries'. Squires was, on Dorr's account, 'well versed in Roman lore', and acted as something of a guide, pointing out walls, and the gate, and, near Albano, a 'tall monumental tomb of white marble' which he claimed was that of Pompey the Great.[36] This companion was presumably E. G. Squier, an archaeologist best known for his work on the Americas, and this trip out, like much of the journey, situates Dorr in the typical position of a white European Grand Tourist accompanied by an expert tutor. Such privilege was not always, however, afforded to Black travellers in Europe. An unnamed servant from Mozambique who accompanied the author Maria Graham on her travels through Italy became the subject of curious gazes from the local peasants, who apparently told Graham that his appearance 'would most probably frighten any robbers we might meet; a black man being so rare here that something almost supernatural is attached to his appearance'; the locals insisted on bringing out their children to him 'to be kissed, as a charm against certain infantile diseases'.[37]

Frederick Douglass' visit to Rome came in 1887, when he was about seventy years of age. It was not the first time he had visited Europe: in the 1840s he had toured Britain and Ireland campaigning for the abolition of slavery. In making the journey to Rome, while Douglass followed in the footsteps of a white Western elite, acknowledging southern France and northern Italy as 'the cradle in which the civilization of Western Europe and of our own country was rocked and developed',[38] he simultaneously challenged that narrative. Pointing to Rome in discussions of the American present, including in relation to race, was not new. Thomas Jefferson, for example, had famously contrasted the Roman system of slavery, which enslaved white people, with that of the United States, arguing that the US could not manumit to the same extent as the Romans because Black people were by nature inferior.[39]

Douglass' account of his journey reworks the typical narrative of the white Grand Tourist, so it becomes, in the words of scholar Robert S. Levine, a 'journey towards blackness'.[40] A traveller between Paris and Rome, wrote Douglass, would observe:

> An increase of black hair, black eyes, full lips, and dark complexions. He will observe a Southern and Eastern style of dress; gay colors, startling jewelry, and an outdoor free-and-easy movement of the people.[41]

Douglass evoked further parallels: in France and Italy the people, like Africans, would 'congregate at night in their towns and villages'; they would carry burdens on their heads. At the Palais des Papes in Avignon he noted that 'a difference of religion in the days of this old palace did for a man what a difference of color does for him in some quarters at this day'. Unlike religion, however, which had come to be treated as a matter of freedom of thought, 'light has not dawned upon the color question'.[42] Visiting the amphitheatre at Arles, and reading newspaper reports about prize-fighting, Douglass reflected on the history of human brutality; on the other hand he also found genius, not least that of Alexandre Dumas (also of African descent), who at the Château d'If had 'woven such a network of enchantment that a desire to visit it is irresistible'.[43]

Like so many modern travellers, Douglass was disappointed by his arrival in Termini, although later in his journey he would be more positive about the 'splendid view' of the aqueducts from the train south through the Campagna: 'Few works better illustrate the spirit and power of the Roman people than do these miles of masonry.'[44] At first, however, Rome seemed 'more like an American town of the latest pattern than a city whose foundations were laid nearly a thousand years before the flight of Joseph and Mary into Egypt'.[45] His reference to Joseph and Mary gives an indication of how he would approach

Rome: more as a Christian traveller than through any other of the city's paradigms (though he did quote Byron on the Pantheon).[46] Like Benjamin the rabbi seven centuries before, Douglass made particular note of the monument associated with Titus:

> None of the splendid arches, recalling as they do the glories of Rome's triumphs can, by the reflective mind, be contemplated with a deeper, sadder interest than is indelibly associated with that of Titus, commemorating the destruction of the unhappy Jews and making public to a pagan city the desecration of all that was most sacred to the religion of that despised people. This arch is an object which must forever be a painful one to every Jew, since it reminds him of the loss of his beloved Jerusalem.[47]

It was, however, the history of St Paul that most engaged Douglass. He contrasted Paul's humble preaching with the 'fine silks and costly jewels and vestments of the priests of the present'. There was a certain excitement in occupying the same places:

> It was something to feel ourselves standing where this brave man stood, looking on the place where he lived, and walking on the same Appian Way where he walked, when, having appealed to Caesar, he was bravely on the way to this same Rome to meet his fate, whether that should be life or death.[48]

Continuing on from Rome, Douglass went to Naples and Pozzuoli, where he stood 'upon the spot where the great apostle Paul first landed'.[49] (Douglass is not among those commemorated at that spot today: besides Paul himself, only Pope John Paul II gets that honour.) Douglass followed, moreover, Paul's voyage, seeing Crete, perhaps as the preacher had, and then travelling on to Egypt.[50] Born in Tarsus in what is now south-central Turkey, St Paul had been somewhat adopted in the United States as a saint of colour who had preached to people of all nations.[51] Douglass' interest in his life was not incidental. Nor was his travel to Egypt, which continued his journey closer to blackness. Rome, however, retained its appeal:

> No place is better fitted to withdraw one from the noise and bustle of modern life and fill one's soul with solemn reflections and thrilling sensations. Under one's feet and all around are the ashes of human greatness.

> Here, according to the age and body of its time, human ambition reached its topmost height and human power its utmost limit. The lesson of the vanity of all things is taught in deeply buried palaces, in fallen columns, in defaced monuments, in decaying arches, and in crumbling walls; all perishing under the silent and destructive force of time and the steady action of the elements, in utter mockery of the pride and power of the great people by whom they were called into existence.[52]

The absence of roads from this list of the buried, fallen, defaced and decayed is striking. While much of Rome had crumbled, one part of its greatness still existed, could still be walked upon after millennia. Ending his chapter on the European tour, Douglass hoped that readers would 'rejoice that after my life of hardships in slavery and of conflict with race and color prejudice and proscription at home, there was left to me a space in life when I could and did walk the world unquestioned, a man among men'.[53]

Yet for all Douglass' optimism about that space in life, this was also the height of European empire. Rome and its roads were frequently cited in arguments for European and (white) American superiority. In 1839, the anonymous author of a book on *The Roads and Railroads, Vehicles, and Modes of Travelling, of Ancient and Modern Countries*, described these routes as 'the paths over which civilization has advanced, and is still advancing'.[54] Plenty of space was allocated in this work to discussion of Roman roads, though the author did not assume they were necessarily superior to those constructed elsewhere in the world, and had particular praise for the roads of ancient Mexico.[55] *Roads and Railroads* opened with an epigraph from the eighteenth-century historian Abbé Raynal (author of a book on European settlement and trade in the East and West Indies):

> Let us visit all the countries of the earth, and wherever we find no facilities for travelling from a city to a town, or from a village to a hamlet, we may pronounce the people to be barbarians.[56]

The presence or absence of a road network was thus, to educated Europeans of this period, one marker of civility or barbarity. Grant Allen was firm in his view that in Europe one could find the origins not only of modern art and architecture, but of American 'institutions . . . law . . . thought . . . language'. 'Our whole life,' he wrote, 'is bound up with Greece and Rome, with Egypt and Assyria . . . the lands which lie in the direct line of memory of our own civilisation'. This was, he added with explicit reference to ideas of race, 'the immediate genetic chain of European and American civilisation'.[57] Back in the middle of the century, James Russell Lowell, a prominent American poet, had agreed:

> I cannot help believing that in some respects we represent more truly the old Roman Power and sentiment than any other people. Our art, our literature, are, as theirs in some sort exotics; but our genius for politics, for law, and, above all, for colonization, our instinct for aggrandizement and for trade, are all Roman.[58]

Lowell, it should be noted, was no conservative but a reformer active in the abolitionist cause. The idea of a white, Western genealogy for American culture – one that excluded the continent's indigenous past and confined engagement with African history to an appreciation of Egypt – was widespread, and undoubtedly present in the planning of many European tours.

The Americans, however, had competition for the title of the heirs of Rome. Much later, in the 1950s, H. V. Morton, an English author visiting the city, would find a description of his countrymen in an 1853 book called *Six Months in Italy*. Written by an American, George Stillman Hillard, it portrayed not Americans but Englishmen in Rome as 'the legitimate descendants of the old Romans'. In its time, this had been a hugely popular book, but a century on, Morton (a reporter for the *Daily Express* and bestselling author) found it 'painful reading'.[59] For Hillard, the English were:

> the legitimate descendants of the old Romans, the true inheritors of their spirit . . . They stalk over the land as if it were their own. There is something downright and uncompromising in their air. They have the natural languages of command, and their bearing flows from the proud consciousness of undisputed power . . . They, like the Romans, are haughty to the proud and forbearing towards the weak. They force the mood of peace upon nations that cannot afford to waste their strength in unprofitable war. They are law-makers, road-makers and bridge-makers.[60]

There were visual representations of this parallel, too. Fifteen minutes' walk from my house, a series of frescoes in Manchester Town Hall, painted in 1879–80 by Ford Madox Brown, incorporates both a depiction of the Romans building the local fort, now partially reconstructed at Castlefield, and one of modern Britons constructing the Bridgewater Canal.[61] (The Roman fresco also depicts an enslaved Nubian, an uncomfortable reminder today of how modern Manchester's textile fortunes were made.) Another man with Manchester connections, James Bryce, who had taught at Owens College (forerunner to the University of Manchester) before becoming British ambassador to the United States, saw an explicit parallel between the Roman Empire and the British Empire in India, a topic on which he published a long essay in 1914:

> To make forces so small as those on which Rome relied and those which now defend British India adequate for the work they have to do, good means of communication are indispensable. It was one of the first tasks of the Romans to establish such means. They were the great—indeed, one may say the only—road builders of antiquity. They began this policy before they had completed the conquest of Italy; and it was one of the devices which assured their supremacy throughout that peninsula. They followed it out in Gaul, Spain, Africa, Britain, and the East, doing their work so thoroughly that in Britain some of the Roman roads continued to be the chief avenues of travel down till the eighteenth century. So the English have been in India a great engineering people, constructing lines of communication, first roads and afterwards railways, on a scale of expenditure unknown to earlier ages.[62]

Indeed, a visit to Delhi demonstrates the parallel very clearly. In 1911, the British rulers of India commissioned Sir Edwin Lutyens to design a classically inspired Kingsway (or Rajpath) to be the centre of government for the new imperial capital. Though Lutyens was obliged to make some concessions to local style, with the triumphal arch of India Gate at one end of the boulevard it looks for all the world as if a chunk of Rome has suddenly been dropped into the city.

The civilising mission of the Romans was important enough to feature even in general books for children. *A Picture History of England Written for the Use of the Young*, published in 1866, recorded road building among the achievements of the Romans.[63] A half-century later, C. R. L. Fletcher and Rudyard Kipling's *A History of England* informed its readers that in the decades after Caesar's initial raid on Britain, 'Men began to talk, in the wooden or wattle huts of British Kings . . . of the name and fame of the great empire, of streets paved with marble . . . of the great paved roads driven like arrows over hill and dale, through the length and breadth of Western Europe.'[64] The authors here, of course, omit the existence of the Eastern Roman Empire: what matters in this history is the West. Kipling goes on to narrate, in poetry, the lament of a Roman centurion ordered back from Britain, but longing to stay in his new home country, asking that rather than taking 'the old Aurelian Road through shore-descending pines' he be allowed to 'work here for Britain's sake—at any task you will—/ A marsh to drain, a road to make, or native troops to drill'.[65] It isn't hard to spot the parallel between the Roman soldier posted overseas and the soldiers of the twentieth-century British Empire.

The interest in empire isn't only evident in the texts of the later nineteenth and early twentieth centuries, nor is it solely British. While in the south of France, I take the twenty-minute train ride from Nice to Monaco–Monte Carlo, the starting point for a steep climb up to one of the most spectacular sites of the Via Julia Augusta and another of Napoleon's inspirations: the Trophée des Alpes. It's reached either, sensibly, by bus to the nearby village of La Turbie or, for exercise, by a steep series of paths that lead up the hill from Monaco. It's hot work in September, however charming the pine scent of the 'chemin romain', and I look enviously across at the swimming pools cut into hillside terraces. Luckily there's a sea breeze for some relief. Yet when I get to the top of the hill, I learn in the small site museum that in my quest for the Roman past I've been cheated. There was an ancient arch, but the current monument is largely a creative reconstruction, a project that began in 1910. The name La Turbie comes, by way of the Latin Turbia, from *tropaeum*, meaning trophy, and the trophy in question, a colonnaded monument atop a hill, marked the subjugation of the Alpine tribes under the Emperor Augustus. Badly damaged by centuries of neglect, during which much of its stone was stripped, it was a suitable candidate for restoration in this age of modern empire, and its inscription was re-carved from words noted by Pliny. The scheme was, however, interrupted by war, and completed in the 1920s and 30s, with financial support from a former American vice-consul in Paris, Edward Tuck, and his wife Julia Stell. The rebuilding of the ancient monuments and the imagining of the Roman Empire was not a matter only for one country, but across the western world.

There were also challenges to this narrative, including from beyond the West. In the later nineteenth century, Urdu poet Altaf Hussain Ali, who had worked at the Government Book Depot in Lahore and then the Anglo-Arabian College in Delhi, portrayed the early Muslims as great builders much in the manner of the ancient Romans or modern British. His *Musaddas on the Flow and Ebb of Islam* appropriates the metaphors of imperial greatness from the European powers.[66] Discussing the public works of the Muslims, for example, he wrote that:

> These level roads, these spotless highways with the shade of trees unbroken on both sides / The signs for mile and league set up at intervals, with wells and serais prepared by the roadside, / In these things all made copies of them, and these are all marks which that caravan left.[67]

This could very easily be a description of the roads of Roman Egypt: once again, this history proved malleable enough that it might be applied to all sorts of empires, including those that Western observers often wrote out of civilised history.

PART 5

Marching on Rome, 1900–Present

15
Via Mussolinia

As the nineteenth century turned to the twentieth, tourists continued to visit Rome, as did those studying its heritage. Art and archaeology in the city has always been an international business. The second time I lived there, in 2009–10, I was a Fellow of the British School at Rome, one of a group of international research institutes founded in those first years of the twentieth century. An early director, Thomas Ashby, created an important photographic record of the roads out of Rome, cycling or walking for the best views of the historic landscape, even as regeneration projects began to encroach on the ancient routes.[1] From the British School, it's a fifteen-minute walk to another city institution. Down the hill, past the Galleria Nazionale d'Arte Moderna, opened in 1914 to showcase the national modern art collection, across the tram lines and lanes of speeding cars that fill the Valle Giulia, and up the wide stone steps to the Borghese Gardens. Here I could turn left, a walk I've done hundreds of times, through the dust of pine needles, past fountains and pedalos and skateboarders and out to see the sun set behind St Peter's from the balcony on the Pincio hill that overlooks Piazza del Popolo. This time, however, I cut down the hill instead, past the teens snogging beneath the pine trees, and down some dilapidated brick steps just outside the city walls. A little way to my right is the end of the Via Flaminia. I take the crossing and head through the Porta del Popolo to the grand piazza with its fountain and stone lions. Three streets stretch out from its far side, two domed churches between them. I take the street to my left, Via del Babuino.

The Hotel de Russie here has accommodated guests since the 1820s. The building was constructed in parallel with the remodelling of the Piazza del Popolo, by the same architect, Giuseppe Valadier, and until the Second World War was the residence of choice for many wealthy international travellers, including royalty from Russia, Sweden and Bulgaria as well as cultural figures including Picasso, Jean Cocteau and Sergei Diaghilev.[2] After the war it was for a while the headquarters of the Italian state broadcaster RAI, but since the turn of the millennium it has once again been a hotel, offering exclusivity and tranquillity in the busy city centre. If the Grand Hotel in Genoa had an excess of bolsters, here there are not only excess bolsters, but housekeeping twice a day, once to move the cushions off the bed so you can go to sleep, and once to put them back. This is the distinction between four- and five-star: you don't have to move your own cushions. There are grapes in the bedroom and fresh flowers in the bathroom, but the hotel's great secret are its gardens. All but invisible from the surrounding streets, they're terraced up the Pincio, a private match for the more vulgar public staircase that leads up from Piazza del Popolo. They're green and lush and gorgeous, fountains flowing down what must be the equivalent of half a dozen floors. There's a grotto, lit at night now in electric colours, a few worn stone capitals (probably the real thing), palm trees, umbrellas over restaurant tables, little table lights in the Stravinskij bar.

Ruskin was a guest here in 1874,[3] and the gardens are recorded in a 1920 painting by Duncan Grant, one of the Bloomsbury Group of artists and writers. Grant had a residency at the Villa Medici, up the hill, and his lover Vanessa Bell stayed at the hotel.[4] Italy remained a popular destination for British travellers. Winston Churchill spent time in Rome in 1926, when he painted the Forum and the Arch of Constantine. Vanessa Bell returned in 1935 with her son Quentin.[5] But as Ruskin had appreciated, not everyone could afford to travel. Ivy, Lady Chamberlain, wife of a British Foreign Office minister, picked up the idea, first touted by an Italian critic, that an exhibition of Italian art should be hosted in London.[6]

Benito Mussolini, Italy's new leader, agreed. Travelling exhibitions were providing excellent propaganda for the Fascist regime that had taken power in 1922. He sent out a directive requiring the loan of works 'without any exception whatsoever'.[7] In December 1929, shortly before the opening of the exhibition, the London magazine *Punch* published a cartoon showing Mussolini in Renaissance dress with a Botticelli-esque woman labelled 'Italian art', and John Bull (representing England) kneeling. Playing on the nickname of Renaissance patron Lorenzo de' Medici, its caption read: 'MUSSOLINI THE MAGNIFICENT. For the Exhibition of Italian Art which is to open at Burlington House . . . we have in great measure to thank the energy and enthusiasm of Signor Mussolini.'[8]

At the start of the First World War, Italy had been part of the Triple Alliance with Germany and Austria-Hungary. At the outbreak of conflict, however, it declared neutrality and in 1915 entered the war on the side of Britain and France with the aim of securing more natural borders. Italian victory in the 1918 Battle of Vittorio Veneto was crucial to the defeat of the Habsburg Empire, but Italy emerged from the war with only part of the territory it had hoped for, a poor consolation for heavy losses. There followed the *Biennio Rosso*, two 'red years' of social conflict, characterised by strikes and factory occupations in Italy's newly industrialised north. Yet the militancy was not translated to political power, and as the struggle dwindled the Fascist movement of Benito Mussolini gained ground.

At a crucial moment in 1922, its leadership set up headquarters in one of those luxury hotels: the Brufani Palace, in Perugia. Sitting atop the Rocca Paolina, a fortress constructed in the sixteenth century under Pope Paul III, the Brufani was founded in 1884 to cater to international tourists, and remains an upmarket option with splendid views over the Umbrian countryside. (A few years ago I was a lecturer on a tour that used this hotel as its base. 'Anyone know why this hotel's famous?' I asked the clients on the first night. No one did, so I saved the story for the end of the week. Personally, I would have been quite annoyed to spend that much on a holiday and then discover I'd been put up in the Fascist destination of choice.)

It was on the roads to Rome that the Fascist party staged its 'March on Rome'. This was to see supporters – the *squadristi* or squad members – travel from across Italy towards the capital and assemble just outside. Once the order came from Perugia, they would then march into Rome. Many, including Mussolini himself, in fact took the train to the outskirts.[9] One column of the March moved in from the east, along the route of the ancient Via Tiburtina, across a new bridge at Ponte Mammolo. As a sympathetic writer observed a decade later, along that road were scattered 'numerous ancient remains . . . villas, tombs, fragments of wall—and on the road itself Roman paving stones appear from time to time by the side of the tarred strip'.[10] Once again the Roman roads were a stage set, if this time for a more sinister performance.

It has often been said that the army could have fought off the Fascists, had the king decided to declare that Rome was under siege, but this narrative has been challenged by historians who argue that it underplays the violence of the March. It was convenient for post-war consensus-building to claim that Fascism happened rather by accident.[11] Either way, the Fascists' dominance of the roads was symbolically important. It emphasised their confidence: to march openly left them vulnerable to attack, but that made any martyred Fascists all the more heroic.[12] Some observers, including Carleton Beals, an American journalist, made explicit parallels between this March and those of ancient invaders. Chatting to the 'grumpy-eyed youths . . . with heavy cudgels and guns' who were hanging out in the entrance to the Fascist headquarters in Rome, Beals was told that five kilometres out on the Via Nomentana, which leads north from the city, there were 20,000 Fascisti 'with cannons and machine-guns'. It was raining that day, though, and Beals retreated to his room where, rather than go and investigate, he mused on history:

> Out there, I recall vaguely, near the Mons Sacer, the seceding Plebs had camped twenty-three hundred years ago . . . Over that road had passed the legions of conquering Caesars, coming to take Rome, the Eternal City, the center of the world. How many times? How many times in a year? How many times in a century?—And by that road in 1870 the troops of the house of Savoy had come to batter down the walls at Porta Pia, to found a new nation . . .[13]

Other viewers emphasised instead the modernity of Fascism, and its contrast with the past as the old Roman roads became racetracks for a new regime fascinated by motor transport and a cult of speed.[14]

Not six months later, on 26 March 1923, Mussolini inaugurated a grand road-building project. Europe's first motorway was to run between Milan and the Northern Lakes. The new prime minister did not just pose with a pickaxe, but was reported in *La Stampa* to have struck forty-one blows.[15] Opened the following year, this was the first of several motorways to be built in the following decade, including stretches linking the commercial centre of Milan with Bergamo and Brescia in one direction and Turin in another; leading from Florence to the sea; and connecting Venice and Padua plus, in the south, Naples and Pompeii.[16] There was already considerable enthusiasm for motoring tours of Italy. Francis Miltoun was the author of multiple travel guides to Europe, among them a book on *Italian Highways and Byways by Motor Car*. Published in 1909, it provided a helpful list of those Roman routes that motorists could follow in the present day.[17] The old Appian Way, he explained, 'is still there, loose ended fragments joined up here and there with a modern roadway which has become its successor'.[18] Four years later, in an article for *Scientific American*, Miltoun emphasised the importance of the old Roman network to Europe's road-building progress: 'It is remarkable the wide interest that the road question has for all classes in Europe, and it is this unity of purpose that builds on the network legacy left by the Romans.'[19]

D. H. Lawrence likewise pointed to Roman heritage when he described the experience of motoring through Italy in his *Sea and Sardinia*, published in 1923:

> These automobiles in Italy are splendid. They take the steep, looping roads so easily, they seem to run so naturally. And this one was comfortable, too.
>
> The roads of Italy always impress me. They run undaunted over the most precipitous regions, and with curious ease. In England almost any such road, among the mountains at least, would be labelled three times dangerous and would be famous throughout the land as an impossible climb. Here it is nothing . . . There seems to be a passion for high-roads and for constant communication. In this the Italians have a real Roman instinct, *now*. For the roads are new.[20]

Others were similarly enthusiastic. For Aldous Huxley, 'even the train has become a means of travelling too inconvenient to be much employed', though he was rather jealous of the Alfa Romeo that powered up the Mont Cenis Pass while his ten-horsepower

Citroën struggled.[21] Friedrich Noack, who in the early years of the twentieth century spent extended periods researching Goethe's life in Rome, thought the motor car – in which he travelled down the Via Cassia, across the Ponte Molle and through Porta del Popolo – came closer to his subject's experience than the train with its 'swarms of Philistines'.[22]

Road builders benefited from tax subsidies.[23] Piero Puricelli, whose family firm came to specialise in road construction, was a key figure in the process, setting up a racetrack that remains in use in the grounds of the former Habsburg Royal Villa in Monza, and in 1925 endowing a chair in road engineering at the Polytechnic University of Milan. In 1929 he was appointed senator.[24] According to their advocates, including men like Luigi Vittorio Bertarelli, president of the Italian Touring Club, the new autostradas worked to everyone's benefit. The motorist could drive safely, saluted by the military personnel who staffed the new highways in an echo of the early *cursus publicus*. Those seeking a quieter day out, walking or cycling, could enjoy the peace of Italy's beautiful countryside along the minor roads without being troubled by long-distance traffic.[25]

The motorway construction of the 1920s, while of evident propaganda value to the Fascist regime, was in some senses a catch-up project. At the point of unification the Italian road network had been poor by international standards, partly for lack of investment and partly for the emphasis on railways. Efforts to improve it, including a 1914 plan for a new route along the line of the Via Appia, incorporating a tunnel under the Apennines to carry both trams and motor cars, had largely failed.[26] Now, official lists of roads made a point of using the old Roman names where they could in an attempt to link what might be disruptive or contentious to valued historical tradition.[27] There was even a plan for a 'Via Mussolinia', an extension of the Venice–Trieste route to Fiume in Istria (now the Croatian city of Rijeka), which had been annexed by Italy in 1924.[28] It was no accident that the Duce's name was to be attached to this most explicitly imperial of road projects. For the Fascists, roads could both incorporate new territory and assist in the maintenance of social order, demonstrating the benefits of the regime, at least for those who could afford to run a car.[29]

The early enthusiasm for building, however, faltered. Motorways were expensive and there simply weren't enough cars and drivers in Italy to fill them. An embarrassed expert from the Polytechnic in Milan complained that visiting international guests often raised eyebrows at the lack of traffic.[30] With the economic crash of 1929 came an end to any more ambitious projects, bar one state-funded route between Genoa and Serravalle, just 50 km long. On a more modest level, there were also significant improvements to state roads. Luigi Villari, a writer supportive of the regime, enthused that in the Campagna (the countryside around Rome) there had only been 100 km of roads in 1905, 'most of them very bad', and another 65 km added between 1908 and 1922. Walking the area before the Great War, he had 'found practically no roads, except the main ones bearing famous classical names'. In contrast, 'by 1927, the road system had expanded to 550 km . . . the main roads are tarred or asphalted . . . there is now hardly a hamlet or *casale* which cannot be reached by an excellent or fairly good road'.[31] His comments on the state of the Via Tiburtina, notorious for its 'carts heavily laden with huge blocks of travertine' that were 'chawing up its surface', curiously echo the situation of two millennia before, when the road was widened. 'Now, however,' wrote Villari, 'it has been relaid and tarred, and is very well kept'. Its 'ramshackle steam tram' had been replaced by 'comfortable motor buses'.[32] While Villari was clearly evangelising, there is no doubt that these years indeed saw significant improvements to infrastructure.

As the son of an Italian father and British mother, Villari's background as a journalist and author, as well as his experience as an Italian vice-consul in several US cities, made him the ideal candidate to propagandise in England for the Fascist regime.[33] In 1932, his book *On the Roads from Rome* was published by the London firm Maclehose. In it, Villari wove a story of his travels around the Campagna into a discussion of the many interventions now being undertaken by the government to improve the area. 'Those who are really interested in the Campagna,' he wrote, should 'visit it not once or twice in hurried excursions, but many times, and get steeped in its atmosphere.' Reading books could only do so much.[34] Despite his enthusiasm for 'modern progress' when it came to agricultural techniques and the eradication of malaria, Villari was no great admirer of the motor car: 'alas,' he wrote, it was 'gradually displacing the horse', but horseback was still 'the most satisfactory means of locomotion in the Campagna'.[35] Visitors might explore the 'many lovely bits of woodland landscape', including the 'group of fine oaks at Marco Simone between the Via Tiburtina and the Nomentana, and the famous Sacred Grove off the Via Appia'.[36] (This was a reference to the Grotto of Egeria that so many writers had visited before.) The electric lights, though, were brighter than ever. At night:

> the darkness is lit up here and there by the bright gleaming eyes of Frascati, Rocca di Papa, Tivoli, Montecelio, and a dozen other hill towns, and by the white haze of the arc lights of Rome. About the Campagna itself are frequent bonfires, and every now and then the lurid flames of a passing train or the white flashes produced by the electrically-driven trains and trams give a touch of life to the scene. Many of the *casali* and farm-houses are now lit by electricity, and thus add to the fairy-like glimmer which bespatters the darkness.[37]

Villari was, however, keen to emphasise the long shadow of the past: 'the social and economic problems of to-day are directly linked up with the customs and institutions of the Middle Ages and even of classical times'. He was dealing with a 'struggle between modern progress and ancient traditions'.[38] The Campagna's past was important, but so was its future.

The roads for which the regime is most famous today, however, are not the motorways but those in Rome itself. In 1925, Mussolini gave a speech on 'The new Rome'. 'In five years,' he said, 'Rome must appear marvellous to all peoples of the world: vast, ordered, and powerful, as it was in the time of Augustus' first empire.' This demanded major changes to 'create space' around a series of historic ruins: 'The thousand-year-old monuments of our history must rise like giants from their necessary solitude.' The 'foolish contamination of the trams' was to be removed and from Ostia to the tomb of the unknown soldier at the Altare della Patria would lead 'a straight road . . . the longest and widest in the world'.[39] Though early Fascists were not straightforward enthusiasts for ancient Rome, and sometimes identified themselves as much as barbarians or iconoclasts, through the emphasis on road building these interventions created a direct relationship between the Fascist present and the Roman past.[40] Two new roads were to change the city landscape. One, the Via del Mare, would run south-west to connect Rome with the sea at Ostia (its first section is now the Via del Teatro di Marcello). The other, originally to be called Via dei Monti or dei Colli (Street of the Mountains or Hills), now Via dei Fori Imperiali, would cut through the historic sites of the Roman Forum to create a vista from the Colosseum to Palazzo Venezia (on the piazza of the same name), where Mussolini had his city headquarters.[41] Today, that view is the background to thousands of tourist photographs, many of them no doubt taken with no knowledge of the twentieth-century history.

The street through the Forum was not an idea original to Mussolini or any of the Fascist planners. It had been touted fifty years before, in the first Master Plan for Rome's development.[42] The risk that its construction might damage valuable archaeological evidence was dismissed: surveys were commissioned but what they found was, conveniently, 'not important enough to require a deviation of the road'.[43] To build it, one of Rome's famous seven hills, the Velia, had to be flattened: again, so be it.[44] When diggers found the remains of an elephant, archaeologist Giuseppe Marchetti Longhi cited that as evidence for the area's centrality to 'world empire'.[45] For him the road was an 'expression of fated evolution in the past, present and future of our race'.[46]

Construction of both roads proceeded at considerable cost to the local inhabitants. It was estimated that 138 buildings would be demolished in the construction of the Via dei Monti,[47] while the Via del Mare destroyed further historic sites, among them Piazza Aracoeli and Piazza Montanara, a picturesque part of Rome's Jewish ghetto,[48] which Goethe had enjoyed on his visit to the city a hundred years before. Hawthorne had seen the ruins of the Theatre of Marcellus too, describing them as 'very picturesque, and the more so from being close linked in—indeed, identified—with the shops, habitations and swarming life of modern Rome'.[49] Sydney Lee's 1927 painting of the Theatre, now in Liverpool's Walker Art Gallery,[50] captures the area just before the demolitions, a green-shuttered house close up to the ancient building, clothes and food on sale in its lower arches, a woman walking by with a burden on her head, and a carter waiting for a load. Now, however, the later buildings were to be cut away, so that as far as possible the ancient theatre – like the Arch of Augustus in Rimini – would stand alone. Even writers broadly favourable to Fascism showed some concern. Villari thought the changes to Piazza Montanara 'unfortunate', though he was more positive about the clearance of 'saddlers and blacksmiths' who had once done 'a busy trade' around the Theatre of Marcellus: now, instead 'the arches are re-opened and the stately ancient pile is being restored'.[51] Pietro Fedele, who had been a minister of education for the regime, complained to the city governor about the impact, but Mussolini intervened to insist that they 'continue to demolish and, if necessary, demolish the melancholy of Mr Fedele, who is ridiculously moved by [the destruction] of a pile of lavatories'.[52] Taking up his pickaxe once again, Mussolini marked the start of construction outside the Theatre of Marcellus in 1926, and the road was opened two years later, built by the same Puricelli company responsible for many autostradas.[53] In a nod to the ancient past, it supposedly followed the Via Ostiense,[54] beginning at the foot of the Tarpeian Rock, 'over which the ancient Romans threw dissidents and criminals to their deaths'.[55]

The impact of this remodelling was not only devastating for the residents and traders forced out of homes and shops, it was to change fundamentally the experience of travellers to Rome. In Goethe's day, and indeed through the nineteenth century, it was only by wandering through the twisting medieval streets that they might find the Colosseum, probably getting lost in the process.[56] Now the road to the monument was itself a landmark, no longer, in the words of one Fascist observer, 'suffocated by superstructures, hovels and alleys'.[57] (The same was true of the construction of the new Via della Conciliazione, which likewise opened up a vista to St Peter's, formerly accessible only through the tight streets of the Borgo.)[58] Such was the change to the experience of the Forum that guidebooks had to be rewritten.[59] As the official journal of the Roman municipal government explained: 'The new roads opened between the sacred ruins have revealed previously hidden magnificence and have brought the dynamicism of modern life amongst the glories of the past, providing, in a sense, an urban function to the ruins.'[60] This was not only about new roads: it was also about reshaping Romans themselves. In the words of Antonio Muñoz, an art historian who from 1928 to 1944 was the city's inspector general of fine art and antiquities, the 'souls of its inhabitants' were likewise to be 'built with solid principles . . . Harmony, order, clarity, cleanliness: these are the characteristics of the Rome of Mussolini.'[61]

I take a walk through the archaeological site at the foot of the Theatre of Marcellus. Today's interpretive panels avoid mention of the F-word, though they do explain what was done: medieval and Renaissance buildings were removed to create clear views of the ancient monuments in the same way that the 1930s demolitions in Rimini were passively carried out. Mostly, however, it's left to the discretion of tour guides to explain or not. When I do spot a mention, it's generally original. In Ostia, for example, a plaque still records 1927 restorations, complete with reference to 'Duce Benito Mussolini'. One of the consequences of the many demolitions was that the Via del Mare became a scenic route, from which those monuments could now be viewed from a car. The schemes, however, prompted dispute with the Vatican, which was concerned that some proposed works might damage the catacombs and, more broadly, over the emphasis the regime was placing on the ancient 'pagan' sites over Christian ones.[62] Mussolini took his children motorbike racing along this modern highway, from Palazzo Venezia to a cabin on the royal estate near the ancient port ruins on the coast.[63]

On the train to Ostia Antica, I hope for a view of the extended Via del Mare, which runs alongside the track, but the windows are so dirty all I get is a glimpse of passing traffic, maybe a motorbike. On the train back are a group of lads in black, beers in hand, hanging out the doors at every stop to take another puff of whatever they're smoking in their king-size Rizlas. One has an AS Roma scarf tied around his waist: there's a match this evening and Roma are playing Atalanta, a team from Bergamo, in the north near Milan. 'We hate Bergamo,' they sing, and something about the *carabinieri* with the broad sense of 'all cops are bastards', possibly the 2010 song by the rapper Fedez, a recent revival of which has prompted complaints of incitement to anti-police violence. (Fedez pointed out that his opinions have changed, like those of many people including Giorgia Meloni, front-runner to be prime minister, who in her younger days explicitly praised Mussolini.)[64]

In 1931, the Fascist regime produced a new Master Plan for Rome.[65] Like the earlier interventions it was not universally popular, criticised in practical terms for encouraging 'reckless driving' and, on more ideological grounds, for its overt militarism.[66] The road through the Forum was formally opened the following year as part of celebrations for the tenth anniversary of the March on Rome.[67] Mussolini cut the ribbon while still mounted on his horse, before leading a military parade. As its own imperial pretensions grew, his regime increasingly linked itself to the ancient empire, and in a last-minute change the Via dei Monti was instead named Via dell'Impero (Empire Street).[68] In April 1934, four maps were added to the wall beside the street, showing the expansion of the Roman Empire. On 9 May 1936, Mussolini proclaimed the re-establishment of the Roman Empire from his balcony in Piazza Venezia, and in October that year, following the Italian conquest of Ethiopia, the regime put up a fifth map to illustrate its own success.[69] (These maps are now gone as redevelopment proceeds to accommodate Line C of the metro, but the first four were still there when I was in Rome fifteen years ago.) For the governor of Rome, Giuseppe Bottai, Italy's troops were 'invincible warriors and at the same time builders of roads'.[70] Yet the resonance of military parades along the Via dell'Impero was not only with the ancient past: it also recalled the more recent experience of those soldiers who fought in the First World War.[71]

I've seen a lot of memorials, to both the Great War and imperial enterprises, on my travels. In Monte Sant'Angelo, near the cave church of San Michele, battles in Eritrea (1895–6) and Libya (1911–15) are memorialised on the side of a monument primarily dedicated to those lost in the First World War. In the cathedral at Bari, a plaque dated 1936 mourns the loss of members of the armed forces in the struggle to reinforce Italy's borders and to create a 'halo of imperial power'. In Durrës, on the other hand, multiple plaques around the town square commemorate the Albanian partisans' struggle against the Italian troops who invaded in 1939. And if the maps in the Forum have gone, there's still a reminder here of who was responsible for this road. The monument that marked the opening of the Via dell'Impero stands at its beginning, behind the Altare della Patria. A round pillar, after the fashion of a Roman milestone, unassuming by comparison to the surrounding monuments, on which is written:

REGNANDO	IN THE REIGN OF
VITTORIO EMANUELE III	VITTORIO EMANUELE III
BENITO MUSSOLINI	BENITO MUSSOLINI
CAPO DEL GOVERNO	HEAD OF GOVERNMENT
FRANCESCO BONCOMPAGNI	FRANCESCO BONCOMPAGNI
LUDOVISI	LUDOVISI
GOVERNATORE DI ROMA	GOVERNOR OF ROME
FU APERTA QUESTA VIA	THIS VIA DELL'IMPERO
DELL'IMPERO	WAS OPENED
COMPIENDOSI	ON THE OCCASION OF
IL DECENNALE DELL'ERA	THE DECENNIAL OF THE
FASCISTA	FASCIST ERA
XXVIII OTTOBRE MCMXXXII	28 OCTOBER 1932

16
Viale Adolfo Hitler

A few months before the opening of the Via dell'Impero, in July 1932, Mussolini's government received a message. The leader of Germany's National Socialist Party would like to visit. Adolf Hitler, soon to hold a majority in parliament, was keen to see, 'if it is not too hot, the monuments and museums of Rome'. The note added that 'he is very impressionable and a warm welcome could leave a lasting effect on him'.[1] Politicians of all stripes were interested in seeing the city's sights. Mahatma Gandhi had visited in 1931, taking the train down from Milan for a reception by Mussolini. The Pope declined to see him, possibly for reasons to do with English diplomacy, but Gandhi did visit the Vatican Museums. A Pathé newsreel shows him being greeted with the straight-armed salute characteristic of the Fascist regimes (despite the lack of any documented ancient origin – it first appears in art in the eighteenth century – it's also known as the 'Roman salute', which has given more than one person caught using it an excuse to distance themself from the political associations). Gandhi watched a parade of young Italian cadets, bayonetted guns in hand, a somewhat odd choice with which to entertain a famous advocate of non-violence. The visit was a short one. After dinner Gandhi took a train to Brindisi – rail having superseded the entire route of the Via Appia – and from there a ship to Bombay.[2] The Suez Canal, opened in 1869, was now making that journey rather easier than it had been in ancient times, but even then traders had stepped off the Roman roads and onto ships to India.[3] Hitler's trip would be logistically easier, but he had to wait for an invitation.

The Fascist project of road building, meanwhile, was being accompanied by attempts at land reclamation, not least in the Pontine

Marshes, by far the largest of the various projects. Reclamation was a long-running initiative: in the half-century since unification there had been on average a new law every year on this theme![4] The fact that the legislators kept returning to the topic, however, points to the challenge of both delivering the project and ensuring its maintenance. Touring in his motor car in 1909, on a 'modern roadway which has become [the Via Appia's] successor' and amid a 'very appreciable traffic', Francis Miltoun noted that it is 'more or less a marvel that a decent road could have been built here at all', and that despite multiple attempts at improvement 'the morass is still there in spite of the fact that a company calling itself Ufficio della Bonificazione delle Paludi Pontine [Office for the Improvement of the Pontine Marshes] is to-day working continuously at the same problem'.[5] In the 1930s the regime built five New Towns, including Littoria (now Latina) in the Pontine Marshes, inaugurated in 1934.[6] These were intended to emphasise a commitment to social improvement. Writers on the Campagna frequently commented on the area's backwardness. Around the turn of the century, the writer Ugo Fleres, a leading figure in Roman cultural circles who became director of the city's modern art gallery, had described the area as 'perennial and unchanging under the weight of millennia, peopled by ruins and buffalo and sheep and foals and herdsmen still clothed in pelts like ancient fauns'.[7] Francis Miltoun observed that 'round about, save for a few squalid huts and droves of cattle, sheep and goats, a wayside inn, a fountain beneath a cypress and a few sleepy, dusty hamlets and villages, there is nothing to indicate a progressive modern existence. All is as dead and dull as it was when Rome first decayed.'[8] At the inauguration ceremony for Littoria, Mussolini proclaimed: 'This is the war we prefer.'[9]

Indeed, because the marshes were familiar to an educated international audience who knew their Horace, and had read their Grand Tour accounts, the project had considerable propaganda value.[10] Dickens had described the marshes in his *Pictures from Italy*:

> wearily flat and lonesome, and overgrown with brushwood, and swamped with water, but with a fine road made across them, shaded by a long, long, avenue. Here and there, we pass a solitary guard-house; here and there, a hovel, deserted, and walled up. Some herdsmen loiter

> on the banks of the stream beside the road, and sometimes a flat-bottomed boat, towed by a man, comes rippling idly along it. A horseman passes occasionally, carrying a long gun cross-wise on the saddle before him, and attended by fierce dogs; but there is nothing else astir save the wind and shadows, until we come in sight of Terracina.[11]

Ruth Sterling Frost, a correspondent for the *Paris Tribune*, praised the modernisation in the 1934 edition of the *Geographical Review*. Outlining the multiple attempts to drain the marshes since ancient times, she concluded that: 'Indeed, the transformation seems little short of miraculous. Everywhere one is struck by the beautiful order and the Utopian quality of the work.'[12] Even after the war, writing up the Allied victory, US war correspondent Michael Stern could praise Mussolini for turning them into 'one of Italy's richest agricultural areas, demonstrating that he, too, was good for something'.[13] That said, it was not enough to drain the marshes: the reclamation needed continuous upkeep to be sustainable.[14] It would be all too easy for the new landscape to collapse.

The year 1937 saw the 2,000th anniversary of the Emperor Augustus' birth, and an ideal opportunity for the new Italian Empire to celebrate its antecedents. Among the events organised was a massive archaeological exhibition, the 'Mostra Augustea della Romanità' (Augustan Exhibition of *Romanità*, a word that the English 'Romanity' or 'Romanness' doesn't quite convey).[15] Radio broadcasts promoting the exhibition promised that visitors would 'learn about the road system of ancient Rome' as well as its other public works. This wasn't just an exhibition for archaeologists, they promised: 'Whatever your background, wherever your interests lie, you will find things of great interest.'[16]

Experts at the Istituto di Studi Romani (Institute for Roman Studies) backed up the regime's enthusiasm. 'The road is the means through which one communicates one's own civilization to peoples both near and far,' wrote Pietro Romanelli, an archaeologist. 'No people in antiquity had this sense more than the Romans, and no people left, as they did, the broadest, most organic, most robust network of roads, laid to bind and connect the known world together in one system.'[17]

The minister for education, Giuseppe Bottai, concurred: 'In every place that an aqueduct reaches, where a bridge lies, where a military road stretches, where an arch or a vault was raised, there is Rome.'[18] In 1938 the Institute published an extended study of the great roads of the Roman world. This volume, *Le grandi strade del mondo romano*, brought together an international group of historians and archaeologists, and is revealing not only of the roads themselves, but of contemporary attitudes towards them. The fifteen sections covered both the usual western routes and also those in Bulgaria, Czechoslovakia, Romania, Anatolia, Asia and North Africa. Albert Grenier, author of the section on Gaul, observed that 'of all the works of Rome in the world, certainly the grandest and most majestic, and thus the most fruitful, was the conception and organisation of the vast system of imperial roads'.[19] In the section on Britain, Eugénie Strong, an archaeologist and art historian and former assistant director of the British School at Rome, commented:

> For we English who claim descent from the ancient Britons, the allusion to them as barbarians might seem at first glance less than flattering. But when we study those words in the light of history, we must recognise that the recorded defeat was only a transitory event, while the submission of Britannia to the Romans marks our entry into the orbit of Latin civilization, and is the seal that was to leave a permanent imprint on our life as a civilised people.[20]

Strong here, in fact, abandons the metaphor of engrafting that writers from Camden onwards had used to explain Britain's relationship to Roman civilisation, in favour of the straightforward statement that submission to a foreign power was, in certain circumstances, no bad thing.

In 1938, Mussolini's regime hosted its most spectacular visit yet: that of Adolf Hitler. No trip to Rome had come to pass after his initial interest in 1932, but the pair had met in Venice two years later. Their personal relations had been frosty at first but slowly warmed in light of British opposition to the 1935 Italian invasion of Ethiopia. Mussolini had visited Germany in September 1937, and invited his host, now of course Chancellor of Germany, on a return trip.[21] In the background was a certain competitive one-upmanship between the two leaders. The invitation was not so much about practical diplomatic outcomes as about image, spectacle, creating an impression. A special committee had six months to make the arrangements before Hitler and his party took the train south across the Brenner Pass, reaching Rome on 3 May 1938. Arriving at the Stazione Ostiense, Hitler and other diplomatic guests were to be dazzled by the new, monumental city. Just outside the station were both the Porta San Paolo and the Pyramid of Gaius Cestius, and the route continued past the Obelisk of Axum, Fascist loot from the recent conquest of Ethiopia. The street leading to the station was named Viale Adolfo Hitler[22] – Adolf Hitler Avenue – and the visiting party progressed in a horse-drawn carriage past the Circus Maximus onto the first of the new roads in the area: the Via dei Trionfi (Triumph Street). This took them through the Arch of Constantine and past the Colosseum, before they crossed the Forums on the Via dell'Impero, passed Piazza Venezia and took the final hill to the royal residence on the Quirinale. King Vittorio Emanuele III still outranked Mussolini, the dictator.[23] The impression was enhanced by a spectacular electric light show. Forty-five thousand electric lamps were employed for the purpose: the Colosseum glowing, mainly red in an allusion to the German flag.[24]

For the remainder of the week, Hitler toured the sites of Rome, from the tomb of the unknown soldier, along the Via Appia to Centocelle (where he watched a military fly-past), to the Galleria Borghese, and twice to the Pantheon.[25] Yet as much as the ancient sites, the new road building was a part of the experience. Hitler, for whom the German autobahns were a source of considerable pride, not only practical but aesthetic, toured in a Mercedes-Benz to experience the regime's construction for himself.[26] An expert art historian, Ranuccio Bianchi Bandinelli, was tasked with acting as guide. Later, Bandinelli claimed that the tour might have offered an opportunity for an attack, but his 'generic' anti-Fascist friends had none of the contacts that might have made it happen.[27] (Some caution is needed with this source, however, which was published by his family in the 1990s and has a sense of rationalising after the event.) While Rome's ancient imperial experience – and its interaction with the Fascist present – was key to the visit, it did not neglect other histories. Parallels were also drawn between Hitler and Goethe, and with the Holy Roman Emperors who had once been crowned in Rome,[28] though at no point did Hitler visit the Vatican. From Mussolini's point of view, the spectacle worked. If the diplomatic entourage was somewhat irritated at the lack of political specifics, Hitler was duly impressed. In a telegram to the king of Italy, he said the trip would 'belong to the most precious memories of my life'.[29] He referred to the city more than once as 'the crystallization of a world empire'.[30]

The importance of Roman roads was already present in the minds of those responsible for developing the autobahn network. Fritz Todt, the general inspector of German roadways, was well aware of roads' symbolic power: 'Roads are cultural goods. Every road we take has its own history and meaning.'[31] Making the case for the 'gigantic project of Adolf Hitler's roads', he cited not only Herodotus, but also Napoleon, whose roads, he wrote, 'expressed, in their orientation and merciless layout, the brutal will to power of a great conqueror'.[32] According to an article on the cultural significance of the Reichsautobahnen, published in 1938, the Reich's roads 'must . . . become a monument on the landscape of history'.[33] So far were these roads inspired by the ancient imperial model that the design of their bridges and viaducts was determinedly Roman.[34] Indeed, contemporaries attributed to Hitler the idea that 'the beginnings of every civilisation express themselves in terms of road construction' and suggested he intended to take the Roman road network as a model for those he planned in Russia.[35] These ideas were not just the province of the officials concerned with roads, but enjoyed wider circulation.

Though the Rome–Berlin axis was formed in 1936, and the military Pact of Steel between Italy and Germany in 1939, it was not until 10 June 1940 that Mussolini declared war on France and Britain. British organisations in Rome closed down, or hid. Vera Cacciatore, curator of the Keats-Shelley House, had its signage taken down. German officers who enquired were informed that the keys were with the Italian ministry responsible for art and culture. This ministry was located in the north, and with communications badly disrupted, it was nobody's priority to check. The house's collections were, in fact, safe inside. Only in December 1942, as the risk of war in Italy increased, were two boxes of the most prized artefacts sent out of Rome. Just as in the

Napoleonic Wars the Pope had planned to dispatch the treasures of Loreto south to Terracina, now, 'Severn's last drawing of Keats, Keats's own drawing of a Grecian urn, locks of Keats's and Shelley's hair, and letters' were to be safely housed at the monastery of Montecassino.[36] Meanwhile, diplomatic families took refuge in the Vatican, enjoying tennis at the college linked to the Ethiopian church of Santo Stefano that lay within its territory. They were allowed the privilege of trips out along the Via Aurelia to the beach at Fregene, although by August 1943 they were meeting 'scores of southbound German vehicles'.[37]

It was not until after Allied victory in North Africa, in May 1943, that the Italian campaign began in earnest. In July troops landed in Sicily. Allied bombers targeted transport links: airfields, rail bridges and train marshalling yards. On 19 July, in what has been described as 'the largest single bombing raid in history to date', involving over 540 aircraft and 1,000 tons of bombs, their targets included the yard outside Termini. Adjoining the working-class district of San Lorenzo, this was a choice that inevitably led to civilian casualties: estimates suggest 2,000 to 3,000 people were killed and many more injured. The bombs brought, as one writer put it, 'a scorching wind of death'.[38] Leaflets airdropped in September promised that Allied troops would be in Rome within a week, but that proved false.[39]

One air raid shelter, located on a promontory dividing the two small south-facing bays on the north coast of the Bay of Naples, had famous ancient origins. One of four road tunnels attributed to the Roman engineer Lucius Cocceius Auctus, it's now known as the Grotta di Sejano. It was a private access road to an imperial residence on the coast, 700 metres long and cut through two types of volcanic rock, which required two different construction methods to accommodate their relative softness. Three side tunnels allowed for ventilation, essential given that those passing through would have needed to use torches. Although the Grotta was mentioned in the fifteenth century (when the humanist Giovanni Gioacchino Pontano wrongly linked it to the imperial minister Sejanus), and it seems unlikely that knowledge of its existence was ever lost locally, it was not until 1841, under the Bourbon king Ferdinand II, that restoration work began. A century on, as the bombing of Naples continued, local residents divided its length into little rooms, hanging sheets from its arches, converting one of the side tunnels into toilets.

Today, this is the only one of Cocceius' four tunnels accessible to the public. Enter at first through high arches, and there's no light at the end: the tunnel has a curve in the middle. There are several theories, explains Noemi, our guide from the association Gaiola, which looks after the site. One is that the two ends were dug by two different crews, whose tunnels didn't quite meet up. Another is that the curve went round a particularly tough bit of rock. The third is that the curve avoided a through draught that might have blown out candles or torches. At the far end, we see the remains of two imperial theatres, one large, one small, and views across the bays of Pozzuoli and Baiae in one direction and towards Vesuvius in the other. Seneca's description of one of the Neapolitan tunnels gives a sense of its ancient atmosphere:

> No place could be longer than that prison; nothing could be dimmer than those torches, which enabled us, not to see amid the darkness, but to see the darkness. But, even supposing that there was light in the place, the dust, which is an oppressive and disagreeable thing even in the open air, would destroy the light; how much worse the dust is there, where it rolls back upon itself, and, being shut in without ventilation, blows back in the faces of those who set it going![40]

How much worse it must have felt beneath the bombs.

As the Allied campaign intensified, key members of Mussolini's government turned against him. After a vote of no confidence, on 25 July 1943, Mussolini was first dismissed and then arrested on the orders of King Vittorio Emanuele III. The Allied bombing, however, continued in August. On 8 September, the king and his new prime minister, Marshal Pietro Badoglio, announced an armistice, and fled south to territories now held by the Allies. The following day, already in control of Sicily, Allied troops landed at Salerno, a port town south-east of Naples. (The Amalfi Coast lies between them.) From the north, however, German troops pushed south. Christopher Buckley, a *Telegraph* correspondent who accompanied British troops to Italy, described the Italian retreat in his 1945 book, *Road to Rome*:

> A column of damaged armoured cars and lorries limped slowly down the great Via Flaminia, which enters the city from the north. They had been in action against the Germans at Monte Rotondo, ten miles north of Rome. The officer in charge of the column told the bystanders that the Germans had opened fire on the Italian troops.[41]

To the north of Rome, one group of Italians mined a road and bridge – as Garibaldi's men had done decades before – delaying the German entry to the city.[42] The biggest battle, however, took place at Porta San Paolo, close to the newly restored Ostiense station and the pyramid that overlooks the Non-Catholic Cemetery. As the Germans advanced further, the Italians fell back to make a final defence there, though to no avail. On 12 September the Germans broke Mussolini out of his temporary prison in a ski resort hotel that should, on account of its location, have been easy to defend. His puppet regime, the Republic of Salò, provided cover for a German occupation of north and central Italy, including Rome, supported by sections of the Italian army and authorities that had stayed loyal to Mussolini.[43] Many Italians would now fight with the Allies or as part of the resistance.

On the coast south of Salerno, Paul Kennedy, an American field surgeon, was not enjoying his arrival in Italy. The night of Wednesday, 22 September 1943 was, he wrote, the worst 'of all the miserable nights I have ever spent . . . Just 100 yards off the beach, no blankets, nothing but a towel to wrap up in. I shivered practically all night and got about 10 minutes' sleep.'[44] He was quickly in demand at the field hospital, however, in the short time before he was posted on to Naples 'in a British lorry loaded to the ceilings'. There, Mount Vesuvius was 'belching a large column of black smoke'. It was the first of the usual tourist sites he'd seen in Italy, but a far cry from the Grand Tour excursions to Pompeii. His party arrived in Naples 'in pitch darkness' and camped for the night 'in a corridor of the postal telegraph building – a really modern and beautiful place'.[45]

When I first went to Naples, almost sixty years after Kennedy, my guidebook also recommended a visit to the Palazzo delle Poste, a fine example of Fascist architecture with a spectacular curved facade. And when I came back to Naples to research this book, I stayed in another legacy of that regime: the Hotel Palazzo Esedra. Originally built as offices for the Mostra d'Oltremare – a great exhibition in 1937 aimed at showing off Italy's new empire – the building has been restored as a hotel, keeping much of its modernist design. There are black-and-white mosaic floors, a classically inspired courtyard with a central water feature, its tiles the only place any colour is allowed, and the furniture has been picked to match, with square leather seats and curving metal around the desks. Its architect, Marcello Canino, was a supporter of the regime who'd failed to get the contract for the Palazzo delle Poste.[46] I didn't plan it this way, but the nights I stay in the Palazzo Esedra are the two nights before the Italian elections, and there's a spooky parallel between the restoration of this place and the revitalisation of the post-Fascist party leading in the polls. It's monumental, grand, all white or pale travertine, nothing like the Roman painted houses in Pompeii. Here I am, sitting in fully polished, luxury ex-Fascism. It's clean, dapper, sharp: it's got gloss, tech, future. Don't think too hard about it or you might forget to enjoy your trip. The restaurant cutlery balances nicely in my hands. No pictures bar two great frescoes on the wall of the breakfast room. The hotel website tells me they're by Emilio Notte. In the corner of one are two figures, one turbaned, one Black, bending their knees before a priest with a cross. It's 24 September 2022, just short of a century since the March on Rome, and this is what we get: Fascist aesthetics as fashionable hotel vibes.

Kennedy, the surgeon, had a lucky escape. The retreating German forces had left time bombs in that modernist post office. They exploded two days later, killing a hundred people who had taken shelter there. Inside, now, there's a monument to the fallen. Kennedy's hope of getting to Pompeii 'to buy some cameos' was thwarted when the troops were ordered 'to stay close to home in case a big push is starting'.[47] In the end, more than 2,000 Allied soldiers were killed at Salerno, and a further 11,000 wounded or missing. They had, however, as one historian put it (no one can resist the metaphor), 'an unshakable foothold on the road to Rome'.[48]

In Rome, meanwhile, some of the old institutions came into their own. William Newnan, a US Army Ranger, described how the wily Father Superior of the French seminary, Father Monier, had fooled the Italian (Fascist) troops sent to close it down into thinking it had diplomatic immunity as a papal institution, and then ran it as a hostel to pay the bills, accommodating 'a lot of Italian Jews . . . some Italian priests that had been bombed out of Frascati . . . five young Frenchmen who had come down from France to escape the labour draft'. Elsewhere, the 'jolly Irish seminary . . . was running full blast in Rome, with good times and plenty of food and jolly good fellows'.[49]

More direct resistance soon began. Italian partisans targeted the occupiers' road transport, with a weapon we've already met in this story: the ancient Roman caltrop, which I saw first in the Corbridge Museum near Hadrian's Wall, only for it to turn up again in the Museo della Liberazione in Rome. On the nights of 10 to 13 October, teams of partisans from the towns of the Alban Hills scattered four-pointed nails across the Via Appia, Via Casilina and Via Ardeatina. That attack alone damaged twenty German trucks. Consisting of two small L-shaped iron rods, pointed at either end and soldered together at right angles, however the nails fell, one prong would point upwards, puncturing the tyres of any passing vehicle. They were, moreover, easily made by local blacksmiths in areas that still relied heavily on horse-drawn transport. The Central Military Committee of the Italian Communist Party, which organised its members in resistance, directed them to:

> Begin with the simplest acts, those that require only a few men, for example; spreading four-pointed nails along the roads most frequently used by enemy traffic (you should have a model nail, if not we will send one) . . . Where possible, provoke landslides to interrupt the flow of traffic. String metal wires across roads to saw the heads off the drivers and passengers of enemy motorcycles; these are all actions that you can do with the scarce means at your disposal.[50]

Disruption of the roads and of their traffic was key to resistance. The occupiers, however, swiftly made production and possession of the caltrops punishable by death and, moreover, issued a formal, written police threat of reprisals 'against those who live along the roads and in the areas where such acts are repeated'.[51] (Since the early twentieth century, such retaliation against bystanders had been a war crime under international law, a fact that would eventually catch up with the German commander in Italy, Albert Kesselring.)

Later that week in the autumn of 1943, the round-up of Jews in Rome began. At dawn on Saturday, 16 October, SS police officers arrived at houses across the city. Jews living in the ghetto, forced to leave their homes still in night clothes, were made to wait in the rain in the Theatre of Marcellus.[52] Other Roman Jews were taken directly in trucks to the Italian Military College near the Vatican. (A book by Susan Zuccotti on the Pope and the Holocaust is titled *Under His Very Windows*: it is impossible that no one saw what was going on.) By the end of the day the SS police, led by Herbert Kappler, formally a police attaché at the German Embassy but in fact working for the Gestapo and Foreign Intelligence, had arrested 1,259 people.[53]

When I visit the archaeological area outside the Theatre of Marcellus, in the autumn of 2021, there is no mention of this moment in the Theatre's history on the information panels there. One does discuss the restoration of the area, but as with the arch in Rimini, entirely in the passive voice. The demolitions were carried out. We don't learn by whom. The ancient history has been tidily separated out from the memorialisation that I find up a flight of steps in what is now Piazza 16 Ottobre 1943. I'm at the end of the main street of the ghetto. It's packed with restaurants. The buskers – one on an accordion, one a double bass – have worked into their medley the partisan song *Bella Ciao*. Eight hundred years before, when the rabbi Benjamin had travelled from Spain to Rome and beyond, he had found a Jewish community of about 200 people. That was before the ghetto, established in 1555, but antisemitic sentiment can be found even in the ancient texts. Juvenal's third *Satire* slates the Grotto of Egeria off the Appian Way as 'fake-looking caves', observing 'how much more present the spirit of the waters would be, if grass enclosed the pool with a green border and marble did not profane the native tufa'. The suggestion of foreign marble profaning native tufa here is subtle by comparison to his comment that the 'sacred spring and its shrine are [now] given over to Jews'.[54]

Around the piazza several plaques commemorate the deportation, the principal one erected in 1964, another on a school from which

112 pupils were sent to the death camps.[55] Up a side street paved with Rome's distinctive *sampietrini*, brass plaques known as 'stumbling stones' or in German *Stolpersteine* have been inlaid outside houses from which residents were deported, recording their fates. Settimio Spagnoletto, born 1895, arrested 27 March 1944, murdered at Auschwitz 23 May 1944. Leone Pavoncello, born 1902, arrested 13 April 1944, murdered at Auschwitz October 1944. In total more than 2,000 people were deported to the Nazi camps. The first were identified by records maintained under Italy's racial laws; later deportations, however, relied on denunciations.[56] One recent book describes the people who supplied this information as the *Italian Executioners*: its original Italian edition used even stronger language, labelling them *Italian Butchers*, a counterweight to the prevailing stories of Italians who saved their Jewish neighbours.[57]

Rather than deportations, Kappler had at first tried extortion, demanding that the Jewish community of Rome produce fifty kilograms of gold. The Vatican offered (or was asked for, and agreed to) a loan, but it was not necessary. Later Kappler would testify that he was hoping to persuade his superiors of the potential for financial exploitation: if he was fundamentally concerned about his orders to deport the Jews, it seems likely that that was only because it might increase hostility to the German occupiers.[58] Some Roman Jews managed to escape the round-up, sometimes thanks to neighbours' warnings, sometimes by their own evasive action. Others had already gone into hiding, among them the leaders of Delasem, an organisation assisting foreign Jewish refugees in Rome, which with the support of sympathetic priests organised a secret network of hiding places. The Nazis had hoped to deport eight times more people than in fact they did.[59] Yet despite Radio London's reports on the existence of concentration camps, the local leadership and many of their followers struggled to believe that they might become victims. Even the man initially chosen to translate their captors' orders, Arminio Wachsberger, believed at first what he was saying: that they were being sent north to a labour camp. On Monday, 18 October, just over 1,000 prisoners were transported across Rome to the cargo terminal at Tiburtina station. Still in existence, the station is located on the Via

Tiburtina, the old road to Tivoli. The train travelled north, via Orte and the station at Terontola.

I didn't plan to follow that journey, but at one point I find myself on the same line, albeit travelling in the opposite direction. At Terontola, south of Arezzo, north of Orvieto, a plaque on the station wall catches my eye. It records the role of cycling champion Gino Bartali, twice winner of the Tour de France, who stopped here multiple times in 1943–4 while training with rides between Florence and Assisi 'to help victims of racist and ideological persecution during the Second World War'. The Bartali story is controversial: accepted at first, it has more recently been criticised for lack of corroboration in the documentary sources,[60] though this has not stopped it becoming the basis for a new West End show. The roads, and railroads, garner as many myths as they do histories. I understand, though, why we might want tales of heroes. The truth is hard.

Back in 1943, six hours after leaving Rome, the train reached Florence. It arrived at Padua the following midday. By this time the people on board had not had anything to drink for two days, and only after threats of violence against the Nazis from Fascist militiamen were the Jews given water.[61] From Padua the train crossed into Germany and then Poland, reaching Auschwitz at almost midnight on Friday. All but 196 of the prisoners were sent to the gas chambers; of those 196 (forty-seven of them women), fewer than twenty survived. The only woman among them, Settimia Spizzichino, dedicated her life to Holocaust education. A bridge over the railway line in Rome's southern garden suburb Garbatella is now named after her.[62]

17
Highway 7

Three months later, in January 1944, Peter Tompkins was hiding just off the Via Aurelia about a hundred miles north of Rome. His place of concealment was 'the bailiff's house of a Roman nobleman's estate'.[1] Tompkins, a secret agent of the US Office of Strategic Services, had made his way there after landing on the coast in a rubber dinghy. He was supposed to meet a contact who would take him to Rome, but no one turned up. Obliged instead to bribe a pair of limousine chauffeurs, claiming their employer was a friend, Tompkins, an Italian companion, and a boy known as T., who ran errands between this safe house and Rome, crammed into the car in the unwelcome company of two Italian saboteurs: 'and off we went into the night, heading down the Aurelia towards Montalto de Castro and Tarquinia'.[2]

Tompkins had with him 'phony papers, 300 gold sovereigns . . . my own secret codes and radio crystals which would produce certain wave lengths, a Beretta 9mm automatic and, foolishly, a small Minox camera'.[3] The chauffeurs had papers from both the German Embassy and the Department of the Fascist Republican Army, and Tompkins wondered if they might, in fact, be working for the German occupiers, but was reassured when one of them recognised one of the saboteurs as a former army comrade. 'The feeling of relief', he wrote, 'was general.' They drove through the night, cutting cross-country away from the Aurelia, Tompkins dozing and disorientated from lack of sleep. Past 'the gray-brown battlements of Viterbo', they joined the Via Cassia as dawn approached. (The medieval town, strategically located on the road and railway north from Rome, had been a target for Allied bombings, which damaged many of its historic buildings.) A German truck passed as they stopped to refuel with black-market petrol, but the troops only ordered them to switch off their headlights, and they made it through a roadblock with no more than a cursory look at their papers. Tompkins feared a further stop, but as they reached the Ponte Milvio they saw only an empty piazza. They had arrived in occupied Rome.[4]

Once in the capital, Tompkins was tasked with dealing with the partisans who from early in the occupation had been leading the resistance. Within a week of the 16 October deportations, the largest group, Bandiera Rossa (in English 'Red Flag'), had attacked an Italian Fascist military base, hoping to appropriate some weapons. The mission, however, ended with the capture of twelve partisans, of whom eleven were swiftly executed. Subsequent actions were more successful. On one occasion the group succeeded in stopping a set of executions by disguising themselves as German police, setting up a roadblock (once again, control of roads matters) and stealing the uniforms and truck of the Italian Africa Police firing squad as it made its way to Fort Bravetta. Fooling both Italian and German guards, the partisans freed the captives, took hostages to secure their safe exit and – back in their stolen truck – screeched up the Via Aurelia to a safe house in Cerveteri. If that was spectacular, even more modest activity could be useful: partisans from the Patriotic Action Groups (GAP) removed the road signs from key routes out of Rome including the Via Casilina in the hope of confusing the enemy.[5]

The Allied advance up the Italian peninsula, meanwhile, was proceeding slowly. War throws up new geography: the defensive lines of the Second World War did not follow the roads but cut across them. The Gustav Line, for example, began near the mouth of the Garigliano river (about fifty miles north of Naples, the point where the Via Appia turns inland from the coast), and ended eighty-four miles to the east, at the mouth of the Sangro river, about thirty miles south of Pescara on the Adriatic. Combining minefields, earthworks, barbed wire and bunkers, the line also benefited from the natural geography of Italy. Its peaks included the monastery of Montecassino, 1,700 feet up, the destination over a millennium earlier of that anonymous deaf-mute English pilgrim. Kesselring assured Hitler the Gustav Line could be defended for six months.[6]

The Allies broke the Barbara Line, between ten and twenty miles to the south of the Gustav and more lightly defended, in November 1943. On 1 December the US Fifth Army began a new offensive against the Gustav Line. Ten days of fighting, however, did not secure their key targets: Montecassino and, thirty miles up the Via Casilina, the town of Frosinone.[7] John Smallwood, a South African soldier, recorded the 'nightmare journey' along the road to Rome in his diary:

> Tanks, guns, half-tracks and ambulances were mixed up with three-ton lorries, carriers and more tanks. An endless column, nose to tail, either waiting with engines running in the overpowering heat and dust or tearing through narrow lanes trying to catch the vehicle in front. Trees and bushes are smashed and twisted. Houses are either completely collapsed or have huge rents in them. Civilians in ragged clothes stand in small groups staring pathetically at the never-ending stream. Enemy equipment is everywhere. Broken trucks, burned-out tanks, guns upside down are scattered about. Great broken cobwebs of barbed wire and telephone lines are tangled in the hedgerows and above all hangs a thick, nauseating blanket of dust and the stench of the dead.[8]

As observers reported the conflict, they turned to the roads to make sense of what was going on. Headline writers could not resist the resonance of the phrase 'Roads to Rome'. 'DOUBLE ASSAULT ON ROADS TO ROME: GERMANS CLINGING TO BATTERED DEFENCES' trumpeted the *Dundee Courier* on 18 December 1943. 'The Fifth Army . . . is fighting bitterly for the lower stretches of the Appian Way, gateway to Rome.' Two days later, Cyril Bewley, war correspondent for the Aberdeen *Press and Journal* at Allied HQ in North Africa, could report that: 'The Fifth Army have captured San Pietro, the last remaining mountain fortress in the series which once blocked our progress along the main Capua–Rome road to Cassino.'[9] Securing roads, in fact, was key to the Allied campaign and for ease of reference, rather than the ancient names, they were given numbers. The *Aberdeen Journal* provided a list for the convenience of its readers. Working clockwise around Rome, Via Aurelia, which followed the coast north, became Highway 1; Via Cassia (part of which overlapped with the Via Francigena) was Highway 2; Via Flaminia (north-east to Rimini) Highway 3; and Via Salaria Highway 4. Via Tiburtina (east to Tivoli) became Highway 5; Via Casilina (south through the Liri valley) Highway 6 and the Via Appia Highway 7. Highway 8 was the Via Ostiense, connecting Rome with its ancient port.[10]

The landscape south of Rome, however, provided the occupying Germans with solid natural defences against the Allied advance. As we've seen, the Appia ran across the Pontine Marshes and in places close up to the coast; the Via Casilina was located between twelve and twenty miles inland. Between them were hilly – sometimes mountainous – areas, their highest peaks, in the Aurunci Mountains, rising to 5,000 feet. Advancing troops were vulnerable to observation, and attack, from higher ground, but there was no choice: these were the only routes that could support modern supply lines.[11] Of the two, the Via Casilina was preferable: the Liri valley was relatively wide, while the Appia, at times, was tightly built into steep cliffs.[12] The geography that had challenged first Roman road-builders, then popes through the centuries, now faced twentieth-century armies.

The failure to break through the Gustav Line meant new tactics were needed. As Peter Tompkins observed, looking back on the campaign many years later, 'a head-on attack up the ancient avenues to Rome, the Casilina and Appian highways, previously employed by Hannibal and Belisarius, appeared hopeless'. (He assumed his readers would know that only one of those two – Belisarius – had been successful. Hannibal had resorted to bringing his elephants over the Alps, which was hardly an option for the Allies.) If, wrote Tompkins, the Allies could seize the Alban Hills, twenty miles south of Rome, which lay in between the two roads – and overlooked them – their position would be vastly improved.[13] Thus the Allied commanders settled on an amphibious assault, in which their troops would land well north of the Gustav Line. The chosen locations were Anzio and, just along the beach, Nettuno, seventeen miles from Cisterna, a town further inland on the Via Appia sometimes associated with the ancient way station of Tres Tabernae but here important for its strategic hilltop setting. There was considerable scepticism about the Allied commanders' decision, which remains a subject for debate among military historians, but Winston Churchill was in favour, and his view prevailed.[14] The story of Anzio takes us back to a familiar place: the Pontine Marshes, just to the south of the chosen landing point. Although drained in the recent reclamation project, and criss-crossed by roads, they were still far from ideal territory for the movement of heavy military equipment, especially in a rainy winter. Yet that was also a problem for the Germans, who relied on Highway 7, the Via Appia, to supply their troops at the front line.[15]

Just after midnight, in the early hours of 22 January 1944, the first Allied vessels anchored off Anzio. Their air forces had done their best to cut off communications from the north of Italy to Rome, bombing railway lines and airfields, though these were swiftly repaired.[16] A decoy operation in Corsica and Sardinia would, the Allies hoped, deceive the Germans as to the likely location of their attack. Whether or not that particular tactic worked, the landings did come as a surprise.[17] The Germans were not, however, entirely unprepared: this was one of a number of Allied options for which they had planned, and as the Allies landed first two divisions, then more, they deployed a scenario known as 'Case Richard'.[18] In their first three days, the Allies consolidated a beachhead stretching out from Anzio in a semicircle with a perimeter of twenty-six miles. With the Germans holding the Alban Hills to their north, however, they were vulnerable to artillery attack.[19] Michael Stern, the war correspondent, explained the challenge of the area to his son as they drove through the Pontine Marshes after the war: the Germans held the mountains that descended sharply to the road and any advance would have been met with artillery fire. 'It was suicide', he recalled, 'to try to move unless we pushed them out.' Nor was the valley on the other side of the hills an option: 'Monte Cassino is there and again they held the high ground.'[20]

The Allies continued their landings on the coast: by 29 January they had 69,000 troops there; by mid-February about 100,000. The Germans built up defensive lines to protect both Cisterna and the smaller town of Campoleone, mobilising 120,000 men to this new front.[21] Among them was Lance-Corporal Joachim Liebschner from Silesia, then aged just eighteen. He worked as a runner, carrying messages by bicycle up and down the roads between his own company and headquarters. He later recalled:

> We were issued with a bicycle and it was really a great big joke because when we moved forward, the harder the artillery fire became and we

> were then attacked by aeroplanes. When everybody jumped into the ditches to the left and right I was left with the bicycle. Eventually I went to the Sergeant Major and said look when am I going to use my bicycle here, and he said 'You signed for it, you're responsible for it!' typical German kind of answer to a question . . . I left it against a tree and thought I could find the tree again when we get to the front line. Not only had the bicycle gone but the tree had gone as well.[22]

Today, the Anzio landings are commemorated in a small museum in the town itself, filled with photos and memorabilia, with donated uniforms, framed newspapers, bags and kit, petrified guns, encrusted with molluscs after being ditched in the harbour. The attendant steps up on a chair to start a compilation of black and white film footage showing the destruction wreaked by the campaign, not only on the town, which was bombed by both sides, but in the countryside, where the checkered pattern of fields was pockmarked with bomb craters. Outside the museum stands a memorial, topped with a white stone cross, a sword pointing down its upright, 'in proud memory of the officers, warrant-officers, non-commissioned officers and men of the 2nd Battalion the Sherwood Foresters who gave their lives in the fighting in the Anzio beachhead'. Visiting at the same time as me are a British couple: his father was at Anzio. For veterans and their families this and other locations – including the international cemeteries that now dot southern Italy – have become modern sites of pilgrimage.[23]

William L. Newnan, the US Ranger, told his story of the campaign to friends and family shortly after he returned to the USA in 1945. His battalion had been tasked with an attack on Cisterna. It was, he explained:

> a natural point for us to attack for this reason: it was astride the Appian Way, one of three main roads south to Cassino, and had the Allies controlled the Appian Way to Cassino the Jerries would have been very embarrassed, because it would have been very difficult to bring in food and ammunition, and also reinforcements.[24]

The attack, however, was thwarted: 'The Jerries had a great deal more strength than we thought they had there.' The Rangers succeeded in sneaking through the German lines on the night of 31 January–1 February, but failed to take the town before they ran out of ammunition. All but a handful of Newnan's battalion were killed or captured. The prisoners were taken to Rome, 'to the old Coliseum, then put off the trucks and marched in triumph through the streets'.[25] The remodelled roads had a new use. The captured soldiers were transported north through Italy, but in Tuscany Newnan managed to escape. With the help of farmers and other escapees he headed south to Rome, 'convinced that the Anzio beachhead would be extended shortly'.[26] Avoiding major roads, picking his way through the Tuscan countryside he discovered that the area around Chiusi 'did not have roads, it was just full of little paths'.[27] A CIA report of December 1960 noted that across the Adriatic, Yugoslav partisans had likewise benefited from the absence of modern highways: they 'found refuge in rugged uplands' from which they successfully ambushed and blockaded roads. 'Many of the major roads of today', observed the report's author, 'follow routes developed by the Romans.'[28]

A little further on, south of Montefiascone (which lies on the Via Cassia), Newnan spotted what he later learned was Mount Soratte, site of Carloman's monastery, cited by Horace, noted by the Grand Tourist Samuel Rogers. It was, wrote Newnan, 'one of the few single mountains in Italy . . . a natural point for anybody moving from north to south to use as a guide'.[29] (It isn't clear from Newnan's account whether he knew that Mount Soratte was also the location of a massive military bunker, built by the Italian government in the late 1930s but since September 1943 the headquarters of the occupying German forces.) The closer Newnan got to the major roads, however, the harder he found it to get help:

> good roads meant Jerries, and if there were Jerries near or Jerries that could be brought in the Italians wouldn't do much for you. They had too much at stake themselves. However, if there weren't roads, they were in their own little castles and very independent.[30]

Eventually, inevitably, Newnan, now accompanied by another escapee, was obliged to cross a major road: 'we felt like desperate conspirators,' he wrote, noting, however, that 'nobody was paying a darn bit of attention and unless we had walked right into a Jerry we were perfectly okay'.[31] With the help of 'an Italian Communist, the big Communist of that area', he made it to Rignano Flaminio. As the name suggests, it lies on the Via Flaminia. It was also on the train line from Viterbo to Rome, and at 4 a.m. Newnan managed to get into the city on a train.[32] This Communist partisan helped Newnan to hide in an apartment on the Via Flaminia, where he could hear 'all the Jerries . . . marching up and down that road at night, moving troops in and empty trucks out . . . I heard a lot of horse-drawn stuff come by.'[33]

Having arrived in Rome the day before the Anzio landings, Peter Tompkins had begun his work of gathering intelligence. Just as Newnan had realised the significance of roads, so had Tompkins. On the night following the landings, that of 22–23 January, he received a report of 'intense southbound traffic through Rome, out Via Appia. All available German units in a radius of 90 kilometers north of Rome have been ordered south . . . Road followed: Appia Antica, Albano, Via Anziate.' Other units were 'astride Albano-Anzio road on perimeter of Beachhead', while 'trenches and field defenses [were] being thrown together just south of Rome (Porta S. Paolo on Ostia road)'. The traffic on the Via Appia amounted to '270 vehicles, most intense between 1900 [hours] and dawn'.[34]

Tompkins and his commanders made best use of the fact that all roads led to Rome. In the absence of the ring road that today enables traffic to avoid the city, it was a bottleneck, not just for road traffic but for rail lines. 'I realised that . . . if properly organized,' he wrote, 'we could keep a continuous check on them, not only by day but by night (when no air reconnaissance was possible) and that these counts could be quickly and systematically radioed both to Caserta and the beachhead.' (The enormous eighteenth-century royal palace at Caserta, outside Naples, was currently Allied headquarters.) Partisans from the Socialist party, already organised underground on the basis of city sectors 'each with a secret headquarters to which members of the various cells could report', took on the task of watching in shifts.[35]

News of the landings gave hope to those living at the north end of the roads, in occupied Rome. On the Via Casilina, the 'people's republic of Torpignattara and Certosa' was for a few weeks in February an effective partisan enclave, where volunteers trained, and the local police took orders from their underground organisations, not the Nazis.[36] Back at the Anzio beachhead, however, there had been heavy casualties on both sides. On 22 February Allied commander Major General John P. Lucas was replaced by General Lucian Truscott. The campaign settled into stalemate.[37] The Germans turned off the drainage pumps and reflooded the Pontine Marshes. That provided a sound natural defence for the Axis army. It also encouraged the malarial mosquitoes, with devastating consequences for civilians returning after the war.[38] Peter Tompkins, writing forty years later, was among the critics of the conduct of the Anzio campaign. Kesselring, he noted, had observed that 'only a miracle' could save the Germans, and yet in their lack of boldness the Allied generals Alexander and Clark had failed to take advantage. Rather than heading for the Alban Hills, they had focused on consolidating the beachhead.[39] After the war both Kesselring and his chief of staff conceded that the Allies could well have taken Rome, as did the German commander of the city, Lieutenant General Kurt Maeltzer.[40] Michael Stern said it was 'hard to explain' to his son that the Anzio plan had been 'disastrous, not because of the strategy, which was excellent, but because of faulty execution and poor leadership'.[41] Much later, John T. Cummings, a US lieutenant tasked with reconnaissance, would claim that he and his driver had managed to drive right up the Via Appia, past the hills, spotting no Germans until they came within sight of the Tiber. Assuming Cummings' memory is accurate, his report was either not passed on, or not acted upon.[42] Churchill complained that: 'I thought we should fling a wild-cat ashore and all we got was an old stranded whale on the beach.'[43] On the other hand, more recent analysis has suggested that Lucas' lack of boldness was reasonable given the available forces and the available intelligence.[44] After all, the last successful conquest of Rome from the south had been 1,400 years before, that of Belisarius. Even Hannibal had failed.[45] Either way, the stalemate was cold comfort for the 'people's republic'. After about three weeks, as prospects of help from the south disappeared, the Germans rounded up the organisers, killing twenty-five and deporting others.[46]

Perhaps that fuelled Roman determination. On 23 March 1944, as the third battle for Montecassino raged, partisans from the GAP in Rome bombed a police convoy making its way down Via Rasella, near Palazzo Barberini in central Rome. The attack killed thirty men from a military unit of the German police and at least two Italian civilians who happened to be nearby. Via Rasella is an unprepossessing street, narrow and steep between high buildings, still with its *sampietrini*. When I walk down in the autumn of 2021 I don't see any reference to what happened here. Goethe's house, and Shelley's, and Keats' can have a plaque, but this is not so easy to remember. Indeed, as John Foot has argued, there have long been in Italy two competing narratives of the Via Rasella attack, one regarding it as a heroic act of resistance with the broad backing of the people of occupied Rome, the other perceiving it as pointless provocation.[47] In response to the bombing, the occupiers issued an order to round up ten times the number of men killed (a further three troops died after the initial thirty). Among them were residents of the area around Via Rasella, seventy-five men already detained as Jews, and many political activists, including Uccio Pisino, who had trained partisans in the 'people's republic', Valerio Fiorentini, an organiser for the GAP, and twenty-two of the Socialist intelligence agents who had worked with Tompkins to monitor the roads to Rome.[48]

'When we crucify criminals,' wrote Quintilian, a rhetorician and teacher of oratory in the second century CE, 'the most frequented roads are chosen, where the greatest number of people can look and be seized by this fear. For every punishment has less to do with the offence than with the example.'[49] In the aftermath of Spartacus' revolt, according to Appian's history of the *Civil Wars*, 6,000 rebels were crucified along the road from Rome to Capua.[50] Yet while the reprisals for the Via Rasella attacks were clearly meant as an example, the action itself was hidden away from public view, off the Via Ardeatina.

Early in the twentieth century, when the historian Giuseppe Tomassetti wrote his great survey of the Roman campagna, he could reasonably open his discussion of the Ardeatina with the observation that of the suburban roads, it was 'one of the least regarded, and, relatively speaking, the least known'. It had once led to the town of Ardea, twenty-four miles from Rome, but thanks to both the early decline of that city and the 'commercial competition of the adjacent roads', the Ardeatina fell into relative disuse, though it must have been a route up to at least the year 1130 when Ardea was granted city status.[51] In the early nineteenth century, there had been a shrine on the road dedicated to the Madonna of Divine Love, patroness of laundresses, which attracted brightly dressed women pilgrims on her feast day.[52] A century on, however, Tomassetti found the countryside 'desolated'. He and his companions were attacked by a pack of six mastiffs. Luckily for them, they had a shotgun to scare off the dogs.[53]

Tomassetti could not have predicted the road's modern notoriety. The reprisals here were not the first (those were on 22 October 1943, at Pietralata, commemorated at the tenth kilometre of the Via Tiburtina), but they were by far the bloodiest. The killings took place in the tunnels of a disused quarry just off the Via Ardeatina; it's an eerie walk from the nearby ancient catacombs. The mausoleum at Fosse Ardeatine now marks the site of one of the most infamous acts of the Second World War in Italy: the massacre on 24 March 1944 of 335 men. They weren't precise about the numbers.

The modern memorial is based on the U-shaped cave in which the massacre took place. After the shootings, its two entrances were mined and blown up so as to prevent access to the site of the atrocity. Now the craters made in the explosion open to the sky and the caves are reinforced with stone walls. Inside is a little chapel, and above on the hillside a small museum. The text in the museum tells me that at this time in Rome rations were cut to 100g and then 50g of bread. I try to imagine cutting my bread-maker's small loaf into ten slices and one slice being my food for the day.

It's very quiet. I'm the only person here when I arrive.

The tomb itself – the tombs, 335 tombs – lie under a great concrete slab. The tombs are made of granite, on each one an iron laurel wreath and the name of the martyr: that's the word they use here. And they have holders for little photographs. On some of them the names are newly carved: the latest identity was uncovered only in March this year, 2021.

The stalemate at Anzio ended on the night of 11–12 May. The Allies had built up their forces: on the beachhead alone were seven divisions; a further eighteen were south of the Gustav Line. Although the commanders were principally British and American, the troops involved included multiple nationalities: from Canadians to Indians to Algerians, South Africans and New Zealanders as well as Frenchmen, Italians and Poles.[54]

Joachim Liebschner thought at first he had held off an American advance:

> I was given 10 youngsters and one experienced man and two heavy machine guns and was ordered to defend, or stop the onslaught along the Via Appia – Route 7 . . . I took over very good fortified positions already dug. I put a machine gun nest either side of the road and stayed with one on the right hand side . . . At between 8 and 9 the following morning the whole field in front of us was filled with hundreds of Americans, their rifles slung across their shoulders or at their hip, walking towards us as though it were peacetime. We held our fire until they were 100 to 120 yards on top of us. Then we let go and caused an incredible amount of havoc. They were just falling like nine pins and the rest withdrew back into the woods. It took them about half an hour to sort out where we were and then they hammered us with their artillery . . . I had never lived through anything like this.[55]

Later, travelling south out of Rome, the US Ranger Newnan saw 'where about seven of our tanks had been knocked out along the road by well placed anti-tank guns. The tanks had just come steaming in ahead of everything else, and of course channelized on the road. The Jerry guns had just knocked 'em off.'[56] Liebschner was captured and dispatched to a prisoner-of-war camp. Later he recalled:

> This was the first time that I thought we could not win the war because of all the war materiel I could see the Americans moving forward – the roads were simply full of tanks, lorries, jeeps – and moving during day time. We couldn't move a bicycle in the daytime without being shot at. The roads were jammed with traffic, they were moving this huge mass of war materiel, guns and tanks.[57]

The offensive broke the Gustav Line within a week. Allied troops seized Montecassino on 18 May. The monastery had already been all but flattened by bombing: the Allies mistakenly believed that German troops were hiding there. When Paul Kennedy, the field surgeon, took a trip to Cassino, 'or rather what was Cassino', he described it as 'nothing more than a disorganized rock pile. I have never seen such complete destruction.'[58]

Today, the monastery at Montecassino has risen again from the ruins, painstakingly reconstructed in the 1950s. The artefacts belonging to the Keats-Shelley House were ironically saved by being brought back to occupied Rome in October 1943, concealed in the personal baggage of the Montecassino archivist, Dom Mauro Inguanez, who had secured a lift to the city in a car driven by a German medical officer. Dom Mauro took the treasures to the convent of St Anselmo on the Aventine hill, from where the curator collected them less than a year after they'd been sent to Montecassino for safekeeping.[59] What you see now at Montecassino is a simulacrum, for the most part, an image of the history. Only underground do you get the real thing, in the bizarre but captivating not-quite-Egyptian-style crypt. That survived. The same is true elsewhere, in Anzio, for example, where much of the city centre had to be rebuilt after the war.

In May 1944, outside Naples, Kennedy was waiting for news. On the 22nd he observed drily in his diary that: 'There's a war going on right now – you can actually see tracers firing from our own machine guns – that's just a little too close.' He was optimistic, though, that 'soon we shall see Rome'. Before that, however, he had to deal with heavy casualties: 200 surgical admissions in the aftermath of the battle for Cisterna, in which the Allies successfully cut off German supply lines down the Via Appia, Highway 7.[60] Later, as Newnan headed south out of Rome, he saw 'Truck after truck of German equipment . . . burning alongside of the road.' 'Finally,' he wrote, 'we got to a place that was just a pile of rubble and the General said, "Do you recognize this?" I said, "No." He said, "This is Cisterna." Just flattened – absolutely nothing left.'[61]

The war reporters were, unsurprisingly, more eloquent, and when they came to write their books on the conflict made ample reference to the famous Roman roads. Christopher Buckley, the *Telegraph* correspondent, reported the American advance from the south across the Pontine Marshes.

> American troops had taken Terracina on May 24. Early next morning their armoured cars raced forward without opposition for twenty miles

> along the dead-straight line of the Appian Way and at seven-thirty they made contact with the sappers of the beach-head force at Borgo Grappa five miles east of the Mussolini Canal, which ever since January had formed the front line of the Anzio position.[62]

Michael Stern was another to use the ancient past in his writing. In a narrative peppered with references to Rome's roads, pines, churches and ruins, he compared his own arrival in Rome through death and destruction to an ancient precedent:

> Beyond the roofs of the city in the plains to the south winds Via Casilina, the ancient Roman road used by the military two centuries before Christ. It was along the embankments of this road that Pompey raised the crucifixes bearing the six thousand bodies of prisoners taken in the battle against Spartacus. And it was along this road that I travelled in another, more recent war ... bearded, haggard from lack of sleep ... Men about me were being killed.[63]

Other versions of the Spartacus story place the crucifixions along the Appian Way.[64] Probably the imagery mattered more to later storytellers than the fact. And yet, like Belisarius, the Allies had succeeded from the south. As Stern wrote, 'The road to Rome was open.'[65]

British war correspondent Richard McMillan, in his book *Twenty Angels over Rome*, published in August 1944 while the wider war still raged, raided the same store of metaphors:

> The Via Appia – the road along which Roman conquerors had returned in triumph from so many conquests – was making history again. More than 2,000 years before, this highway, which was to become one of the main arteries of the Roman Empire, ancient and modern, began to take form under slave labour conscripted by the blind Censor, Appius Claudius Caecus.
>
> The arteries from the main stem sprawled out until the highway linked with the chief cities of the south; and today Italy's modern road system follows the lines traced by that first great national thoroughfare which aided succeeding Emperors to lay the foundations of their power throughout the Mediterranean.
>
> Amidst the shades of dead Caesars, in the dust they had trodden, amongst the temples and arches that, blurred by time, still commemorated

> forgotten triumphs, British and Americans fought from shell-hole to shell-hole against the legions of the modern aspirant to world mastership![66]

The story of the progress up the roads was recounted with more ironic appreciation of those references in a semi-autobiographical novel, *The Skin*, by Curzio Malaparte, a journalist (and formerly a Fascist) who was acting as interpreter for Allied troops. In Malaparte's tale, a French general discusses the available guides to Rome, preferring Stendhal to Chateaubriand. As he moves north with the Americans, they find the Appia Nuova blocked, but take the Appia Antica instead, 'a longer route, but it's more picturesque'. Malaparte, mocking the ignorance of the Americans, tells them not only that this is 'the noblest road in the world', but also that the tombs lining it are those of Caesar, Sulla, Cicero and Cleopatra. Belying his jokes and lyrical description of the scenery, however, is a brutal incident: as the Americans pour into a joyful Rome, a man is run over by a Sherman tank.[67] A similar moment is recorded in the memoirs of Roberto Bassi: there the dead man is a Jewish teenager, Claudio Amato, who had been in hiding with Roberto in a city orphanage.[68] Even that happiest of days could not escape a shadow.

In October 1943, Roberto Bassi's family had fled Venice for Rome, hoping that Allied troops would soon reach the capital. They had arrived on the 18th of the month, just as their Roman relatives were being deported to Auschwitz, and spent almost nine months in hiding before liberation finally came on 3 June 1944. Roberto was ill in bed that day:

> Wrapped up in a blanket, I sat there at the bedroom window, watching the road which runs along the Tiber. Throughout the morning and into the early hours of the afternoon that road was crammed by unbroken lines of German soldiers heading north . . . Most of the soldiers were on foot, looking threadbare and exhausted: only a few of them were wearing the helmet which had become such a hated symbol of the Reich.[69]

Another teenager in Rome, Harold H. Tittmann III, son of the American Chargé d'Affaires at the Holy See, had been keeping a diary. On that same night, 3 June, unable to sleep, he watched from the roof of the Santa Marta guest house inside the Vatican complex as the German troops retreated north, up the Via Aurelia, near the Vatican walls.

> One could tell that the Germans were lacking motor transport, for they were extensively using horses to draw wagons and every kind of contraption you could think of. Some were even on bicycles. They had stolen all Rome's horse drawn cabs . . . Some had to carry machine guns on their shoulders. They looked terribly depressed.[70]

The campaign of 1943–4 had cost the lives of about 60,000 Allied troops, and twice that number of Italian civilians.[71] Casualties – including both dead and wounded – are estimated at 336,000 for the Germans, and 313,000 for the Allies.[72] For all that the ancient roads were built in the service of conquest, the modern destruction plumbed new depths.

18

Roman holidays

Thus, in 1944, Rome found itself with some unexpected tourists as Allied troops found themselves in the city with time to spare. GIs were provided with a *Soldier's Guide to Rome* and their British counterparts with an equivalent, *Rome: Allied Soldiers' Souvenir Guide*.[1] Just like the Grand Tour guides of centuries past, these handy pamphlets recommended appropriate trips out. A visit to the Via Appia via the Baths of Caracalla was among them: the *Soldier's Guide* highlighted not only the catacombs but also the church of San Paolo fuori le Mura (St Paul Outside the Walls).[2] Besides guidebooks, there was historical advice, including a *Soldier's Outline of Italian History*.[3] Tourism was encouraged, both as a constructive way to occupy the time of soldiers while they waited either to advance or return home, and in the interests of projecting soft power. The US authorities were keen to ensure that Italy (which had a substantial Communist Party active in the Resistance) would become a friendly liberal democracy.[4]

The interactions of GIs with Italians even inspired fiction. In 1949, Alfred Hayes, who had worked for the US Army Special Services, published *The Girl on the Via Flaminia*, the tale of an American soldier who pretends that the girl in question, Lisa, is his wife. The book makes no mention of the road's ancient origins, except to note that the Ponte Milvio was 'a very old and very much-used bridge'. For his setting, Hayes was more concerned with the brutal modernity of a road on which speeding military vehicles routinely ran down pedestrians, leaving them to bleed out in the gutters.[5]

The war continued, of course, further north. The Brenner Pass, a key resupply route for Germany, remained a target.[6] Meanwhile, as Rome recovered, there were swiftly new memorials, including at the

Fosse Ardeatine, which GIs were informed they could visit: although at this stage the caves had a 'No Entry' sign, Allied soldiers were exempt from that rule.[7] Indeed, while 'dark tourism' might seem a very modern practice, it has ancient roots. Germanicus, a prominent general and nephew of the Emperor Tiberius, is said to have visited a battlefield where the general Publius Quinctilius Varus and his troops had suffered an infamous ambush almost a decade before, in order to pay his respects. Navigating 'wet marshes and treacherous plains, they entered the mournful site, grotesque to behold and for its memories'.[8]

The Fosse Ardeatine attracted mourners almost from the start. Perhaps 7,000 or more of them walked down the Via Ardeatina to lay flowers at the site each Sunday.[9] Among the early visitors, in 1945, was the US journalist Michael Stern, who set the site in deep historical perspective:

> The English priest and I drove through the Aurelian Wall at the turreted gateway of San Sebastiano. Peter had walked here, his feet treading the very stones my jeep was now bumping over, as he fled a Roman pogrom some two thousand years ago. He had reached a point on the Appia Antica about a mile from the gate when Jesus appeared before him and asked '*Domini* [*sic*], *Quo vadis?*' Ashamed at having deserted his faithful followers, Peter turned back to martyrdom and sainthood.
>
> At the church of Domini Quo Vadis, erected on the spot where the Roman soldiers had seized St Peter, I turned right onto Via Ardeatina.[10]

A formal memorial was opened on 24 March 1950, the sixth anniversary of the atrocity.[11] H. V. Morton, author of a popular English book on Rome, also visited; he ran into a German and wondered 'if it were a case of a murderer returning to the scene of his crime'.[12] Given Morton's wider reputation, it's tempting to read that as rather lurid xenophobic speculation, but in fact Erich Priebke, an SS captain involved in the massacre, did go back to Rome as a tourist, not once but twice. He was tried in the 1990s, at first found guilty but left unpunished owing to his subsequent good conduct and because he had been 'following orders'. Only after an outcry was he retried and jailed.[13]

The shifting landscape of memory in Rome is also apparent in the multiple changes to road names made in the post-war years. The Via dell'Impero (Empire Street) became the Via dei Fori Imperiali (Street of the Imperial Forums), the ancient empire less toxic to opinion than the modern one. One street I regularly walked down as a resident of the British School at Rome, Viale Bruno Buozzi, acquired its name in honour of an anti-Fascist trade unionist killed by the Nazi occupiers in 1944. It had previously been Via dei Martiri Fascisti (Street of the Fascist Martyrs).[14] The piazza outside Ostiense train station is now the Piazza dei Partigiani (of the Partisans); the Viale Adolfo Hitler is the Viale delle Cave Ardeatine.[15]

Within a few years of the war, institutions were getting back to normal. Lydian Russell Bennett, a teacher of Latin, arrived in Italy in July 1947 to attend a summer school at the American Academy in Rome (counterpart of the British School).[16] Her ship docked at Naples, where she was shocked by the poverty of the local population, among them soldiers who had lost limbs in the war, and children, 'their almost naked bodies covered with sores'. On Bennett's account, 'our pity was only exceeded by our fright', testimony to the fact that even while one might expect ill children to inspire some sense of sympathy, to Bennett the people of Naples were different, other, an attitude redolent of earlier Grand Tourists. The war had changed the tourist landscape. Bennett's lunch at 'the famous Santa Lucia Hotel . . . the usual spaghetti, wine, and fruit' was eaten in a room where 'the pockmarks of bombing and the smell of fresh concrete were very obvious'. Heading north to Rome, her party saw 'the typical Italian countryside with groves of ancient olive trees, neat vineyards, and multi-colored farm houses'. She was thrilled 'to pass Minturnae and its famous excavations'. Yet her journey north wasn't all so pretty:

> All along the way evidences of bombed-out villages met our eyes. Among the most memorable were Terracina and Formiae. At one village the brave sign '*Banca*' was displayed above two crates covered by a plank, where men were endeavoring to carry on the financial business of the day.
>
> As we neared Rome in the deepening twilight, less and less signs of war damage were seen. Sometimes we were travelling on the ancient

> Appian Way, and then again parallel to the old on the new Appian Way, built to facilitate troop movements. Over the entire distance the road was in good condition, except for temporary bridge spans which brought to mind the newspaper stories of the stand the Germans made as they retreated northward from river to river.[17]

If sometimes Bennett echoed writers of centuries before, her roads to Rome had acquired a new veneer of history.

Rebuilding, however, went on and tourism grew, helped by a hit 1953 film, *Roman Holiday*. Starring Audrey Hepburn and Gregory Peck, it won three Oscars and was one of a series of Hollywood movies filmed at Rome's Cinecittà studios in the 1950s and 60s. Along with *Three Coins in the Fountain*, which came out the following year, it presented Rome as a romantic but also fun contemporary destination.[18] Growth in air travel made intercontinental holidays increasingly practical. By 1955 half of US travellers to Italy were flying, and by 1960 that figure had risen to three-quarters. From 1958, jet planes cut journey times and made direct flights between New York and Europe feasible (earlier flights would stop in Newfoundland, Shannon or both, taking only the very shortest route across the Atlantic). By now women were as likely to take these tours as men, and Frommer's *Europe on $5 a Day*, published in 1957, provided helpful tips for those on a budget taking advantage of the new economy-class fares.[19] Such travel was positively encouraged by the US State Department, which was keen on transatlantic friendship-building and went so far as to provide applicants for US passports with advice on how to help their country while abroad.[20] Fears of communism persisted.

Besides tours of Rome, Italy offered a variety of holidays: art, history and culture could be found in the cities, but there were also seaside and mountain resorts (including skiing in the north), plus hot springs and spas.[21] All of these, of course, had some historical precedent. The ancient Romans had enjoyed their hot baths, but so had Pope Pius II. The Romantics had delighted in mountain views. The entire court of Ravenna had moved to the seaside. For sports fans, it was hoped that the 1960 Olympics would put Italy back on the world stage. While it was awkward to have to use a sports complex, the Foro Italico, designed to glorify the Fascist regime, once the place was integrated into Rome's wider historic landscape the impact of the iconography was somewhat diluted, though the obelisk featuring in giant letters the words 'Mussolini Dux' was left standing, as it still stands today. The marathon route took in some of the Fascist-period roads around the Forum (it's impossible to avoid them if you want to incorporate the sights), along with Rome's most celebrated road, the Via Appia.[22]

That said, the cheap 'sea and sun' tourism of the 1960s presented new challenges for Italy. Aimed at lower-middle-class and working-class travellers who – following wartime service – were now more familiar with aircraft, these inclusive tours from northern to southern Europe made trips to unfamiliar places easy. The clientele, however, was (rightly or wrongly) perceived to be more interested in the beach than in a cultural experience.[23] That was tough for Italy, best known for its history and art. Though it had seaside resorts, its holidays were twice the price of those to Spain and about twenty-five per cent above those to Austria, Yugoslavia and Greece. While in the 1920s tourists had come for a fortnight, by 1965 the average stay was just six days. Air services did not compete effectively and in the late 1980s and early 90s eighty per cent of international travellers arrived by car.[24] Certainly during my childhood Italy did not feel in reach as a holiday option. That changed only with the late 1990s advent of cheap – if environmentally problematic – flights.

Most of my experience of travel to Rome has involved those flights. They have their downsides, and not only in the form of carbon emissions. I get fifteen minutes of the Alps at best if it's not cloudy, and I never see ground level: when I first take the train I realise how much wider the valleys are than they seem from the air. I imagine that's the opposite observation to those of past tourists, who more likely commented on the height of mountains. I didn't try a land route until I could put at least a part of the cost on expenses, driving from England to Italy and back in 2011, as I first considered writing about the journey.

One of the few Italian resorts to enjoy international success was Rimini, at the far end of the Via Flaminia. It developed seaside baths in the 1840s, and thrived in the 1920s and 30s when it abandoned an upmarket image to pursue a more middle-class clientele with all-inclusive packages.[25] The location's popularity with Fascist supporters, however, proved a handicap after the war, and the Kursaal (entertainment hall) and original baths – by that time owned by the local council – were eventually demolished.[26] Its airport, opened in 1938, became the leading Italian charter flight destination from the late 1950s, but in the face of competition from elsewhere in the Mediterranean, Rimini came to rely on domestic tourism and later – after a disastrous year in which algae prevented sea bathing – on conference facilities and theme parks.[27]

Today, the town combines a charming historical centre with a modernised beach resort and attractive seafront boardwalk. As I discover when the GPS tries to send me on the motorway out of Rimini rather than on the Via Flaminia, there have also been substantial improvements to the roads. The context for these post-war routes was a wider interest across Europe in road building as a means of peace-building. Better links and easier movement of people would, the motorways' proponents hoped, improve relations across the continent. An international Working Party on Highways was convened in Geneva in 1948.[28] Italy had come out of the war with a badly damaged railway system, which contributed to a significant increase in road traffic. Plans for a national motorway network gained parliamentary approval in 1955, and by 1981 there were 5,900 km of *autostrade*, compared to just 500 km in 1939. Alongside this expansion of infrastructure went a vast increase in the use of private vehicles, a process known in Italy as *motorizzazione di massa* or 'mass motorisation', facilitated by the development of cheap cars like the Fiat 500 (launched in 1957) and ending only with the oil crisis of 1973 and the accompanying spike in petrol prices. So serious was that crisis, in fact, that driving on Sundays was temporarily banned.[29]

The expansion of the motorways was also part of a wider campaign of social modernisation. In Oria, near Brindisi, a local doctor who had left home to study at Padua in the north and then returned, told visiting journalist Charles Lister in 1960 that: 'Down here it doesn't seem like Europe at all sometimes . . . Still, I expect it will be better when the motorway comes.'[30] Even in the later twentieth century, the idea of roads as a means to civilise persisted. What counted as civilisation, though, was not always consistent. Count Marzotto, proprietor of the Jolly Hotel in Benevento, was apparently tempting tourists with 'two young ladies . . . in permanent residence', which calls to mind the earlier facilities for sexual encounters on the pilgrim routes. The count told Lister that he hoped to expand his business with the expanding motorway network.[31] This is perhaps not quite what the authors of the 1958 coffee table book, *Roads to Rome* (translated from an Austrian edition of the same year, *Wege nach Rom*) were thinking when they enthused over the links between roads ancient and modern:

> It is only in our age of motor travel that the roads to Rome are regaining something of the importance which they lost around the middle of last century with the construction of the railway. The roads now travelled by car, coach and scooter are still the old Roman roads; ancient sites and places of pilgrimage lie on their border and are now visited again.[32]

Not all visitors, however, were admirers of the new developments. Hepburn and Peck might look glamorous on a Vespa but to H. V. Morton, motor traffic was a nuisance. Only by rising early could he avoid it:

> At this time in the morning I had some idea of what Rome must have looked like to the travellers of a hundred years before . . . The old palaces with their iron-bound lower windows, their walls of burnt sienna, yellow, and Roman red, the archways leading to courtyards where wall fountains dripped into moss-grown bowls, though triumphantly Renaissance, stood in dark and narrow lanes which recalled an older, mediaeval world. This moment of silence and dignity, which our ancestors knew, does not last long. Soon the first motors and scooters come hooting and exploding down the road.[33]

As for the papal motorcade, its 'three black touring cars' were accompanied by a 'tremendous roar of motor-cycles and twenty young men in blue uniforms'.[34] Even the institution with the best claim to continuity from the ancient world had embraced modernity.

And then there were the buses. Tourist coaches, Morton commented, surely 'owe something to mechanized warfare and the experience gained in transporting infantry by road'.[35] He described a bus, 'usually half empty', that took passengers from the Colosseum to the Via Appia, 'under a railway arch and [across] a miserable trickle of a stream. It is difficult to believe this is the romantic Almone.'[36] Charles Lister also had some caustic observations on the buses, here observing one at Ariccia, the stop made famous by Horace:

> You can hear Italian buses long before you see them. This one is snorting with exhaustion over by the parapet wall, and if its wheels were legs would be on its knees, for it is old and ill, with tortured skin and gaseous innards giving spasmodic asthmatic hisses, its roof decked with all the southern impedimenta that pass for luggage – home-made crates, splitting suitcases and shapeless cardboard boxes growing spaghetti loops of string and yards of frayed rope – and around it are gathered the passengers-to-be, all bubbling out their excited intimacies as if this were the final journey for all time.[37]

Yet Morton occasionally found the calm past that he was seeking. Passing the villas of the Via Appia, he observed: 'you think that this road cannot have been altered since our ancestors of the nineteenth century drove out here in their carriages'.[38] This spot, where the road 'narrows between old garden walls and vine trellises', was one of the parts of Rome that 'remind one of the tranquillity of the Roman scene as described by writers of the last century'.[39] Morton's book is evidence for the continuing fascination, even post-war, even in the dying years of the European empires, with the Roman roads. The Capitoline, he noted, 'looked down over the heart of the Roman world, that centre of civilization to which all roads led and whence they began'.[40]

That appreciation for the ancient roads informed continuing battles to protect the Via Appia from 'abusive' development by property owners who disregarded planning rules to build just off the main road. Since Canova's interventions in the early nineteenth century, there had been a series of projects to conserve the area's heritage. In 1824, Giuseppe Valadier, architect of the Hotel de Russie, had been granted permission to gather together fragments and inscriptions on the wall beside the Mausoleum of Caecilia Metella. In the middle of the century, Luigi Canina took over, aiming to protect the ancient remains in a great open air museum, and in 1869, the Secretary General of the

Ministry of Commerce, Fine Art, Industry, Agriculture and Public Works praised the reopening of the Via Appia as the greatest of the various papal projects for preservation of Rome's ancient heritage.[41] Multiple initiatives to create an archaeological park followed, and in 1953, the stretch of the Via Appia Antica between Porta San Sebastiano in Rome and Fratocchie/Bovillae (where the side road can now be seen beneath McDonald's), was formally declared to be 'of notable public interest'.[42] Despite restrictions, however, illegal building projects continued well into the twenty-first century.[43] The best prospect for securing the road's future is its addition to the UNESCO World Heritage list, for which its candidacy now has formal sponsorship by the Italian government.[44]

The travellers kept coming. Charles Lister traced the Appian Way in 1960, though he published the story only in 1991.[45] Dora Jane Hamblin, a former Rome bureau chief for *Life* magazine, and Mary Jane Grunsfeld published their version in 1974. They sketched their own histories over Rome's existing layers. By this time, they might have seen the sword-and-sandals epics popular at the cinema, including in 1960 *Spartacus*, perhaps inspired by the many correspondents who had repeated the story in the course of reporting on the Second World War. Some aspects of Italian history, however, proved less comfortable to remember. Lister observed that 'the Italians have little taste for books on war or campaign memories', that they 'felt ashamed' of the likes of Curzio Malaparte.[46] Hamblin and Grunsfeld told a more conventional story, from Charlemagne to Hawthorne and Melville, to Garibaldi. So, no doubt, did many travellers who wrote nothing of their journeys down.

A very different version of the roads appeared in Federico Fellini's 1972 film *Roma*, which through a series of loosely connected scenes tells the story of two journeys to Rome, one in the 1970s and one in the 1930s. Fellini was Riminese, and *Roma* opens with a scene on the Via Flaminia in which a group of women ride their bicycles past a milestone marked 'Rome, 340 km'.[47] This, the narrator tells us, was 'the first image of Rome, a stone consumed by time'. If it isn't quite the usual ancient milestone, it alludes to one, and the subsequent scenes are no less engaged with the past. At school the boys visit the

Rubicon, shouting '*a Roma*' – to Rome; a young Fellini watches a slide show of the city's sights – the bronze Capitoline wolf, Santa Maria Maggiore, the tomb of Caecilia Metella on the Appian Way – until a schoolboy prank throws the showing into chaos: one of the boys has slipped in a slide of an almost-naked woman. This vision of ancient Rome contrasts with the 1970s sequences, where we see a modern motorway toll area, road signs to the Via Salaria, a traffic jam around the Colosseum. A new metro tunnel is going under the Appia Antica, not far from Porta San Sebastiano: the builders have had to skirt a necropolis and they run into a Roman house filled with sculptures and frescoes, only for the air to destroy the ancient art. Back in the 1930s, the young Fellini visits a brothel. While he waits in reception, behind him on the wall hangs a huge painting of pines and aqueducts: the characteristic landscape of the Via Appia.

Seven years later, viewers would learn from Monty Python's *Life of Brian* that the roads went without saying. Not in Italy, though, where the film was banned until 1991.[48]

My last journey to Rome also follows the Via Appia, in my case north from Bari to Benevento. Plenty of tourists made their way to the south. From the middle of the eighteenth century, the remains of Pompeii were a key attraction, but even earlier so were the southern cities, despite the need to navigate the stony roads. In 1753, Luigi Vanvitelli, the leading Italian architect of his day, complained of the state of them: 'unimaginably bad and one risks being overturned, so uneven are the stones ... Poor Via Appia!'[49] Although today's train takes a more northerly route than either the Via Traiana or the older Via Appia, the journey gives a sense of the territory. The first stretch north from Bari to Foggia is an easy ride, flat and close to the coast. Benevento, however, can only be reached through hillier country, nowadays traversed in tunnels. Still, the railway doesn't reach the old centre. It's late enough when I arrive that I take a taxi to my flat rather than walk.

In 1717, George Berkeley, Bishop of Cloyne, came here and saw the 'streets paved with marble' and 'many fragments of antiquity in the walls of houses'.[50] The principal monument, however, is the Arch of Trajan, commemorating the construction of the Via Appia Traiana between Benevento and Brindisi. Vanvitelli and Jean-Claude Richard de Saint-Non, a painter and printmaker travelling in 1781, both appreciated the sight. 'Exceedingly beautiful', noted the former, despite the fact that 'the barbarity of our age has had a city gate built within this splendid arch'.[51] It was 'one of the best-preserved monuments to be found in Italy', wrote the latter.[52] Almost two centuries on, Charles Lister likewise saw the arch: 'square and dominant, wrinkled by a hundred detailed carvings to show the emperors' triumphant passage through history, and said to be the finest Roman arch in Christendom'.[53] The decorative scheme, in fact, records the pacification of Germany and the Danube regions, as well as Trajan's reorganisation of the army and the subjugation of Dacia.[54]

Beside the monument is a plaque with a quotation from Giovanni de Nicastro, a local historian, dated 1723:

> Everyone must admire the arch so as you all admire the bones of giants. Everyone must relive its wonder and almost worship it with silence. We must consider that this huge work has never been so revered as it is now. Indeed, it will be more and more venerable and venerated in the next centuries.

Look at its setting now, and that prediction has been borne out. The area around the arch has been cleared and it's framed by the ubiquitous lines of modern architecture. Square and dominant maybe, but that view isn't ancient. It's a Fascist cityscape again, the arch tiny at the vanishing point of the street, a reminder of how closely the roads have been tied to militarism ancient and modern.

I take the high-speed train for the last leg of my journey. Two hours only, and one stop. The train cuts through in tunnels; you have to imagine for yourself the Appia slinking through cuttings and over hills. At Caserta, it stops almost right outside the Reggia, the royal country residence outside Naples, once Allied headquarters. From there north, the railway runs closer to the Via Casilina than to the Appia, up the Liri valley, passing to my left haunted mountains with their wartime cemeteries. Step out of the train at Termini. I've been here often enough that I don't mind the lack of view. Ignore the buses, take a taxi. I'm in Rome.

Epilogue: On the roads today

Yoshio Markino, an artist, visited Rome early in the twentieth century. He was underwhelmed at first and wondered why. Then it came to him: 'To the European, Rome is the revelation of their ancestors. To us Japanese, Rome is only a strange town.'[1] Perhaps it takes an outsider to spot the mentality that makes the Romans the ancestors of other Europeans rather than – or as well as – our conquerors. Certainly, in my home country, the Roman road network has been absorbed into the landscape. Its moss and myths are inscribed in the green of meadows, freckled with the brown of autumn leaves. Fosse Way runs 220 miles between Lincoln and Seaton in Devon, long stretches still evident. From Kent, Watling Street crosses the Thames at London, and rises through the Midlands to reach the Roman city near Wroxeter. We have Ermine Street and Dere Street; along Hadrian's Wall runs Stanegate. Roads barely remembered rise from the flat as field boundaries beside hedgerows. Until the coming of the motorways, this network of routes was the basis for much of Britain's road system.[2]

Yet focus only on the numbers, the construction, the sheer distance and engineering – how many miles again? – and you overlook the cultural power of these seemingly common stones. It's rare that you can pick up an object this old without setting off the museum alarm, but across Europe and beyond you can walk on Roman roads. There's an undeniable magic about sharing these places with the people of the past. Every so often, a map overlaying the ancient roads onto modern ones goes viral. As I was writing this book, my phone's algorithm spotted my interest and sent me story after story about the Roman roads. From Stirling to Cádiz to Istanbul, travelling these roads, going overland, makes for a sense of connection that flights don't allow. Yet this isn't the whole story. The actual Roman road network was not simply European: the Mediterranean was at the empire's heart. You might think stones don't lie but the canon of roads has shifted over time, from the original circuit of the inland sea to become more and more a western one, and north-western at that, as north-west Europe became rich. The story of the roads has become a European one. It's a tale of uniformity, of an empire of towns, each remembering its amphitheatre, forum, baths, theatre, road and arch, connected by conquest, coercion and co-option into a remarkable heritage.

While road-building projects were certainly praised, both by the Romans themselves on inscriptions and by outside observers, it's harder to tell what those beyond the elite made of the new network in its first centuries. Maybe people welcomed easier travel from A to B; maybe they resented the appropriation of their land for road building and the forced labour so evocatively described by Tacitus. Perhaps there was a bit of both. We don't know, but look at any modern road-building scheme and you'll see objections. Even once the new bypass is built, some people will still say it's a shame those trees had to be cut down. Roads have a cost. And that's roads with some democracy in the planning process. Though we have only hints of ancient complaint, they're enough to conclude that it existed. There was almost a millennium between the 'fall' – or, better, slow decline – of the Western Roman Empire and the revival of interest in the ancient roads. That renaissance coincided with the rise of the first European empires that not only reconquered sections of the Roman world but went out to find new territory. Imperial history was newly useful. The discourse of the roads as something 'the Romans did for us' has been absorbed so far into European culture that we tend to forget that historical gap. The modern fascination with the Roman roads began at a point when the roads were beyond memory, so far into a mythologised past that few stories remained to interfere with a narrative of appreciation. If Tacitus' 'make a desert and call it peace' is now a well-known phrase, his accompanying allusion to forced labour in road building is not. Rome's past has been usable history for popes and princes, for modern emperors, for activists, for politicians. Rome itself has been remade, and it's been made elsewhere, with arches and domes and roads and their successors: railways. Rome offers a lesson in the history of empires – not only directly but through the many subsequent empires that have found in it inspiration.[3] Yet in the interpretation of the roads, that history is rarely subject to much critical interrogation. We are still with Lassels, with roads as the 'greatest Proofs of the *Romans* Greatness and Riches'.

We should recall, though, the moments of subversion. In the seventeenth century, Tadhg Ó Cianáin's travel narrative was clear that the Romans – and by implication those who sought to follow them – were the persecutors. In 1968, Nikki Giovanni, an African-American poet, responded to the recent assassinations of Martin Luther King and Malcolm X by flipping the old civilising narrative of Roman history:

> they killed the Carthaginians
> in the great appian way
> And they killed the Moors
> 'to civilize a nation'[4]

As I write, the Via Appia 'Regina Viarum' (Queen of the Roads) is on the tentative list of UNESCO World Heritage Sites. The description cites its 'outstanding feats of engineering', the 'revolution in road construction brought about by the Romans', the 'truly innovative' legal status of Roman roads and its importance 'in the history of architectural restoration for the many works aimed at reclaiming and restoring it'.[5] This is all fair enough, but we might ask *why* there were so many works from the sixteenth century onwards to reclaim and restore it. The histories of this road, and the choices made to intervene on it, are not neutral. The listing reflects an ambivalence about empire that is very characteristic of present-day Europe.

Yet the potential listing also represents an opportunity to reconsider the history of the Roman roads and how they're presented to tourists. The Appia isn't the only historic route to be accorded cultural status. Beginning in 1987 with the Santiago de Compostela pilgrim route – since 1993 also a World Heritage Site – the Council of Europe has recognised 'Cultural Routes' across Europe, adding the Via Francigena in 2004. A foundation has been established to develop the ancient Via Egnatia as a walking route. The roads offer a remarkable opportunity to talk about two millennia of history, not to mention a chance to experience gorgeous landscapes at a slower pace. Their ruins and renovations are filled with the memories of a continent.

What stories might we tell about the roads? For a start, I'd like to know more about the people who did the work of building them. In the absence of records, the only way to cross that gulf is through feats of imagination, rather than historical research, but such exercises are important. Remember the rabbis? Once upon a time, being snarky about what the Romans did for us would get you a death sentence. It's no wonder people kept their mouths shut. That shouldn't mean we can't discuss it now. We should talk about the political uses of the roads, why emperors from Charlemagne to Napoleon thought to revive them, why new roads and new cityscapes around old ones became so important under Fascism, and why the roads became a source of inspiration for writers and artists. Roman roads encapsulate ideas about technological superiority, military prowess, and mastery of nature, but embedded in the landscape for centuries they allow that history to appear picturesque. They offer a lesson in the exercise of power across the centuries: if we understand how they've been used and misused we might be better placed to think through how today's great political projects work for those who fund and commission them, for those who are intended to benefit, and for those who along the way lose out. We might also understand better the importance of this heritage to the creation of Western and European identities, and its role in the stories that we tell ourselves about who we are.

After eighteen months of staying home, I make my first trip back to Rome in November 2021. When I leave, after three weeks, it's dawn. The sun washes over the facade of the Lateran and glazes the top floors of apartment blocks. To reach Ciampino from Rome's centre you head down past the fountain at Repubblica, down the line of metro A, past the stop called Re di Roma, named for the ancient kings of Rome. Past a pizza shop that bears that royal name. Out onto the Via Appia Nuova, a dual carriageway, not so romantic, to either side car showrooms, furniture stores and supermarkets.

Lines of aqueducts in slender brick, and now a tomb. The ubiquitous pines break into the sky. The Appia Antica. Two thousand years beneath us. A plane descends towards the airport. The road leads east. We're driving almost into the light.

Acknowledgements

More than any book I have written, this one has been the work of many hands. I am grateful to my agent Catherine Clarke, editors Will Hammond and Alice Skinner, copyeditor Duncan Heath, managing editor Graeme Hall and publicist Susie Merry. Thanks also to Stephen Parker for the original hardback cover design, and to Chris Wormell and Amelia Tolley for the illustration and design of the paperback. I owe a particular debt to the staff, fellows and scholars of the British School at Rome – especially but not only my own class of 2009–10 – without whom I would know far less about the city and its history than I do. When I visited in autumn 2021, Clare Hornsby provided a very helpful introduction to historic guidebooks from the School's collections.

The early work for this book was done during the coronavirus lockdowns of 2020–21, during which time I was very grateful for the research assistance of Luke Daly-Groves on Napoleon, Garibaldi, and the Second World War; Lauren Wainwright on the Byzantine Empire; Luisa Izzi on early medieval Rome; and Charlotte Gauthier and Edward Caddy on pilgrims and crusaders. Student research interns on Manchester Metropolitan University's RISE scheme provided further assistance: they included in 2020 Connor Jephcott, Larissa Brettingham-Smith, Lauren Gannon and Roisin Loughrey; and in 2022 Samuel Jolly, Caitlin Ryan Denholm, Mattia Franchina and Henrieta Montvilaite. Thanks to Manchester Met's wider student internship scheme, Filorida Semere Tesfay researched locations and travel arrangements, Lucy Hopkinson researched pictures, and Lagoon Myers assisted with publicity. Emma Glendhill shared references; April Pudsey, Luisa Izzi, Kathryn Hurlock, Jérémy Filet, Anna Mercer and Luke Daly-Groves kindly read and commented on drafts.

The staff of both my own university library at Manchester Metropolitan University and that of the neighbouring University of Manchester made a huge effort to keep services running safely through extended restrictions on social mixing. Once I could travel again, my work was made possible by the hundreds of people who staff heritage sites, museums, hotels, trains, travel agencies, bus companies, restaurants and cafés across the footprint of the Roman road network. My journeys were much smoother thanks to the comprehensive guide to international train travel at seat61.com. I'm grateful that the UK's decision to leave the European Union did not also involve us leaving Interrail, and frustrated that it did require me to spend hours of my time checking visa rules when a few years ago I could have exercised my right to work across the EU.

As I was completing this book I learnt of the untimely deaths of two old friends, Alan McArthur and Andrea Spreafico, for whose support at different points of my writing career I would like to record my gratitude. I could not have asked for better companions on my journey.

The Travel

Summer 2021

Bath — Cirencester — Wall — Wroxeter Roman City — York — Corbridge — St Mary Whitekirk — The Antonine Wall

November 2021

From Bern to Rome, via the Simplon Pass — Narni

April 2022: Via Julia Augusta

Cádiz — Seville/Italica — Córdoba — Valencia — Tarragona — Barcelona — Nîmes — Turin

September 2022: Via Francigena, Via Julia Augusta, Via Emilia, Via Flaminia, Via Appia

Paris — Avignon — Orange — Arles — Monaco — Nice — Genoa — Pavia — Rimini — Ravenna — Furlo — Viterbo — Rome — Pozzuoli — Terracina — Anzio — Cassino

October 2022: Via Militaris (Diagonalis), Via Egnatia, Via Traiana/Appia

Vienna/Carnuntum — Sofia — Plovdiv — Istanbul — Thessaloniki — Durrës — Bari — Monte Sant' Angelo — Benevento — Rome

Through fourteen countries: UK, Spain, France, Switzerland, Italy, Belgium, Germany, Austria, Hungary, Romania, Bulgaria, Turkey, Greece, Albania.

List of Illustrations

1. *Arch of Augustus*, Rimini, Emilia Romagna, Italy. © Gacro74 / Alamy.
2. *Round milestone from the Ephesus area*, Asset ID: 1426322156. © Z. Ayse Kiyas Aslanturk / Shutterstock.
3. *Votive Deposit of Vicarello*, probably first century CE. One of four silver cups, each bearing an itinerary from Cádiz to Rome. © Ryan Bauman / Flickr. Used under a CC-BY-2.0-DEED licence.
4. *Slab with feet in relief and dedicatory inscription to the goddess Caelestis*. Marble, third century CE. Musei Capitolini, Palazzo Senatorio, Galleria Lapidaria. Inventory no. 2416. © Sovrintendenza Capitolina / Foto in Comune.
5. *Rome and Central Italy, from the Peutinger Table,* thirteenth-century copy of a fourth-century original. © DEA Picture Library / Getty.
6. *Bibliothèque de Genève, ms. fr. 85, William of Tyre, History of the Crusades*. f. 130v. c. 1460–65. © www.e-codices.ch
7. *On the Road to Emmaus*, Jesus and two disciples, Duccio di Buoninsegna, c. 1308–11, Museo dell'Opera del Duomo, Siena. © Wikimedia Commons.
8. *A wood-cut map of Germany,* Erhard Etzlaub, Nuremberg, c. 1492. © British Library Board / Bridgeman.

9. *Courtyard of an Inn with Classical Ruins*, c. 1621–47, Viviano Codazzi and Domenico Gargiulo, Walters Art Museum. Acquired by Henry Walters with the Massarenti Collection, 1902. © Creative Commons Licence.
10. *Exit from cave Crypta Neapolitana (or Grotta di Posillipo) on the coast of Pozzuoli*, Louis Ducros, 1778. © Sepia Times / Universal Images Group / Getty.
11. *Napoleon Bonaparte crossing the Saint Bernard in 1800*, Paul Delaroche, 1848, Louvre Museum, Paris. © Leemage / Corbis / Getty.
12. *View of Rome from the Arco Oscuro,* 1831, (oil over graphite on paper), André Giroux. © Fitzwilliam Museum, University of Cambridge / Bridgeman.
13. *Fosse Way*, Gloucestershire, 2018. Aerial view of the Roman road looking north-east towards Northleach. © English Heritage / Heritage Images / Getty.
14. *Mussolini with a Pickaxe on the cover of 'La Domenica del Corriere'*, 1935. © Stefano Bianchetti / Corbis / Getty.
15. *Hand-drawn postcard from Aldous Huxley to Matthew Huxley*, 1924. Aldous and Laura Huxley papers. © UCLA Library Special Collections. By kind permission of the Huxley estate.
16. *Roman Holiday*, Audrey Hepburn and Gregory Peck in front of the Colosseum, directed by William Wyler, 1953. © Archivio di Augusto Di Giovanni / Bridgeman.

Bibliography

Archive and newspaper sources, and the few printed sources I was unable to check directly, are cited in full in the notes.

Printed primary sources

Addison, Joseph. 1718. *Remarks on Several Parts of Italy*. 2nd edn. London.

Alberti, Leandro. 1550. *Descrittione di Tutta Italia*. Bologna.

Allen, Grant. 1899. *The European Tour*. New York.

The Anglo-Saxon Chronicle according to the several original authorities. 1964. Ed. by B. Thorpe. Milwood.

Anon. 1668. 'Vita Ex MS. Beneuentano.' In *Acta Sanctorum Volume 06: Mar. I*, 340-264. Antwerp.

——. 1839. *The Roads and Railroads, Vehicles, and Modes of Travelling, of Ancient and Modern Countries*. London.

——. 1882. *Le Voyage de La Saincte Cyté de Hierusalem*. Ed. by M. Ch. Schefer. Paris.

——. 1958. *Roads to Rome: From Pisa, Bologna and Ravenna to the Eternal City*. London and New York.

Bandinelli, Ranuccio Bianchi. 1995. *Hitler e Mussolini, 1938: il viaggio del Führer in Italia*. Rome.

Bassi, Roberto. 2014. *Skirmishes on Lake Ladoga. Venice to Rome: In Flight from the Racial Laws*. Trans. by Jeremy Scott. New York.

Beals, Carleton. 1932. *Rome or Death: The Story of Fascism*. London.

Beard, Thomas, and Thomas Taylor. 1648. *The Theatre of Gods Judgements*. London.

Beckford, William. 1783. *Dreams, Waking Thoughts and Incidents*. London.

——. 1834. *Biographical Memoirs of Extraordinary Painters*. London.

Bede, the Venerable. 1723. *The Ecclesiastical History of the English Nation*. London.

Benjamin of Tudela. 1907. *The Itinerary of Benjamin of Tudela*. Ed. by Marcus Nathan Adler. New York.

Bennett, Lydian Russell. 1948. 'A Roman Summer'. *The Classical Journal*, 43.6: 359–65.

Berkeley, George. 1948. *The Works of George Berkeley Bishop of Cloyne*. Ed. by A. A. Luce and T. E. Jessup. 9 vols. London.

Biondo, Flavio. 1927. *Scritti inediti e rari*. Rome.

Bonaparte, Napoleon. 1856. *The Confidential Correspondence of Napoleon Bonaparte with His Brother Joseph*. 2 vols. New York.

Bordeaux Pilgrim (*c*.333 CE), *The Bordeaux Pilgrim*. Trans. by Andrew Jacobs. Online at: https://andrewjacobs.org/translations/bordeaux.html.

Boswell, James. 1867. *The Life of Samuel Johnson, LL.D.* London.

Bracciolini, Poggio. 1993. *De Varietate Fortunae*. Ed. by Outi Merisalo. Helsinki.

de la Brocquière, Bertrandon. 1807. *The Travels of Bertrandon de La Brocquière*. Trans. by Thomas Johnes. Hafod.

de Brosses, Charles. 1885. *Lettres Familières Écrites d'Italie En 1739 et 1740*. Paris.

Bryce, James. 1914. *The Ancient Roman Empire and the British Empire in India*. London.

Buckley, Christopher. 1945. *Road To Rome*. London.

de Busbecq, Ogier Ghiselin. 1968. *The Turkish Letters of Ogier Ghiselin de Busbecq, Imperial Ambassador at Constantinople, 1554–1562*. Oxford.

Byron, Lord. 1828. *The Works of Lord Byron*. 4 vols. London.

Camden, William. 1695. *Camden's Britannia newly translated into English, with large additions and improvements*. Trans. by Edmund Gibson. London.

Canova, Antonio. 1825. *Napoleon and Canova: Eight Conversations Held at the Chateau of the Tuileries, in 1810*. London.

Carducci, Giosue. 1897. 'Per la morte di Giuseppe Garibaldi', in *Letture del Risorgimento italiano scelte e ordinate da Giosue Carducci*. Vol. 2, 540–49. Bologna.

Cassiodorus, Magnus Aurelius. 1886. *The Letters of Cassiodorus*. Ed. by Thomas Hodgkin. London. Online at: https://www.gutenberg.org/files/18590/18590-h/18590-h.htm

Cavour, Camillo. 1962–2012. *Epistolario*. 21 vols. Florence.

de Chateaubriand, François-René. 1828. *Travels in America and Italy*. 2 vols. London.

Chaucer, Geoffrey. 1870. *The Treatise on the Astrolabe of Geoffrey Chaucer*. Ed. by Andrew Edmund Brae. London.

Chetwode Eustace, John. 1819. *A Classical Tour Through Italy*. London.

Codex Theodosianus. 1923. Ed. by P. Krueger. Berlin.

Corpus Velazqueño: Documentos y Textos. 2000. Ed. by the Dirección General de Bellas Artes y Bienes Culturales. 2 vols. Madrid.

Coryat, Thomas. 1905. *Coryats Crudities*. 2 vols. Glasgow.

Coxe, Henry (John Millard). 1815. *Picture of Italy; Being a Guide to the Antiquities and Curiosities of That Classical and Interesting Country*. London.

Crosland, Camilla (Mrs Newton). 1871. *The Diamond Wedding, A Doric Story, and Other Poems*. London.

The Deeds of the Franks and Other Jerusalem-Bound Pilgrims: The Earliest Chronicle of the First Crusades. 2011. Ed. by Nirmal Dass. Lanham, MD.

Dickens, Charles. 1846. *Pictures from Italy*. London.

Dorr, David F. 1999. *A Colored Man Round the World*. Ed. by Malini Johar Schueller. Ann Arbor, MI.

Douglass, Frederick. 1892. *The Life and Times of Frederick Douglass*. Boston.

Doyle, Gregory. 1910. *Incidents of European Travel*. Syracuse, NY.

Dulcken, H. W. 1866. *A Picture History of England Written for the Use of the Young*. London.

Egeria. 1999. *Egeria's Travels*. Ed. by John Wilkinson. 3rd edn. Warminster.

Eliot, George. 1889. *Middlemarch*. Chicago.

——. 1998. *The Journals of George Eliot*. Ed. by Margaret Harris and Judith Johnston. Cambridge.

Elliot, Frances. 1872. *Diary of an Idle Woman in Italy*. Leipzig.

Epitaphium Ansae reginae. 1878. Ed. by Ludwig Bethmann and Georg Waitz, MGH, *Scriptores rerum Langobardicarum et Italicarum saec. VI–IX*. Hanover, pp. 191–2.

Estienne, Charles. 1552. *La guide des chemins de France*. Paris.

Eusebius Pamphilus. 1845. *The Life of the Blessed Emperor Constantine*. London.

Fabri, Felix. 1896. *The Book of the Wanderings of Brother Felix Fabri*. Trans. by Aubrey Stewart. 2 vols. London.

Fenimore Cooper, James. 1838. *Gleanings in Europe*. 2 vols. Philadelphia.

Fisher Jr, Ernest F. 1993. *Cassino to the Alps*. Washington, DC.

Fletcher C. R. L., and Rudyard Kipling. 1911. *A History of England*. New York.

Forster, E. M. 2000. *A Room With A View*. Ed. by Malcolm Bradbury. London.

Frederick I, Holy Roman Emperor. 2016. *The Crusade of Frederick Barbarossa: The History of the Expedition of the Emperor Frederick and Related Texts*. Ed. by G. A. Loud. London.

Freud, Sigmund. 1953–74. *The Standard Edition of the Complete Psychological Works of Sigmund Freud*. Ed. by James Strachey and Anna Freud. 24 vols. London.

Frost, Ruth Sterling. 1934. 'The Reclamation of the Pontine Marshes', *Geographical Review*, 24.4, 584–95.

Fulcher of Chartres. 2017. *Fulcher of Chartres: Chronicle of the First Crusade*. Trans. by Martha Evelyn McGinty. Philadelphia.

Fuller Ossoli, Margaret. 1852. *Memoirs*. 3 vols. London.

Galen. *Claudii Galeni Opera Omnia. Volume 10*. 2011. Ed. by Karl Gottlob Kühn. Cambridge.

Gamucci, Bernardo. 1565. *Libri Quattro Dell'antichità di Roma*. Venice.

Geoffrey de Villehardouin. 1908. *Memoirs or Chronicle of the Fourth Crusade and the Conquest of Constantinople*. Trans. by Frank T. Marzials. London.

Gilles, Pierre. 1729. *The Antiquities of Constantinople: With a Description of Its Situation, the Conveniencies of Its Port ...* London.

Giovanni, Nikki. 1968. *The Great Pax Whitie*. Online at: https://www.poetryfoundation.org/poems/48221/the-great-pax-whitie

Goethe, Johann Wolfgang von. 1885. *Goethe's Travels in Italy*. Trans. by Alexander James William Morrison and Charles Nisbet. London.

——. 1977. *Roman Elegies*. Trans. by David Luke. London.

Gogol, Nikolai. 2020. *The Nose and Other Stories*. Trans. by Susanne Fusso. New York.

Graham, Maria. 1820. *Three Months Passed in the Mountains East of Rome, During the Year 1819*. London.

Graves, Robert. 1934. *Claudius the God and His Wife Messalina*. Harmondsworth.

Gray, Thomas. 1935. *Correspondence of Thomas Gray*. Ed. by Leonard Whibley and Paget Jackson Toynbee. 3 vols. Oxford.

Gregorius. 1987. *The Marvels of Rome*. Trans. and ed. by John Osborne. Toronto.

Grenier, Albert. 1938. *Le Strade romane nella Gallia ... II edizione*. [Quaderni dell'Impero. Le grandi strade del mondo romano. no. 1.] Rome.

Hali. 1997. *Hali's Musaddas: The Flow and Ebb of Islam*. Trans. by Christopher Shackle and Javed Majeed. Delhi.

Hawthorne, Nathaniel. 1901. *The Marble Faun*. 2 vols. Boston.

——. 1980. *The French and Italian Notebooks*. Ed. by Thomas Woodson. Ohio.

Hayes, Alfred. 2007. *The Girl on the Via Flaminia*. New York.

Hazlitt, William. 1826. *Notes of a Journey Through France and Italy*. London.

Hillard, George Stillman. 1881. *Six Months in Italy*. Boston.

Hitler, Adolf. 1973. *Hitler's Table Talk, 1941–44: His Private Conversations*. Trans. by Norman Cameron and R. H. Stevens. 2nd edn. London.

Howells, W. D. 2004. *Italian Journeys*. Online at: https://www.gutenberg.org/files/14276/14276-h/14276-h.htm

Huxley, Aldous. 1948. *Along the Road: Notes and Essays of a Tourist*. London.

Informacõn for Pylgrymes unto the Holy Londe. 1824. Ed. by George Henry Freeling. London.

Isabella d'Este. 2017. *Isabella d'Este: Selected Letters*. Ed. and trans. by Deanna Shemek. Tempe, AZ.

James, Henry. 1875. *Transatlantic Sketches*. Boston.

——. 1909. *Italian Hours*. London.

Jefferson, Thomas. 2006. *Notes on the State of Virginia*. Chapel Hill, NC. Online at: https://docsouth.unc.edu/southlit/jefferson/jefferson.html

Jerome, Saint. 2013. *Jerome's Epitaph on Paula: A Commentary on the Epitaphium Sanctae Paulae*. Ed. and trans. by Andrew Cain. Oxford.

Kempe, Margery. 2000. *The Book of Margery Kempe*. Ed. by B. A. Windeatt. Harlow.

——. 2015. *The Book of Margery Kempe*. Ed. by Anthony Bale. Oxford.

Kennedy, Paul A. 2016. *Battlefield Surgeon: Life and Death on the Front Lines of World War II*. Lexington, KY.

Klein, Harry. 1969. *Light Horse Cavalcade: The Imperial Light Horse, 1899–1961*. London.

Lassels, Richard. 1697. *An Italian Voyage, or, A Compleat Journey through Italy*. London.

Lawrence, D. H. 1923. *Sea and Sardinia*. London.

Le Huen, Nicole. 1517. *Le grant voyage de Jherusalem*. Paris.

Lister, Charles. 1991. *Between Two Seas: A Walk down the Appian Way*. London.

The Lives of the Ninth-Century Popes (Liber Pontificalis): The Ancient Biographies of Ten Popes from A.D. 817–891. 1995. Trans. by Raymond Davis. Liverpool.

Ludwig, Emil. 1950. *Colloqui Con Mussolini*. Trans. by Tomaso Gnoli. Milan.

McMillan, Richard. 1945. *Twenty Angels Over Rome: The Story of Fascist Italy's Fall*. London.

Maillet, Thomas (?). 2007. *Les proverbez d'Alain*. Ed. by Tony Hunt. Paris.

Malaparte, Curzio. 2013. *The Skin*. Trans. by David Moore. New York.

Medieval Italy: Texts in Translation. 2009. Ed. and trans. by Katherine Ludwig Jansen, Joanna H. Drell and Frances Andrews. Philadelphia.

Melena, Elpis. 1861. *Recollections of General Garibaldi, Or, Travels from Rome to Lucerne*. London.

Melville, Herman. 1989. *Journals*. Evanston, IL.

Mesarites, Nicholas. 2017. *His Life and Works (in Translation)*. Trans. by Michael Angold. Liverpool.

Miltoun, Francis. 1909. *Italian Highways and Byways from a Motor Car*. Boston.

——. 1913. 'Europe's Good Roads', *Scientific American*, 108.2: 36–54.

Montaigne, Michel. 1903. *The Journal of Montaigne's Travels in Italy*. Trans. by W. G. Waters. 3 vols. London.

Moore, John. 1820. *The Works of John Moore, MD, with Memoirs of his Life and Writings*. 7 vols. Edinburgh.

Morgan, Sydney (Lady). 1821. *Italy*. 2 vols. London.

Morton, H. V. 1957. *A Traveller in Rome*. New York.

Moryson, Fynes. 1907. *An Itinerary Containing His Ten Yeeres Travell: Through the Twelve Dominions*. 4 vols. Glasgow.

Munday, Anthony. 1980. *The English Roman Life*. Oxford.

Muñoz, Antonio. 1935. *Roma di Mussolini*. Milan.

Murray, John (Firm). 1853. *Rome and Its Environs*. London.

Mussolini, Benito. 1951–62. *Opera omnia di Benito Mussolini*. Ed. by Edoardo Susmel and Duilio Susmel. 35 vols. Florence.

N. D. R. 1929. 'Il concorso per il Palazzo delle Poste e Telegrafi a Napoli'. *Architettura e Arti Decorative*, Fascicolo 1, September 1929. Online at: https://opac.sba.uniroma3.it/arardeco/1929/29_I/Art1/I1T.html

Newnan, William Loring. 1945. *Escape in Italy: The Narrative of Lieutenant William L. Newnan*. Ann Arbor, MI.

Nithard. 1970. *Carolingian Chronicles: Royal Frankish Annals and Nithard's Histories*. Ed. by Bernhard Walter Scholz. Ann Arbor, MI.

North, Thomas. 2020. *Thomas North's 1555 Travel Journal: From Italy to Shakespeare*. Ed. by Dennis McCarthy and June Schlueter. Lanham, MD.

Nugent, Thomas. 1749. *The Grand Tour. Containing an Exact Description of Most of the Cities, Towns, and Remarkable Places of Europe*. London.

Ó Cianáin, Tadhg, and Paul Walsh. 1915. 'The Flight of the Earls'. *Archivium Hibernicum*, 4: iii–268.

Odo of Deuil. 1948. *De Profectione Ludovici VII in Orientem = The Journey of Louis VII to the East*. New York.

The Origins of the Grand Tour: The Travels of Robert Montague, Lord Mandeville (1649–1654), William Hammond (1655–1658), Banaster Maynard (1660–1663). 2004. Ed. by Michael G. Brennan. London.

Palmer Putnam, George. 1838. *The Tourist in Europe*. New York.

Parker, John Henry. 1883. *The Via Sacra. Excavations in Rome from 1438 to 1882*. Oxford.

Paul the Deacon. 1878. *Historia Langobardorum*. Hanover.

Peabody Hawthorne, Sophia. 1869. *Notes in England and Italy*. New York.

Phocas, Joannes. 1889. *The Pilgrimage of Joannes Phocas in the Holy Land*. Trans. by Aubrey Stewart. London.

Piccolomini, Aeneas Sylvius (Pius II). 1947. *The Commentaries of Pius II: Books IV and V*. Trans. by Florence Alden Gragg, and ed. by Leona C. Gabel. Northampton, MA.

——. 1988. *Secret Memoirs of a Renaissance Pope: The Commentaries of Aeneas Sylvius Piccolomini Pius II*. Trans. by Florence Alden Gragg, and ed. by Leona C. Gabel. London.

Piozzi, Hester Lynch. 1789. *Observations and Reflections Made in the Course of a Journey through France, Italy and Germany*. 2 vols. London.

Playfair, Robert Lambert. 1877. *Travels in the Footsteps of Bruce in Algeria and Tunis*. London.

Potter, Olave M., and Yoshio Markino. 1910. *The Colour of Rome*. Toronto.

Priorato, Galeazzo Gualdo. 1658. *The History of the Sacred and Royal Majesty of Christina Alessandra, Queen of Swedland*. Trans. by John Burbury. London.

Raymond d'Aguilers. 1968. *Historia Francorum Qui Ceperunt Iherusalem*. Trans. by J. H. Hill and L. L. Hill. Philadelphia.

Raymond, John. 1648. *An Itinerary: Contayning a Voyage, Made Through Italy, in the Yeare 1646, and 1647*. London.

Riggs Miller, Anna. 1777. *Letters from Italy*. 2nd edn. 2 vols. London.

Riqueti, Victor, Marquis de Mirabeau. 1762. *L'Ami des hommes, ou Traité de la population*. New corrected edn. 4 vols. Avignon.

Rogers, Samuel. 1828. *Italy: A Poem. Part the Second*. London.

——. 1956. *The Italian Journal of Samuel Rogers*. Ed. by J. R. Hale. London.

Romanelli, Pietro. 1938. 'Le grandi strade romane nell'Africa settentrionale', *Le grandi strade del mondo romano*, 13. Rome.

Ruskin, John. 1909. *Works of John Ruskin*. Ed. by E. T. Cook and Alexander Wedderburn. 39 vols. London.

——. 1972. *Ruskin in Italy: Letters to his Parents*. Ed. by H. I. Shapiro. Oxford.

Sandys, George. 1615. *A Relation of a Journey Begun an Dom. 1610. Foure Bookes Containing a Description of the Turkish Empire, of Aegypt, of the Holy Land, of the Remote Parts of Italy, and Ilands Adjoyning*. London.

Sanudo Torsello, Marino. 2011. *Marino Sanudo Torsello, the Book of the Secrets of the Faithful of the Cross = Liber Secretorum Fidelium Crucis / Marino Sanudo Torsello*. Trans. by Peter Lock. Farnham.

Scudder, Horace. 1901. *James Russell Lowell: A Biography*. 2 vols. Boston.

Shelley, Mary Wollstonecraft. 1844. *Rambles in Germany and Italy in 1840, 1842, and 1843*. 2 vols. London.

Shelley, Percy. 1880. *Prose Works of P. B. Shelley*. 4 vols. London.

Smollett, Tobias. 1907. *Travels through France and Italy*. Ed. by Thomas Seccombe. Oxford.

de Staël, Madame. 1833. *Corinne, or Italy*. Trans. by Isabel Hill. London.

Starke, Mariana. 1800. *Letters from Italy, between the Years 1792 and 1798*. 2 vols. London.

Stendhal. 1997. *The Charterhouse of Parma*. Trans. by Margaret Mauldon. Oxford.

Stephanus, Eddius. 1927. *The Life of Bishop Wilfrid*. Ed. by Bertram Colgrave. Cambridge.

Stern, Michael. 1964. *An American in Rome*. New York.

Sterne, Laurence. 2003. *A Sentimental Journey And Other Writings*. Ed. by Ian Jack and Tim Parnell. Oxford.

Strong, Eugénie. 1938. 'Viaggio attraverso le strade della Britannia romana', *Le grande stradi del mondo romano*, 6. Rome.

Suchem, Ludolf von. 1895. *Ludolph Von Suchem's Description of the Holy Land: And of the Way Thither. Written in the Year A.D. 1350*. Trans. by Aubrey Stewart. London.

Theophanes. 2006. *The Journey of Theophanes: Travel, Business, and Daily Life in the Roman East*. Ed. and trans. by John Matthews. New Haven, CT.

Thomas, William. 1963. *The History of Italy (1549)*. Ithaca, NY.

Three Byzantine Saints: Contemporary Biographies. 1996. Trans. by Elizabeth Dawes and Norman H. Baynes. Crestwood, NY. Online at: https://sourcebooks.fordham.edu/basis/theodore-sykeon.asp

Tittmann Jr., Harold H. 2004. *Inside the Vatican of Pius XII: The Memoir of an American Diplomat During World War II*. Ed. by Harold H. Tittmann III. New York.

Tomassetti, Giuseppe. 1979. *La Campagna romana antica, medioevale e moderna*. Ed. by Luisa Chiumenti and Fernando Bilancia. 7 vols. Florence.

Tompkins, Peter. 1962. *A Spy in Rome*. New York.

Trevelyan, George Macaulay. 1933. *Garibaldi*. 3 vols. London.

Twain, Mark. 1879. *The Innocents Abroad*. Hartford, CT.

Vanvitelli, Luigi. 1976. *Le lettere di Luigi Vanvitelli della Biblioteca Palatina di Caserta*. Ed. by Franco Strazzullo. Galatina.

Vegetius Renatus, Flavius. 1993. *Vegetius: Epitome of Military Science*. Trans. by N. P. Milner. Liverpool.

——. 2004. *Epitoma rei militaris*. Trans. by Michael D. Reeve. Oxford.

Verri, Alessandro. 1860. *Le notti romane del conte Alessandro Verri*. Turin.

Villari, Luigi. 1932. *On the Roads from Rome*. London.

Vita sanctae Arthellaidis. 1668. Ed. by Jean Bolland and others. BHL 719. In *Acta Sanctorum Volume 06: Mar. I*, 264. Antwerp.

Waller, Edmund, and John Denham. 1857. *The Poetical Works of Edmund Waller and Sir John Denham*. Ed. by George Gilfillan. Edinburgh.

Wilde, Oscar. 1962. *The Letters of Oscar Wilde*. Ed. by Rupert Hart-Davis. London.

William of Malmesbury. 1998. *Gesta regum Anglorum*. Ed. and trans. R. A. B. Mynors; completed by R. M. Thomson and M. Winterbottom. Vol. 1. Oxford.

William of Tyre. 1943. *A History of Deeds Done beyond the Sea*. New York.

Williams, Hugh William. 1820. *Travels in Italy, Greece, and the Ionian Islands*. 2 vols. Edinburgh.

Wilmot, Catherine. 1920. *An Irish Peer on the Continent (1801–1803): Being a Narrative of the Tour of Stephen, 2nd Earl Mount Cashell, through France, Italy, Etc*. Ed. by Thomas U. Sadleir. London.

Wordsworth, William. 1984. *The Illustrated Wordsworth's Guide to the Lakes*. Ed. by Peter Bicknell. Exeter.

Wortley Montagu, Lady Mary. 1893. *The Letters and Works of Lady Mary Wortley Montagu*. London.

Wotton, Henry, and Logan Pearsall Smith. 1907. *The Life and Letters of Sir Henry Wotton*. Oxford.

Wright, Edward. 1730. *Some Observations Made in Travelling through France, Italy, &c*. 2 vols. London.

Secondary literature

Adams, C. E. P., and Ray Laurence. 2011. *Travel and Geography in the Roman Empire*. London.

Adams, C. E. P. 2011. '"There and Back Again": Getting Around in Roman Egypt'. In Adams and Laurence, pp. 138–66.

Adams, J. N. 2003. *Bilingualism and the Latin Language*. Cambridge.

Agazarian, Dory. 2015. 'Victorian Roads to Rome: Historical Travel in the Wake of the Grand Tour'. *Nineteenth-Century Contexts*, 37.5: 391–409.

Ahmed, Talat. 2019. *Mohandas Gandhi: Experiments in Civil Disobedience*. London.

Albanese, Giulia. 2019. *The March on Rome: Violence and the rise of Italian Fascism*. Trans. by Sergio Knipe. London.

Alcock, Susan E., John Bodel, and Richard J. A. Talbert. 2012. *Highways, Byways, and Road Systems in the Pre-Modern World*. Chichester, West Sussex; Malden, MA.

Allen, E. John B. 1972. *Post and Courier Service in the Diplomacy of Early Modern Europe*. The Hague.

Allen, Rosamund, ed. 2004. *Eastward Bound: Travel and Travellers, 1050–1550*. Manchester.

Anderson, Carolyn. 2011. 'Cold War Consumer Diplomacy and Movie-Induced Roman Holidays'. *Journal of Tourism History*, 3.1: 1–19.

——. 2019. 'Accidental Tourists: Yanks in Rome, 1944–1945'. *Journal of Tourism History*, 11.1: 22–45.

Armellini, Mariano. 1887. *Le chiese di Roma dalle loro origini sino al secolo XVI*. Rome.

Arthurs, Joshua. 2012. *Excavating Modernity: The Roman Past in Fascist Italy*. Ithaca, NY.

Asbridge, Thomas S. 2004. *The First Crusade: A New History*. New York; London.

Ayres, Philip. 1997. *Classical Culture and the Idea of Rome in Eighteenth-Century England*. Cambridge.

Bacciolo, Andrea. 2020. '"Belonging of Right to Our English Nation". The Oratory of Domine Quo Vadis, Reginald Pole, and the English Hospice in Rome'. *RIHA Journal*, article no. 0238.

Badin, Donatella Abbate. 2007. *Lady Morgan's Italy: Anglo-Irish Sensibilities and Italian Realities*. Bethesda, MD.

Baigent, Elizabeth. 2004. 'Nugent, Thomas (c. 1700–1772), writer and traveller'. *Oxford Dictionary of National Biography*. Oxford.

Baker, Paul R. 1964. *The Fortunate Pilgrims: Americans in Italy, 1800–1860*. Cambridge, MA.

Barlow, Paul. 1996. 'Local Disturbances: Madox Brown and the Problem of the Manchester Murals'. In *Reframing the Pre-Raphaelites: Historical and Theoretical Essays*, ed. by Ellen Harding, pp. 81–97. Aldershot.

Barnard, John Levi. 2017. *Empire of Ruin: Black Classicism and American Imperial Culture*. Oxford; New York.

Barnish, S. J. B. 1987. 'Pigs, Plebeians and *Potentes* : Rome's Economic Hinterland, *c.* 350–600 A.D.'. *Papers of the British School at Rome*, 55: 157–85.

Barrington Atlas of the Greek and Roman World. 2000. Ed. by Richard J. A. Talbert, in collaboration with Roger S. Bagnall et al. Princeton, NJ.

Bartlett, Robert. 2013. *Why Can the Dead Do Such Great Things? Saints and Worshippers from the Martyrs to the Reformation*. Princeton, NJ.

Baskins, Cristelle. 2014. 'Popes, Patriarchs, and Print: Representing Chaldeans in Renaissance Rome'. *Renaissance Studies*, 28.3: 405–25.

Bate, Jonathan. 2004. 'Hazlitt, William (1778–1830), writer and painter.' *Oxford Dictionary of National Biography*. Oxford.

Battilani, Patrizia. 2009. 'Rimini: An Original Mix of Italian Style and Foreign Models?' In Segreto et al., pp. 104–24.

Baumgartner, Karin. 2015. 'Packaging the Grand Tour: German Women Authors Write Italy, 1791–1874'. *Women in German Yearbook*, 31: 1–27.

——. 2014. 'Travel, Tourism, and Cultural Identity in Mariana Starke's Letters from Italy (1800) and Goethe's Italienische Reise (1816–17)'. *Publications of the English Goethe Society*, 83.3: 177–95.

Baxa, Paul. 2010. *Roads and Ruins: The Symbolic Landscape of Fascist Rome*. Toronto.

Belke, Klaus. 2002. 'Roads and Travel in Macedonia and Thrace in the Middle and Late Byzantine Period'. In Macrides, pp. 73–90.

——. 2008. 'Communications: Roads and Bridges'. In *The Oxford Handbook of Byzantine Studies*, ed. by Elizabeth Jeffreys, John F. Haldon, and Robin Cormack, pp. 295–308. Oxford; New York.

Berechman, Joseph. 2003. 'Transportation-Economic Aspects of Roman Highway Development: The Case of Via Appia'. *Transportation Research Part A: Policy and Practice*, 37: 453–78.

Bisaha, Nancy. 2023. *From Christians to Europeans: Pope Pius II and the Concept of the Modern Western Identity*. Abingdon.

Blennow, Anna. 2019. 'Wanderers and Wonders. The Medieval Guidebooks to Rome'. In *Rome and The Guidebook Tradition*, ed. by Anna Blennow and Stefano Fogelberg Rota, pp. 33–88. Online at: https://doi.org/10.1515/9783110615630

Bossy, John. 1964. 'Rome and the Elizabethan Catholics: A Question of Geography', *Historical Journal*, 7: 135–49.

Bosworth, R. J. B. 2011. *Whispering City: Rome and Its Histories*. New Haven, CT.

Bourhill, James. 2011. *Come Back to Portofino: Through Italy with the 6th South African Armoured Division*. Johannesburg.

de Bourrienne, L.-A. F. 1829. *Mémoires de M. de Bourrienne, Ministre d'État; sur Napoléon, le Directoire, le Consulat, l'Empire et la Restauration*, Vol. IV. Paris.

Bowes, Kim, and Afrim Hoti. 2003. 'An amphitheatre and its afterlives: survey and excavation in the Durrës amphitheatre'. *Journal of Roman Archaeology*, 16: 380–94.

Boyer, Marjorie Nice. 1964. 'The Bridgebuilding Brotherhoods', *Speculum*, 39.4: 635–50.

Bradley, Mark. 2010. *Classics and Imperialism in the British Empire*. Oxford.

Bradley, Mark. 2010. 'Tacitus' *Agricola* and the Conquest of Britain: Representations of Empire in Victorian and Edwardian England'. In Bradley, pp. 123–57.

Breitman, Richard. 2002. 'New Sources on the Holocaust in Italy'. *Holocaust and Genocide Studies*, 16.3: 402–14.

Brigden, Susan, and Jonathan Woolfson, 2005. 'Thomas Wyatt in Italy', *Renaissance Quarterly*, 58: 464–511.

Broder, David. 2023. *Mussolini's Grandchildren: Fascism in Contemporary Italy*. London.

Brodersen, Kai. 2011. 'Geographical Knowledge in the Roman World'. In Adams and Laurence, pp. 7–21.

Bronstein, Judith. 2007. 'The Crusades and the Jews: Some Reflections on the 1096 Massacre'. *History Compass*, 5.4: 1268–79.

Brown, John S. 2019 (May). '"Sad Sacks" First Unit to Fight Into Rome'. *Army*, 63–6.

Buchanan, Andrew. 2016. '"I Felt like a Tourist Instead of a Soldier": The Occupying Gaze – War and Tourism in Italy, 1943–1945'. *American Quarterly*, 68.3: 593–615.

Buck, Pamela. 2011. 'Collecting An Empire'. *Prose Studies*, 33.3: 188–99.

Buzard, James. 1993. *The Beaten Track: European Tourism, Literature and the Ways to Culture, 1800–1918*. Oxford.

Cacciatore, Vera. 2005. 'The House in War-Time'. In *Keats in Italy: A History of the Keats-Shelley House in Rome*, pp. 68–71. Rome.

Caddick-Adams, Peter. 2013. *Monte Cassino: Ten Armies in Hell*. Oxford.

Campedelli, Camilla. 2021. 'The Impact of Roman Roads and Milestones on the Landscape of the Iberian Peninsula'. In *The Impact of the Roman Empire on Landscapes: Proceedings of the Fourteenth Workshop of the International Network Impact of Empire (Mainz, June 12–15, 2019)*, pp. 111–30. Leiden.

Canny, Nicholas P. 1971. 'Historical Revision XVI: The Flight of the Earls, 1607'. *Irish Historical Studies*, 17.67: 380–99.

Caprotti, Federico. 2007. *Mussolini's Cities: Internal Colonialism in Italy, 1930–1939*. Youngstown, NY.

Carroll, Clare. 2018. *Exiles in a Global City: The Irish and Early Modern Rome, 1609–1783*. Leiden.

Carucci, M. 2017. 'The Danger of Female Mobility in Roman Imperial Times'. In Lo Cascio and Tacoma, pp. 173–90.

Cassibry, Kimberly. 2021. *Destinations in Mind: Portraying Places on the Roman Empire's Souvenirs*. New York.

Casson, L. 1974. *Travel in the Ancient World*. London.

Chapoutot, Johann. 2016. *Greeks, Romans, Germans: How the Nazis Usurped Europe's Classical Past*. Trans. by Richard R. Nybakken. Berkeley, CA.

Chazan, Robert. 1996. *In the Year 1096: The First Crusade and the Jews*. Philadelphia.

Chevallier, Raymond. 1989. *Roman Roads*. Trans. by N. H. Field. London.

Chiurco, G. A. 1929. *Storia della rivoluzione Fascista*. 5 vols. Florence.

Clark, Lloyd. 2013. *Anzio: The Friction of War*. London.

Clark, Martin. 2013. *The Italian Risorgimento*. 2nd edn. London.

Clark, W. G. 1861. 'Naples and Garibaldi'. In *Vacation Tourists and Notes of Travel*, ed. by Francis Galton, pp. 1–75. London.

Clegg, Jeanne. 2021. 'From Dead End to Central City of the World: (Re) locating Rome on Ruskin's map of Europe'. *Papers of the British School at Rome*, 89: 279–317.

Coarelli, Filippo, James J. Clauss, Daniel P. Harmon, J. Anthony Clauss, and Pierre A. Mackay. 2014. 'Via Appia'. In *Rome and its Environs: An Archaeological Guide*, ed. by Filippo Coarelli, pp. 365–400. Berkeley, CA.

Cobb, Matthew. 2015. 'The Chronology of Roman Trade in the Indian Ocean from Augustus to the Early Third Century CE'. *Journal of the Economic and Social History of the Orient*, 58: 362–418.

Coffin, David R. 1979. *The Villa in the Life of Renaissance Rome*. Princeton, NJ.

Colbert, Benjamin. 2014–20. 'Mariana Starke, 1762–1838'. *Women's Travel Writing, 1780–1840: A Bio-Bibliographical Database*. Online at: https://btw.wlv.ac.uk/authors/1135 (accessed 24 August 2023).

Colville, John. 1985. *Fringes of Power: Downing Street Diaries 1939–1955*. London.

Comfort, Anthony. 2019. 'Travelling Between the Euphrates and Tigris in Late Antiquity'. In Kolb 2019a, pp. 109–31.

Connelly, Charlie. 4 August 2022. 'HV Morton: Terrific Writer ... Terrible Man'. Online at: https://www.theneweuropean.co.uk/hv-morton-terrific-writer-terrible-man/

Consoli, Gian Paolo. 2003. 'Dal primato della città al primato della strada: il ruolo del piano di Armando Brasini per Roma nello sviluppo della città Fascista'. In *L'architettura nelle città italiane del XX secolo: dagli anni Venti agli anni Ottanta*, ed. by Vittorio Franchetti Pardo, pp. 202–11. Milan.

Corp, Edward. 2010. 'The Location of the Stuart Court in Rome: The Palazzo Del Re'. In *Loyalty and Identity: Jacobites at Home and Abroad*, ed. by Paul Monod, Murray Pittock, and Daniel Szechi, pp. 180–205. Basingstoke.

Coulston, Jon. 2011. 'Transport and Travel on Trajan's Column'. In Adams and Laurence, pp. 106–37.

Craig, Leigh Ann. 2003. '"Stronger than Men and Braver than Knights": Women and the Pilgrimages to Jerusalem and Rome in the Later Middle Ages'. *Journal of Medieval History*, 29.3: 153–75.

D'Arco, Carlo. 1857. *Delle arti e degli artefici di Mantova*. 2 vols. Mantua.

Davies, Hugh E. H. 1998. 'Designing Roman Roads'. *Britannia*, 29: 1–16.

——. 2008. *Roman Roads in Britain*. Oxford.

Davis, John A. 2006. *Naples and Napoleon: Southern Italy and the European Revolutions, 1780–1860*. Oxford.

De Blois, Lukas. 2015. 'Invasions, Deportations and Repopulation. Mobility and Migration in Thrace, Moesia Inferior, and Dacia in the Third Quarter of the Third Century AD'. In Lo Cascio and Tacoma, pp. 42–54.

De Lange, N. R. M. 1978. 'Jewish attitudes to the Roman Empire'. In *Imperialism in the Ancient World*, ed. by P. D. A. Garnsey and C. A. Whittaker, pp. 255–82. Cambridge.

Del Lungo, Stefano. 2014. *Roma in età carolingia e gli scritti dell'anonimo Augiense: (Einsiedeln, Bibliotheca Monasterii Ordinis Sancti Benedicti,* 326 [8 Nr. 13], IV, ff. 67v–86r). Rome.

Del Nero, Domenico. 1997. 'La via Francigena in Toscana'. In *La Via Francigena: atti della giornata di studi: la Via Francigena dalla Toscana a Sarzana, attraverso il territorio di Massa e Carrara: luoghi, figure e fatti: Massa, 5 maggio 1996*, pp. 9–17. Modena.

Della Portella, Ivana, ed. 2004a. *The Appian Way: From Its Foundation to the Middle Ages*. Trans. by Stephen Sartarelli. Los Angeles.

——. 2004b. 'Wanderings Along the Appian Way', pp. 8–10; 'From Benevento to Brindisi', pp. 146–85; 'The Via Appia Traiana', pp. 186–229; in Della Portella 2004a.

Derose Evans, Jane, ed. 2013. *A Companion to the Archaeology of the Roman Republic*. Chichester.

De Seta, Cesare. 1996. 'Grand Tour: The Lure of Italy in the Eighteenth Century'. In Wilton and Bignamini, pp. 13–20.

Diehl, Charles. 1888. *Études sur l'administration Byzantine dans l'exarchat de Ravenne (568–751)*. Paris.

Douglass, Laurie. 1996. 'A New Look at the Itinerarium Burdigalense'. *Journal of Early Christian Studies*, 4.3: 313–33.

Dyson, Stephen L. 2008. *In Pursuit of Ancient Pasts: A History of Classical Archaeology in the Nineteenth and Twentieth Centuries*. New Haven, CT.

——. 2019. *Archaeology, Ideology and Urbanism in Rome from the Grand Tour to Berlusconi*. Cambridge.

Easton, M. G. 1897. *Illustrated Bible Dictionary*. 3rd edn. London. https://www.ccel.org/e/easton/ebd/ebd3.html (accessed 22 April 2023).

Edwards, Catharine. 1996. 'The Roads to Rome'. In *Imagining Rome: British Artists and Rome in the Nineteenth Century*, ed. by Michael Liversidge and Catharine Edwards, pp. 8–19. London.

Ehrlich, Michael. 2006. 'The Route of the First Crusade and the Frankish Roads to Jerusalem during the Twelfth Century'. *Revue Biblique (1946–)*, 113.2: 263–83.

Eidelberg, Shlomo, ed. 1977. *The Jews and the Crusaders: The Hebrew Chronicles of the First and Second Crusades*. Madison, WI.

Elliot van Liere, Katherine. 2007. '"Shared Studies Foster Friendship": Humanism and History in Spain'. In *The Renaissance World*, ed. by John Jeffries Martin, pp. 242–61. London.

Ellis, Heather. 2023. 'The Indian Civil Service, Classical Studies, and an Education in Empire, 1890–1914'. *The Historical Journal*, 66: 593–618.

Emiliani, Vittorio. 2004. 'The Appian Way as Literary Journey'. In Della Portella 2004a, pp. 11–13.

Erskine, Andrew. 2010. *Roman Imperialism*. Edinburgh.

Evangelista, Matthew Anthony. 2020. 'Myron Taylor and the Bombing of Rome: The Limits of Law and Diplomacy'. *Diplomacy & Statecraft*, 31.2: 278–305.

Fafinski, Mateusz. 2021. *Roman Infrastructure in Early Medieval Britain*. Amsterdam.

Fagrskinna: A Catalogue of the Kings of Norway. 2004. Ed. and trans. by Alison Finlay. Leiden.

Failmezger, Victor. 2020. *Rome – City in Terror: The Nazi Occupation 1943–44*. Oxford.

Falcasantos, Rebecca Stephens. 2017. 'Wandering Wombs, Inspired Intellects: Christian Religious Travel in Late Antiquity'. *Journal of Early Christian Studies*, 25.1: 89–117.

Fauri, Francesca, and Matteo Troilo. 2020. 'The "Duce Hometown Effect" on Local Industrial Development: The Case of Forlì', *Business History*, 62.4: 613–36.

Ferguson, Gary. 2016. *Same-Sex Marriage in Renaissance Rome: Sexuality, Identity, and Community in Early Modern Europe*. Ithaca, NY.

Ferrari, Aldo. 2021. '"Most of Them Are Honourable". Luigi Villari e gli armeni durante la "guerra Armeno-Tatara" Del 1905–1906', *Studi Slavistici*, 18: 257–73.

Fiore Melacrinis, Francesco M. S. 2023. 'Annual wages in the Kingdom of the Two Sicilies from 1800 to 1860 and the beginning of the Italian regional divide', *European Review of Economic History*, advance article.

Fletcher, Catherine. 2015. *Diplomacy in Renaissance Rome: The Rise of the Resident Ambassador*. Cambridge.

Foot, John. 2000. 'Via Rasella, 1944: Memory, Truth, and History'. *Historical Journal*, 43: 1173–81.

——. 2021. 'San Gino'. *LRB Blog*, online at: https://www.lrb.co.uk/blog/2021/february/san-gino (accessed 26 April 2023).

——. 2023. 'The March on Rome Revisited. Silences, Historians and the Power of the Counter-Factual'. *Modern Italy*, 28: 162–77.

Formica, Sandro, and Muzaffer Uysal. 1996. 'The Revitalization of Italy as a Tourist Destination'. *Tourism Management*, 17.5: 323–31.

Foubert, Lien. 2018. 'Men and Women Tourists' Desire to See the World: "Curiosity" and "a Longing to Learn" as (Self-) Fashioning Motifs (First–Fifth Centuries C.E.)'. *Journal of Tourism History*, 10.1: 5–20.

Foxhall Forbes, Helen. 2019. 'Writing on the Wall: Anglo-Saxons at Monte Sant'Angelo Sul Gargano (Puglia) and the Spiritual and Social Significance of Graffiti'. *Journal of Late Antiquity*, 12.1: 169–210.

Frauzel, Flavia. 2013. 'From Canterbury to Rome: Plures de Gente Anglorum Ad Petri Limina. Pilgrimage as a Worldwide System of Connectivity during the Late Antiquity and the Early Middle Ages'. In *SOMA 2012: Identity and Connectivity: Proceedings of the 16th Symposium on Mediterranean Archaeology, Florence, Italy, 1–3 March 2012*, ed. by Luca Bombardieri et al., pp. 1087–94. Oxford.

Gabriele, Matthew. 2011. *An Empire of Memory: The Legend of Charlemagne, the Franks, and Jerusalem before the First Crusade*. Oxford.

Galatariotou, Catia. 1993. 'Travel and Perception in Byzantium', *Dumbarton Oaks Papers*, 47: 221–41.

Galliazzo, Vittorio. 1994. *I Ponti Romani. II. Catalogo Generale*. Treviso.

Games, Alison. 2008. *The Web of Empire: English Cosmopolitans in an Age of Expansion, 1560–1660*. Oxford.

Gameson, Richard. 1999. *St Augustine and the Conversion of England*. Stroud.

Gates-Foster, Jennifer. 2012. 'The Well-Remembered Path: Roadways and Cultural Memory in Ptolemaic and Roman Egypt'. In Alcock et al., pp. 202–21.

Geissler, Erhard, and Jeanne Guillemin. 2010. 'German Flooding of the Pontine Marshes in World War II: Biological Warfare Or Total War Tactic?' *Politics and the Life Sciences*, 29.1: 2–23.

Ghirardo, Diane. 1989. *Building New Communities: New Deal America and Fascist Italy*. Princeton, NJ.

Gikandi, Simon. 2014. *Slavery and the Culture of Taste*. Princeton, NJ.

Gleadhill, Emma. 2018. 'Improving Upon Birth, Marriage and Divorce: The Cultural Capital of Three Late Eighteenth-Century Female Grand Tourists'. *Journal of Tourism History*, 10.1: 21–36.

Goodden, Angelica. 2008. *Madame de Staël: The Dangerous Exile*. Oxford.

Graham-Campbell, Angus. 2004. 'Where Byron Stayed in Rome: The "Torlonia Letter" Rediscovered'. *The Keats-Shelley Review*, 18.1: 102–3.

Green, Roger Lancelyn, and Walter Hooper. 2002. *C. S. Lewis: A Biography*. London.

Grosholz, Emily. 2015. 'Letter from Rome'. *The Hudson Review*, 68.2: 189–93.

Haldon, John. 2006. 'Roads and Communications in the Byzantine Empire: Wagons, Horses and Supplies'. In *Logistics of Warfare in the Age of the Crusades*, ed. by John Pryor, pp. 131–58. Aldershot.

Hallenbeck, Jan T. 1982. 'Pavia and Rome: The Lombard Monarchy and the Papacy in the Eighth Century'. *Transactions of the American Philosophical Society*, 72: 1–186.

Hardacre, P. H. 1953. 'The Royalists in Exile During the Puritan Revolution, 1642–1660'. *Huntington Library Quarterly*, 16.4: 353–70.

Hardwick, Lorna, and Christopher Stray. 2008. *A Companion to Classical Receptions*. Oxford.

Harris, Jonathan. 2017. *Constantinople: Capital of Byzantium*. 2nd edn. London.

Harvey, Margaret. 1999. *The English in Rome, 1362–1420: Portrait of an Expatriate Community*. Cambridge.

Haskell, Francis. 2000. *The Ephemeral Museum: Old Master Paintings and the Rise of the Art Exhibition*. New Haven, CT.

Hauken, Tor. 1998. *Petition and Response. An Epigraphic Study of Petitions to Roman Emperors 181–249*. Bergen.

Herrin, Judith. 2021. *Women in Purple: Rulers of Medieval Byzantium*. Princeton, NJ.

Higgins, Valerie. 2013. 'Rome's Uncomfortable Heritage: Dealing with History in the Aftermath of WWII'. *Archaeologies*, 9.1: 29–55.

Hitchin, Keith. 2014. *A Concise History of Romania*. Cambridge.

Hitchner, R. Bruce. 2012. 'Roads, Integration, Connectivity, and Economic Performance in the Roman Empire'. In Alcock et al., pp. 222–34.

Holland, Robert. 2018. *The Warm South: How the Mediterranean Shaped the British Imagination*. New Haven, CT.

Holum, Kenneth G. 1990. 'Hadrian and St Helena: Imperial Travel and the Origins of Christian Holy Land Pilgrimage'. In *The Blessings of Pilgrimage*, ed. by Robert Ousterhout, pp. 66–81. Urbana, IL.

Hudson, Roger. 2014. 'The Vendôme Column, 1871'. *History Today*, online at: https://www.historytoday.com/archive/vendôme-column-1871

Humm, Michel. 1996. 'Appius Claudius Caecus et la construction de la via Appia'. *Mélanges de l'École Française de Rome. Antiquité*, 108.2: 693–746.

Ingamells, John. 1996. 'Discovering Italy: British Travellers in the Eighteenth Century'. In Wilton and Bignamini, pp. 21–30.

Inglis, Erik, and Elise Christmon. 2013. '"The Worthless Stories of Pilgrims"? The Art Historical Imagination of Fifteenth-Century Travelers to Jerusalem'. *Viator*, 44.3: 257–327.

Izzi, Luisa. 2014. 'Anglo-Saxons Underground: Early Medieval *graffiti* in the Catacombs of Rome'. In Tinti, pp. 141–77.

Jaques, Susan. 2018. *The Caesar of Paris – Napoleon Bonaparte, Rome, and the Artistic Obsession That Shaped an Empire*. New York.

Johns, Christopher M. S. 1998. *Antonio Canova and the Politics of Patronage in Revolutionary and Napoleonic Europe*. Berkeley, CA.

Kaicker, Abhishek. 2010. 'Visions of Modernity in Revisions of the Past: Altaf Hussain Hali and the "Legacy of the Greeks"'. In Bradley, pp. 231–48.

Kalla-Bishop, P. M. 1971. *Italian Railways*. Newton Abbot.

Kallis, Aristotle. 2014. *The Third Rome, 1922–43: The Making of the Fascist Capital*. Basingstoke.

Kaplan, M. 2000. 'Quelques remarques sur les routes à grande circulation dans l'empire Byzantin du VIe au XIe siècle'. In *Voyages et voyageurs à Byzance et en Occident du VIe au XIe siècle*, ed. by Alain Dierkens and Jean-Marie Sansterre with Jean-Louis Kupper, pp. 83–100. Geneva.

Karmon, David. 2011. *The Ruin of the Eternal City: Antiquity and Preservation in Renaissance Rome*. Oxford.

Katz, Robert. 2003. *The Battle for Rome: The Germans, The Allies, The Partisans and the Pope, September 1943–June 1944*. New York.

Keynes, S. 1997. 'Anglo-Saxon Entries in the "Liber Vitae" of Brescia'. In *Alfred the Wise: Studies in Honour of Janet Bately on the Occasion of Her 65th Birthday*, ed. by Jane Annette Roberts, Janet L. Nelson, Malcolm Godden, and Janet M. Bately, pp. 99–119. Woodbridge.

Keyvanian, Carla. 2015. *Hospitals and Urbanism in Rome, 1200–1500*. Leiden.

Kirk, Terry. 2011. 'The Political Topography of Modern Rome, 1870–1936'. In *Rome: Continuing Encounters Between Past and Present*, ed. by Dorigen Sophie Caldwell and Lesley Caldwell, pp. 101–28. Farnham.

Kitzes, Adam H. 2017. 'The Hazards of Professional Authorship: Polemic and Fiction in Anthony Munday's English Roman Life'. *Renaissance Studies*, 31: 444–61.

Klynne, Allan. 2009. 'Where have all the ruins gone? Chasing the past along Via Tiburtina'. In *Via Tiburtina: Space, Movement & Artefacts in the Urban Landscape*, ed. by Hans Bjur and Barbro Santillo Frizell, pp. 165–80. Rome.

Kolb, Anne. 2011. 'Transport and Communication in the Roman State: The Cursus Publicus'. In Adams and Laurence, pp. 95–105.

——. 2019. 'Via Ducta – Roman Road Building: An Introduction to Its Significance, the Sources and the State of Research'. In *Roman Roads: New Evidence – New Perspectives*, ed. by Anne Kolb, pp. 3–21. Berlin.

Krautheimer, Richard. 1980. *Rome, Profile of a City, 312–1308*. Princeton, NJ.

Kuelzer, A. 2002. 'Pilgrimage to the Holy Land'. In Macrides, pp. 149–61.

Kulikowski, Michael. 2006. *Rome's Gothic Wars: From the Third Century to Alaric*. Cambridge.

Larmour, David H. J., and Diana Spencer. 2007. *The Sites of Rome: Time, Space, Memory*. Oxford.

Larnach, Matthew. 2016. 'All Roads Lead to Constantinople: Exploring the Via Militaris in the Medieval Balkans, 600–1204'. University of Sydney, doctoral thesis.

Laurence, Ray. 1999. *The Roads of Roman Italy: Mobility and Cultural Change*. London.

——. 2011. 'Geography in Roman Britain'. In Adams and Laurence, 67–94.

——. 2013. 'Roads and Bridges'. In Derose Evans, pp. 296–307.

Leask, Nigel. 2006. 'Bruce, James, of Kinnaird', in *Oxford Dictionary of National Biography*. Oxford.

Levine, Robert S. 2002. 'Road to Africa: Frederick Douglass's Rome. In *Roman Holidays: American Writers and Artists in Nineteenth-Century Italy*, ed. by Robert K. Martin and Leland S. Person, pp. 226–45. Iowa City.

Levis Sullam, Simon. 2018. *The Italian Executioners: The Genocide of the Jews of Italy*. Trans. by Oona Smyth with Claudia Patane. Princeton, NJ.

Lo Cascio, Elio, and Laurens Ernst Tacoma, eds. 2017. *The Impact of Mobility and Migration in the Roman Empire. Proceedings of the Twelfth Workshop of the International Network Impact of Empire (Rome, June 17–19, 2015)*. Leiden.

Lowe, Benedict. 2018. 'Manilius and the Logistics of Salting in the Roman World'. *Journal of Maritime Archaeology*, 13.3: 467–80.

Lyth, Peter. 2009. 'Flying Visits: The Growth of British Air Package Tours, 1945–1975'. In Segreto et al., pp. 11–30.

Maas, Michael, and Derek Ruths. 2012. 'Road Connectivity and the Structure of Ancient Empires: A Case Study from Late Antiquity'. In Alcock et al., pp. 255–64.

McCabe, A. 2002. 'Horses and Horse-Doctors on the Road'. In Macrides, pp. 91–7.

MacCannell, D. 1973. 'Staged Authenticity: Arrangements of Social Space in Tourist Settings'. *American Journal of Sociology* 79: 589–603.

McCavitt, John. 1994. 'The Flight of the Earls, 1607'. *Irish Historical Studies*, 29.114: 159–73.

McCormick, Michael. 2002. *Origins of the European Economy: Communications and Commerce AD 300–900*. Cambridge.

McDonough, Frank. 2019–21. *The Hitler Years*. 2 vols. London.

McGeary, Thomas. 2014. 'British Grand Tourists Visit Rosalba Carriera, 1732–1741: New Documents'. *British Art Journal*, 15.1: 117–19.

Mack, Robert L. 2000. *Thomas Gray: A Life*. New Haven, CT.

McKechnie, Paul. 2019. *Christianizing Asia Minor: Conversion, Communities, and Social Change in the Pre-Constantinian Era*. Cambridge.

McKitterick, Rosamond, John Osborne, Carol M. Richardson, and Joanna Story, eds. 2013. *Old Saint Peter's, Rome*. Cambridge.

Macrides, R. J., ed. 2002. *Travel in the Byzantine World: Papers from the Thirty-Fourth Spring Symposium of Byzantine Studies, Birmingham, April 2000*. Aldershot.

Madgearu, Alexandru. 2010. 'Narses'. In *The Oxford Encyclopedia of Medieval Warfare and Military Technology*, ed. by Clifford J. Rogers. Online edition.

Magoun Jr., Francis Peabody. 1940. 'The Rome of Two Northern Pilgrims: Archbishop Sigeric of Canterbury and Abbot Nikolás of Munkathverá'. *Harvard Theological Review*, 33.4: 267–89.

——. 1944. 'The Pilgrim-Diary of Nikulas of Munkathverá: The Road to Rome', *Mediaeval Studies*, 6: 314–54.

Mailloux, Steven. 2013. 'Narrative as Embodied Intensities: The Eloquence of Travel in Nineteenth-Century Rome'. *Narrative*, 21.2: 125–39.

Mairs, Rachel. 2020. 'Interpretes, Negotiatores and the Roman Army: Mobile Professionals and Their Languages'. In James Clackson et al., eds., *Migration, Mobility and Language Contact in and around the Ancient Mediterranean*, pp. 203–29. Cambridge.

Malamud, Margaret. 2009. *Ancient Rome and Modern America*. Oxford.

Manacorda, Daniele. 2000. 'Archeologia e storia di un paesaggio urbano'. In *Museo Nazionale Romano Crypta Balbi*, pp. 7–47. Milan.

Manera, Carles, Luciano Segreto, and Manfred Pohl. 2009. 'Introduction. The Mediterranean as a Tourist Destination: Past, Present and Future of the First Mass Tourism Resort Area'. In Segreto et al., pp. 1–10.

Mari, Zaccaria. 1983. *Tibur: Pars Tertia*. Florence.

Marraro, Howard R. 1944. 'Unpublished American Documents on Garibaldi's March on Rome in 1867'. *The Journal of Modern History*, 16.2: 116–23.

Matheus, Michael. 2000. 'Borgo San Martino: An Early Medieval Pilgrimage Station on the Via Francigena Near Sutri'. *Papers of the British School at Rome*, 68: 185–99.

Mauri, Enzo. 2021. 1979. 'Esce fra le polemiche Brian di Nazareth, il film che i Monty Python non volevano fare. Acclamato all'estero, in Italia è distribuito dopo dodici anni'. *70-80.it*, online at: https://www.70-80.it/1979-esce-fra-le-polemiche-brian-di-nazareth-il-film-che-i-monty-python-non-volevano-fare-acclamato-allestero-in-italia-e-distribuito-dopo-dodici-anni/ (accessed 22 April 2023).

Mayer, Roland. 2007. 'Impressions of Rome'. *Greece & Rome*, 54.2: 156–77.

Meyenberg, Roger, and Vincent, Patrick. 2001. 'Wordsworth's Route Over the Simplon in 1790: A Reconstruction'. Online at: http://romantic-circles.org/reference/misc/simplon/index.html (accessed 21 February 2023).

Midura, Rachel. 2021. 'Itinerating Europe: Early Modern Spatial Networks in Printed Itineraries, 1545–1700'. *Journal of Social History*, 54.4: 1023–63.

Milkova, Stiliana. 2015. 'From Rome to Paris to Rome: Reversing the Grand Tour in Gogol's "Rome"'. *The Slavic and East European Journal*, 59.4: 493–516.

Mitchell, Stephen. 1999. 'The administration of Roman Asia from 133 BC to AD 250'. In *Lokale Autonomie und Ordnungsmacht in den kaiserzeitlichen Provinzen vom 1. bis 3. Jahrhundert*, ed. by Werner Eck, pp. 17–46. Munich.

——. 2020. 'The Mansio in Pisidia's Döşeme Boğazı: A Unique Building in Roman Asia Minor'. *Journal of Roman Archaeology*, 33: 231–48.

Moi, Toril. 2006. *Henrik Ibsen and the Birth of Modernism: Art, Theater, Philosophy*. Oxford.

Moraglio, Massimo. 2007. 'Between Industry and Tourism: The Turin–Savona Motorway, 1956–2001'. *The Journal of Transport History*, 28.1: 93–110.

——. 2009. 'Real Ambition or Just Coincidence?: The Italian Fascist Motorway Projects in Inter-War Europe'. *The Journal of Transport History*, 30.2: 168–82.

——. 2017. *Driving Modernity: Technology, Experts, Politics, and Fascist Motorways, 1922–1943*. New York.

Morley, Neville. 2010. *The Roman Empire: Roots of Imperialism*. London.

Moskal, Jeanne. 2000. 'Politics and the Occupation of a Nurse in Mariana Starke's Letters from Italy'. In *Romantic Geographies*, ed. by Amanda Gilroy, pp. 150–64. Manchester.

——. 2001. 'Napoleon, Nationalism, and the Politics of Religion in Mariana Starke's Letters from Italy'. In *Rebellious Hearts: British Women Writers and the French Revolution*, ed. by Adriana Craciun and Kari Lokke. Albany, NY.

Munby, Julian. 2008. 'From Carriage to Coach: What Happened?' In *The Art, Science and Technology of Medieval Travel*, ed. by Robert Bork and Andrea Kann, pp. 41–53. Aldershot.

Murray, Alan V. 2018. 'The Middle Ground: The Passage of Crusade Armies to The Holy Land By Land and Sea (1096–1204)'. In *A Military History of the Mediterranean Sea*, ed. by Georgios Theotokis and Aysel Yıldız, pp. 185–201. Leiden.

Nasrallah, Laura S. 2017. 'Imposing Travelers: An Inscription from Galatia and the Journeys of the Earliest Christians'. In *Journeys in the Roman East: Imagined and Real*, ed. by Maren R. Niehoff, pp. 273–96. Tübingen.

Nicassio, Susan Vandiver. 2009. *Imperial City: Rome under Napoleon*. Chicago.

Nilsson, Mikael. 2021. *Hitler Redux: The Incredible History of Hitler's So-Called Table Talks*. Abingdon.

Nuti, Lucia. 2015. 'Re-Moulding the City: The Roman Possessi in the First Half of the Sixteenth Century'. In *Ceremonial Entries in Early Modern Europe*, ed. by J. R. Mulryne, pp. 113–33. Farnham.

O'Callaghan, R. T. 1953. 'Vatican Excavations and the Tomb of Peter'. *The Biblical Archaeologist*, 16: 70–87.

O'Connor, Anne. 2016. 'A Voyage into Catholicism: Irish Travel to Italy in the Nineteenth Century'. *Studies in Travel Writing*, 20.2: 149–61.

O'Connor, Thomas, and Mary Ann Lyons, eds. 2010. *The Ulster Earls and Baroque Europe: Refashioning Irish Identities, 1600–1800*. Dublin.

Olcelli, Laura. 2015. 'Lady Anna Riggs Miller: The "Modest" Self-Exposure of the Female Grand Tourist'. *Studies in Travel Writing*, 19.4: 312–23.

Onuf, Peter, and Nicolas Cole, eds. 2011. *Thomas Jefferson, the Classical World, and Early America*. Charlottesville, VA.

Ord, Melanie. 2007. 'Venice and Rome in the Addresses and Dispatches of Sir Henry Wotton: First English Embassy to Venice, 1604–1610'. *The Seventeenth Century*, 22.1: 1–23.

Ortenberg, Veronica. 1990. 'Archbishop Sigeric's Journey to Rome in 990'. *Anglo-Saxon England*, 19: 197–246.

O'Sullivan, Firmin. 1972. *The Egnatian Way*. Newton Abbot.

Painter, Borden W. 2005. *Mussolini's Rome: Rebuilding the Eternal City*. New York.

Paris, Rita, ed. 2001, *La via Appia, il bianco e nero di un patrimonio italiano*. Milan.

Pazos, Antón M. 2020. *Nineteenth-Century European Pilgrimages: A New Golden Age*. London.

Pelteret, David A. E. 2014. 'Not All Roads Lead to Rome'. In Tinti, pp. 17–41.

Pelù, Paolo. 1997. 'Aspetti della via Francigena nel territorio di Massa di Lunigiana'. In *La Via Francigena: Atti della giornata di studi: Massa, 5 maggio 1996*, pp. 19–30. Modena.

Pennock, Caroline Dodds. 2023. *On Savage Shores: How Indigenous Americans Discovered Europe*. London.

Pepper, Simon, and Nicholas Adams. 1986. *Firearms and Fortifications: Military Architecture and Siege Warfare in Sixteenth-Century Siena*. Chicago.

Perowne, Stewart. 1973. *The Journeys of St Paul*. London.

Pfister, Manfred. 1996. *The Fatal Gift of Beauty: The Italies of British Travellers*. Amsterdam.

Piana, Pietro, Charles Watkins, and Ross Balzaretti. 2018. 'Travel, Modernity and Rural Landscapes in Nineteenth-Century Liguria'. *Rural History*, 29.2: 167–93.

Picciotto, Liliana. 2009. 'The Shoah in Italy: Its History and Characteristics'. In *Jews in Italy under Fascist and Nazi Rule, 1922–1945*, ed. by Joshua D. Zimmerman, pp. 209–23. Cambridge.

Pinto, John A. 2016. 'Speaking Ruins: Travelers' Perceptions of Ancient Rome'. *SiteLINES: A Journal of Place*, 11.2: 3–5.

Pirro, Deirdre. 2019. 'Mahatma Gandhi's Italian Visit'. *The Florentine*, 6 February, online at: https://www.theflorentine.net/2019/02/06/mahatma-gandhi-italian-visit-mussolini/

Popkin, Maggie L. 2022. 'The Vicarello Milestone Beakers and Future-Oriented Mental Time Travel in the Roman Empire'. In *Future Thinking in Roman Culture: New Approaches to History, Memory, and Cognition*, ed. by Maggie L. Popkin and Diana Y. Ng. Abingdon.

Portelli, Alessandro. 2007. *The Order Has Been Carried Out: History, Memory, and Meaning of a Nazi Massacre in Rome*. Basingstoke.

Pryor, John, ed. 2006. *Logistics of Warfare in the Age of the Crusades*. Aldershot.

Pucci Donati, Francesca. 2018. *Luoghi e mestieri dell'ospitalità nel Medioevo: Alberghi, taverne e osterie a Bologna tra Due e Quattrocento*. Spoleto.

Quilici, Lorenzo. 2002. 'Da Roma alle foci del Garigliano: Per un parco regionale della Via Appia Antica'. In *Ancient History Matters: Studies presented to Jens Erik Skydsgaard on his seventieth birthday*, ed. Ascani et al., pp. 77–86. Rome.

Rautman, Marcus Louis. 2006. *Daily Life in the Byzantine Empire*. Westport, CT; London.

Redigonda, Abele L. 1960. 'Leandro Alberti'. *Dizionario biografico degli italiani*, online at: https://www.treccani.it/enciclopedia/leandro-alberti_(Dizionario-Biografico) (accessed 23 August 2023).

Rehm, Ulrich. 2016. 'The critical fortunes of "Vasari's Botticelli" in the nineteenth century'. In *Botticelli Reimagined*, ed. by Mark Evans and Stefan Weppelman, pp. 48–9. London.

Reilly, Benjamin James. 2019. 'Northern European Patterns of Visiting Rome, 1400–1850'. *Journal of Tourism History*, 11.2: 101–23.

Riall, Lucy. 2007. *Garibaldi: Invention of a Hero*. New Haven, CT.

Richards, Greg, ed. 2007. *Cultural Tourism: Global and Local Perspectives*. Binghamton, NY.

Richardson, L. 1992. *A New Topographical Dictionary of Ancient Rome*. Baltimore.

Ridley, Ronald. 2009. *The Eagle and the Spade: Archaeology in Rome during the Napoleonic Era*. Cambridge.

Riganelli, Giovanni. 1999. 'Il corridoio bizantino nelle vicende storichee dell'Umbria altomedievale'. In *Il corridoio bizantino e la via Amerina in Umbria nell'alto Medioevo*, ed. by Enrico Menesto, pp. 117–44. 2 vols. Spoleto.

Ritter, Max. 2018. 'Panegyric Markets in the Byzantine Empire'. In Despoina Ariantzi and Ina Eichner, eds, *Für Seelenheil und Lebensglück: Das byzantinische Pilgerwesen und seine Wurzeln*, pp. 367–82. Heidelberg. Online at: https://books.ub.uni-heidelberg.de/propylaeum/reader/download/495/495-30-85025-1-10-20190513.pdf

Robb, Graham. 2016. *The Discovery of France*. London.

Roe, Nicholas. 2012. *John Keats: A New Life*. New Haven, CT.

Rossiaud, Jacques. 1988. *Medieval Prostitution: Family, Sexuality and Social Relations in Past Times*. Oxford.

Rowell, Diana. 2012. *Paris: The 'New Rome' of Napoleon I*. London.

Rowlandson, Jane, ed. 1988. *Women and Society in Greek and Roman Egypt: A Sourcebook*. Cambridge.

Rubinstein, Ruth. 1988. 'Pius II and Roman Ruins'. *Renaissance Studies*, 2.2: 197–203.

Russell, Amy. 2014. 'Memory and Movement in the Roman Fora from Antiquity to Metro C'. *Journal of the Society of Architectural Historians*, 73.4: 478–506.

Salvadore, Matteo. 2017. 'African Cosmopolitanism in the Early Modern Mediterranean: The Diasporic Life of Yohannes, the Ethiopian Pilgrim who became a Counter-Reformation Bishop'. *The Journal of African History*, 58.1: 61–83.

——. 2022. 'The Narrative of Zaga Christ (Ṣägga Krəstos): The First Published African Autobiography (1635)'. *Africa*, 92.1: 1–41.

Salway, Benet. 2011. 'Travel, Itineraria, and Tabellaria'. In Adams and Laurence, pp. 22–66.

Samuels, Ernest, with Jayne Newcomer Samuels. 1987. *Bernard Berenson: The Making of a Legend*. Cambridge, MA.

Sandrock, Kirsten. 2015. 'Truth and Lying in Early Modern Travel Narratives: Coryat's Crudities, Lithgow's Totall Discourse and Generic Change'. *European Journal of English Studies*, 19: 189–203.

Sartorio, Giuseppina Pisani. 2004. 'Origins and Historic Events', pp. 14–39, and 'The Urban Segment from Porta Capena to Casal Rotondo', pp. 40–83, in Della Portella 2004a.

Savill, Benjamin, ed. 2021. *Cult of Saints in Late Antiquity database*. Online at: http://csla.history.ox.ac.uk

Scheidel, Walter. 2013. 'The Shape of the Roman World'. Online at SSRN: http://dx.doi.org/10.2139/ssrn.2242325

Schipper, Frank. 2009. *Driving Europe*. Amsterdam.

Schobesberger, Nikolaus. 2016. 'Mapping the Fuggerzeitungen: The Geographical Issues of an Information Network'. In *News Networks in Early Modern Europe*, ed. by Joad Raymond and Noah Moxham, pp. 216–40. Leiden.

Scobie, Alexander. 1990. *Hitler's State Architecture: The Impact of Classical Antiquity*. University Park, PA.

Segreto, Luciano, Carles Manera, and Manfred Pohl, eds. 2009. *Europe at the Seaside: The Economic History of Mass Tourism in the Mediterranean*. New York.

Seymour, W. A., ed. 1980. *A History of the Ordnance Survey*. Folkestone. Online at: https://www.ordnancesurvey.co.uk/documents/resources/os-history.pdf

Simmons, Laurence. 2006. *Freud's Italian Journey*. Amsterdam.

Sinisi, Lucia. 2014. 'Beyond Rome: The Cult of the Archangel Michael and the Pilgrimage to Apulia'. In Tinti, pp. 43–68.

Smith, Melanie K., and Mike Robinson, eds. 2006. *Cultural Tourism in a Changing World: Politics, Participation and (Re)presentation*. Clevedon.

Spotts, Frederic. 2003. *Hitler and the Power of Aesthetics*. Woodstock, NY.

Stabler, Jane. 2013. *The Artistry of Exile*. Oxford.

Staccioli, Romolo Augusto. 2003. *Roads of the Romans*. Rome.

Stenhouse, William. 2005. 'Visitors, Display, and Reception in the Antiquity Collections of Late-Renaissance Rome'. *Renaissance Quarterly*, 58.2: 397–434.

Stevens Crawshaw, Jane. 2016. 'The Places and Spaces of Early Modern Quarantine'. In *Quarantine: Local and Global Histories*, ed. Alison Bashford, pp. 20–29. London.

Stevenson, Jane. 2022. *Siena: The Life and Afterlife of a Medieval City*. London.

Stopani, Renato. 1992. *La via Francigena del sud: l'Appia Traiana nel Medioevo*. Florence.

——. 1998. *La via Francigena in Toscana. Storia di una strada medievale*. Florence.

Strong, Roy. 1984. *Art and Power: Renaissance Festivals 1450–1650*. Woodbridge.

Sweeney, James Ross. 1973. 'Basil of Trnovo's Journey to Durazzo: A Note on Balkan Travel at the Beginning of the 13th Century'. *The Slavonic and East European Review*, 51.122: 118–23.

Sweet, Rosemary. 2012. *Cities and the Grand Tour: The British in Italy, c. 1690–1820*. Cambridge.

——, Gerrit Verhoeven and Sarah Goldsmith, eds. 2017. *Beyond the Grand Tour. Northern Metropolises and Early Modern Travel Behaviour*. London.

Talbert, Richard J. A., with Tom Elliot, Nora Harris and Martin Steinmann. 2010. *Rome's World: The Peutinger Map Reconsidered*. Cambridge.

——. 2012. 'Roads Not Featured: A Roman Failure to Communicate?', in Alcock et al., pp. 235–54.

Terrenato, Nicola. 2019. *The Early Roman Expansion into Italy: Elite Negotiation and Family Agendas*. Cambridge.

Thessaloniki and its Monuments. 1985. Ed. by the Thessaloniki Ephorate of Byzantine Antiquities. Thessaloniki.

Thomas, Rebecca. 2020. 'Three Welsh Kings and Rome: Royal Pilgrimage, Overlordship, and Anglo-Welsh Relations in the Early Middle Ages'. *Early Medieval Europe* 28: 560–91.

Thommen, Lukas. 2012. *An Environmental History of Ancient Greece and Rome*. Cambridge.

Tinti, Francesca, ed. 2014. *England and Rome in the Early Middle Ages: Pilgrimage, Art, and Politics*. Turnhout.

Tompkins, Peter. 1985. 'What really happened at Anzio'. *Il Politico*, 50.3: 509–28.

Towner, John. 1985. 'The Grand Tour: A Key Phase in the History of Tourism'. *Annals of Tourism Research*, 12.3: 297–333.

Treharne, Elaine. 2014. 'The Performance of Piety: Cnut, Rome and England'. In Tinti, pp. 343–64.

Tresoldi, Lucia. 1975–77. *Viaggiatori tedeschi in Italia*. 2 vols. Rome.

Underwood, Lucy. 2012. 'Youth, Religious Identity, and Autobiography at the English Colleges in Rome and Valladolid, 1592–1685'. *The Historical Journal*, 55.2: 349–74.

Van Allen, Susan. 2021. 'What did the ancient Romans eat?' Online at: https://www.bbc.com/travel/article/20210719-what-did-the-ancient-romans-eat (accessed 23 August 2023).

Vasori, Orietta. 1980. *I monumenti antichi in Italia nei disegni degli Uffizi*. Ed. by Antonio Giuliano. Rome.

Vego, Milan. 2014. 'The Allied Landing at Anzio-Nettuno, 22 January–4 March 1944: Operation SHINGLE'. *Naval War College Review*, 67.4: 1–60.

Ventre, Francesca. 2004. 'From the Alban Hills to Cisterna Latina', pp. 84–105, and 'From the Pontine Plain to Benevento', pp. 106–45, in Della Portella 2004a.

Vingtain, Dominique, and Claude Sauvageot. 1998. *Avignon: Le Palais Des Papes*. Saint-Léger-Vauban.

Voaden, Rosalynn. 2004. 'Travels with Margery: Pilgrimage in Context'. In R. Allen, pp. 177–95.

Vout, Caroline. 2012. *The Hills of Rome: Signature of an Eternal City*. Cambridge.

Wacher, John. 2000. *A Portrait of Roman Britain*. London.

Wade, Janet. 2022. 'Expeditions from Rome: Thomas Ashby, his BSR companions and the Roman roads of Italy'. *Papers of the British School at Rome*, 90: 267–95.

Wade, Janet, and Alessandra Giovenco. 2022. 'Road trips, rail journeys and landscape archaeology: reconstructing research itineraries and travel excursions in Italy through the British School at Rome's photographic collections'. *Papers of the British School at Rome*, 90: 297–324.

Ward-Perkins, J. B. 1957. 'Etruscan and Roman Roads in Southern Etruria'. *The Journal of Roman Studies*, 47.1/2: 139–43.

Warnock, Robert. 1942. 'Boswell on the Grand Tour'. *Studies in Philology*, 39.4: 650–61.

Webb, Diana. 2002. *Medieval European Pilgrimage c.700–c.1500*. Gordonsville, VA.

Weber, Elke. 2004. 'Sharing the Sites: Medieval Jewish Travellers to the Land of Israel'. In R. Allen, pp. 35–52.

Weingarten, Susan. 1999. 'Was the Pilgrim from Bordeaux a Woman? A Reply to Laurie Douglass'. *Journal of Early Christian Studies*, 7.2: 291–7.

Wildvang, Frauke. 2007. 'The Enemy Next Door: Italian Collaboration in Deporting Jews during the German Occupation of Rome'. *Modern Italy*, 12: 189–204.

Williams, Michael E. 1979. *The Venerable English College, Rome: A History: 1579–1979*. London.

Wilson, Mark. 2009. 'The Route of Paul's First Journey to Pisidian Antioch'. *New Testament Studies*, 55: 471–83.

Wilton, Andrew, Ilaria Bignamini, Tate Gallery, and Palazzo delle Esposizioni. 1996. *Grand Tour: The Lure of Italy in the Eighteenth Century*. London.

Winter, Jay. 2008. 'Sites of Memory and the Shadow of War'. In *Cultural Memory Studies: An International and Interdisciplinary Handbook*, ed. by Astrid Erll and Asgar Nünning, pp. 61–74. Berlin.

Wyatt, Michael. 2005. *The Italian Encounter with Tudor England: A Cultural Politics of Translation*. Cambridge.

Zaldini, Mara. n.d. 'Il monastero di San Felice'. Online at: http://www-wp.unipv.it/biblioteche/wp-content/uploads/2012/09/SanFeliceZaldini.pdf (accessed 23 August 2023).

Zei, Constantino. 1917. 'Le terme romane di Viterbo'. *Bollettino d'Arte*, 11: 155–70.

Zilcosky, John. 2017. 'Learning How to Get Lost: Goethe in Italy'. *Eighteenth-Century Studies*, 50.4: 417–35.

Zuccotti, Susan. 1996. *The Italians and the Holocaust: Persecution, Rescue, and Survival*. Lincoln, NE.

Notes

Abbreviations

CIL *Corpus Inscriptionum Latinarum*
ILS *Inscriptiones Latinae Selectae*
LCL Loeb Classical Library
MGH *Monumenta Germaniae Historica*

All websites accessed 13 December 2023. Translations are from the Loeb editions unless otherwise stated.

INTRODUCTION

1. Maillet, 128. Chaucer, 20.
2. Cassius Dio, *Historiae Romanae* 54.8.4 (LCL 83: 300–01); Richardson 1992, 254. Plutarch, *Galba* 24.4 (LCL 103: 260–61).
3. Statius, *Silvae* 2.2.
4. Graves, 147–8.
5. Thommen, 74; Hitchner, 222–3.
6. Dionysius Halicarnassensis, *Antiquitates Romanae* 3.67.5 (LCL 347: 240–41).
7. Thommen, 71.
8. Casson, 174.
9. Humm, 741.
10. The date of the later section is uncertain: see Laurence 2013, 296.
11. Humm, 734, 737.
12. Lister, 10 repeats it; for the qualification see Van Allen.
13. Laurence 1999, 13–21; for the currency, Humm, 733.
14. Laurence 1999, 197–9.
15. Sartorio, 68; Coarelli, 394.
16. For an example of the latter, see Hardwick and Stray.
17. For context see Goodden 153–80.
18. De Staël, 63; this translation from Pinto, 3.
19. Rogers 1956, 219–20.
20. Mailloux, 126 notes how Rome offered 'an imaginative landscape' for nineteenth-century American visitors. I discuss these ideas further in a forthcoming essay on public historical practices on the Roman roads.
21. Dickens, 169.

1: ROMANS ON THE ROADS

1. Staccioli, 17.
2. Richardson 1992, 254.
3. Staccioli, 34.
4. Mari, 366–7; Klynne 168.
5. Thommen, 74. Ward-Perkins, 140.
6. Staccioli, 49.
7. Terrenato, 232–6.
8. Polybius 1.58. Translation online at perseus.tufts.edu
9. Polybius 3.50, 3.55. Translation online at perseus.tufts.edu
10. Chevallier, 85.
11. Humm, 713.
12. Appian, *Bella civilia* 1.120 (LCL 5: 238–9).
13. Byron, vol. 1, 249.
14. Staccioli, 55.
15. Siculus Flaccus 110–11, trans. in Chevallier 65; Laurence 1999, 59–61.
16. Capitoline Museums, inv. no. NCE 476.
17. Laurence 1999, 144.
18. Laurence 2013, 303.
19. Chevallier, 83 suggests this refers to a specific variant of the Via Appia, while Laurence 1999, 65 sees Statius as describing an ideal rather than a routine project. Stat., *Silv.* 4.3, trans. from Chevallier (also at LCL 206: 242–3).
20. Berechman, 473.
21. Davies 2008, 32–3, 37.
22. Davies 1998, 8–9, 14; Humm, 719–20.
23. Diodorus Siculus 20.36.1–4, translation from Sartorio, 26 (also at LCL 390: 236–7); see also Humm, 696.
24. Laurence 2013, 296.
25. Humm, 704.
26. Plutarch, Gaius Gracchus 7.1–2; translation from Casson, 166 (also at LCL 102: 212–13).
27. Laurence 2013, 299.
28. Green and Hooper, ch. 11, unpaginated digital edition.
29. CIL (*Corpus Inscriptionum Latinarum*) XI: 6625–7.
30. Davies 1998, 9–10.
31. Davies 2008, 38–9, 41.
32. Staccioli, 123.
33. Montaigne, vol. 3, 12. The inscription is CIL XI: 6106.
34. For an analysis of the relationship between Meloni's party and the original Fascists, see Broder.
35. Translation as given on interpretive panel.
36. Talbert 2012, 241.
37. Staccioli, 79–80.
38. Galen, vol. 10, 633. Translation from Della Portella 2004b, 8.
39. ILS (Dessau, *Inscriptiones Latinae Selectae*) 5863, trans. in Erskine, 120–21.
40. Capitoline Museums, inv. no. NCE 2416.
41. Laurence 2013, 304–5.
42. Salway, 32.
43. Suetonius, *Divus Iulius* 57 (LCL 31: 110–11) and Pliny (the Elder), *Naturalis Historia* 7.84 (LCL 352: 560–61); for context Laurence 1999, 81.

44. Laurence 1999, 82.
45. Kolb 2011, 101.
46. For vehicles worth more than 15,000 asses. Laurence 1999, 136.
47. Laurence 1999, 138–41.
48. Laurence 1999, 172–3.
49. Scheidel, 4.
50. Foubert, 5–6.
51. Casson, 147.
52. Seneca (the Younger), *Epistulae* 104.13 (LCL 77: 198–9); *De tranquillitate animi* 2.13 (LCL 254: 220–21); see also Foubert, 9–10.
53. Casson, 139.
54. Pliny the Younger, *Epistulae* 2.17 (LCL 55: 132–3).
55. Laurence 1999, 84.
56. Laurence 1999, 103–4.
57. Martial, *Epigrammata* 3.47.15, trans. in Casson, 146 (also at LCL 94: 220–23).
58. https://www.ostia-antica.org/dict/topics/severan-emperors/statio-32.htm
59. https://www.ostia-antica.org/regio2/2/2-3.htm
60. Livy, *Periochae* 107 (LCL 404: 132–3); see also Ventre, 87–9.
61. Laurence 1999, 179.
62. Ventre, 96.
63. Horace, *Satirae* 1.5.3–13 (LCL 194: 64–5).
64. Seneca (the Elder), *Suasoriae* 6.17, translation from Ventre, 132.
65. Thommen, 76–8.
66. Strabo, *Geographica* 5.3.8, trans. in Staccioli, 7 (also in LCL 50: 404–5).

2: JOURNEYS THROUGH THE EMPIRE

1. Popkin, 113; Cassibry, 34.
2. Chevallier, 49.
3. Cassibry, 35–6.
4. Strabo, *Geog.* 3.4.9 (LCL 50: 93–7); Campedelli, 115.
5. Popkin 121; Cassibry, 34.
6. Campedelli, 111, 122, 127.
7. Cassibry, 51.
8. Coarelli, 167.
9. Manacorda, 11–12; Kallis, 95.
10. Cicero, *Epistulae ad familiares* 415 (X.32), (LCL 230: 358–9).
11. Cicero, *Pro Balbo* 29 (LCL 447: 660–63); Chevallier, 226, fn. 18.
12. Lowe, 469.
13. Cassibry, 59.
14. Livy, *Ab Urbe Condita* 39.29.8–10, (LCL 313: 294–5).
15. C. E. P. Adams, 154.
16. Apuleius, *Metamorphoses* 1.15, (LCL 44: 26–7).
17. Apuleius, *Met.* 8.15, (LCL 453: 72–3).
18. Suet., *Tiberius* 3.37, (LCL 31: 364–5).
19. Laurence 1999, 144.
20. Mitchell, 246.
21. *P.Mich.inv.* 1367/Recto, https://quod.lib.umich.edu/a/apis/x-1409/1367r.tif. University of Michigan Library Digital Collections. Translation Carucci, 182–3, adapting Rowlandson, 148.
22. Sen., *De Ira* 3.20, (LCL 214: 306–7).

23. Brodersen, 12.
24. Vegetius, *De re militari* 3.6, cited and translated Salway, 31; see also Larnach, 29.
25. Chevallier, 34.
26. Salway, 34, 59.
27. Brodersen, 18; Salway, 30; Blennow, 58.
28. Talbert 2010, 7.
29. Talbert 2010, 135–6.
30. Rautman, 142.
31. Talbert 2010, 139.
32. Talbert 2012, 250.
33. https://banc.memoria.gencat.cat/en/results/espais_memoria/45
34. Chevallier, 78.
35. Musée Départemental Arles Antique, FAN 1992.520.
36. Musée de la Romanité, Nîmes, interpretive material.
37. Cassibry, 42.
38. Erskine, 61.
39. J. N. Adams, 275, 552–3 and 617–18.
40. Mairs.
41. Velleius Paterculus, *Historiae Romanae* 2.120.2–3 (LCL 152: 302–5).
42. Morley, 43, 82.
43. Campedelli, 112.
44. Suet., *Divus Augustus* 49.2, LCL 31: 228–9.
45. Kolb 2011, 95–6, 98–9.
46. Museum of Burdur, inv. no. 2670, text online at https://www.judaism-and-rome.org/edict-governor-galatia-requisitioning-transport-and-accommodation; cited in Kolb 2011, 97.
47. Eusebius, *Vita Constantini* 4.36.4; for discussion Kolb 2011, 102.
48. C. E. P. Adams, 145.
49. Laurence 1999, 58–9. *XII Tabulae sive Lex XII Tabularum*, 7.6 (LCL 329: 470–71); for the widths see also Varro, *De Lingua Latina* 7.15 (LCL 333: 282–3).
50. Davies 2008, 42.
51. *Codex Theodosianus*, 282–95.
52. Kolb 2011, 98.
53. Laurence 2011, 75, 87.
54. Laurence 2013, 307.
55. Strabo, *Geog.* 5.3.8, trans. in Talbert 2012, 238–9 (also in LCL 50: 404–5).
56. Plut., *Moralia. Praecepta gerendae reipublicae* 10.55 (Stephanus 811B), LCL 321: 222–5, as adapted by Valerius Maximus, *Factorum et dictorum memorabilium libri IX* 3.7.ext5 (LCL 492: 314–15).
57. Tacitus, *Annales* 1.20 (LCL 249: 280–81).
58. Tac., *Agricola*, 30–31 (LCL 35: 80–82, which however uses 'desolation' rather than the more common 'desert').
59. Shabbat 33b, https://www.sefaria.org/Shabbat.33b.5?lang=bi&with=About&lang2=en. For context: de Lange, 268.
60. De Blois, 53; examples from Hauken, 40 and 205–6.
61. Krautheimer, 3.
62. Staccioli, 86.
63. Casson, 165.
64. Maas and Ruths, 255–6.

3: EARLY CHRISTIAN TRAVEL

1. Isaiah 11:16, 35:8, 40:3, 62:10. Easton, entry for 'Highway'.
2. Bartlett, 410–11.
3. Frauzel, 1088; Blennow, 70.
4. Webb, 1, 11; Frauzel, 1087.
5. Galatians 1:17–18, 21, 2:1; see Perowne, 29.
6. Wilson; Nasrallah.
7. Chevallier, 21.
8. Acts, 28:15–16.
9. McKechnie, 151.
10. McKechnie, 279–81.
11. McKitterick et al., 2.
12. For Paul VI see https://www.vatican.va/content/paul-vi/it/audiences/1968/documents/hf_p-vi_aud_19680626.html (accessed 23 August 2023); for an early example of expert caution, O'Callaghan 71.
13. Holum, 66.
14. Holum, 76, argues that she 'vastly increased its scope'.
15. For an English translation see Bordeaux Pilgrim (trans. Jacobs).
16. Talbert 2010, 139–40; Larnach, 31, 72; Belke 2008, 302.
17. Thommen, 74, Chevallier, 165–70.
18. For the discussion see L. Douglass; Weingarten; Falcasantos.
19. Anonimus post Dionem, 15, *Digital Fragmenta Historicorum Graecorum* IV, p. 199.
20. Online at https://edh.ub.uni-heidelberg.de/edh/inschrift/HD043084. My thanks to Julia Hillner for identifying the source.
21. Vout, 3 lists multiple cities that make the claim.
22. Kuelzer, 157.
23. *Barrington Atlas*, map 58.
24. Egeria (ed. Wilkinson), 3. Blennow, 63–4.
25. Egeria, 7.
26. Egeria, 100.
27. Egeria, 100.
28. Egeria, 101, 103.
29. Theophanes (ed. Matthews), 72.
30. Theophanes, 62.
31. Theophanes, 49.
32. Theophanes, 53–5.
33. Theophanes, 123.
34. Theophanes, 126.
35. Theophanes, 49.
36. Theophanes, 50.
37. Larnach, 166.
38. Mitchell 2020.
39. Staccioli, 127.
40. Coulston, 109–10 and 112–13.
41. McCabe, 91.
42. McCabe, 92, 95–7.
43. Strabo, *Geog.* 17.1.45 (LCL 267: 120–21); for discussion C. Adams, 141.
44. Comfort, 126.
45. Cornelius Nepos, *De excellentibus ducibus exterarum gentium* 18.8.7 (LCL 467: 222–3).
46. Comfort, 111, 118, 119.
47. For ongoing research on the roads in Anatolia, see www.anatolianroads.org

48. Jerome (ed. Cain), 51.
49. Jerome, 51–63.
50. Jerome, 65.
51. Jerome, 313: editor's commentary.
52. Gameson, 8–12: the quotation is from Bede, ch. 23.

4: BYZANTIUM AND THE VIA EGNATIA

1. *Vita sanctae Arthellaidis*; for context Sinisi, 51.
2. Kulikowski, 38.
3. Procopius, *De Bellis* (*or De Bello Gothico*), 5.14.6 (LCL 107: 142–3).
4. Procop., *Goth.* 5.14.11 (LCL 107: 144–5).
5. Archaeological Museum of Thessaloniki: https://www.amth.gr/en/exhibitions/exhibit-of-the-month/1809. I am grateful to Gareth Harvey for drawing this detail to public attention.
6. Chevallier, 140, Erskine, 28–9.
7. Laurence 2013, 305, citing Cicero *De provinciis consularibus* 2.2 (LCL 447: 542–3); *In Pisonem*, 17(40), (LCL 252: 188–9). Casson gives the date as 'shortly after 148 BC', 164.
8. Erskine 28–9.
9. Larnach, 25.
10. Belke 2008, 304.
11. Belke 2008, 300.
12. Belke 2008, 304.
13. McCormick, 69; Haldon, 136.
14. Haldon, 137; McCormick, 68.
15. Haldon, 136.
16. Samantha Lock and agencies, 'Greece and Turkey trade blame after 92 naked migrants rescued at border', *The Guardian*, 17 October 2022, online at https://www.theguardian.com/world/2022/oct/17/greece-and-turkey-trade-blame-after-92-naked-migrants-rescued-at-border
17. *Thessaloniki and its Monuments*, 9–10.
18. Rautman, 141; Ritter.
19. Pryor, 4–5; O'Sullivan, 28.
20. Apul., *Met.* 1.1, (LCL 44: 4–5).
21. Chevallier, 85.
22. Bowes and Hoti.
23. CIL IX: 6052.
24. Sidonius Apollinaris, *Epistulae* 9.3.1–2, (LCL 420: 508–9).
25. Sartorio, 29, citing CIL X: 6850–52 = ILS 867; Cassiodorus 2.32–3.
26. Pelteret, 20.
27. Pelteret, 21.
28. Stephanus, *Life of Bishop Wilfrid* (ed. Colgrave), 51.
29. Pelteret, 22.
30. Pelteret, 21.
31. Barnish, 171; Cassiodorus, 8.33.
32. Webb, 17–18.
33. https://www.edoardotresoldi.com/works/basilica-di-siponto/
34. Sinisi, 43.
35. Foxhall Forbes, 183.
36. Izzi, 147 and 172; Foxhall Forbes, 191.
37. Madgearu.
38. Hallenbeck, 7–8. Diehl, 68–9.

39. Diehl, 69–70.
40. Riganelli, 141–2.
41. Hallenbeck, 146–8, 160. Nithard, 49.
42. Krautheimer, 107.
43. Riganelli, 144.
44. McCormick, 397.
45. Herrin, 75, 78–9, 98–100, 114, 117–18, 126–8.
46. Webb, 130.
47. Horace, *Odes* 1.9 (LCL 33: 40–41).
48. Nithard, 38.
49. McCormick, 395.
50. McCormick, 399.
51. McCormick, 445.
52. McCormick, 478–9.

5: PILGRIMS AND THE VIA FRANCIGENA

1. Paul the Deacon, 229; trans. from Bartlett, 412.
2. Fafinski, 52.
3. Fafinski, 62–3.
4. Fafinski, 57–9, 81.
5. Izzi, 149–55.
6. Savill, record no. E05710, online at http://csla.history.ox.ac.uk/record.php?recid=E05710.
7. Keyvanian, 80–81; Ortenberg, 204–5.
8. Pelteret, 25, where this translation is provided.
9. Pelteret, 33.
10. Voaden, 181.
11. R. Thomas, 564; Keynes 112–14.
12. R. Thomas, 561.
13. R. Thomas, 562, 566.
14. Pelteret, 28–9.
15. *Anglo-Saxon Chronicle* ed. Thorpe, discussed in Frauzel, 1090.
16. https://www.lombardiabeniculturali.it/architetture/schede/PV240-00123/
17. *Epitaphium Ansae reginae*, 192; Bartlett, 436.
18. Zaldini.
19. Blennow, 66–7.
20. Blennow, 42–3. It is Franz Alto Bauer who suggests the more specific dating.
21. Blennow, 53.
22. Blennow, 53–5.
23. Blennow, 41. Del Lungo provides a transcription of the manuscript.
24. *Liber Pontificalis* 107: 53.
25. Matheus, 185.
26. Del Nero, 9.
27. Matheus, 186; Del Nero, 9–11; Stevenson 34–5; for in-depth study see Stopani 1992 and Stopani 1998.
28. Matheus, 187.
29. Webb, 129.
30. Matheus, 187.
31. Webb, 130; Matheus, 188; Magoun 1940, 269–70.
32. Magoun 1940, 276; on the Schola see Keyvanian, 80–82.
33. Ortenberg, 200.
34. Ortenberg, 228–9.
35. Bartlett, 417.
36. Gates-Foster, 214.
37. Now cared for by the Churches Conservation Trust.

https://www.visitchurches.org.uk/static/uploaded/5f6b1f35-1f92-450f-a18e44f110873301.pdf

38. Vasori, 185–6; Zei, 166.
39. Treharne, 344–5.
40. *Fagrskinna* 164; Treharne, 359.
41. MGH (*Monumenta Germaniae Historica*), *Epistolae Karolini Aevi II* ed. E. Dümmler, Berlin 1895, p. 145.16–20. For discussion Pelteret, 28; McCormick, 275.
42. William of Malmesbury, 326–7, translation slightly modified by Treharne, 346.
43. Magoun 1944, 314–36; see also Webb, 131–2.
44. Magoun 1944, 337, 350.
45. Magoun 1944, 345–6.
46. James 1875, 195.
47. Magoun 1940, 280.
48. Weber, 39.
49. Benjamin, 1–5.
50. Benjamin, 6–9.
51. Benjamin, 10.
52. Benjamin, 11.
53. Benjamin, 11–12.
54. Benjamin, 12.
55. Strabo, *Geog*, 5.4.5 (LCL 50: 444–5). On tunnel construction see Davies 1998, 9–10 and for further descriptions Strabo, *Geog*, 5.4.7 (LCL 50: 450–51) and Seneca *Ep. ad Luc.* 57.1–2 (LCL 75: 382–3).
56. 'Mozart & Material Culture: Naples: Grotta di Pozzuoli', online at https://mmc.kdl.kcl.ac.uk/entities/place/naples-grotta-di-pozzuoli-also-known-crypta-neapolitana/
57. Benjamin, 12.
58. Benjamin, 12–15.
59. von Suchem, 8.
60. de la Brocquière, 70.
61. Leask; Playfair.
62. Webb, 24–5.
63. Webb, 25. Blennow, 71–2.
64. Blennow, 82.
65. Blennow, 78.
66. Mayer, 164, who amends Osborne's translation of Gregorius.
67. Lucan, *De Bello Civili*, 3, 84–92.
68. Webb, 25.
69. Webb, 116, 134.
70. Pucci Donati, 107.
71. Pucci Donati, 110.
72. Pucci Donati, 111.
73. Pucci Donati, 112.
74. Pucci Donati, 115.
75. Pelù, 25.
76. Vingtain, 17.
77. *Medieval Italy: Texts in Translation*, 295, translated from *Chronicon Estense*, 148–9.
78. Craig, 166–7.
79. MGH, *Epistolae Merowingici et Karolini Aevi, Epistola ad Cuthiberthum archiepiscopum Cantabrigensem*, no. 78, 354–5. For discussion Frauzel, 1089.
80. *Three Byzantine Saints*, ch. 3.
81. Strabo 17.1.16 (LCL 267: 60–61). Trans. from C. Adams, 145.
82. Staccioli, 7, citing Pliny, *Naturalis Historia*, 36.2. My thanks to Rob Boddice for identifying Staccioli's source.
83. Fabri 1.1, 163; for context Craig, 172–3.

84. Fabri, 1.1, 110; for context Inglis and Christmon, 263.
85. Translation from Voaden, 185.
86. *Voyage de la saincte cyté de Hierusalem*, 56, trans. in Inglis and Christmon, 271.
87. Windeatt, Introduction, in Kempe 2000, 13.
88. Windeatt, Introduction, in Kempe 2000, 10–11.
89. Bale, Introduction to Kempe 2015, xviii–xix.
90. Kempe 2000, 96–99.
91. Kempe 2000, 101.
92. Kempe 2000, 111.
93. Kempe 2000, 112–13; for context, Bartlett, 438.
94. Rossiaud, 33.
95. Webb, 121.
96. Kempe, 115.
97. Craig, 171–2.
98. Kempe, 116. On the English hospice, Harvey, 55–66.

6: CRUSADERS AND THE VIA MILITARIS

1. Bartlett, 414; Asbridge, 39.
2. Suchem, 4.
3. McCormick, 69–70.
4. McCormick, 73.
5. Larnach, 117.
6. Haldon, 137.
7. Haldon, 138.
8. Larnach, 8, 12.
9. Belke 2002, 77.
10. Kaplan, 93.
11. McCormick, 549–50.
12. McCormick, 551.
13. *Deeds of the Franks*, 28.
14. *Deeds of the Franks*, 25.
15. Gabriele, 41–2.
16. Larnach, 117.
17. Belke 2002, 79; Belke 2008, 298; Larnach 117–18.
18. Davies 2008, 47.
19. Murray, 186–8.
20. Murray, 189.
21. Asbridge, 149.
22. Belke 2008, 301, 305.
23. Larnach, 145–7.
24. Asbridge, 91–2.
25. Sanudo Torsello, 214.
26. Asbridge, 105–6.
27. Eidelberg, 22; Bronstein, 1268.
28. Chazan, ix–x.
29. Bronstein, 1270–71.
30. Fulcher, 22.
31. Asbridge, 89, 95.
32. Murray, 186–7.
33. Asbridge, 105–6.
34. Larnach, 45.
35. Asbridge, 92–3; Murray, 187.
36. Belke 2002, 82.
37. Raymond d'Aguilers, 6.
38. Raymond d'Aguilers, 16.
39. Galatariotou, 226–7; Mesarites, 228.
40. Raymond d'Aguilers, 16.
41. Raymond d'Aguilers, 17.
42. Sanudo Torsello, 73.
43. Schipper, 209.
44. Larnach, 138–9.
45. William of Tyre, vol. 1, 122.
46. Larnach, 143, 254; Murray, 189.
47. Hitchin, 17–19.
48. *Crusade of Frederick*, 70.
49. *Crusade of Frederick*, 7.
50. *Crusade of Frederick*, 46.

51. *Crusade of Frederick*, 46.
52. *Crusade of Frederick*, 60.
53. *Crusade of Frederick*, 60.
54. *Crusade of Frederick*, 66.
55. *Crusade of Frederick*, 70.
56. *Crusade of Frederick*, 71.
57. Odo of Deuil, 33.
58. Geoffrey de Villehardouin, 91. https://bulgariatravel.org/asens-fortress-and-the-city-of-asenovgrad/
59. Sweeney, 118.
60. Sweeney, 119.
61. Sweeney, 120.
62. Sweeney, 121.
63. Larnach, 63, 242.
64. Haldon, 138–9.
65. *Deeds of the Franks*, 33.
66. Ehrlich, 270.
67. Ehrlich, 266, 269–70.
68. Ehrlich, 266, 272.
69. Ehrlich, 273–82.
70. Ehrlich, 282–3.
71. Phocas, 17.
72. Phocas, 26.
73. Sanudo Torsello, 412–16.
74. Belke 2002, 83.
75. Belke 2008, 298.
76. Belke 2002, 90.

7: THE RENAISSANCE OF THE ROADS

1. Bracciolini 9, 97, 99, 189.
2. Karmon, 54–7.
3. Caprotti, xxv.
4. Leonardo da Vinci, 'A map of the Pontine marshes, 1515', Royal Collection, inv. no. RCIN 912684, online at: https://www.rct.uk/collection/themes/exhibitions/leonardo-da-vinci-a-life-in-drawing/derby-museum-and-art-gallery-derby/a-map-of-the-pontine-marshes
5. Karmon, 67.
6. Karmon, 65.
7. Karmon, 75.
8. D'Arco, vol. 2, 44, trans. in Karmon, 75.
9. Stenhouse, 413.
10. Bisaha, 2–4, 37.
11. Piccolomini 1988, 94.
12. Piccolomini 1947, 350.
13. Piccolomini 1988, 293.
14. Galliazzo, 37.
15. Piccolomini 1988, 297–8.
16. Piccolomini 1988, 70.
17. Piccolomini 1988, 184.
18. Piccolomini 1988, 309.
19. Piccolomini 1988, 310–11.
20. Piccolomini 1988, 300.
21. Rubinstein, 199–202.
22. Piccolomini 1998, 28–9.
23. Piccolomini 1988, 29–31.
24. Piccolomini 1988, 31.
25. Piccolomini 1988, 31.
26. Piccolomini 1988, 140.
27. Erhard Etzlaub, '"Romweg", map of central Europe', British Library.
28. Examples from this period include *Informacōn for Pylgrymes* and Le Huen.
29. Alberti, 259r.
30. Alberti, 121v.
31. Isabella d'Este, 385.
32. Stenhouse, 397, 405, 410.
33. Elliot van Liere, 248.
34. Elliot van Liere, 242.

35. Sartorio, 46–7; Coffin, 64–5.
36. Biondo, 155.
37. Pepper and Adams, 23–7.
38. Ventre, 126.
39. Coffin, 38.
40. https://www.landmarktrust.org.uk/search-and-book/properties/sant-antonio-11845/#Overview
41. Coffin, 257.
42. Coffin, 152–3, 167, 150.
43. Coffin, 171.
44. Gamucci, 137; translation from Coffin, 178.
45. North, 206.
46. North, 193–4.
47. Piccolomini 1988, 161–2.
48. Nuti, 119–22.
49. Karmon, 108.
50. Karmon, 102–3; Rowell, 133; Strong, 83.
51. Fletcher, 126.
52. Bacciolo, para. 17.
53. Karmon, 105–7.
54. E. J. B. Allen, 3–4, 9, 13.
55. Midura, 1028.
56. Schobesberger, 239.
57. Isabella d'Este, 495–6.
58. For further discussion, see Fletcher, ch. 5.
59. Midura, 1026–9.
60. Fletcher, 115.
61. Calculation from orbis.stanford.edu

8: EXPLORERS, SPIES AND PRIESTS

1. Sartorio, 58.
2. Bacciolo.
3. W. Thomas, 50.
4. W. Thomas, 41.
5. North, 190.
6. North, 203.
7. Estienne; for context Chevallier, 57.
8. Underwood, 349; Williams, 4–6.
9. Munday, xiv–xv, 5.
10. For discussion of this interest see Wyatt.
11. Kitzes, 444.
12. Bossy, 135–8; M. E. Williams, 7.
13. Munday, 6.
14. Brigden and Woolfson, 485–7.
15. Fletcher, 118.
16. Munday, 7, 9.
17. Munday, 11–12.
18. Munday, 17.
19. Munday, 21.
20. Munday, 35–6.
21. Munday, 41–2.
22. Munday, 25.
23. Munday, 38–40.
24. Munday, 46.
25. Munday, 65.
26. Munday, 70–73.
27. Munday, 49–50.
28. Munday, 95.
29. Munby.
30. Montaigne, vol. 1, 80.
31. Montaigne, vol. 1, 90–91.
32. Montaigne, vol. 1, 103.
33. Montaigne, vol. 1, 108.
34. Montaigne, vol. 1, 115. CIL 3: 5987.
35. Montaigne, vol. 1, 116.
36. Montaigne, vol. 2, 1.
37. E. Wright, vol. 1, 111; for discussion Ingamells, 22.
38. Stevens Crawshaw.
39. Montaigne, vol. 2, 4.

40. Montaigne, vol. 2, 36, 41.
41. Montaigne, vol. 2, 54.
42. Montaigne, vol. 2, 69.
43. Montaigne, vol. 2, 70–71.
44. Montaigne, vol. 2, 71.
45. Montaigne, vol. 2, 73.
46. Montaigne, vol. 2, 75, 80–82.
47. Montaigne, vol. 2, 131.
48. Montaigne, vol. 2, 165–6.
49. Montaigne, vol. 2, 181–2.
50. Montaigne, vol. 2, 182–3.
51. Montaigne, vol. 3, 22, 27.
52. Montaigne, vol. 3, 42.
53. Montaigne, vol. 3, 190.
54. Ferguson, 85.
55. Ferguson, 77.
56. Ferguson, 88–92.
57. Ferguson, 79, 123.
58. Beard and Taylor, 281.
59. Moryson, vol. 1, 212, 222, 224, 231.
60. Redigonda.
61. Moryson, vol. 1, 266–7.
62. Wotton, vol. 1, 70, note 3; for discussion see Ord, 3–4.
63. Ord, 2–3.
64. Coryat, vol. 1, 158.
65. Coryat, vol. 1, 160, 165.
66. Coryat, vol. 1, 171.
67. Coryat, vol. 1, 170.
68. Coryat, vol. 1, 203.
69. Coryat, vol. 1, 206.
70. Coryat, vol. 1, 211–14.
71. Coryat, vol. 1, 216.
72. Coryat, vol. 1, 228.
73. Coryat, vol. 1, 259, 263, 268.
74. Coryat, vol. 1, 281–5.
75. Sandrock, 192.
76. Sandys, 1.
77. Addison, 126.
78. Sandrock, 192.
79. Midura, 1051; Chevallier, 59.
80. Wilton and Bignamini, 99.

9: ROYAL REFUGEES

1. McCavitt; for an older but still revisionist argument see Canny. O'Connor and Lyons provide extensive context.
2. Ò Cianáin, ed. Walsh, ix. Carroll, 26.
3. Ò Cianáin, 88.
4. Ò Cianáin, 91.
5. Ò Cianáin, 123.
6. Carroll, 23; Ò Cianáin, 169.
7. Carroll, 26.
8. Ò Cianáin, 201.
9. Ò Cianáin, 251.
10. Ò Cianáin, 209.
11. Ò Cianáin, 209–11, 239.
12. Salvadore 2022.
13. Salvadore 2022, 28.
14. Salvadore 2022, 4.
15. Armellini, 622.
16. Salvadore 2017.
17. Baskins, 405.
18. Translation by David Bowles, cited in Pennock, 29.
19. Corpus Velazqueño, vol. 1, p. 1650, no. 267.
20. Priorato, 96–8.
21. Priorato, 95.
22. Priorato, 105.
23. Priorato, 119.
24. Priorato, 122.
25. Priorato, 176.
26. Priorato, 211.
27. Priorato, 213.
28. Priorato, 239, 275–6.

29. Priorato 301–3.
30. Priorato, 311.
31. Priorato, 326.
32. Wilton and Bignamini, 99.
33. Waller and Denham, 247; for context see Hardacre, 356.
34. Raymond, 120.
35. Raymond, 123–4.
36. *Origins of the Grand Tour*, 260.
37. Games, 37–8.
38. De Seta, 13.
39. Lassels, 159.
40. Sweet, Verhoeven and Goldsmith, Introduction.
41. McGeary, 117.
42. Towner, 304.
43. Bartlett, 434.
44. Reilly: death rates 102, route and timing 109–11.
45. Addison, 141–2.
46. Milkova, 499.
47. Warnock, 652.
48. Morgan, vol. 1, 262–3.
49. Busbecq, 16.
50. Busbecq, 15 and note.
51. Busbecq, 48.
52. Busbecq, 36–7.
53. Gilles, 147.
54. Wortley Montagu, 288.
55. Wortley Montagu, 291–2. The gate has recently undergone a controversial restoration: https://ancientbulgaria.bg/listings/gate-trajan
56. Harris, 194–9.
57. Busbecq, 241; Larnach, 63.
58. Chora: https://muze.gen.tr/muze-detag/kariye. The official website of the Basilica Cistern museum notes that the cistern remained known to locals even while a sixteenth-century western topographer claimed its rediscovery. https://yerebatan.com/en/basilica-cistern/about-us/.
59. Camden, 87; for discussion Ayres, 86.
60. Ayres, 87–8.
61. Cited in Ayres, 110–11.
62. Ayres, xiv.
63. Corp.

10: THE GRAND TOUR

1. Gray, vol. 1, 145; Mayer, 167.
2. Rogers 1956, 207; Mayer, 168.
3. Gray, vol. 1, 146; Mayer, 167.
4. Gray, vol. 1, 156, 159; Mack, 246–9.
5. Brosses, 318.
6. Nugent, vol. 3, 341.
7. Riggs Miller, vol. 2, 286.
8. Riggs Miller, vol. 2, 39.
9. Warnock, 654–5, 657.
10. Riqueti, vol. 1, 91, translation from Robb, 222; Hitchner, 223.
11. Gleadhill, 23. Olcelli, 312–13.
12. Riggs Miller, vol. 2, 20–21.
13. Smollett, 246.
14. Sweet, 15.
15. Baigent.
16. Nugent, vol. 3, 61.
17. Nugent, vol. 3, 65.
18. Nugent, vol. 3, 210.
19. Sartorio, 64–8.
20. Nugent, vol. 3, 211.
21. Nugent, vol. 3, 212.
22. Nugent, vol. 3, 279–80.
23. Brosses, 316.

24. Smollett, 203.
25. Starke, vol. 1, 3.
26. Smollett, 203.
27. Laurence 1999, 41.
28. Tacitus, *Annales* 3.31 (LCL 249: 572–3).
29. Dio 59.15 and 60.17 (LCL 175: 304–5 and 408–9), cited in Laurence 1999, 46.
30. Ingamells, 21–2; Rogers, ed. Hale 1956, 79–81.
31. Sweet, 16.
32. Smollett, 72.
33. Gogol, 260.
34. See the forthcoming edition of servants' Grand Tour journals, edited by Richard Ansell.
35. Hazlitt, 331.
36. Baumgartner 2015, 11 and note 31.
37. Translation of Recke's *Tagebuche* vol. 1, 221, in Baumgartner 2015, 12.
38. Translation of Lewald, *Italienisches Bilderbuch*, 36, in Baumgartner 2015, 13.
39. Riggs Miller, vol. 2, 390–91.
40. Sterne, 101.
41. Gleadhill, 21.
42. Games, 37.
43. Moore, vol. 2, 424–5; for context Gleadhill, 24.
44. Riggs Miller, vol. 2, 118.
45. Piozzi, vol. 2, 66–7.
46. The classic work on this theme is MacCannell; see also Richards; Smith and Robinson.
47. Verri, 246–51; Sartorio, 34.
48. Stendhal, 238.
49. Buzard, 69–70.
50. Colbert.
51. Starke, vol. 1, 330–31, 351, 341.
52. Starke, vol. 2, 3–5.
53. Starke, vol. 1, 336.
54. Starke, vol. 1, 335.
55. Starke, vol. 2, 51–9.
56. Towner, 321–2.
57. Kempe 2000, 18.
58. Nugent, vol. 3, 269.
59. Starke, vol. 2, 61; Riggs Miller, vol. 2, 17.
60. Towner, 324.
61. https://www.royalvictoria.it/en/the-hotel/
62. Starke, vol. 2, 98.
63. Fenimore Cooper, vol. 1, 165.
64. Starke, vol. 2, 64.
65. Starke, vol. 2, 107–8.
66. Starke, vol. 2, 170.
67. Starke, vol. 2, 178.
68. Baumgartner 2014, unpaginated online edition.
69. Gikandi, 115–18.
70. Beckford 1783, 196–7.
71. Mack, 236. Translation from Mack.
72. Gray, vol. 1, 163, cited in Mack, 249.
73. Cavour, vol. 17, 2483, translation from M. Clark, 122.
74. Starke, vol. 2, 57.
75. Boswell, 266.
76. Morgan, vol. 1, 23. Badin, 7.

11: NAPOLEON

1. Starke, vol. 1, 25–47.
2. Starke, vol. 1, 153; for the outline of Starke's travels in relation

to the invasions see Moskal 2001, 162–6.
3. Bonaparte, vol. 1, 41.
4. Bonaparte, vol. 1, 42.
5. Bonaparte, vol. 1, 43.
6. Nicassio, 21. Dyson 2019, 35.
7. Nicassio, 16.
8. Ventre, 109, 118–19.
9. Gregorovius, cited in Ventre, 109.
10. Starke, vol. 1, 8.
11. Chetwode Eustace, 452.
12. Chetwode Eustace, 112, 121.
13. Nicassio, 16.
14. de Bourrienne, vol. 4, 52, trans. from Rowell, 65.
15. Rowell, 7.
16. Rowell, 11–12.
17. Rowell, 91, 133.
18. Jaques, Part 3, ch. 4, unpaginated digital edition.
19. Rowell, 17.
20. Rowell, 43.
21. Rowell, 39.
22. Cited in Hudson.
23. Wilmot, 11; for context Buck, 190.
24. Wilmot, 72; for context Buck, 192–3.
25. Starke, Introduction; Moskal 2001, 176.
26. Starke, vol. 1, 137; Moskal 2001, 181.
27. *Journal de Paris*, No. 309, 27 July 1798:1295, trans. in Rowell, 11; original text in Rowell, 168.
28. Ridley, 29.
29. Paris, 11.
30. Ridley, 51–2, 84.
31. Dyson 2019, ch. 2.
32. Coxe, 187–8.
33. Piozzi, vol. 2, 157.
34. Dyson 2019, 55.
35. Jaques, Part 3, ch. 2, unpaginated digital edition; Johns, 106–12.
36. Canova, 37–8.
37. Melena, 128–9.
38. Jaques, Part 3, ch. 2.
39. Rogers 1956, 274, fn. 1.
40. *Liverpool Mercury*, 89, Friday, 12 March 1813, p. 7, 'Miscellaneous Extracts', no. LX.
41. Davis, 174.
42. Davis, 197.
43. Calculations are tricky because workers were paid in kind as well as cash. My rough estimate here is based on the figures in Fiore Melacrinis.
44. *Caledonian Mercury*, 27 February 1815, 'London News Continued'.
45. Coxe, 8.
46. Rogers 1956, 159–60.
47. Anon., *Roads and Railroads*, 19.
48. Rowell, 30–31.
49. Rowell, 13.
50. Chateaubriand, vol. 2, 227.
51. Chateaubriand, vol. 2, 231.
52. Chateaubriand, vol. 2, 256–7.

12: THE ROMANTICS

1. Meyenberg and Vincent.
2. Wordsworth, online at: https://www.poetryfoundation.org/poems/45552/the-simplon-pass
3. Towner, 313–14.
4. For a survey, see Tresoldi.

5. Baumgartner, 2014, unpaginated online edition.
6. Goethe 1885, 123–4.
7. Goethe 1885, 118.
8. Goethe 1885, 119.
9. Goethe 1885, 119.
10. Zilcosky, 421, 422, 426–7.
11. Goethe 1977, elegy XVIII, p. 83, although as the editor notes (p. 10), the name is a conventional one; for the Osteria, see elegy XV, p. 73 and note.
12. Arthurs, 77. 'Vita popolare della vecchia Roma – Piazza Montanara', in *L'illustrazione popolare* vol. XXIII, no. 46, Milan, 14 November 1886.
13. Nicassio, 17 for the timeline.
14. Coxe (Millard), xxi: for context Sweet, 11–12.
15. Morgan, vol. 1, 262.
16. Morgan, vol. 1, 263.
17. H. W. Williams, vol. 1, 353.
18. Wilmot, 117.
19. Towner, 310. Jonathan Bate, 'William Hazlitt, 1778–1830', *ODNB*.
20. Hazlitt, 245–9.
21. 'Discus upon the Appian Way', *Sussex Advertiser*, 4 December 1815, p. 2.
22. Charlotte Higgins, 'Lavish ancient Roman winery found at ruins of the Villa of the Quintilii near Rome', *The Guardian*, 17 April 2023, online at: https://www.theguardian.com/world/2023/apr/17/ancient-roman-winery-found-ruins-villa-of-quintilii-rome
23. H. W. Williams, vol. 2, 114.
24. Wilmot, 125.
25. 'Letter from Italy', in the *Scots Magazine*, 1 September 1818, p. 16.
26. Rogers 1956, 207.
27. https://keats-shelley.org/about
28. I am grateful to Anna Mercer for this information.
29. Interpretive material at the Keats-Shelley House.
30. Holland, 95; Roe, 388.
31. Holland, 79.
32. Rogers 1828, 19.
33. Graham-Campbell; Holland, 86.
34. Interpretive material, Casa di Goethe.
35. *Stone Pines on Monte Mario, with a View of Rome from near the Villa Mellini*, 1819, Tate Britain, D16337; Turner Bequest CLXXXIX 11.
36. Lorrain: English Heritage, The Wellington Collection, Apsley House. WM.1599-1948. Marlow: Tate Britain, T03602. Wilton and Bignamini, 23.
37. Beckford 1834, 54–8.
38. P. Shelley, vol. 4, 63.
39. Boyer, 635.
40. Morgan, vol. 1, 23–4.
41. M. Shelley, vol. 2, 214.
42. Dickens, 144.
43. Dickens, 163–4.
44. Letter to Stepan Shevyrev, 10 August 1839. Trans. in Milkova, 493.
45. Milkova, 497.
46. Gogol, 247.

47. Towner, 316.
48. Wordsworth, 197.

13: THE AMERICANS

1. Piana et al., 169.
2. Palmer Putnam, 28.
3. Palmer Putnam, 37.
4. Putnam, 34 (incorrectly paginated as 43).
5. Piana et al., 187.
6. Pazos, ch. 4, unpaginated digital edition.
7. Pazos, ch. 4. For the painting see: https://collections.mfa.org/objects/31228
8. On the complex reception of the classics in early America, see Malamud; Onuf and Cole.
9. James 1875, 7.
10. G. Allen, 28–9.
11. *Roman Fish Market. Arch of Octavius*. Albert Bierstadt, 1858. De Young Museum, San Francisco. Accession no. 1979.7.12. Online at: https://www.famsf.org/artworks/roman-fish-market-arch-of-octavius
12. 'The Road to Rome', *Daily Telegraph*, 12 December 1866.
13. John Murray, 246.
14. Dyson 2008, 37–8, 40–41.
15. John Murray, 250.
16. John Murray, 271.
17. John Murray, 288, 306.
18. John Murray, 304.
19. John Murray, 325.
20. Piana et al., 187.
21. Baker, 27–8.
22. Hawthorne 1980, 905–8.
23. Peabody Hawthorne, 250.
24. Fuller Ossoli, vol. 3, 161.
25. Melville, 111; for context Mailloux, 126–7.
26. Hawthorne 1901, vol. 2, 79.
27. Hawthorne 1901, vol. 2, 83–4.
28. Hawthorne 1901, vol. 2, 208, 210.
29. Hawthorne 1980, 117.
30. Twain, 274.
31. Piana et al., 181; Kalla-Bishop, 24–6.
32. M. Clark, 36, 49.
33. Trevelyan vol. 1, 157–8.
34. Trevelyan, vol. 1, 243.
35. Trevelyan, vol. 1, 312.
36. Riall, 98–9.
37. M. Clark, 82.
38. W. G. Clark, 51–2.
39. Cavour, vol. 17, part 5, 2482, translation from M. Clark, 121.
40. This was Gen. Lewis Cass, Democratic senator for Michigan; Riall, 110, note 50.
41. Carducci, 541.
42. Trevelyan, vol. 1, 5, 282.
43. Kalla-Bishop, 27–8.
44. Parker, vol. 3, x.
45. Kalla-Bishop, 44.
46. James 1875, 74.
47. Sartorio, 71.
48. Kalla-Bishop, 38.
49. Howells, ch. 12, unpaginated online edition.
50. Ruskin 1909, vol. 5, 370; Piana et al., 169.
51. Ruskin 1909, vol. 8, 159.
52. Ruskin 1972, 198. This was a trip in 1845. For context see Piana et al., 170.
53. Melena, 112.

54. W. G. Clark, vii; 15.
55. Eliot, 1998, 341; Mayer, 171.
56. 'The Road to Rome', *Daily Telegraph*, 13 December 1866.
57. Potter and Markino, 254.
58. Potter and Markino, xix.
59. Dyson 2008, 38.
60. Doyle, 58.
61. Crosland, 278–9.
62. Eliot 1998, 343.

14: NEW NARRATIVES, OLD EMPIRES

1. James 1875, 63.
2. Forster, ed. Bradbury, xii.
3. Marraro, 118–19.
4. Giuseppe Mazzini, 1906–90. *Scritti editi et inediti di Giuseppe Mazzini*. 106 vols, Imola; vol. 29, 92–4, cited in Riall, 65.
5. Laurence 2013, 299; Quilici.
6. Agazarian, 392.
7. Agazarian, 395–6.
8. Agazarian, 398–9.
9. Elliot, 72, 81–2; for context Agazarian, 401–3.
10. G. Allen, 263.
11. Rehm; Samuels and Samuels, 215.
12. Zilcosky, 430.
13. Moi, 83.
14. Eliot 1998, 348–9; Wilde, 41–2, 824.
15. Baxa, 90.
16. James 1875, 62.
17. James 1875, 136.
18. Melena, 8.
19. Melena, 103.
20. Melena, 107.
21. James 1909, 225.
22. For discussion see Clegg.
23. Ruskin 1909, vol. 37, 405.
24. Seymour, 63.
25. Seymour, 173–5.
26. Eliot 1889, 182.
27. Simmons, 15.
28. Simmons, 23–4.
29. Freud, vol. 4, 317, 194, 195, 196; Simmons, 121, 133, 134, 136, 138–9.
30. Simmons, 140.
31. O'Connor, 159.
32. Rogers 1956, 207.
33. Levine, 234.
34. Dorr, 12.
35. Dorr, xi.
36. Dorr, 102.
37. Graham, 180.
38. F. Douglass, 681; Levine, 231.
39. Levine, 234; Jefferson.
40. Levine, 232.
41. F. Douglass, 682.
42. F. Douglass, 686–7.
43. F. Douglass, 688–9.
44. F. Douglass, 693, 701.
45. F. Douglass, 693–4.
46. F. Douglass, 694–5.
47. F. Douglass, 695–6.
48. F. Douglass, 699–700; for context Mailloux, 129.
49. F. Douglass, 702.
50. F. Douglass, 713–14.
51. Levine, 241.
52. F. Douglass, 714.
53. F. Douglass, 716.
54. Anon., *Roads and Railroads*, iii.
55. Anon., *Roads and Railroads*, 59.
56. I have not identified the original source of this comment but it is attributed to Abbé Raynal in

multiple editions of the *Encyclopaedia Britannica* from at least 1796.

57. G. Allen, 11–12.
58. Scudder, vol. 1, 342; for background see Baker, 209.
59. Morton, 196–8; Baker, 29. On Morton's popularity, see Connelly.
60. Hillard, 442–3, summarised in Morton, 197.
61. Edwards, 18. Barlow, 91–2, suggests an element of satire in the representation of the Nubian, but even if that was the painter's intention I am sceptical that viewers would have perceived it that way.
62. Bryce, 20. For context see Ellis.
63. Dulcken, 10. For background, Bradley, 152–5.
64. Fletcher and Kipling, 14–15.
65. Fletcher and Kipling, 18.
66. Kaicker, 247–8.
67. Hali, 131, stanza 77.

15: VIA MUSSOLINIA

1. Wade; Wade and Giovenco.
2. https://press.roccofortehotels.com/hotel-de-russie-fact-sheet/
3. Ruskin 1909, vol. 37, 98.
4. Scarlett Conlon, 'Creative set: Fendi celebrates the Bloomsbury legacy', *The Guardian*, 23 January 2022, online at https://www.theguardian.com/fashion/2022/jan/23/creative-set-fendi-celebrates-the-bloomsbury-legacy. I was unable to consult the reviewed work directly.
5. *The Forum in Rome, with the Arch of Constantine*, National Trust, Chartwell. Online at: https://artuk.org/discover/artworks/the-forum-in-rome-with-the-arch-of-constantine-218679. For the paintings by the Bells see https://artuk.org/discover/artworks/the-forum-rome-73760 and https://artuk.org/discover/artworks/the-forum-rome-with-the-facade-and-campanile-of-san-francesca-romana-santa-maria-nuova-220626/
6. Haskell, 109.
7. Haskell, 114.
8. *Punch*, 18 December 1929, reprinted in Haskell, fig. 31.
9. Albanese, 91–3.
10. Villari, 189–90.
11. For a discussion of the historiography, Foot 2023.
12. Baxa, 38–9.
13. Beals, 291–4; Baxa, 52.
14. Baxa, 49.
15. Moraglio 2017, 1.
16. Moraglio 2017, 26; Moraglio 2009, 175.
17. Miltoun 1909, 66.
18. Miltoun 1909, 183.
19. Miltoun 1913, 36.
20. Lawrence, 176–7.
21. Huxley, 16–21.
22. Interpretive material, Goethe house exhibition.
23. Fauri and Troilo, 613.
24. Moraglio 2017, 14–15.

25. Moraglio 2017, 7, 10.
26. Moraglio 2017, 27–9, 42.
27. Moraglio 2017, 95.
28. Moraglio 2017, 158.
29. Moraglio 2009, 171.
30. B. Bolis, 'Ancora in tema di autostrade, di camionabili, e di strade automobilistiche', *Le strade* 3 (1954), 66, trans. in Moraglio 2009, 177.
31. Villari, 181–2.
32. Villari, 187.
33. Ferrari, 257.
34. Villari, vii.
35. Villari, 17, 6.
36. Villari, 11.
37. Villari, 15–16.
38. Villari, 17.
39. Mussolini, vol. 22, 48; translation adapted from Kirk, 122.
40. Baxa, 10–11.
41. Kirk, 123.
42. Painter, 22.
43. Arturo Bianchi, 'Il centro di Roma: La sistemazione del Foro Italico e le nuove vie del mare e dei monti', in *Architettura* 12.3 (1933): 149. Translation from Arthurs, 63.
44. Baxa, 84.
45. Giuseppe Marchetti Longhi, 'La via dell'Impero nel suo sviluppo storico-topografico e nel suo significato ideal', *Capitolium* 10.2 (1934): 62. Translation from Arthurs, 66–7.
46. Marchetti Longhi, 54. Translation from Arthurs, 66.
47. Arthurs, 59.
48. Baxa, xiv.
49. Hawthorne 1980, 106.
50. Sydney Lee, *Theatre of Marcellus, Rome*, 1927. Walker Art Gallery, accession number WAG 2880. https://artuk.org/discover/artworks/theatre-of-marcellus-rome-97785
51. Villari, 4–5.
52. Consoli, 208; translation from Kallis, 84–5.
53. Bosworth, 174; Moraglio 2017, 82.
54. Kallis, 84.
55. Baxa, xi.
56. Baxa, 12, 71–2.
57. *Casabella* 85 (January 1935), 13, trans. in Painter, 22.
58. Baxa, 84.
59. Baxa, 85.
60. Ceccarius, 'L'isolamento della Mole Adriana', *Capitolium* 1934: 209–10. Trans. in Baxa, 13.
61. Muñoz, xi, trans. in Arthurs, 59–60.
62. Baxa, 128–9.
63. Ludwig, 31; for context Baxa, 85.
64. Enrico Spaccini, 'Fedez e la denuncia per vilipendio per i versi sui carabinieri', 10 September 2022, online at: https://www.open.online/2022/09/10/fedez-canzone-carabinieri-denuncia-vilipendio-risposta-video/
65. Baxa, 54.
66. Baxa, 79–80, 92–3.
67. Baxa, 112.
68. Kallis, 85.
69. Kirk, 123; Painter, 24.
70. 'La carta marmorea dell'Impero Fascista', *L'Urbe* 1 (1936): 3–4, trans. in Baxa, 11.
71. Baxa, 94.

16: VIALE ADOLFO HITLER

1. Archivio Centrale dello Stato, JAJA, Job 170, Mussolini's Secretariat, trans. in Baxa, 141.
2. Pirro. For further context Ahmed, 111–14; for the film see: https://www.youtube.com/watch?v=3PXfoxs8UbY
3. Cobb.
4. Ghirardo, 40, cited in Caprotti, xxv.
5. Miltoun 1909, 183, 72.
6. Caprotti, 81; for background, see Ghirardo, 46–58.
7. Cited in Sartorio, 34.
8. Miltoun 1909, 183.
9. Painter, 161.
10. Caprotti, 86.
11. Dickens, 234.
12. Frost, 595.
13. Stern, 132.
14. Caprotti, 96.
15. Arthurs, 92.
16. Translations from Arthurs, 105, citing MCR MAR b. 201, fasc. 7, sotto 'Radio'.
17. Romanelli, 4, translation from Arthurs, 129–30.
18. Bottai, 'Roma e la scuola italiana', *Roma* 17.1 (1939): 6, cited and translated in Arthurs, 131.
19. Grenier, 3.
20. Strong, 5. My translation.
21. Kallis, 240. McDonough, vol. 1, ch. 6, unpaginated digital edition.
22. Painter, 153.
23. Baxa, 149–50; Painter, 120; Kallis, 241; Scobie has a contemporary map, 25.
24. Mayer, 175.
25. Baxa, 143; Kallis, 241–2.
26. Baxa, 144–5, 155.
27. Bandinelli, 18–19, cited in Baxa, 145.
28. Baxa, 142, 153.
29. Scobie, 34, fn. 134.
30. Scobie, 20.
31. Fritz Todt, ed., *Deutschlands Autobahnen* (Bayreuth: Gauverlag Bayerische Ostmark, 1937), 22, trans. in Chapoutot, 237.
32. Todt, 3, 6, trans. in Chapoutot, 238.
33. Emil Maier-Dorn, 'Die kulturelle Bedeutung der Reichsautobahnen', *Die Strasse* 5, no. 23 (1938): 736, trans. in Chapoutot, 239.
34. Chapoutot, 240.
35. Hitler, 537–8, cited in Chapoutot, 237. For important caveats relating to this source, see Nilsson.
36. Grosholz, 192; Cacciatore, 68–9.
37. Tittmann Jr, 90, 176.
38. Cited in Evangelista, 294–5.
39. Anderson 2019, 24.
40. Seneca, *Ep. ad Luc.* 57.2 (LCL 75: 382–3).
41. Buckley, 188.
42. Failmezger, ch. 4.
43. Evangelista, 298.
44. Kennedy, 59.
45. Kennedy, 63.

46. For his shortlisting see N. D. R., online at: https://opac.sba.uniroma3.it/arardeco/1929/29_I/Art1/I1T.html. The eventual contract went to Giuseppe Vaccaro.
47. Kennedy, 64.
48. Katz, 48.
49. Newnan, 36–7.
50. Documenti della resistenza romana, 909, cited and translated in Katz, 59–60.
51. Katz, 87–8.
52. Except where otherwise noted, I rely here on the account in Zuccotti, 101–25.
53. For Kappler, Breitman, 402.
54. Juvenal 3.10–20, discussed in Larmour, 192.
55. Higgins, 44.
56. Wildvang, 191.
57. Levis Sullam.
58. Breitman, 404.
59. Wildvang, 191.
60. Foot 2021.
61. Zuccotti, 121.
62. Picciotto, 213. I am grateful to Agnes Crawford for drawing the bridge to public attention.

17: HIGHWAY 7

1. Tompkins 1962, 23.
2. Tompkins 1962, 33.
3. Tompkins 1962, 26–7.
4. Tompkins 1962, 34–7.
5. Failmezger, ch. 12.
6. Vego, 98.
7. Vego, 103.
8. Klein, 141; for context Bourhill, 129 and Caddick-Adams, 267.
9. '5th Open Road To Rome', *Aberdeen Journal*, 20 December 1943.
10. 'Eight Roads To Rome', *Aberdeen Journal*, 3 June 1944.
11. Fisher Jr, 28–30.
12. Caddick-Adams, 16.
13. Tompkins 1985, 510–11.
14. Vego, 104.
15. Vego, 105–6.
16. Vego, 115.
17. Vego, 123–4.
18. Vego, 128.
19. Vego, 126.
20. Stern, 131.
21. Vego, 131; Brown, 63–4.
22. Joachim Liebschner interview, Sound Archive 8878, Imperial War Museum, edited in L. Clark, 112.
23. For context: Winter, esp. 67.
24. Newnan, 1.
25. Newnan, 2.
26. Newnan, 13.
27. Newnan, 16.
28. 'The Roads of Yugoslavia', CIA/RR GR 60/3, pp. 2, 7, online at https://www.cia.gov/readingroom/docs/CIA-RDP79T01018A000300040001-7.pdf
29. Newnan, 16.
30. Newnan, 17.
31. Newnan, 23.
32. Newnan, 24.
33. Newnan, 29.
34. Tompkins 1962, 70.
35. Tompkins 1962, 84–5; Tompkins 1985, 516–17.
36. Portelli, 63.
37. Vego, 134; Brown, 64.
38. Geissler and Guillemin, 4.

39. Tompkins 1985, 513.
40. Tompkins 1985, 515–16.
41. Stern, 131.
42. Katz, 151.
43. Colville, 476.
44. Vego, 138.
45. Katz, 65.
46. Portelli, 63.
47. Foot 2000, 1175–7.
48. Portelli, 63; Tompkins 1985, 524.
49. [Quintilian], *Declamationes minores*, 274 (LCL 500: 258–9).
50. Appian, *Bella civilia*, 1.120 (LCL 5: 238–9).
51. Tomassetti, vol. 2, 481.
52. Nicassio, 110.
53. Tomassetti, vol. 2, 483.
54. Brown, 64.
55. Joachim Liebschner interview, Sound Archive 8878, Imperial War Museum, edited in L. Clark, 309.
56. Newnan, 46.
57. Joachim Liebschner interview, Sound Archive 8878, Imperial War Museum, edited in L. Clark, 310.
58. Kennedy, 131.
59. Grosholz, 192; Cacciatore, 69.
60. Kennedy, 113.
61. Newnan, 47.
62. Buckley, 328.
63. Stern, 3.
64. Ventre, 141.
65. Stern, 8.
66. McMillan, 129.
67. Malaparte, 278, 289–91, 298.
68. Bassi, ch. 25, unpaginated digital edition.
69. Bassi, ch. 27, unpaginated digital edition.
70. Tittmann Jr, 209.
71. Evangelista, 298.
72. https://www.nam.ac.uk/explore/italian-campaign

18: ROMAN HOLIDAYS

1. Anderson 2019, 31–2.
2. Anderson 2019, 35.
3. Anderson 2019, 44.
4. Buchanan, 595–6.
5. Hayes, 1.
6. Evangelista, 293.
7. Anderson 2019, 35.
8. Tac. *Ann.* 1.61., translation adapted from Foubert, 11.
9. Portelli, 209.
10. Stern, 17.
11. Painter, 155.
12. Morton, 139.
13. Foot 2000, 1180–81.
14. Bosworth, 193.
15. Painter, 153.
16. Bennett, 359.
17. Bennett, 361–2.
18. Anderson 2011, 7.
19. Anderson 2011, 4–5.
20. Anderson 2011, 2–3.
21. Formica and Uysal, 324.
22. Higgins, 32.
23. Lyth, 11–13.
24. Formica and Uysal, 326–7; Manera et al., Introduction 7–8.
25. Battilani, 105–6.
26. Battilani, 107–8.
27. Battilani, 107–16.
28. Schipper et al., 192–3.
29. Moraglio 2007, 93, 105.
30. Lister, 293.
31. Lister, 114.

32. Anon., *Roads to Rome*, unpaginated edition.
33. Morton, 8.
34. Morton, 302–3.
35. Morton, 20.
36. Morton, 137–8.
37. Lister, 26–7.
38. Morton, 139.
39. Morton, 177.
40. Morton, 31.
41. Paris, 10–12.
42. Paris, 15.
43. Paris, 22.
44. 'Italy seeks UNESCO World Heritage Status for Appian Way', online at https://www.wantedinrome.com/news/italy-unesco-world-heritage-status-appian-way.html
45. Lister, 1.
46. Lister, 208.
47. For background: Emiliani, 12.
48. Mauri.
49. Vanvitelli, 257, no. 159, translation from della Portella 2004b, 149.
50. Berkeley, vol. 7, 270.
51. Vanvitelli, 257, no. 159, translation from della Portella, 150.
52. Jean-Claude Richard de Saint-Non, *Voyage pittoresque, ou Description des Royaumes de Naples et de Sicile*, 5 vols, Paris, 1781–6. Translation from della Portella, 186.
53. Lister, 119.
54. Della Portella 2004b, 189–90.

EPILOGUE: ON THE ROADS TODAY

1. Potter and Markino, xxi.
2. Wacher, 32, 121–2.
3. Higgins, 49.
4. Giovanni, online at: https://www.poetryfoundation.org/poems/48221/the-great-pax-whitie; for discussion see Barnard, 175–7.
5. https://whc.unesco.org/en/tentativelists/349/

Index

Places are in England or Italy unless otherwise stated.